TASTING BEER

TASTING BEER

AN INSIDER'S GUIDE TO THE WORLD'S GREATEST DRINK

RANDY MOSHER

Storey Publishing

This book is dedicated to my father.

Not much of a beer man himself,
he patiently taught me from a very early age
how to figure out the way everything in
the world works.

The mission of Storey Publishing is to serve our customers by publishing practical information that encourages personal independence in harmony with the environment.

Edited by Margaret Sutherland, Molly Jackel, and Sarah Guare
Art direction and book design by Dan O. Williams

Cover photography by © Randy Mosher, except © Ben Harris-Roxas: front cover, bottom left, and © Jonathan Levin Photography: author
Cover illustrations and ephemera courtesy of the author
Interior photography credits appear on page 240

Indexed by Christine R. Lindemer, Boston Road Communications

Printed in China by R. R. Donnelley
20 19 18 17 16 15 14 13 12

Library of Congress Cataloging-in-Publication Data
Mosher, Randy.
Tasting beer / Randy Mosher.
p. cm.
Includes index.
ISBN 978-1-60342-089-1 (pbk. : alk. paper)
1. Beer tasting. 2. Beer—History. 3. Brewing—History. I. Title.
TP577.M68 2009
641.2'3—dc22

2008040676

CONTENTS

ACKNOWLEDGMENTS

A book like this could only happen in a community such as the one that swirls around great beer in North America. Its creators and sustainers are far too numerous to mention. You know who you are.

As far as specifics, thanks to Lyn Kruger and Keith Lemcke of the Siebel Institute for plenty of technical information and for allowing me to hone my skills and story on their students. Thanks go out to my technical editor Stan Heironymous and to a number of other people who reviewed part or all of the book: Ed Bronson, Steve Hamburg, and Tom Schmidlin. Thanks to Dick Cantwell, Adam Ellis, Ken Grossman, Jim Koch, Marty Jones, Mark Linsner, Andy Musser, and Charlie Papazian for various tidbits. Special thanks to Jonathan Levin for the portrait photo.

Others who helped get the book off the ground include Sam Calagione and my agent, Clare Pelino, along with the fine folks at Storey: Margaret Sutherland, Molly Jackel, Sarah Guare, and Dan Williams. Thanks to Ray Daniels for his insights, friendship, and keeping me honest. Thanks also to the late Michael Jackson, who provided me with some pithy insights into the publishing world, along with everything else he did so well.

It couldn't have happened without the warm and supportive community of brewers, both craft and amateur, including my own Chicago Beer Society. And of course immeasurable thanks go to my wife, Nancy, and the rest of my family. Cheers to all.

FOREWORD

WHEN I met Randy Mosher he was coming at me with a hammer in his hand and a maniacal smile on his face. We were at Chicago's Real Ale Festival in 1998 and he was helping prepare casks of unfiltered, unpasteurized, naturally carbonated real ale for serving. His enthusiasm was infectious — as lively as the beers contained in those casks. I have gotten to know Randy better in the last five years as we have served together on the board of directors of the Brewers Association. He earned his seat at the table representing the American Homebrewers Association, but in time it became apparent that his perspective, knowledge, and passion encompassed the whole world of beer lovers and makers: enthusiasts, amateurs, pros, and beyond. Randy is a true beer evangelist. In this book, and in all aspects of his beer-soaked life, he is saving souls one pint at a time.

Tasting Beer tackles the experience of choosing and imbibing beer with just enough technical and scientific information to explain the events but not so much that the beer novice feels overwhelmed. Randy doesn't preach his personal preferences here. He celebrates the fact that our individual palates are as unique as snowflakes. *Tasting Beer* is like a collection of many fine books bound together. Beer history, the science of brewing, the disciplines of tasting and evaluation, the wide array of beer styles, pairings of food and beer, beer terminology — it's all in here. This book is like an imperial pint full of knowledge, and Randy's cup runneth over. I am hopeful that *Tasting Beer* will find a home with professionals in addition to beer enthusiasts. I can think of no better single tool for brewers, bartenders, connoisseurs, chefs, salespeople, and everyone else in the beer trade for enhancing their beer IQ.

Despite the fact that beer's history is as ancient as wine's and that there are more styles and flavors of beer than wine, beer is still considered a less complex beverage by too many foodies and connoisseurs. Randy helps to dispel this myth in *Tasting Beer*. Much of the beer sold throughout the world is some slight variation on the light lager style, but Randy points out that centuries before the *Reinheitsgebot,* beers were being brewed with diverse ingredients such as honey, bog myrtle, cranberries, and coriander. Craft breweries today have reinvigorated this ancient tradition, using spices, herbs, sugars, fruits, and more. Randy gives equal time to each of the diverse, exciting beers that drinkers are trading up to, from the exotic eccentrics to the popular classic styles.

As international beer culture evolves, the brewers of these exciting craft beers are achieving growth and recognition disproportionate to that of the industrial, conglomerate light beer producers. After reading this book it is easy to see why. Beer culture is tremendously diverse, distinguished, and nuanced. As Randy writes, "Like any art, beer needs a proper context to be truly compelling." *Tasting Beer* gives us this context in spades. Drink up as you read up on the world's most storied and beloved adult beverage. Cheers.

—Sam Calagione
Owner of Dogfish Head Craft Brewery
and the author of *Brewing Up a Business*

PREFACE

As you read these words, consider the beer-filled glass in your hand. Look closely. Study the rich color and slight viscosity of the liquid. Observe the way the light plays on the shimmering highlights. Watch the bubbles as they form and rise lazily through the beer, adding to the creamy foam on top, hushed and peaceful as a snowfall.

Lift the glass to your lips, but first, pause to inhale and ponder the aroma. Draw in the bready, caramelly, or toasty foundation of malt, the brisk green counterpoint of hops, and the swirling cupboard of spices and fruit, earth and wood. These scents can fire off neurons in the forgotten happy corners of your memory, as powerful an experience as any art form.

Finally, have a taste. The beer floods in, cool and crisp or warm and rich. Observe the first blush of flavor and the tart tingle of carbonation. As the beer warms in your mouth, it releases a new round of flavors and sensations: malty sweetness, bright herbal hops, a touch of toast, all building to a bittersweet crescendo. It's not one single taste; it's an ever-evolving cinematic experience unspooling as you drink. A soft inward breath stirs a new layer of beery perfume. This pleasure has been savored for millennia.

If you can read the meaning in these sensations, the whole history of brewing opens up, and the long process reveals itself in the beer, from golden barley fields to steam-filled brewhouse to the tireless working of man's first domesticated microbe — yeast.

The grand finale comes as a long-fading aftertaste, with lingering wisps of resin, toast, or honey, concluding perhaps with a gentle, warming alcohol sensation in your throat. The empty glass, now spent, is clad in an immodest slip of lace. . . .

WELCOME TO BEER

I WISH IT were always this ecstatic, and when it's good it really can be. Truth be told, we don't always give our beer the attention it deserves, and we are the poorer for it. Like any aspect of a consciously lived life, enjoying beer to the fullest takes education, experience, and a proper frame of mind.

That isn't to say that learning to understand and appreciate beer is hard work. It is among the most enjoyable things you can do. But to get the most out of beer you have to put a little effort into it. This book lays out the experience of beer in all its glory, in a logical and systematic way. Beer may be humble, but it is not simple.

Beer is brewed nearly everywhere that grain grows except, ironically, in its own homeland of the Middle East. It spans the full range of the sacred and the profane, a participant with equal gusto in ancient religious mysteries and raucous frat-house revelries. Whether it provides essential nutrition and a safe source of water or is a rare and costly luxury, there is a beer to satisfy every need or whim. It may be harvested with sickles, brewed in baskets, and drunk through reeds, or conjured up with a simple push of a button in automated space-age breweries. It can be a faceless, industrial commodity or an artistic creation as treasured and transfixing as the finest wine. Light, dark, strong, weak, fizzy, flat, canned, bottled, or draft, beer has fluidly adapted to serve every role it has been asked to play, and it has done so with extraordinary grace. Beer is *the* universal beverage.

Yet despite this impressive résumé, it is surprising how little most people know about it. Even the most basic concepts are fuzzy: "What is beer?" "What is it made from?" "Why is dark beer dark?" If we remain uninformed, we can be trapped in our own limited beer world, not knowing what delights we're missing, like which beer might be perfect with a barbecue sandwich, or when it's okay to send a bad beer back. It takes a little information to open up the extraordinary universe of beer.

Beer is a complicated subject, more difficult to grasp than wine in terms of what is actually in the glass. It can be brewed from dozens of ingredients processed in hundreds of different ways. Unlike the vintner, the brewer actually constructs a recipe to yield a product to suit his or her vision. Every brew requires choice after choice, each of which you can taste in the glass if you understand the process. The many dozens of styles are not fixed beacons, but shifting shoals that change with the tide of generations, each with its own past, present, and future. Finally, bad information abounds — a *lot* of bad information.

"The oyle of malt and juyce of sprightly nectar
Have made my muse more valiant than Hector."

— Richard Brathwaite, *Barnabae Itinerarium*, 1638

The Depth and Breadth of Beer

In a concise and visual way, this book aims to introduce you to the wide world of beer and to give you the tools to understand and, more importantly, enjoy it.

Beer has a history that predates civilization, and in its own way, beer has shaped us as much as we have shaped it. Our relationship with beer is the key to understanding beer's many roles in society, which in turn helps make sense of the bewildering array of colors, strengths, and flavors that form the family of beer.

Beer is democratic. It does not depend on the finest real estate or limited geographical designations. The many choices made by the maltster and brewer create aromas, flavors, textures, and colors, transforming a few simple commodities into exquisite works of art. Anyone with skill, passion, and creativity can learn to make great beer. As a taster, each glance, each telltale whiff and studied sip of a beer can be like peering into the soul of the man or woman who brewed it. This dependence on a human rather than a heavenly touch is one of beer's great delights.

As a passionate fan of beer, you will sometimes be called upon to introduce others to its charms. Like anything, presentation is half the game. It's not cheating. A great beer poured into a perfect glass at just the right temperature, in the best possible setting, should always be the goal. Anything less cheats the brewer and drinker alike.

By the end of the book, and with a lot of practice on your own, you'll be on your way to understanding all the many things that come together to form the wonderfulness of a well-brewed — and thoroughly enjoyed — beer.

Sack makes men from words
Fall to drawing of swords,
And quarreling endeth their quaffing:
Whilst Dagger ale barrels
Bear off many quarrels,
And often turn chiding to laughing.

— from *In Praise of Ale*, 1888, a collection of old English beer poetry, author unknown

The Community of Beer

Gemütlichkeit is a German word meaning "coziness," and it is most often used to describe the warm and cheery atmosphere of the log- and taxidermy-decorated bars in places like Wisconsin. It's a great word, for it has a broader and more important connotation that I like to think of as "cousin-ness." I'm referring to a sense of easy community, where people in a certain space have decided to put aside differences and suspicions and consciously work at being convivial. The Czechs, Dutch, Russians, and Danes have similar concepts in their languages, but English has to borrow the German term.

There is definitely something about beer. Look at the mirth just bursting out of those Breughel paintings as Flemish peasants drink beer and dance despite their rough and challenging lives. Civilization as well as civility thrive where there is a pot of beer. Beer brings people together on common ground, and has been doing so for thousands of years.

The business of beer has a good deal of the same camaraderie. In an era when market competitors in most businesses loathe each other like Cold War rivals, such antipathy is hard to find in brewing. Marketing people may go at it hammer and tongs, but brewers are pals. Maybe it's just the satisfaction of being a member of the small club of people who absolutely, posi-

***The Harvesters*, 1565, Pieter Bruegel**
Whether it's wheat or barley they're harvesting, some of the grain will undoubtedly find its way into the local beer. Note the large jugs of beer assisting with the process.

tively know that what they do for a living makes a lot of people happy.

Beer Today

THESE ARE INTERESTING TIMES for beer. Pockets of true classic styles remain, but everywhere in Europe the classic styles struggle against the hundred-year flood of mass-market Pilsner. The big get bigger, blander, and more international. For the not-so-big, things are especially tough. Many classic old breweries have been gobbled up by large ones unappreciative of their charms, often with disastrous results. Fabled breweries close and their beloved beers change beyond recognition. But as the past fades, a new future for beer is taking shape. Small brewers are producing inspiring products full of character for a limited but highly appreciative clientele.

In England, real ale, once the national drink, has become a specialty beer and there is an alarming shift away from drinking in pubs, driven by cost, driving restrictions, and other factors. The fantastic, classic Belgian beers we love represent just 15 percent of their home market. Germany rightly loves its beers, but given the sameness of many, the place is ripe for consolidation.

The late — and sorely missed — Michael Jackson was fond of shocking audiences in Europe by saying that the United States was the best place on the planet to drink beer. He was right. There are more styles, more choices, and more beers bursting with flavor and personality here than anywhere else. It wasn't always so. By the mid-1970s there were pitifully few American beers worth drinking. The lack of a living beer tradition worth preserving left us free to build a new beer culture from scratch.

Come, fill me a glass, fill it high,
A bumper, a bumper I'll have:
He's a fool that will flinch, I'll not bate an inch,
Though I drink myself into my grave.
Come, my lads, move the glass, drink about,
We'll drink the whole universe dry,
We'll set foot and drink it all out,
If once we grow sober we die.

— Mr. Philips, "Bachanalian Song," from *In Praise of Ale*, 1888

A new generation of American brewers took to the task with passion and imagination.

Despite many examples of sublime subtlety, most craft beers are bold, even brash, an antidote to so much that is bland and faceless out there. The great brewing traditions of Britain, Germany, and Belgium may be brewed with reverential attention to authenticity or as just a loose starting point for flavor piled on top of flavor. Either way, the beers are delicious and there is something for every taste.

And where there are historic local traditions, craft brewers are looking to do something meaningful with them. From Alaska to the Carolinas, brewers are turning out stock, sparkling, and cream ales, pre-Prohibition Pilsner, aniseed-tinged Pennsylvania Swankey, and Kentucky common beer. There's also interest in creating beers that incorporate local ingredients such as sorghum in the South, spruce tips in Alaska, white sage in the Southwest, and all manner of local fruits and honey.

Around the country, brewers are working with the many parts and pieces of Belgian brewing, looking to rearrange them into something new and uniquely American. A freewheeling disregard for styles, barrel-aging, *Brettanomyces*, and wild, lambic-style fermentations are all in their tool kits, and they're just getting going.

Fruit beer has finally gotten serious. A few brewers are creating beers with a fruity impact more along the lines of a fine wine. Sugar, too, is out of the closet, and brewers are using exotic types like piloncillo, rapadura, and Belgian brewer's caramel to lighten the body and enhance the drinkability of stronger beers. Wheat, rye, buckwheat, and other unusual adjunct beers abound. Pumpkin ales are popular around Halloween, and chile beers pop up from time to time, as do the ancient techniques of stone beer and smoked malt. Bourbon barrels have found their way into breweries, yielding vanilla and toasted coconut notes to strong beers after a few months of aging.

There is an arms race going on, too. From the use of massive blasts of hops to the "imperializing" of every imaginable style, craft brewers are piling on the flavor. At the top are super-gravity beers currently weighing in at as much as 27 percent alcohol, right up there with port and close to the level of spirits. Some, like the Samuel Adams Utopias, sell for upward of $200, stratospheric for the beer world but still a bargain by the heady standards of the exotic spirits world.

Beer really is the world's best beverage. It may be quenching or nourishing, cooling or warming, simple or worthy of deep meditation. It is a drink of a thousand aromas, a rainbow of color, and a range of character as diverse as the people who brew and enjoy it. It has ten thousand years of history, with gods, goddesses, heroes, and songs to celebrate its glories. It brings us together. Beer makes us happy.

In *Tasting Beer* it is my hope to help guide you to a better understanding of the many things that make beer and our relationship with it so magical. With effort and information, you can gain the power to peer knowingly into its amber depths, approach it with keener senses, and find within the meaning of beer.

CHAPTER 1

THE STORY OF BEER

BEER is the great family of starch-based alcoholic beverages produced without distillation. Today in the industrialized world, beer is usually brewed from barley malt, with other grains such as rice, corn, wheat, or oats thrown in for reasons of cost, texture, or tradition, and seasoned with hops. This is but a small subset of all possible beers. In the vast span of history, and in the diverse cultures of preindustrial societies, many other variations are possible. Every imaginable starchy vegetable product has been used, even manioc and millet.

THE STARCH IN GRAIN is not readily fermentable by brewer's yeast, so some chemical process must be used to break down the starches into fermentable sugars. For Andean *chicha,* women chew up maize, and enzymes in their saliva do the trick. In sake (yes, it's beer, not wine), *Aspergillis* fungus is used to provide the necessary enzymes. Fortunately, grains such as barley and wheat contain enzymes that are capable of doing the job if given the opportunity.

We know beer as a delicious treat; these days it is not essential for survival. But in the days of poor sanitation — just a century or two ago — beer was one of the few cheap, safe sources of potable water. Beer can also contain a lot of protein and carbohydrates, depending on how it is brewed, and this has earned it the nickname "liquid bread." Beer also contains alcohol, long prized for its ability to ease social tensions and create a sense of well-being, despite the risks to those who overindulge.

Beer may be brewed to suit many different tastes, and for a host of different purposes. It is typical to see, in most cultural contexts, a range of beers from weak to strong filling different roles in the day, the year, or the society.

Those who study the birth of civilizations and beer note that the two happened at just about the same time. Barley was one of the earliest cultivated grains, and the fact that it emerged in domesticated form with just the right characteristics for brewing tells us a lot. Leaving the nomadic life behind for a pot of gruel is one thing, but toss in beer and it's a hard deal to turn down.

It is my belief that squeezing people into cities generates a certain amount of itchy friction, but this can be eased by a social lubricant like beer, served up in that other beloved institution, the tavern, which appeared on the scene not long after beer.

Beer, in many times and places, was not a casual consumer choice, but something much more meaningful. The ancient Middle Eastern peoples had gods and goddesses dedicated to the stuff, and they wove the creation of beer into their own epic tales. In Egyptian legend, it saved the world. Through the millennia, beer has been accorded the highest possible status in culture after culture. We owe it to beer to understand it, to nurture it, to respect it. Like all human art forms, it survives only at our pleasure. We get out of it what we put into it.

A Little Beer History

THE HISTORY OF BEER is a wide and deeply fascinating subject and deserves a great deal more attention than I'm going to be able to give it in this short chapter. All I can hope to do here is lay out the broad strokes so that the rest of the pieces, especially with regard to styles, will fit into the framework I'm providing.

The story begins around 10,000 BCE, just after the glaciers of the last Ice Age retreat to the north. As they do, the vacated land becomes grassland. The Neolithic people in the hill country of what is now Kurdistan start to use the grasses as a good source of nutrition, saving the best seeds and replanting year after year. Eventually, these grasses turn into barley and wheat. This is the beginning of agriculture.

In fairly short order, these clever folks had cajoled various grass plants into producing large, starch-swollen seeds well suited to the foods and drinks they were interested in producing. The early wheat types had a fair amount of the sticky protein called gluten that provides the structure for leavened bread, and even at that time there were varieties that threshed free of the gritty husk. Those characteristics are vital for anything resembling good bread. The barley of the day typically had lower gluten content than wheat, and many varieties threshed with the husk intact, two qualities that

Kurdistan
The grassy hills of this Middle Eastern region is thought to be the birthplace of many domesticated grasses.

are very helpful for brewing. The actual story is fairly complicated, but even in that early era, the fundamentals were there for barley beer and wheaten bread.

It is unclear how the mashing — the enzyme conversion of starch to sugar — was discovered. It is postulated that the essential step of malting (sprouting of the grain, then drying, which also activates the starch-degrading enzymes) was originally done to preserve the grain and to add to its nutritive value. And in a day when the gruel *du jour* must have been monotonous in the extreme, it may have livened things up quite a bit when somebody discovered that if you mix malt with hot water, a few minutes later you get a nutritious broth that is quite sweet — it actually tastes a lot like Grape-Nuts.

Staking their fate on the cultivation of those tiny grass seeds was a bold step for these ancient people. Animal herding was well suited to a nomadic lifestyle, as people followed the herds season to season in search of pasturage. Grain is not particularly portable, so throwing your lot in with this kind of agriculture meant the loss of a certain kind of wind-in-the-hair freedom. Personally, I find this loss much more acceptable when the trade-off is beer, as compared to bread or gruel. Those more scholarly than I make the claim that beer is one thing that allowed people to come together in unnaturally crowded settings, like cities. It's certainly true today that beer helps to take the edge off and makes cities much more livable. I'm not pointing any fingers, but look at the places where beer is absolutely forbidden. It's easy to see the contrast.

It appears that wine and beer developed at about the same time and place. Even in that early day, wine was a much more luxurious product, by and large reserved for royalty and other upper-crusty types, while *everyone* drank beer. Consider this the next time you are banging your head in frustration over the automatic sense of class and status accorded to wine relative to beer. I do believe we have the power to change this to some degree, but it is important to know what we are up against.

The Sumerians were the first great civilization of the ancient Middle East. They were very fond of beer. Their word for beer, *kas,* literally means "what the mouth desires," and this gives us a good idea of how central beer was to their culture. By 3000 BCE, the art of beer was well established, as evidenced by an expansive vocabulary of ingredients, brewing vessels, and beer types. Malt kilns made red, brown, and black beers possible, and there were

This cylinder seal depicts important people sipping what is most likely beer from long straws.

This stone plaque, c. 2550 BCE, shows the Sumerians enjoyed a good beer blast.

fresh and aged, strong and weak, and even a diet beer, the name for which, *eb-la,* literally meant "lessens the waist." Yeast was known as the motive power of beer, but its nature would remain a mystery for another 5,000 years.

In that day, women were the brewers as well as the retailers of beer, a similar situation as in Europe throughout much of the Middle Ages. It's not surprising, then, that the Sumerian deity of beer, Ninkasi, was also a female. She was a daughter of Ninhursag, the Mother Goddess. There is a long and detailed poem, the *Hymn to Ninkasi,* which describes the brewing of beer.

Barley was malted, kilned, and ground. It was then either formed into conical cakes and baked, or used as is. Baking the cakes would have added some caramelization and presumably begun the enzymatic conversion of starch to sugar. The cakes would then have been a sort of "instant mash," and adding them to hot water would have been an easy and portable way to get brewing started. The beer was often drunk out of a communal vessel through long straws typically made of reeds. High-status individuals had straws made of more precious materials.

THE BABYLONIANS, Akkadians, Hittites, and other ancient Middle Eastern people were also beer lovers, but the Semitic people of the Bible were never all that keen on it. The Bible does mention wine frequently, and something called *shekar,* which is usually translated as "strong drink," although it's unclear whether this meant beer or some other alcoholic beverage, such as mead.

But just around the bend in Egypt, we see beer on a grand scale. Breweries were associated with temples there, and were similar in size to the brewpubs of today. Egyptian beer was called *hekt* or *hqt,* and because of its near-industrial scale, brewing was in the domain of men. Beer was such a vital staple of Egyptian life that a model brewery was seen as essential to ensure a happy afterlife. Beer, along with bread and onions, is credited with fueling vast construction projects like the Pyramids. As in Mesopotamia, the beer was often brewed from specially prepared cakes of malted barley. Much of it was bottled in tall clay jars with special clay seals.

Hymn to Ninkasi (excerpt)

Ninkasi, you are the one who spreads
the cooked mash on large reed mats,
Coolness overcomes.
You are the one who holds with both hands
the great sweet wort,
Brewing [it] with honey and wine

— Translated by Miguel Civil

May you have "bread that doesn't crumble, and beer that doesn't go sour."
— Ebers Papyrus, 1552 BCE

THERE IS A TALE from Egyptian mythology that shows the value that culture placed on beer. Sekhmet, the lion-headed woman, was a goddess of destruction, blood, and periodic renewal. Her father, Ra, the big-daddy god of ancient Egypt, felt that humanity was backsliding and not worshipping him in the manner to which he was accustomed. So he sent Sekhmet out to teach the people a lesson. Things got out of hand with a lot of hacking and smacking and drinking of blood. If she continued, humanity would be destroyed. So someone had the bright idea that if they gave her a red beer, she would think it was blood and would drink it. And just to play it safe, they laced it with mandrake root, a powerful sedative. She drank the beer, went to sleep, and humankind was saved. Who wouldn't think kindly of beer after a close call like that?

Vestiges of this ancient beer tradition still survive in Egypt and the Sudan to the south, in the form of a primitive folk brew called *bouza*. Indigenous brewers there still make cakes of malted barley to brew this chunky and nutritious beer.

THE GREEKS had no great use for beer, but that didn't stop them from stealing the very hip god of beer, Sabazius (later Attis), from the beer-drinking Lydians and Phrygians to the north, stripping him of his dignity, dolling him up with a crown of leaves, renaming him Dionysus, and enthroning him as their very own god of wine.

Evidence of the Phrygians' love of beer comes to us by way of their famous ruler, King Midas. Archaeologists in the 1950s dug down through an ancient mound in Gordion, Turkey, into a heavy timber structure; once inside, they found a burial site, determined to be of Midas himself, and the remains of a funerary feast. The objects were recovered and put on display, and scrapings from the cauldrons and drinking vessels were stored away for future analysis. Their time did come a few years later, when a professor from the University of Pennsylvania named Patrick McGovern happened upon them. He was using molecular archaeology to research the early history of wine. Sophisticated analytical methods such as gas chromatography are used to look for individual molecules of substances that would show evidence of the nature of the ancient foods or drinks. What researchers found, in addition to a lamb and lentil stew, was a drink containing barley, grapes, and honey.

To announce the results a party was held, and Sam Calagione of Dogfish Head Craft Brewery was asked to make the beer. This evolved into a regular product, Midas Touch. It is impossible to say how much this modern brew resembles the ancient one, but it is delicious and gives us a tantalizing glimpse into the lives of these ancient, beer-loving people.

This incredibly coarse Ancient Egyptian barley bread was likely destined for the brewhouse.

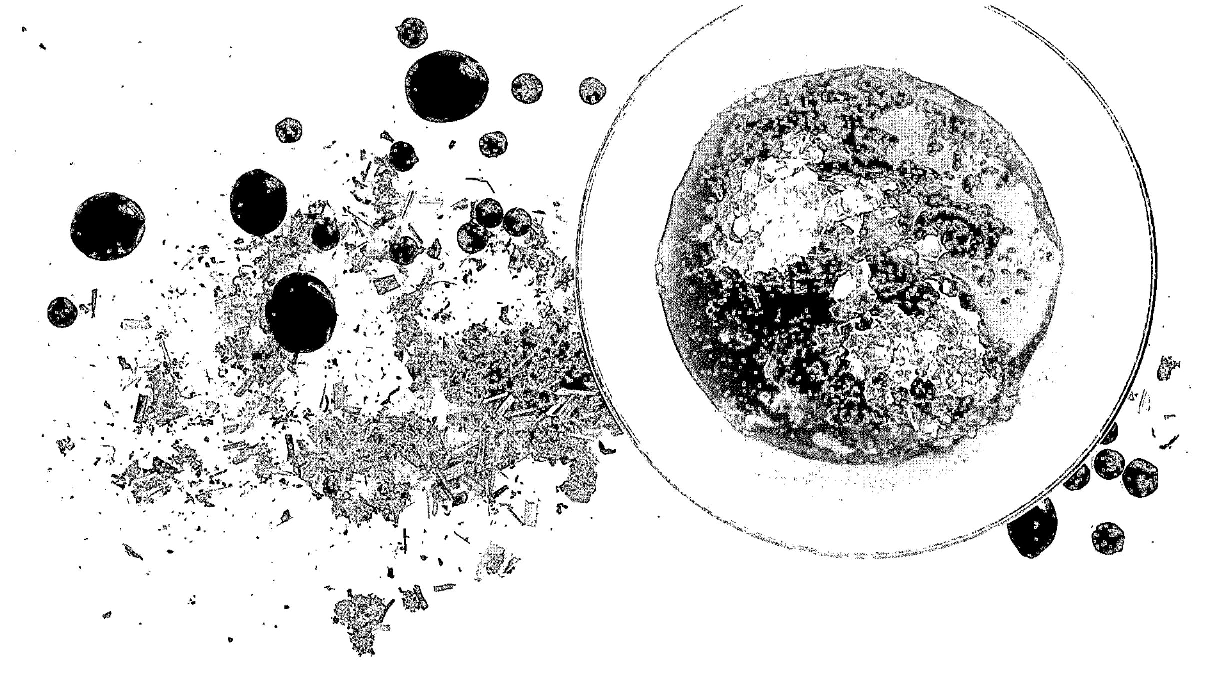

Seasonings of Ancient Northern Beers
Juniper, honey, cranberries, and an herb called meadowsweet were used in beers thousands of years ago, and still find brewing uses today.

LIKE THE GREEKS, whose culture they absorbed, the Romans never did warm up to beer. This points out a key fact of beer geography: There is a line south of which grapes grow well and wine becomes the dominant drink. North of this, ancient Romans encountered enthusiastic beer drinkers at the fringes of their empire.

Based on other research, such mixtures were not uncommon in ancient times, and they occur all through northern Europe. Honey is a willing, if scarce, source of fermentable sugar, and grapes harbor yeast. The dull, waxy haze you see on the surface of grapes is actually brewer's yeast in its natural habitat. This was known in ancient times, and it appears that grapes or raisins were sometimes added for the purpose of kick-starting fermentation in beer.

Other substances found their way into beer and other drinks. Images of poppy pods suggest that opium was involved in Dionysian rituals. Further afield, the Scythians (in present-day Ukraine) seemed to have been enamored of hemp. Greek writers of the time report sauna-like tents with heated rocks inside, upon which they threw hemp seeds, which, Herodotus notes, gave off a "vapor unsurpassed by any vapor-bath one could find in Greece. The Scythians enjoy this so much that they howl with pleasure."

Chemical analysis of scrapings from Bronze Age burials has turned up barley, honey, cranberries, and two herbs, meadowsweet and bog myrtle (*Filipendula ulmaria* and *Myrica gale*). Hops were still far in the future. The *Kalevala,* the national epic of the Finns and Hungarians, has a delightful account of the creation of beer, which took a great deal longer to explain than the creation of the earth. Osmotar, the brewster, aided by the "magic maiden" Kalevatar, is desperately seeking fermentation of the beer she's just brewed. They try pinecones and bear spit before resorting to honey, which worked like a charm: "Upward in the tub of birch-wood/ Foaming higher, higher, higher."

There is also a strong and very old tradition of incorporating juniper in these northern brews, which continues to this day in the unhopped Finnish farmhouse ale called *sahti,* a delicious and unassumingly strong brew made from malt and rye, in which juniper is added to the water, used as a filtering bed, and even made into drinking vessels.

A LITTLE SOUTH in the British Isles, beers seasoned with heather were being brewed by the Picts, the original inhabitants who built Stonehenge before the Celts displaced them. There is a delightfully romantic tale about the last king of the Picts, who allows his son to be flung over a cliff rather than reveal the "secret" of heather ale to the advancing Celts. As it's difficult to find any spot in northern Scotland without heather in sight, it's not hard to fathom what the secret was. But it's still a great story.

The beer-drinking barbarians left the world with many gifts, not the least of which was the wooden barrel. It's a technological achievement of amazing durability, maintaining the same form and construction since its first creation around 0 CE. Barrels were largely phased out for beer until the middle of the twentieth century, but for spirits and wine, nothing else will do.

In the Middle Ages, beer and brewing settles into the familiar premodern pattern. Much brewing is performed on a domestic scale by women called alewives, and it is a reliable source of income for those who may be widowed or otherwise in need of the extra cash. There are also institutional breweries, either monastic or owned by titled gentry. There are some commercial, or "common" breweries, and they become more widespread as time goes on.

Prior to 1000 CE, almost all beer in Europe was brewed without hops, seasoned with a pricey mixture called "gruit," sold by the holder of the local *Gruitrecht,* or "gruit right," which was the usual coterie of bigwigs: church, state, or in between. A lovely example of the power of gruit still stands in Bruges, Belgium, and serves as a medieval folklife museum. I should note that the purchase of gruit was mandatory for brewers, and served as an early form of taxation.

Stone Engraving of Pictish Warrior, Drinking from Horn, c. 900–950 CE
Decorated horns from the now-extinct aurochs cattle were the preferred ceremonial drinking vessel in tenth-century Britain and elsewhere in northern Europe. Could this ancient soldier have been drinking heather ale?

It's not exactly clear what was in gruit, as it was a big secret, and the seasonings were mixed with ground grain to further confound would-be counterfeiters. Bog myrtle, a.k.a. sweet gale, is one herb always mentioned. It's a pretty nicely flavored herb — kind of resiny and piney — not far from hops. Yarrow (*Achillea millefolium*) is another, although it has a rough bitterness that's not to modern tastes. A third, *Ledum palustre*, which sometimes goes by the name of "wild rosemary," seems to have been held in lower regard than bog myrtle. It has a menthol, resiny bitterness, and historically there are suggestions of mind-altering properties, although this appears not to be the case. It does have some toxicity and is a pretty effective bug repellant. This witches' brew was supplemented by whatever culinary seasonings were available: juniper, caraway, aniseed, and possibly more exotic spices such as cinnamon, nutmeg, and ginger. I've tasted a number of homebrewed gruits and I can report that either tastes have changed since then or we're missing some important part of the picture.

Hopped Beer

THE FIRST HOPPED BEERS appear around the year 1000 in the north German Hansa trading league city of Bremen. Many of the early adopters of hops were "free" cities beyond the reach of the church, and as such were not obligated to use gruit. At that time, brewers of gruit beer were known as "red" beer brewers, making brown or amber-colored beers. Those using hops brewed "white" beer, which usually included a fair amount of wheat in the grist along with the barley. The guilds were totally separate, and towns were usually known for one or the other. The brewers of Bremen and Hamburg shipped an awful lot of beer to Amsterdam, which was just getting going at the time and was thirsty for the great, refreshing taste of imported beer. It took about a hundred years before the local brewers figured out that they could brew this hopped, white beer in Amsterdam, and they began exporting to Flanders, repeating the cycle. Hopped beer eventually washed ashore in England with a flood of Flemish immigrants around the year 1500.

Hopped beer was a success not only because it tastes great, but because hops have preservative properties that retard certain beer-spoiling bacteria. This allowed table-strength beer to remain drinkable for a few months rather than a few weeks. Despite some grumblings about the despicable foreignness of it, hopped beer was accepted into England without too much fuss, and by about 1600, all English beer and ale had hops in some quantity.

Eventually, all of northern Europe was flourishing, and hopped beer was the norm. Parts south, such as Italy and Spain, had little or no beer culture. Italy was rightly satisfied with its wonderful wines, and the anti-alcohol Muslims weren't kicked out of Spain until 1614. The brewing action was in the German states,

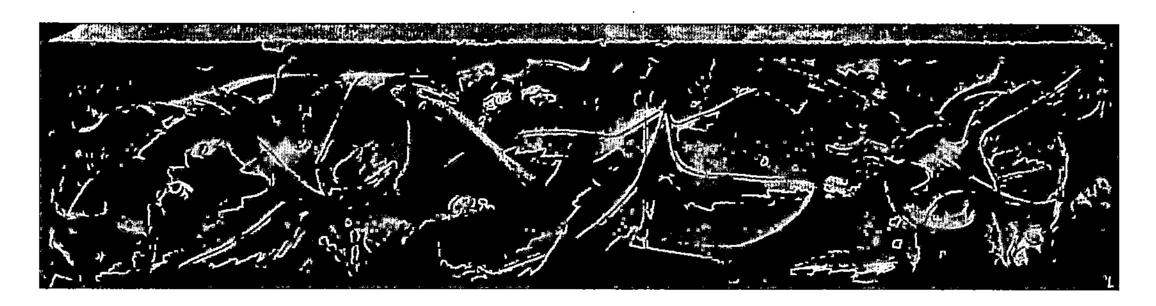

Hops Carved in Oak, **Amiens Cathedral, Thirteenth Century**
Even by this date, hops were an important part of daily life in parts of northern Europe.

Flanders, the Netherlands, and England, and that remains the case 500 years later. These areas are the sources for all the classic styles I'll be covering in detail later in the book.

The Rise of Porter

THE CHANGES that would culminate in the Industrial Revolution began in England in the midseventeenth century. Many large public works projects to open canals and improve harbors would affect brewing, as they changed the availability of raw materials as well as opening distant markets. Farmers were being forced off the land through the restricting of their access to what had previously been common areas of cultivation and grazing. Many of them found new lives in the cities.

London had encountered a patch of tough times: the civil war of 1642 and the subsequent turbulence of Oliver Cromwell's leadership from 1653 to 1658, plague in 1665, and a devastating fire in 1666. The latter actually proved to be a stimulus to new growth and development; peasants and gentry alike flooded into the city to make their fortunes. And there's one thing we all know about hard work: It makes us very thirsty.

About that time, a type of inexpensive brown malt from Hertfordshire was becom-

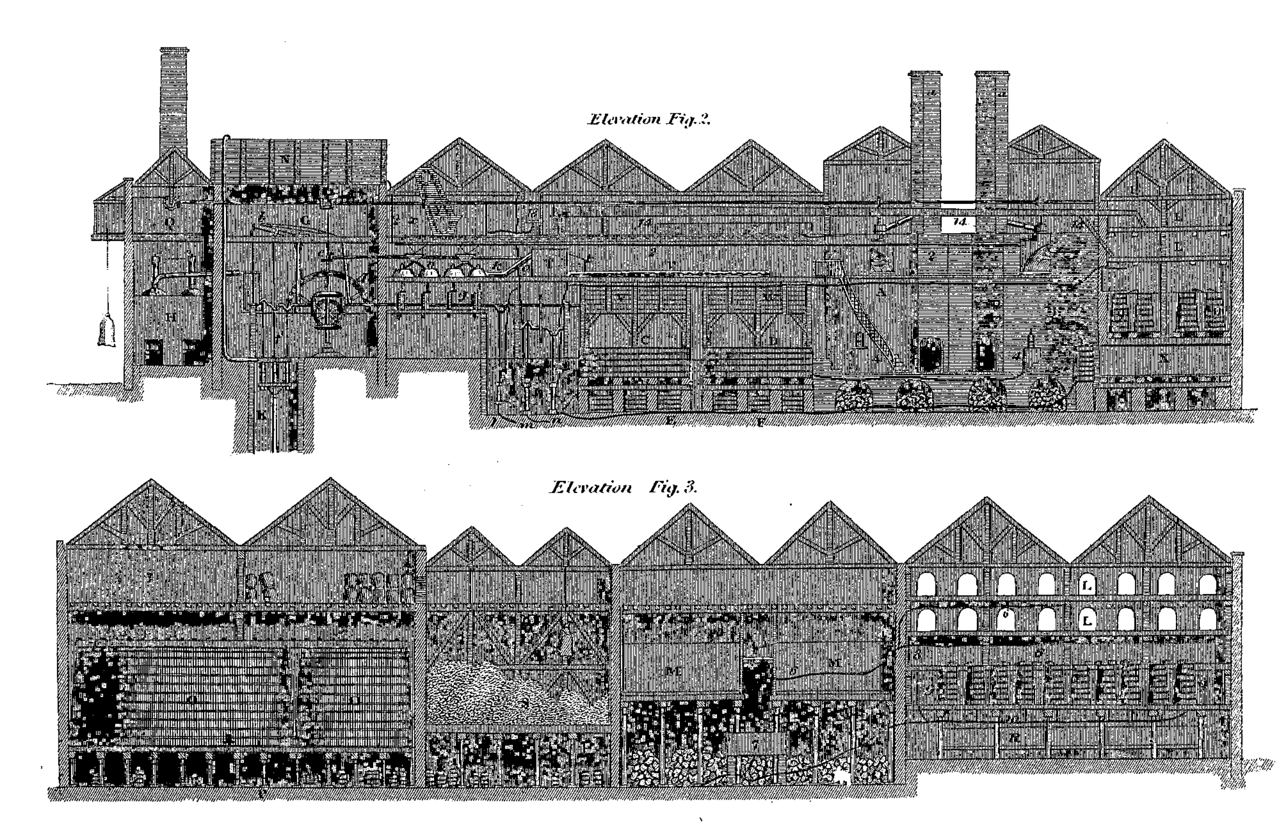

A London Porter Brewery, c. 1800
By this time, many English breweries were large, industrialized operations. Notice the enormous size of the aging vats, "O" in lower left.

ing available in London, and it was adopted as the standard malt there. As always, beers were brewed at different strengths, and the stronger of them were aged long enough to acquire a particular sourish tang. Such aged beer was called "stale," and not in the negative sense, as it sold for a higher price than fresh, or "running," beer. Bar patrons were fond of ordering blends of two, three, or even five separate beers, which must have kept the bar hands busy. The story goes that porter was invented in October 1722 by Ralph Harwood in his Bell Brewery in Shoreditch to replace these blends, particularly one called "three threads." This story, however, is suspect and doesn't appear until 1810 in the book *Picture of London*, nearly a century after the supposed events of 1722.

About this time moneyed people began buying stocks of the new beer and aging it for a year or more, setting the stage for the large-scale enterprises that would soon explode into porter brewing.

Even at that early date, pale ale began to have an influence. Manorial breweries in the countryside had long been famous for strong, pale, hoppy beers and table-strength variants. When the gentry began taking up residence in London and brought a taste for these beers with them, it was a new thing to London brewers, who in the midseventeenth century had been

TECHNOLOGICAL CHANGES IN BREWING, 1700–1900

Steam Power

Although useful steam engines for mining were developed about 1700, the brewing industry had to wait until the improvements of James Watt and others made them practical for such work. The first steam engine installed in a brewery was in 1784 in London. Steam replaced manual, water, and horsepower for many tasks and made brewing on a large industrial scale possible.

The Thermometer

Although the technology had been around for some time, it was Gabriel Fahrenheit who created the first mercury thermometer and standardized scale. The Celsius scale was devised in 1742. James Baverstock was the first brewer to seriously investigate the use of a thermometer, but he had to hide his efforts from his conservative family, who opposed "new-fangled ideas." Michael Combrune wrote the brewing text (1784) detailing its use. The thermometer allowed for a good deal more consistency than the empirical methods in use, and allowed detailed research into the dynamics of brewing procedures.

The Hydrometer

This is an instrument that measures specific gravity and is used to measure the amount of sugar and other dissolved solids in beer wort (the sweet liquid drained from the mash that is fermented to make beer). In 1785, John Richardson wrote the first brewing book detailing brewing measurements made with the hydrometer, which had huge implications for the way beer was brewed and

Reeves & Co. Hydrometer, Ninteenth Century
This instrument, which measured dissolved sugars in unfermented beers, forever changed brewing.

brewing dark, sweet, heavy ales. The new-style pale beer was called "amber" or "twopenny," and it was one of the beers commonly used in the blends. So the public's growing appetite for a crisper, hoppier taste was another factor that drove the creation of porter.

Whatever the reason, the new hoppy brown beer was a huge craze aided by new technologies fueling the largest breweries the world had ever known. By 1796, Whitbread alone was brewing 202,000 thirty-six-gallon barrels a year; combined, London porter breweries brewed 1,200,000 barrels in 1810. At that time it took more money to finance a brewery than any other business except a bank. This new industrial scale is important, because it increased pressure on brewers to find efficiencies that had been insignificant in a smaller setting. In a competitive market, businesses live and die by these efficiencies, but as breweries strive to get the most for the least, the customer doesn't always benefit. The brewing texts are full of wistful quotes telling us how much better the beer was in the good old days. Some of this is simply nostalgia, of course, but if you look at the recipes, changes over time are rarely done with the aim of making the beer taste better.

While the particulars of the rise of pale ale are fascinating enough (and will be discussed in chapter 9), they were very much a

more than any other technology changed the way beer actually tasted by forcing brewers to formulate their recipes with yield in mind.

Yeast and Fermentation

The Dutch microscopist Anton Van Leeuwenhoek first observed and described yeast cells, but their living nature was revealed by three different scientists independently from around 1834 to 1835. Building on the groundbreaking work of Louis Pasteur, Christian Emil Hansen produced the first single-cell culture — as opposed to a mixed-brewing culture. This approach spread slowly, but by the midtwentieth century, this was the norm. Single-cell cultures make for a more consistent and on average better beer. However, many lamented the abandonment of more complex, mixed-culture fermentations even as they acknowledged the necessity of doing so.

Refrigeration

This was a culmination of centuries of work by various luminaries. American Alexander Twining is credited with creating the first commercial refrigeration unit in 1859. German engineer Carl von Linde's advanced dimethyl ether refrigeration machines were installed in the Spaten brewery in 1873. Refrigeration offered an obvious benefit over ice cut from frozen rivers and lakes — until then the only form of cooling available. Not only were the logistics complicated, but natural ice was becoming a health hazard, a result of pollution of the waterways. By 1890, artificial refrigeration was the norm for large-scale brewing everywhere.

Malt Kilning

Over time, there was a gradual transition from direct-fired, wood-fueled kilns to indirectly heated kilns fueled by coal, coke, or other fuels. By 1700, most brewers had switched to smoke-free malts, although brown malt continued to be kilned by crackling hot wood fires into the midtwentieth century (of course, smoked beers are today a specialty item in Bamberg, Germany). The most dramatic invention relative to malt kilning was the cylindrical roaster patented by Daniel Wheeler in 1817 that used a cooling spray to stop roasting before the grain caught fire; this device forever changed the brewing and flavor of porter and stout, as a small amount of this much darker malt was more economical than the large amounts of brown and amber malts used previously. Crystal/caramel malt was a much later development, around 1870.

continuation of the industrialization of beer begun by porter. Both porter and pale ale were hugely influential well beyond the borders of Britain. England was the superpower of the day, and its cultural trends were closely watched and occasionally adopted. Even in tradition-bound Germany, there was an interest in porter, and the globe-drenching success of pale ale was one of the things that pushed the town fathers of Plzeň to create their famous golden lager. But we're getting ahead of ourselves.

Cold-Fermented Lager

THE TRANSITION to cold-fermented lager brewing is a bit murky. The reasons are a mix of the influence of beers imported from farther north and a limiting of brewing to the colder half of the year. The commonly told story of Bavarian monks fermenting in caves in the Alps is plausible enough, but has little to support it. The earliest mention of lager supposedly occurs in 1420, in records from Munich, but this is not well documented. Then, from the city of Nabburg in northeast Bavaria, bordering on Bohemia, we get this: "One brews the warm or top fermentation; but first in 1474 one attempted to brew by the cold bottom fermentation, and to preserve part of the brew for the summer." By 1600, lager must have been pretty dominant in Bavaria and nearby regions such as Bohemia.

Because of its landlocked situation — as well as being host to a good deal of political turmoil over the centuries — Bavaria was a little late to the industrialization party. But by the mid-nineteenth century, things were heating up and the improvements of motive power, instrumentation, and kilning were all put to good use. Progress in microbiology pioneered by Pasteur, followed by the yeast work of Christian Emil Hansen, were especially well received by lager brewers. With their clean, pure flavors, lagers benefit from the consistency of single-cell cultures, so German brewers were quick to adopt them. English brewers of the day tried them out and because of their short brewing cycle found them unnecessary; mixed cultures are still employed today in some English breweries.

In the town of Plzeň in 1842, a number of things came together to create a beer that would eventually dominate the world market beyond anybody's dreams. The beer, Pilsner, was a confluence of ingredients, technology, and a business plan just right for the times.

Community leaders thought it would be a good idea to build a sizable brewery to make lager beer and capitalize on the lager boom and the extraordinarily high quality of the malt and hops of the region. The story goes that a brewer named Josef Grolle actually flubbed the recipe, and instead of a dark Munich-style

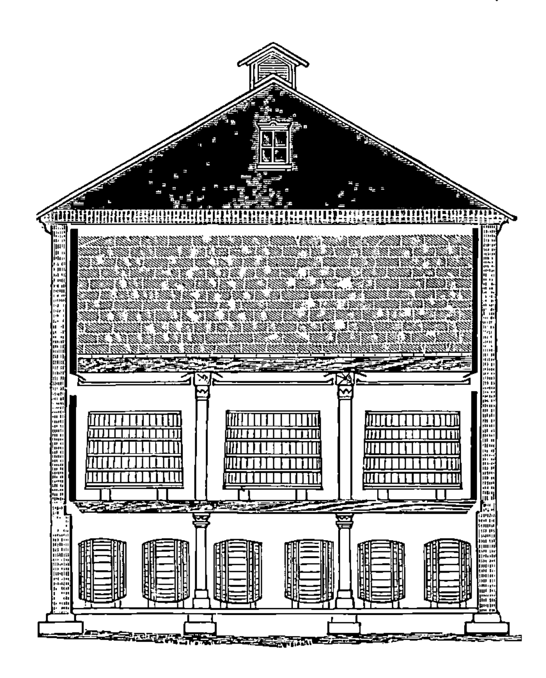

Nineteenth-Century Lager Keller
Before refrigeration, lager breweries used a lot of ice!

Spices
Following an ancient tradition, many Belgian-style beers contain subtle combinations of exotic spices such as coriander, bitter orange peel, grains of paradise, cumin, and star anise.

beer, a much paler beer gushed forth; but this seems very unlikely for a number of reasons. I think when the historians have dug into it a little deeper we will find that the parts and pieces were all there before 1842, and probably the beer, too, on a small scale. What the town fathers of Plzeň did was bet big on it, perhaps seeking to trade on the raging popularity of the English pale ale that seemed to be everywhere in those days. In any event, the pale, crisp, effervescent Pilsner beer was a huge hit, bringing its little hometown worldwide celebrity.

Bavaria joined the German Union in 1871, bringing its restrictive beer purity law with it; by 1879 this *Reinheitsgebot* had the force of law across Germany. Prior to this time, northern Germany's beers had a lot more in common with Belgium than they did with Bavaria. It was white-beer country up north. Beers brewed with a proportion of wheat, often smoked, sometimes sour, and using herbs such as coriander and sugars such as molasses and honey, were very popular. Beers from that time, like *grätzer, lichtenhainer, kotbüsser,* Broyhan, and *gose,* can be lovely beers and deserve to be brewed again — a few of them actually are. Of all the northern German ales, only Berliner Weisse and the lovely specialty ales of the Rhine valley, Kölsch and Düsseldorfer Alt, have survived in any meaningful way.

By the time World War II started rumbling up, all of the classic Germanic lager styles as we know them today were pretty well set in stone.

Belgium and France

THE PICTURE IS DIFFERENT in Belgium. Modernization occurred in the late nineteenth century, but this really only happened for the brewers of Bavarian-style lagers, of which Stella Artois is the best example. Before this invasion, Belgium was known primarily as a brewer of wheat beers. Even those considered barley-malt beers, such as *l'orge d'Anvers* (barley beer of Antwerp), often had a dash of wheat and oats in the grist. This mélange consisted of beers that are familiar to us today: witbier, lambic, and Flanders brown, as well as some that were popular in their day but have disappeared: *uytzet, peetermann, diest,* and many others.

Belgian beer has taproots that go back to the Middle Ages. Those dancing peasants in the Breughel painting are most likely drinking something along the lines of lambic, the sour, wild-fermented beer of the Brussels region. Witbier also has a long pedigree. But many of what we think of as ancient and characteristic beers, such as Trappist Dubbels and Tripels, are actually inventions of the twentieth century, so what you may have heard isn't always the real story.

Belgium has been through a lot. Wedged between vying superpowers, it has been dominated by the French, Dutch, Germans, Spanish, and Austro-Hungarians. Two devastating world wars were fought on its soil, and these brought with them calamitous occupations.

THE BELGIANS love to drink beer. Figures published in an 1851 book *(Lacambre)* state that, ". . . for a population in the neighborhood of four million individuals, [Belgians] brewed no less than eight or nine million hectoliters of beer per year," without exporting a great deal. This works out to a little over a pint a day per person, about twice what it is today. (If you're wondering, the Czechs are the world's biggest beer drinkers, at just over 150 liters [40 gallons] per person per year.)

The Belgian brewing industry was at a low point around 1900, and then came World War I. Despite the hardships, Belgian brewers managed to rebound. The 1920s and '30s saw the introduction of the strong, high-gravity luxury beers that form our impressions of Belgium today. Miraculously, the ancient lambic style managed to survive.

Belgian brewing is subject to the same kind of pilsnerization and consolidation that afflicts many of Europe's traditional brewing regions. But thanks to a strong export market — half of Belgium's beers leave the country — the scene abounds with fascinating artisanal products. Belgium has never had a beer purity law. This means there was never a purge of the ancient spices, herbs, and sugars that were once widespread in European brewing. Coriander, orange peel, cumin, grains of paradise (a pungent, peppery spice), and many kinds of sugars find their way into Belgian beers, often in quite subtle ways. For a beer lover seeking new experiences, Belgium is a wonderland of the highest order.

THE NORTH OF FRANCE, particularly the region of Nord, which borders Belgian Flanders, has a beer tradition that blends

This c. 1920 postcard shows the St. Louis Brewery in Laventie, in France's Nord region.

into Belgium's. Many rustic farm breweries were brewing top-fermented versions of the blondes, *bières de mars* (Märzens), and bocks that were popular as lagers elsewhere in France. These, especially the double versions, have been reborn as the *bières de garde* we know today.

Farther south, France's beer barrel was the Alsace-Lorraine region that bordered Germany to the east. By 1871, when Germany annexed the region after the Franco-Prussian War, Alsace was brewing most of France's beer. Louis Pasteur was among those enraged by this act of war, and he set about to do his part to rebuild the French brewing industry bigger and better with superb, world-class beer, which he called "the beer of revenge." He published his famous *Études sur la Bière* in 1876, which demonstrated the causes of beer spoilage and suggested methods for preventing it. This work was of enormous importance and had effects far beyond France, to every corner of the industrialized beer world.

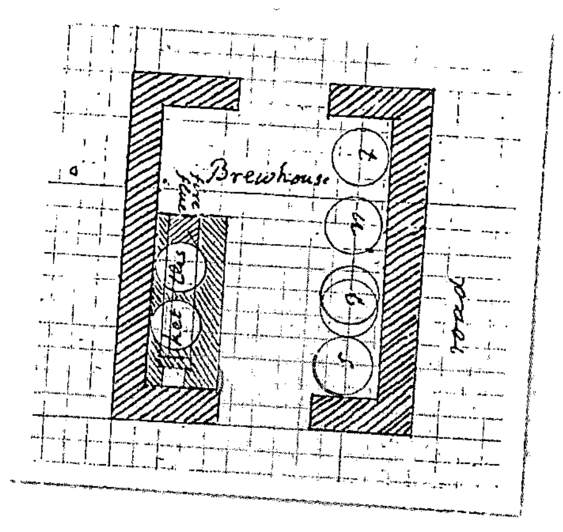

A Brewery at Monticello?
Thomas Jefferson penned this plan for a small brewhouse at his estate in northern Virginia. As far as is known, it was never built.

North America

THE FIRST COLONISTS to America brought with them a taste for beer. But brewing was extremely difficult in the New World for a number of reasons. Malt didn't grow well in southern regions like Virginia or in northern New England. There was some imported malt, but it was very expensive and only occasionally available. People continued to make the effort in the seventeenth and early eighteenth centuries, but after many generations, people's tastes do change; with beers made from molasses, dried pumpkin, and as one ditty says, "walnut-tree chips," it's not hard to see why. The commercial viability and easy access to cheap spirits helped rum and whiskey displace beer in most regions, and per capita consumption of spirits was ten times that of beer in 1800. That figure is in gallons. When you figure it based on the amount of alcohol consumed, it's more like 200 to 1.

Beer never did all that well on the frontier, and for a long time there were a lot of those wide-open spaces in America. Brewing takes a lot of infrastructure, a cooperative climate, and a steady source of clean water. Beer ingredients are heavy and difficult to transport overland, and the same is true of the finished product. Whether it was West Virginia or North Dakota, whiskey, rum, or other spirits were the logical choices for drinkers and producers alike.

In whatever manner people were getting their alcohol, small beer remained important in early America. George Washington's famous recipe of a little molasses and a handful of bran is probably typical. He was a commercial-scale distiller and had access to imported Madeira and other products for serious imbibing, but still, small beer was vital to the functioning of his estate. The idea was to add just enough flavoring to make it palatable as a source of safe water for slaves, servants, and master alike. After the Revolution, Thomas Jefferson saw beer as a temperate path for a spirits-soaked populace and began brewing experiments at Monticello, but ultimately nothing much came of this.

American Beer Labels, 1890–1919
American brewers tried to re-create all the beers of their Germanic homelands.

The exception to this dearth of beer was in Pennsylvania and parts of New York and Massachusetts. Wherever there were Germans or Dutch, there was a demand for beer, and these immigrants settled into lands that were able to provide the raw materials for their favorite drink. The Dutch arrived in New Amsterdam (New York) in 1630, and brewing commenced there just two years later. Brewing was such an industry that the first paved street in the city was Brouwer (Brewer) Street. After the Dutch ceded New Netherland to the English in 1664, brewing continued, but the center of gravity shifted south. Philadelphia became the Milwaukee of its day, a brewing center famous for its porter and ale right up to the lager revolution.

Canada, having never severed its ties to Britain, maintained its own version of an Anglophile beer culture, at least in English-speaking provinces.

Unrest in Germany and Bohemia, especially political chaos, occasioned by demands for more-democratic governments, forced many to head for America in the 1840s. Those flooding in had a strong affinity for beer, a "culture of pleasure," as writer Maureen Ogle (author of *Ambitious Brew*) puts it. For them, a world without the joys of a few lagers in the garden on a Sunday afternoon was just unthinkable, and as they were men of ambition and skill, they set about rebuilding their beer culture here, pretty much from scratch.

While many brewers remained small and were happy serving their local communities, others had grander plans. Colonel Pabst, Augustus Busch, and the Uehlein brothers of Schlitz were thinking along manifest destiny lines, and dreamed of brands spanning from coast to coast. This was a fairly ridiculous idea at the time, for there were few products of any kind with this sort of wide distribution. But as new technological improvements came along, these men were quick to seize on them as a way to achieve their goals. Steam power, refrigerated railcars, pasteurization, the telegraph, and artificial refrigeration were among these tools. The business vision and organizational skills required to make this happen are awe-inspiring.

AMERICA OF 1890 was filled with a sense of its own destiny, but still trying to coalesce as a people after half a century in which wave after wave of immigrants came ashore from Germany, Ireland, Italy, and elsewhere. While each had its own community, the order of the day was to become a "real American." One path to a shared culture turned out to be national brands of products made in shiny factories that were rock-solid consistent wherever they were found. National brands like Heinz pickles, Folgers coffee, Del Monte canned foods, and Coca-Cola are a few, but there were many more. There was an element of modernity in all this, something, happily, that we've gotten away from, but in those heady days, sliced bread (1928) really was the greatest thing.

The same impulses drove people's taste in beer. In the middle of the 1800s, rich brown Munich lagers predominated. Toward the end

Brewing during Prohibition
Americans have always been ready to roll up their sleeves to get what they need. The same kind of self-reliance fueled homebrewers a generation later.

of the century, pale, crisp Pilsner and other Bohemian-inspired beers started to catch the imagination of the public. Outside of the fact that this quenching style is a natural fit with the warm climate of much of the United States, these beers were seen as simply more modern and fashionable than their heavy brown predecessors, and by the beginning of Prohibition, pale lagers ruled the roost.

It's hard to overestimate the effect that the double whammy of war with Germany followed by Prohibition (the two are not unrelated) had on the brewing industry and especially the beer culture in the United States. Germans basically went underground. The beer gardens were shuttered. Even the royal family of England changed its name. Of the 1,300 or so breweries that were brewing shortly before this disastrous experiment in social engineering, only 756 were open a year after Prohibition was repealed, and many of these were destined to fail.

A whole generation grew up viewing alcohol as forbidden fruit, which makes it all the more tempting, but in a dirty, creepy sort of way. Quality plummeted. Worse, because brewing could only take place in utterly corrupt locales such as Chicago, spirits began to take hold nearly everywhere else, with the cocktail capturing the imagination of the drinker as a sophisticated, modern tipple. Although the beer industry regained its footing by the late 1950s, beer in America still suffers from this ravaged thinking many decades later.

Competition from the soda business was also a factor. From $135 million in sales in 1919, it had grown to $750 million by 1947, and double that a decade later. Soft drinks filled a need for a crisp, refreshing, temperate beverage — the role in which beer had held sole sway for thousands of years.

When Prohibition ended, beer started its slow climb out of the hole. Dark Munich-style lager was pretty well finished by then, replaced by crisp, bottled Pilsners thinned down with additions of rice or corn. Consumption shifted away from saloons to the home. Before Prohibition, 75 percent of beer had been draft and the

Near Beer
An old stereoscopic card summed up America's attitude to substitutes available during Prohibition.

Happy Days
Immediately after Prohibition, beer labels often reflected the optimistic spirit of the era. The beer didn't always live up to the promise.

remainder bottled. By 1945, this had reversed, and three-quarters of all beer was packaged, not draft, and increasingly sold to take home, which meant that beer was more available to women, and more importantly, they became involved in its purchase.

THE FIRST CANNED BEER was released in 1935 by the Kruger Brewing Company of Newark, New Jersey. The new cans were light, quick to chill, and took up less room than bottles in the refrigerator, all of which was very appealing to women. When masses of GIs returned home after World War II, having enjoyed canned beer in the intense arena of war, cans were a comfortable fit at home. They were a big hit.

Cans, by the way, are neutral as far as their effect on the product inside, even though by the 1980s they were snobbishly viewed as a low-class marker for the "Joe Six-Pack" lifestyle. At first made of steel, and now of aluminum, cans are lined with a beer-inert coating and have the real advantages of being totally opaque and recyclable. One small but growing trend is canned craft beers, such as pale ales, which appeal to craft beer's outdoorsy customers.

The other inescapable story in the last century of brewing is of consolidation. The United States had 4,131 breweries in 1873. A century later there were barely over a hundred. This is not unique to the brewing industry, or to the United States. It is a fact of business that over time, the efficiencies of larger operations combined with national marketing, the vulnerability of weak producers, and the need to acquire cash for growth all lead toward the big getting bigger while small producers fall by the wayside.

For reasons related to consolidation and the relatively mature stage of the market, the 1950s and '60s saw a hotly contested race to the bottom in terms of beer quality and price. Bargain brands appeared and then came ultra-bargain brands, the low end of which scraped against the federal government's requirement that beer contain at least 50 percent malt. The real low came first with store brands, and then with generic beer that came in cans with no branding at all.

A NUMBER OF different additives were used to make these discount beers more palatable. Cobalt salts were found to dramatically improve beer foam, and this was hailed as a godsend until people started getting sick and the product was withdrawn. By the late 1980s, most of these additives were gone for good, and it should also be noted that not all breweries resorted to extreme means to slice the price.

All this financial pressure put a great deal of strain on the production process. As malt

No-Name Beer
Things got so bad by the 1970s that there was a market for beer so cheap it didn't even have a brand name.

content lowered, it became difficult to produce a product that resembled beer well enough to deserve the name, and brewers were pressed to move the beer more quickly through the production cycle. Continuous fermentation was, and still is, an obsession among those modernizing beer production. In this process, wort is fed into one end of a fermenter, and finished beer comes out the other. Like a conveyor belt oven, this solves a lot of problems inherent in batch brewing. Brewers at Schlitz thought they were on to something big when they flipped the switch on their continuous fermenter in 1973, and they were. But the first batches of beer proved to be highly buttery and quite unacceptable to the consumer. This one huge misstep, on top of a host of others, doomed the brand to hide forever in the shadows, like a thing undead.

THE FINAL PART of the American industrial beer story is the success of light beer. The idea had been kicking around for some time. Miller bought the sleepy brand Lite, which had initially been Gablinger's and then part of the Meister Brau family. In 1975, Miller did the same thing to Lite that its parent company, Philip Morris, had done to Marlboro a couple of decades before: Take a female-oriented brand and restage it with a huge shot of testosterone, this time with aging sports stars, the cowboys of the day. *Blam!* Lite and its many imitators shot to the top of the charts, exceeding regular beer in barrelage by 2005. Like any successful product, Lite had simply seized the moment and presented its product to a market segment thirsty for its particular qualities.

The trend toward light, pale beer reached its low point with the introduction of Miller Clear in 1993. This water-clear beer, stripped of all color and much of its flavor by a carbon filtration process, was, thankfully, a step too far. It quietly slipped into the dark closet of failed brands.

Europe in the Modern Era

IN EUROPE, similar economic and consumer-preference factors have been at work over the past century, but the specifics have played out differently.

Consolidation and thinning the market of weaker players is a factor, but because there was no one catastrophic purge as we had with Prohibition, this has taken much longer — a death of a thousand cuts. The other thing Europe has, at least in the classic brewing nations, is a near-fanatical fan base for its traditional products such as real ale or all-malt lager. These are by no means in the majority, but they are in some places organized and very vocal.

Even in that holy ground for beer geeks, Belgium, Pilsners account for 70 percent of the market. Over the past century, that style has bulldozed many local specialties out of existence. The forces of big business, economic pressures, modernism, and more than anything, changing cultural patterns have had similar effects throughout the industrialized world. The big get bigger, the midsized get eaten alive, and it is left to the little fish to carry the torch for the interesting and meaningful products. For now, Germany still has its extensive network of local breweries, but the pressure for consolidation is on. In a way, we in the United States are lucky to have gotten through the worst of it a lifetime or two ago. When we hit bottom in terms of brewery numbers and interesting beers in the late 1970s, we had nothing to save and nothing to keep us from reinventing beer as we saw fit.

Nonetheless, pockets of real, character-rich beers have managed to survive, even in Pilsner-drenched Germany. From the cheery session beers of the Rhine to the *Weissbier* of Berlin and Jena to the amusement park that is Bamberg, in northern Bavaria, there are specialty beers

ENGLAND'S CAMRA MOVEMENT

In the late 1960s, the classic product of England's breweries, naturally carbonated cask or "real" ale, was being threatened by large brewers seeking to "modernize" the product by substituting filtered, artificially carbonated kegs or bulk tanks in pub cellars filled from brewery tanker trucks. In 1971, the Campaign for Real Ale (CAMRA) was organized to fight this trend. It seeks to use public and political pressure to ensure that real ale remains a viable choice in Britain's pubs. It also produces publications and conducts a number of real-ale festivals in Great Britain, including the Great British Beer Festival every August. Membership in 2007 was listed at 60,000.

Despite their moral rectitude and formidable constituency, CAMRA has been unable to preserve real ale as the national drink, and it now lags behind lagers and keg beers as a specialty product, with just 11 percent of the on-premise market as of 2007; it is available at less than half the nation's pubs. Economic forces and consumer attitudes can be battled, and may even be shifted a bit, but ultimately larger forces will always win out.

worth talking about, and their stories will be told in chapter 11.

In some places, like Italy and Denmark, where there is not a recent history of meaningful local traditions, small brewers have built an interesting beer scene from scratch. At the moment, Italy seems to be on a Belgian-inspired path, while the Danish craft-beer scene is starting to resemble the hop-spattered playpen of American craft brewing. There's been lots of action in Japan since the government lowered the minimum brewery size to a reasonable level. Craft breweries are popping up in Latin America, with an especially lively scene in Argentina. It's a very exciting time for good beer.

America, 1970 to the Present

IT'S HARD TO IMAGINE NOW, even for those of us who were there, just how destitute the American beer landscape was back in 1977. At that time there were fewer than 50 brewing companies with less than 100 breweries, fewer than at any time in the past 200 years. There were still a few regionals, several of whom survive today, but for the most part, they turned out a bland and timid mix of products aimed at an aging customer base. Some still brewed a seasonal bock beer, but this was often just a pale lager with a dash of caramel color added for visual appeal. Nobody seemed to care about the *product.*

To be fair to the honorable family men who rode these institutions into oblivion, the twentieth century was pretty hard on breweries, especially regional ones. Changing patterns of behavior and a shiny new national culture meant that there just wasn't any real need for them, and the struggle for existence after Prohibition had turned into a decades-long cannibalistic orgy of price cutting, product cheapening, and consolidation. There was some pride here and there, but there honestly wasn't much to base it on.

About that time, way off in a quiet corner of San Francisco, a young man with an inquisitive spirit and deeper pockets than most came upon one of the last of these local breweries still making a historic and interesting product. The brewery was Anchor, and the beer was Steam. In 1965, Fritz Maytag bought the Anchor brewery and invested his life in making it mean something again. Most agree this was the beginning of the craft-brewing movement in America. It's fitting that this first craft brewery was a living link to our authentic beer traditions and has the kind of historic cool that you can't just go out and manufacture.

While Fritz Maytag was busy rescuing San Francisco's Anchor brewery, there were a number of other things happening. Young Americans had been experiencing the classic beers of Europe firsthand, either while stationed in the military or backpacking around. The *Whole Earth Catalog* came out, and even though there was scarcely a word about beer in it, for many of us it pointed a way to a kinder, gentler mercantile future of interesting, handmade products in every category. Michael Jackson was hard at work on his groundbreaking *World Beer Guide,* first published in 1977. Books on homebrewing were leaking out of England, calling for strange ingredients like treacle, and Fred Eckhardt published a small but technically detailed book called *A Treatise on Lager Beer.* Homebrewing was still illegal, an oversight in the law written just after Repeal, but nobody seemed to care too much. It's hard to overstate the importance of homebrewing as a source for the ideas, passion, and people that make craft beer happen. Without it, the beer scene today would look very different.

The first actual microbrewery was the New Albion Brewery in Sonoma, California, which Jack McAuliffe opened in 1976. It didn't last long, but by then homebrewing was getting hot, and with a steady supply of guys making great beer and friends saying, "Man, that is great beer. You really should open a brewery," there were eventually plenty of them that did just that. A trickle turned into a flood, and by the early 1990s there were hundreds of packaging breweries and brewpubs brewing a huge range of charming, and occasionally magnificent, beers.

By the early '90s, craft beer was growing at 45 percent per year and was attracting some unsavory types, and by that I mean people who were looking only at the money aspect of craft brewing, which was not enough for a venture to succeed. Not a single brewery that tried to start large was successful. By the end of the decade there had been a shakeout, but the upside was that there was a lot of nice used equipment available for a cheap price.

The craft beer industry is a lot more sophisticated today. Beer quality is extremely high, marketing is correctly understood as helpful in getting the story out, and generally the business sense has caught up with the passion for beer, without overtaking it. Growth has settled into a robust 10 to 15 percent a year, and the category now commands about 4 percent of the U.S. beer market by barrelage, around 6 percent by dollars. North America is home to the most diverse, creative, and delicious beers on the planet. The late author Michael Jackson was fond of shocking European audiences with that observation.

For well over 100 years, the direction of the brewing industry was determined by its largest players. Today, with big beer stagnant and craft beer continuing to blossom, this is no longer the case. I hope we are headed for an era in which the beer market becomes something along the lines of the selection-rich wine category; when you hear August Busch IV say, "The future of beer in America is all about choices for the consumer," you have to just dig down deep and prove him right.

The Beer Marketplace

Since the earliest times, beer has been sold in a highly regulated system. The Code of Hammurabi threatens alewives with drowning in the river for cheating customers; today's punishments can be nearly as draconian. For thousands of years, governments have felt the need to keep beer contributing to society — as a taxable article and an alcoholic beverage — while not allowing it to do too much mischief. Because of corruptible human nature and what's at stake for all involved, it's inevitable that these efforts can be, at times, misplaced.

In the United States, many aspects of alcoholic-beverage regulation have been left to the individual states, especially when it comes to selling it.

After some serious excesses in the brewery-owned saloon system before Prohibition, a three-tier distribution system was set up in most states after Repeal. With exceptions often made for brewpubs and occasionally for small-packaging breweries and wineries, alcoholic beverages must flow from brewer (or importer) to distributor to retailer. In many states, distributors are protected by franchise laws, which set the limits and obligations of the relationship between these parties.

The positive side is that franchise laws give distributors incentive to invest in the brands they carry, knowing that the brands can't be pulled without cause by a capricious brewer. But the downside is that this investment doesn't always happen, and distributors have been known to lock brands into a sort of dungeon where they are neither supported nor allowed to move to a distributor who would get behind them. Over the years, franchise laws have led to a considerable amount of discontent, and they are constantly at play in state legislatures as both sides struggle to move the balance point in their favor.

Most level heads in the beer industry see a need for distributors. One great argument in favor of the three-tier system is that it keeps the retail system out of the direct control of brewers. For a peek at brewery control of retailing, one need only look to England. There, brewers historically controlled the vast majority of pubs, either through direct ownership or through loans with exceptionally generous terms. In that situation, the marketing strategy becomes to spend your budget making your pubs as comfortable and showy as possible to attract drinkers. This has led to some real dazzlers, but it usually limits the beers available to a handful of a single brewery's products, with the requisite "guest" beer tossed in, often from a sister brewery's portfolio. After the Monopolies Commission forced English breweries to divest, control was snapped up by a small number of large multinational corporations that tend to do business with the largest breweries and keep consumer choice limited. If you've ever tried to get a locally brewed product in an American chain restaurant (and who among us hasn't?), you know what I mean.

America is so completely dominated by the large players (Anheuser-Busch had 48.8 percent of the U.S. beer market as of November 2007) that their ownership of pubs could easily be used to restrict consumers' access to smaller brands.

For startup breweries, distribution is a difficult issue. Early on, most are still getting their footing, trying to find out who makes up their market and struggling with the complexities of the business. In general, distributors are happier with somewhat more mature brands that have already had the kinks worked out in the production and marketing areas. In many states, breweries under a certain size are permitted to self-distribute. Distributors see this as violation of their bedrock right to the three-tier system, but it is arguably better for them to let very small breweries incubate on their own until they are ready for a more sophisticated step up into the market.

Liquor laws in the United States are a crazy quilt of sometimes senseless or game-rigging regulations. As of 2007, 5 percent alcohol by volume is the maximum for lager and the minimum for ale in Texas; Pennsylvania curtails consumption by requiring that beer be bought by the case; no beer in Alabama can come in a package larger than 16 ounces; many states mandate that no beer of more than 3.2 percent alcohol (by weight; 4 percent by volume) can be sold in grocery stores. The list goes on and on. Also in Texas, there is a singular exemption to the three-tier system for a "marine mammal attraction" in a specified county and size, though this only applies so long as an actual, live marine mammal is on the premises. (If you need a clue, it begins with "Sea" and ends with "World," and it just happens to be owned by one of America's larger brewers.)

IT DOESN'T END with states; local governments have the power to control things as they see fit. There are wet, dry, and damp counties (places where alcohol is available only at restaurants or private clubs), a county in Maryland that *is* the distributor, and many other practices that would be laughable if it weren't for the fact that they can seriously cut into your ability to enjoy legal products in the manner of your choosing.

Thanks to a slowly thawing political climate and a lot of hard work by enthusiasts and professionals working together, some of the old laws are falling victim to rationality. Alcohol-content caps for beer in North Carolina and several other states have been removed, and the anticompetitive package-size restrictions in Florida have been lifted. There is plenty more to be done, and neo-Prohibitionist forces are always trying to turn back the clock, so all of us who enjoy good beer need to be vigilant and ready to fight for it. The Brewers Association keeps a list of those who have expressed interest in maintaining their access to good beer and calls upon them as needed to provide grassroots pressure on beer-related issues. If you'd like to get on the list, go online to www.supportyourlocalbrewery.org.

Beer is a great mirror of history. It always amazes me how much of a story every beer has to tell. When I hold up the glass and think about it, every aspect of this malty, hoppy, foamy brew is a consequence of a remarkable chain of events that began some 10,000 years ago. That's a deep drink.

From *Let There Be Beer!*

Joe and his buddy sat down in one of the bare wooden drinking stalls in front of the long polished beer board in the Hofbräu-Haus, a bar as long and polished as life. A straight and narrow road to heaven.

Joe's pal held up two fingers and sung out, "*Zwei dunkels*, Fritz," to the waiter, a pleasant little German gnome, shorter than the boys, active as the yeast in beer.

Came the beer. Joe saw upstanding Würzburger for the first time, and was completely conquered. There was no such drink in the world as that — the foam was like whipped cream, you could eat it with a spoon.

— Bob Brown, 1934

CHAPTER 2

SENSORY EVALUATION

WHY taste beer? Wouldn't the world be a better place if we could simply drink, enjoy, relax? Sure, there are times when an uncritical approach is just the ticket. But there are many other situations in which a more focused and structured approach is called for.

Competitions are the most obvious manifestation of this, where beers are judged either against each other, on their own merits, or against an archetype of a particular style. If you are choosing beer for a restaurant or a private dinner party, some beers will make the list and some won't — probably based mainly on how they deliver in the glass.

BREWERS LARGE AND SMALL must constantly evaluate their beers for consistency, freedom from flaws, and suitability to their slice of the market. In small operations, a casual attitude toward this kind of evaluation can cause problems. Relying on a limited number of tasters can fail to account for everybody's individual shortcomings. Even for the smallest brewers, implementing a structured sensory evaluation program with calibrated tasters can pay back big-time in the marketplace.

If you take the time to develop an approach and a vocabulary, even casually tasted beers may reveal themselves in greater depth, meaning, and eventually, pleasure.

Sensation is a mix of stimulation and perception. At one end, sensory nerves fire when stimulated, and at the other end, thoughts, memories, and images emerge. I like to think of the two parts as hardware and software, but of course there's a gray area in between.

The sensory cells that line your mouth and nose fire when stimulated by particular chemicals in certain ways — a kind of "hardware" triggering that shoots signals to your brain. These stimulations are pretty much hardwired into your body, the result of millions of years of trying to make our way in an unforgiving environment. At the highest level, these sensations pop into our conscious awareness. These conscious thoughts are deeply affected by social, cultural, and highly personal histories, and of course are always changing. They are also influenced by how much we can focus on the experience. In all these ways, they form the "software," or cognitive part of the sensory experience.

There is a lot in between nerve and notion. Sensations go through many levels of neural processing before they reach the conscious brain. Some of this processing is simply a form of organizing, but some of it involves memory and emotion — things that punch through into awareness, but at the same time we don't really control. It is pretty cool stuff and it can be useful in tasting beer, which I will explain more fully in just a bit.

The Sense of Taste

YOUR TONGUE HAS about 10,000 taste buds, and there are lesser quantities in the soft palate, epiglottis, esophagus, nasopharynx, and the inner surfaces of the cheeks and lips. Each one is a sensitive detector that responds to a particular set of chemicals. The sense of taste evolved to give us important clues about good and bad things in our environment, to guide us toward nutritionally desirable foods and away from potential poisons. This sense is so important that it is wired into the brain via three separate paths, so if one becomes damaged there are still two backups for the job, the same amount of redundancy built into spacecraft.

If you look at your tongue, you will see that it is covered in small bumps. These are not taste buds, but papillae, and embedded in them are the buds themselves — between just a few and 250 per papilla, depending on type. The tongue map, which we all learned in grade school, is supposed to show the areas of sensitivity to various flavors: sweet up front, sour along the sides, and so on. This has very little to do with physiological reality, and in fact was created in the late nineteenth century by the same folks who brought us phrenology, the pseudoscience of translating the bumps and valleys of the skull into moral proclivities of all sorts.

There is some slight localization of flavor on the tongue, but most of the tongue is sensitive to all six flavors (see sidebar on the following page). The tongue is covered with filiform papillae, the small bumps you can see and feel. These contain no taste buds and are purely mechanical. There are three areas with different populations of papillae that actually contain taste buds. Interspersed amongst the filiform papillae on the front two-thirds of the tongue are the fungiform (mushroom-shaped) papillae, and these are a little more densely packed at the margins. Each has a number of separate taste buds nestled into its sides, not its top. With only slight variations, these are equally sensitive to sweet, bitter, sour, salty, and umami, and also the newly discovered sense for fat.

Across the back of the tongue is a row of large circumvallate papillae, and along the sides, also at the back of the tongue, are the foliate papillae. The circumvallate papillae seem to be especially sensitive to bitter and fat, which is why swallowing is regarded as part of the beer-tasting process; the foliate are sensitive to fat and especially to sourness, which is why a sip of lemon juice (or a sour lambic) triggers a sharp localized sensation to the sides of the back of the tongue. There are also filiform papillae that cover the tongue everywhere, but

THE BASIC FLAVORS

Sweet

This familiar sensation evolved to alert us to food items with a lot of nutritive value in an environment that used to be fairly sparse in them. Even premature babies automatically respond to sweet tastes with suckling. This sensation serves us rather poorly now that sweet foods and drinks are within an arm's length everywhere. Some deep dark corner of our brains still thinks that sweet foods are good for us, and so we overconsume.

Physiologically, the sweet sensation is fairly complicated, being mediated through similar multistep pathways as bitter, fat, and umami.

There is nearly always some sweetness in beer, although it only becomes a major player in a few rich styles like Scotch ale, doppelbock, and milk stout, in which there is a significant amount of residual sugar. Nevertheless it is present in most beers as a balancing element, although it may be overshadowed by hops, roasted malt, or occasionally acidity.

Sour

These sensors detect hydrogen ions, as all pH meters do. Acidity (or lack thereof) is a pretty reliable indicator of ripeness in fruit and is also a marker for spoiled food, so there may have been some evolutionary pressure along those lines.

The cellular mechanism is fairly simple, which is one reason for the lightning-quick reaction we have to acidic foods and drinks. Beer is a moderately acidic drink, normally with a pH of 4.0 to 4.5, but with the exception of the sour Belgian beers (at pH 3.4 to 3.9), it plays a supporting rather than a starring role. One place to really pay attention to acidity is in fruit beers, where it has a great deal to do with the brightness of fruit character.

Salty

These taste buds respond to sodium ions and, to a lesser extent, potassium. These salts are vital to many cellular processes and have to be obtained from the environment. In beer, salt does not commonly play a role, but when it is present — either from mineral-rich water or added intentionally — it makes flavors richer and bigger.

Bitter

This is a plant's way of telling animals "Don't eat me!" In fact, human beings are the only species not automatically averse to bitterness. Because of the many different kinds of toxic chemicals in the environment, there may be as many as thirty different types of receptors in the cells that detect bitterness. Scientists have found a number of genes that code for bitter receptors. Despite this variety, it is thought that all these different pathways send only one signal to the brain for bitterness, without the nuances of a specific taste. This contradicts our subjective sense that there

these serve a strictly physical purpose and don't have any taste buds or receptors in them.

Each taste bud is made up of many sensory cells whose sensitive threadlike tips extend upward into the central pore of the bud, ready to fire off a signal when the appropriate "tastant" molecule wafts by. Each cell is sensitive to one taste, but there are many tastant-specific receptors present for the more chemically complex sensations such as sweet, bitter, and umami.

Aroma and Olfaction

UNLIKE THE GUSTATORY SYSTEM of the tongue, which senses chemicals dissolved in liquid, the olfactory system is sensitive to airborne molecules. It's a vastly more complex system.

are several subtly different "flavors" of bitterness, so there may be some additional mechanism at work in this case. In many ways, bitterness is a catchall category for detecting toxins as diverse as cyanide and alkaloids.

The cellular processes that trigger a bitter signal are fairly complex, and because of this, bitter-sensing taste buds are slower to respond. This is easy to notice and happens every time you take your first sip of a bitter beer. The first taste sensation is likely to be a mix of sweetness and acidity, but after a beat the bitterness kicks in and builds to a crescendo. And the bitterness takes longer to leave the palate as well, sometimes lingering for several minutes in especially assertive beers.

This flavor does not play much of a part in Western cuisine, although bitter foods are relished in many parts of Asia. For most of us, bitterness is an acquired taste. Look at the way the customer preferences at a newly opened brewpub change. At first, an amber ale or pale lager is the best-selling beer. But by the end of a year, it is often the pale ale. For sure, some people mightily crave bitterness, and a slice of the beer market has sprung up to accommodate these hopheads — one that seems to have become a permanent niche.

Umami (Glutamate)

Although this flavor has been acknowledged for over a thousand years, it wasn't until the year 2000 that a genetic basis for the receptor was discovered, establishing it as a primary taste detected by the tongue. *Umami* translates as "deliciousness" in Japanese, and this word sums up a savory, meaty quality found in many foods and occasionally in beer. The sensations originate with a group of amino acids, the subunits from which proteins are formed. Inosinates, guanylates, and glutamates are mainly responsible and are derived from different food types. Umami is found in aged meat, oily fish, fermented foods, especially soy products, aged cheese (as much as 10 percent by weight in Parmesan), ripe tomatoes, seaweed, and many other foods.

Umami starts to become noticeable in beer after prolonged aging. First, a rich meatiness may show itself, and with enough time, flavor notes reminiscent of soy sauce might show up. It's not well studied at this point, but umami is an important player in beer and food pairing.

Fat

This is the most recently discovered member of the taste family, having been added only with the discovery of its receptor in 2005. Like sugar, this one seeks out nutritionally loaded foods and can wreak havoc in the modern french fry-accessible world. It's not clear if this receptor plays any role at all in beer tasting, as beer is a fat-free product.

The Old Tongue Map
An erroneous product of nineteenth-century quackery, it has proven difficult to purge from the textbooks.

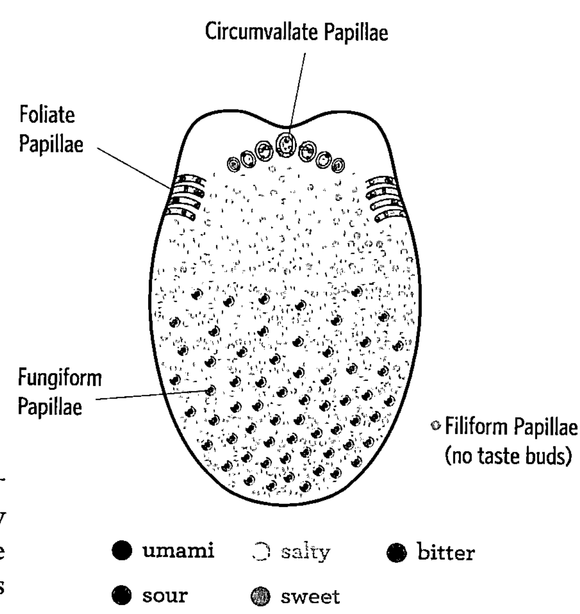

A New Tongue Map
While there are three different taste-sensitive regions on the tongue, the front half of the tongue is equally sensitive to all tastes. Bitterness is perceived a little more intensely in the circumvallate papillae across the back, and the fungiform papillae on the sides are slightly more sensitive to sourness.

Between the upper part of the nasal cavity and the back of the throat, most people have around 9 million olfactory neurons. Humans are relative lightweights in the animal kingdom; dogs have around 225 million. We can perceive about 10,000 perceptible aromas with just 1,000 different receptor types, but exactly how this happens is one of the unresolved (and hotly disputed) areas of science. Clearly, with a tenth as many receptor types as detectable aromas, some combining of signals is needed. Each odorant stimulates a particular set of neurons, each of those at a different intensity, making for a wide variety of possible aromas. The classic explanation of aroma is the lock-and-key model, but there is evidence that something else may be going on. Recent evidence, such as being able to discriminate between the odors of chemically, but not energetically, identical isotopes, suggests that some olfactory cells are able to "read" the energy levels at which the molecules vibrate. No less than five separate mechanisms have been proposed to explain the functioning of the olfactory system, and the real explanation may turn out to involve multiple mechanisms. It's a fascinating area with a lot of research yet to be done.

There are two different sets of olfactory sensors. Some are high up in the nose where you'd expect them to be, and are called the orthonasal receptors. This set seems to be wired more to serve as an analytical tool, where aromas are categorized and eventually identified. There is another set, the retro-nasal, that resides in the soft tissue at the back of the mouth and in the channel that connects the mouth to the nose. It has recently come to light that these two systems are more separate than once thought and are processed by the brain in different ways. The retro-nasal system perceives less as "aroma" and more as "flavor." Additionally, this second system seems to be much more involved in notions of preference or familiarity, so you can blame this one if you never liked broccoli as a child. In beer, this may affect the way that malt or hop character can be perceived as something more complex than purely aromatic. It's also connected with satiation, the sense of having had enough to eat.

The sense of smell is wired into our brains differently from other senses. Rather than proceeding right away to higher centers of cognition, olfactory signals make a detour through some very old and mysterious parts of the brain: the hypothalamus, seat of appetite, anger, and fear; the hippocampus, regulator of memories; and the brain stem, which controls basic bodily functions like respiration.

I would not be bothering you with all this anatomy if it weren't genuinely practical beer-tasting information. Aromas can elicit powerful psychological responses in the form of memories and emotions. One of the most challenging, but crucial, parts of the tasting process is putting a name to an aroma or taste sensation. Having that name literally on the tip of one's tongue is a frustrating experience. I have found that if you can coax up an old memory from a particular aroma, you can often retrieve enough of that memory to look around a little. Is it Grandma's house? Food? Flowers? What's in the backyard — are those roses? And then, *bam!* like a bolt, it comes to you. This kind of mind expansion makes for very entertaining personal growth.

FROM A BREWER'S POINT OF VIEW, these charged psychological experiences offer great leverage for art. If you can formulate a beer that will regularly conjure up happy childhood memories of, say, oatmeal cookies, you can create powerful affinities, even if your audience is not aware of the connection. I tell my recipe formulation students, "As an artist, it's your job to mess with people's heads." It's great to have this kind of tool in your pocket.

Just as our personal histories affect our responses to certain aromas, so do our cultural affinities. Some sensations are universally good or bad: the love of sweetness, the repulsion to rotting meat, and the sensitivity to musty smells, which are among the most powerful odorants known. But many sensations, like the bitterness discussed earlier, are acquired tastes that affect us according to our genes and how we've been brought up, as well as how open-minded we are about seeking their pleasures.

It should be pointed out that in general, women are more sensitive tasters than men, an advantage that increases during pregnancy. Also, as we age, we become less sensitive, but fortunately this can be more than compensated for through training and experience, so there is hope for those of us among the un-young.

And lastly, compared to sight and sound, for example, aroma and taste sensations take longer to register and linger longer. This is another reason to look at taste as having a time dimension — a beginning, middle, and end — rather than being just a single snapshot moment.

Psychological Factors

IN THE STRANGE WORLD of sensory experience, two plus two rarely equals four. Although we are exquisitely sensitive and better than machines for many tasks, we are far from perfect in some very interesting ways.

First, we all vary in our sensitivities to different chemicals. A beer that may seem sickeningly buttery to one taster may be comfortably caramelly to another. Phenol in certain forms is vile in beer, adding an electrical-fire stench, yet up to 20 percent of people may be totally blind to it. If you're a brewer, this should be a very scary thought to you. Most good tasters I know try to get a grip on this either by actually calibrating their palates using a series of different concentrations of specific aroma chemicals, or simply by paying attention when doing critical tasting and comparing their own reactions to those of their peers. If you're always the one person at the table that can't pick up a certain aroma, there's a good chance you have a lower sensitivity than others.

Sensitivity also varies with time of day. Biorhythms may seem like a quacky crock of pseudoscience, but there is real science behind the notion. Midmorning seems to be the time when we're at our sharpest, which is why breweries usually conduct taste panels at this time.

Larger brewers test their taste-panel members on their individual sensitivities to a range of commonly encountered aroma chemicals and factor their strengths and weaknesses into their beer evaluations. By using a series of progressively weaker dilutions of off-flavors spiked into beers, and testing a subject's ability to discriminate between spiked and unspiked beers, each person's threshold can be determined. This is not beyond the reach of serious amateurs and small brewery personnel, although careful observation during the course of normal judging can accomplish much the same thing over time.

SENSORY ENHANCEMENT PRACTICES

- Take a walk or a drive around with your windows open and really pay attention to how smells change from location to location. I think about half of tasting skill is just being able to concentrate. I especially like Chicago around lunchtime.
- Next time you order a beer, make a few notes on your napkin about aroma, flavor, texture, aftertaste. Real beer geeks carry around a notebook, like birders do. It isn't that important whether you save the notes; it is the act of recording them that's important.
- Go to a wine tasting. Sometimes getting away from our comfort zone jolts us into a state of higher awareness.

STRANGE AND STRANGER

There are a number of phenomena that affect the way flavors and aromas are perceived, adding another layer of complexity — and interest — to the taster's task.

Some chemicals change personalities as the amount in a sample changes. That is, if you add more and more, it doesn't just taste like a stronger version of the same thing, but changes its character. One chemical, o-aminoacetophenone, smells like malt in parts-per-billion concentrations, like tacos in parts per million, and enough like Concord grapes in parts-per-thousands that it actually is used in grape soda. This is an extreme example, to be sure, but the same effect happens with diacetyl (a by-product of fermentation), which changes from buttery (think theater popcorn) to butterscotch as the concentration rises.

Another example is the "matrix effect," which involves interactions between flavors that either change each other or give rise to new sensations altogether. Coffee is usually cited as the classic example. Despite the fact that there are over 900 identified flavor chemicals, none of them taste exactly like coffee, and no one really knows what is responsible for "coffeeness." It's a common phenomenon in the Maillard reaction, or caramelization, important in cooked meat and in beer, where kilned malts contribute so much flavor and aroma.

Matrix effects may change the way single chemicals are perceived as well. In pale beer, DMS (a sulfur compound that can cause off-flavors) comes across as creamed corn. In darker beers, however, this often changes to more of a tomato juice aroma — very useful to know if you're judging dark beers.

"Masking" is a phenomenon in which the presence of one chemical hides the flavor of another. In beer, carbonation masks hops, and high levels of ethanol can mask oxidized aromas. Vanilla is a well-known masking substance, having the ability to round the rough edges off just about anything.

"Potentiation" is just the opposite. It occurs when the presence of one chemical enhances or magnifies another. The effects on food of salt and pepper are the most familiar examples; umami is another. Beer itself can do the same thing, which is why it can be great for cooking and as a food companion.

Mouthfeel

In addition to aroma and flavor, there is a further range of sensations that a beer will trigger. We all have the tools to detect temperature, carbonation, viscosity, and cooling or burning sensations from things like mint and chile peppers. In beer, this translates to crispness/dryness, palate fullness, richness, oiliness from oats or rye, and more. The proper technical term is "trigeminal" sensations, after the main nerve of the face that carries these sensations to the brain.

As important as they are in creating the complete experience that is beer, these sensations are perhaps even more important in the context of enjoying beer and food together and can strongly affect the way pairings are put together.

Visual

Beer really is quite beautiful. Humankind has been singing the praises of its deep, clear color and white, creamy foam for thousands of years, and we get no less pleasure from it today. So much of our sensory input comes though our eyes that it's just natural we trust the visual above every other sense. Experienced tasters, though, know not to be too distracted by what they see.

Competitive beer-judging score sheets rarely assign more than 10 percent of available points to the appearance category. But anyone who has ever judged a flight of beers knows what kind of powerful seduction the eyes are capable of bestowing. A little paler or darker than the category description, and you start tasting things that may not actually be there. In judging, of course you want to minimize this effect, but in presenting beer we want to pull out all the stops and take advantage of it. There will be much more to say about this in chapter 6, but for now, just know that the way a beer is presented will profoundly affect the way it tastes.

Someday, you too may be called upon to spread the word about great beer. A well-traveled palate, solid technique, and great vocabulary will be your best tools for guiding people through their beer experience. Having a keen awareness of all the parts and pieces of a given beer allows you to present the most relevant parts to your audience, and allows them to develop confidence as educated tasters. I need hardly mention how much more gratifying your own beer experience will be.

CHAPTER 3

BREWING AND THE VOCABULARY OF BEER FLAVOR

EVERY sensation found in a glass of beer has its origins in the decisions the brewer and maltster made during its manufacture. For instance, the tangy, green perfume of hops? That's the result of the careful choice and deployment of prized aroma hops in the brewhouse or perhaps in the fermenter. The light nuttiness and hints of raisiny fruit? That's lightly kilned pale ale malt and a dab of crystal. And all of this is shaped by the mysterious workings of a particular strain of yeast under certain conditions.

The ability to deconstruct a beer, to get inside the head of a brewer, that separates serious from casual tasters. To those who understand the brewing process a beer is an open book. Beer is so dependent on the actions of its brewer that an understanding of the brewing process is the foundation on which all of your practical beer-tasting experience will build. The goal is more pleasure by way of a more complete grasp of what's in the glass. To get that, we're going to have to get down and dirty with the brewing process.

The gleaming stainless megabreweries of today are doing essentially the same things with malt, water, hops, and yeast as the simple wooden and clay vats of the ancients. The process seems pretty simple, and the fact that it can be carried out to extremely high levels of art by people in their basements and garages with a few oversized pots and pans speaks to this. The advanced technology in industrial breweries is used mostly for consistency, economy, and efficiency, and has very little to do with artistry.

Beer is an agricultural product, but by far the overwhelming majority of brewing's raw materials — barley, hops, water — are bought and sold as commodities. This is very different from the world of wine, in which grapes sitting just yards away from each other can be dramatically different for reasons of microclimate, soil type, access to the sun, and other variables. In wine, the hand of God is foremost. But in brewing,

---

Deconstructing a Beer

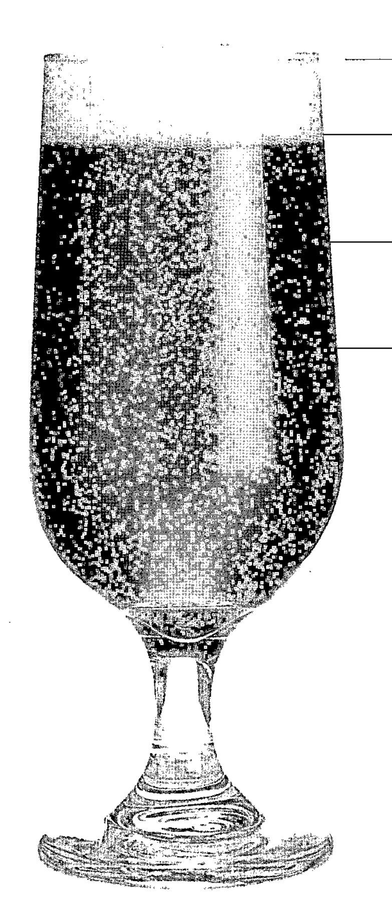

Aroma: Derived from ingredients such as malt and hops, but modified and augmented by yeast.

Head: From the medium-length proteins present in malt and adjunct grains such as wheat, oats, and rye. Affected by mashing, and possibly by filtration.

Color: Primarily from kilning of malts chosen for the brew, but affected by mashing and boiling specifics, and even to some degree by fermentation and filtration.

Carbonation: Carbon dioxide (CO_2) gas, a by-product of fermentation by yeast.

Body and Mouthfeel: Proteins from malts, affected by the brewing, fermentation, and filtering procedures; sweetness from malts, brewhouse decisions, and fermentation.

Flavor: Malt, hops, and brewing water, all affected by many aspects of the brewing process.

Alcohol: More fermentable material means more alcohol, along with everything else.

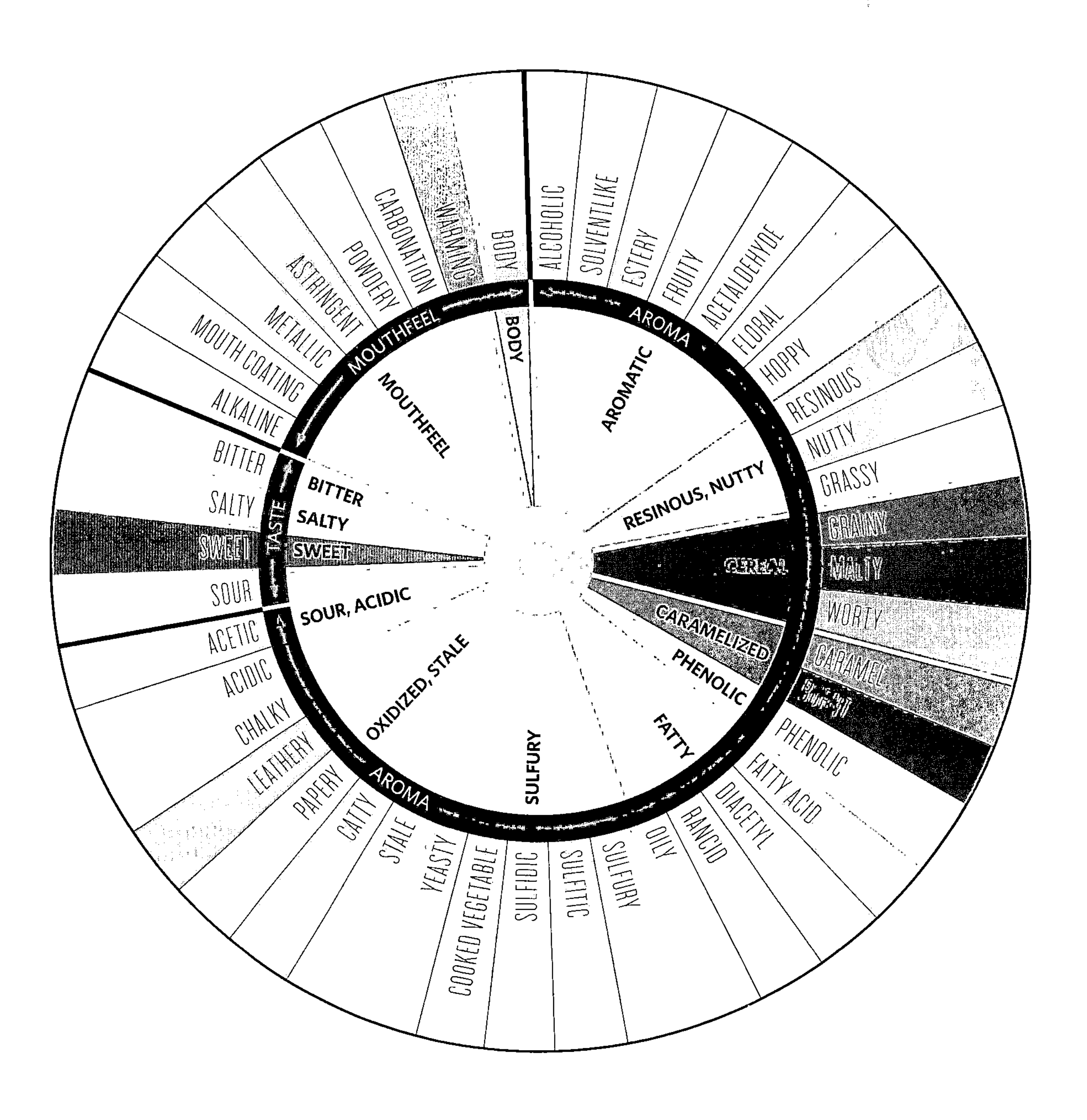

The Flavor Wheel
Beer contains a wide range of different tastes, aromas, and mouthfeel sensations. Designed by sensory scientist Morten Meilgaard in the 1970s, the Flavor Wheel is designed to show the relationships between beer's disparate sensory elements.

it's the hand of man that is clearly visible, and that for me is one of its greatest fascinations. There are a few instances when terroir (the characteristics geography bestows) really matters in beer, and we'll get to that later. Paint is paint; it is the hand that guides the brush that matters. It should be your goal to get to know brewers through their art — their beers.

The choices begin with the maltster. Through a series of steps, the most fertile and uniform barley is coaxed springing to life. As it does, everything changes. Through a fantastically complex series of enzyme-driven transformations, the seed readies its starch reserve to support a new plant, unaware that the maltster has other plans. The particulars of this controlled sprouting have a huge effect on the brewing value of the malt and eventually the flavor of the beer. Heat is applied to stop the process, and it is during this kilning process that the malty flavors of beer are created — from the most delicate, breadlike graininess through dozens of shades of amber and brown to the inkiest espresso of black malts.

And we haven't even started brewing yet.

Yet the choices go on: recipe formulation, brewhouse procedures, yeasts, fermentations, carbonation, filtration, packaging, and much more. Hundreds of little steps work together with tradition, technology, market demands, and sometimes just the rambunctiousness of the brewer to put a particular beer in your glass.

To manage this demanding complexity with a deft hand requires a unique personality. The very best brewers I've known exhibit a mix of curiosity, creativity, and willingness to take risks, coupled with a near-fanatical obsession to every tiny detail; unique people, to be sure, and among the beer world's great pleasures.

While the details of brewing may seem technical, I can assure you they are the heart and soul of any beer. Start looking for them the next time you hoist a brew, and you'll find them just jumping out of the glass.

Water

BEER IS MOSTLY WATER. Of course it's going to have an influence on the flavor.

First of all, water — actually called "liquor" when destined for brewing — is not flavorless. To get into your sip of beer, water sometimes has to travel incredible distances over long time spans. Along the way, it has come in contact with soils, sand, rocks, and other matter. Because water is an unparalleled solvent, it dissolves various minerals on its journey. These show up as ions, half molecules that split apart and float freely in water's magic spell. Many of them you can actually taste. The hard chalkiness of carbonate, the palate-expanding roundness of sodium and chloride, the plastery tang of sulfate all lend their character to beer.

Water minerals bring more than flavor to beer. The ions in brewing water are chemically active and have important effects on the brewing process. Each type of beer and brewing process has its ideal water. It wasn't until about 1900 that brewers learned how to adjust the chemistry of their local water. Before that, they were limited in the types of beer they could brew, and so the limitations imposed by local water was a major factor in the evolution of most of the classic beer styles.

Limestone, a common type of bedrock, is composed mainly of calcium carbonate

SENSORY VOCABULARY: MINERAL

TYPE: taste, aroma (sulfate only)

DESCRIPTORS: mineral, chalky, plaster, drywall, sulfate, salty

THRESHOLD IN BEER: varies; never more than subtle

APPROPRIATENESS: may be noticeable and pleasant in some pale ales, occasionally in Dortmunder lager or pale ale. Excess chalkiness can manifest as unpleasant astringency (see page 40).

SOURCE: mineral ions in brewing water

Water *Does* Matter
Water has flavors of its own, and plays an important role in the chemistry of brewing as well.

(sometimes magnesium carbonate in a similar rock called dolomite), and water traveling over, under, or through limestone often dissolves some of the stone as it passes by. Pure water can't do this. It is only when the atmospheric gas carbon dioxide is dissolved in water that it becomes acidic enough to pick up some of the mineral, creating a slightly alkaline, hard water. Because limestone is common, so is hard carbonate water. It is not the ideal brewing water for many beers. Its alkalinity gives hop bitterness an unpleasant astringent bite and affects the chemistry of the mash. It is only with the addition of dark malts — themselves somewhat acidic — that this chalky, alkaline water starts to work. And when you keep the hop rates down — bingo! You have a winner. The famous dark beers of Munich and Dublin are two such examples.

Gypsum, or calcium sulfate, is a less-common mineral but is key to an important beer style. Brewers in nineteenth-century Burton-on-Trent, England, were delighted to find their well water was just the thing to brew a new style of crisp, dry, and very hoppy beer called pale ale. And even today, in a well-kept draft Bass, you can sometimes get a whiff of that plaster-drywall nose.

For some beers the best minerals are no minerals at all. The Czech town of Plzeň, famous for the pale Pilsner lager that changed the beer world, has extremely soft water, and they coupled that with an elaborate mashing procedure to create one of the world's classics. Mineral-free water is not well suited for most beers or brewing methods, but of course with very soft water it's easy for a brewer to simply add the needed minerals.

Removing minerals is a little more difficult, and until about a hundred years ago, brewers really didn't understand this in any depth. Today, there are many methods that can be used. The beautiful advertising mythology

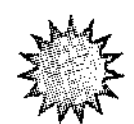

SENSORY VOCABULARY: METALLIC

TYPE: taste*

DESCRIPTORS: metallic, bloody, iron, coppery, bitter

THRESHOLD IN BEER: 0.15 ppm

APPROPRIATENESS: never

SOURCE: Iron, copper, or occasionally other elements present either in water source or from antiquated brewing equipment. Some metallic flavors are thought to be a result of the oxidations of lipids (fats), which may in turn be catalyzed by metal ions.

**It is unclear whether metallic flavors are tastes, aromas, or trigeminal sensations such as electrical effects. To some extent, all three seem to be involved.*

about northern waters or pristine mountain springs is just a big, beautiful lie.

It is important that water for brewing be of good drinking quality, which means free of organic contaminants, pesticides, heavy metals, iron, sulfur, and other noxious stuff. Even if not harmful to humans, some minerals — iron, for example — can be toxic to yeast and contribute to haze formation or add unpleasant tastes. Iron, when present in beer, gives a bloody, metallic flavor. Tiny amounts of metals like copper and zinc, while tasteless, are vital for yeast nutrition, so much so that workers in a new, all-stainless megabrewery had to replace a six-foot length of stainless pipe with copper to ensure healthy conditions for its yeast. Zinc is often added as a yeast nutrient.

The Magic of Barley

BARLEY IS THE PERFECT brewing grain. Not only does it contain a large reserve of starch that can be converted into sugar and a husk that makes a perfect filter bed, but barley also contains the tools — in the form of enzymes — to do the job without adding anything but hot water. The Neolithic people 10 millennia ago knew just what they needed to make beer, selectively replanted wild grasses with just the right qualities, and in relatively short order came up with domesticated barley.

Enzymes are key to many aspects of the brewing process, which would be quite

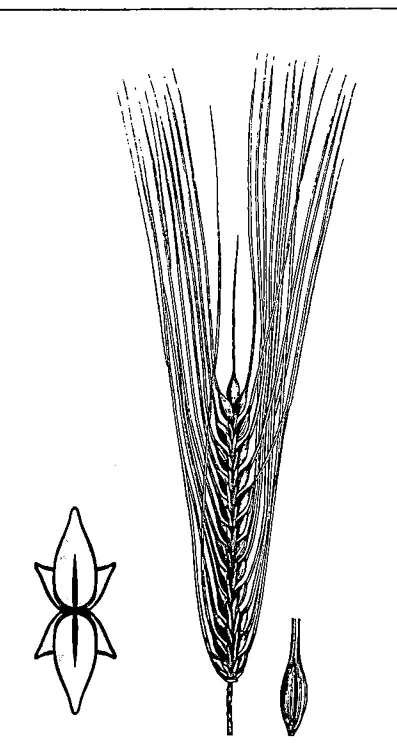

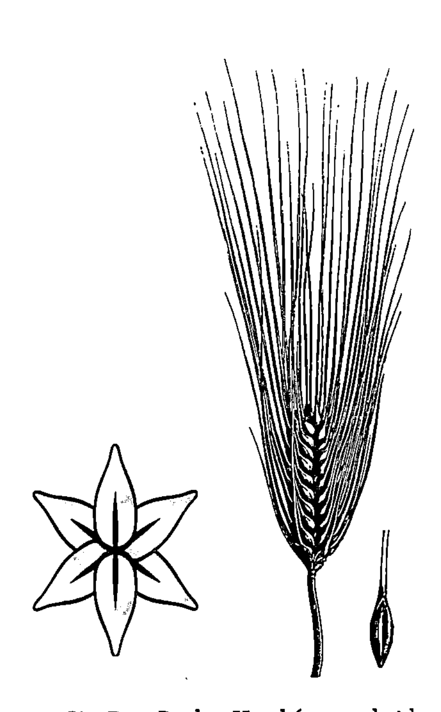

Two-Row Barley Head (top and side views)

Six-Row Barley Head (top and side views)

The seeds of this plant have been used to brew beer for 10,000 years. These two types of barley used in beer vary in how many kernels they have at each node around the center stalk. Two-row produces plumper, lower protein kernels better suited for all-malt beers.

impossible without them. The crucial jobs of malting, brewing, and fermentation all rely on enzymes. Enzymes are specialized proteins that assist chemical reactions. For a chemical reaction to happen, an energy barrier must be crossed, kind of like lifting something over a wall. Enzymes reduce the energy needed to change from one chemical state into another. In brewing, starch must be broken into simpler sugars. While this is possible using the brute force of strong acids or high temperatures, enzymes present in barley have the ability to make these reactions happen with very modest inputs of heat. We'll be seeing enzymes in many parts of the beer-making process.

Barley for brewing comes in two forms, two-row and six-row, so named for the obvious fact that when looking down from above, there are either two rows of kernels or six. Two-row types yield plumper kernels and prefer cooler climates, while six-row kernels are less rotund and are grown in hotter locations. From a brewer's point of view, the main difference is the level of protein. Protein is important in brewing because it indicates the presence of enzymes, adds head-forming and body-boosting qualities, and when broken apart yields nutritious matter for the yeast. But too much protein can cause problems in beer, mostly in the forms of chill haze (a visual cloudiness) and instability on the shelf.

For this reason, all-malt beers are most commonly brewed from two-row malt, while six-row is mainly used in mainstream American-style beers, for which the additional enzymes are used to break down the starches in corn or rice grits, which have no enzymes of their own.

Making Malt

The malting process begins by selecting high-grade barley and soaking it in water for about 24 hours, until it reaches 45 percent water content. This rehydrates the kernel and activates the enzymes within, readying the grain for growth. Then the barley is placed in a cool place and kept well aerated, as the seed needs oxygen at this point. Rootlets appear at one end, and a shoot called an acrospire grows hidden under the husk.

When this sprouting has reached a certain point, the maltster stops the process by applying heat. The length of the shoot is a reliable indicator of the state of the malting process, a measure known as modification. In well-modified malt, the shoot is allowed to grow to the full length of the kernel. Most modern malt is fully modified and can be mashed with relatively simple brewhouse procedures. In the past, not all malt was well modified, which left small "flinty" ends. These flinty bits don't yield their extract easily and need more intensive mashing — usually including a short boil — to gelatinize and fully release their starches.

At this point, the wet, unstable, and relatively flavorless grains are headed for the kiln. Indirect heat is used to first dry the grain, then to toast it. Kilning is the source of nearly all malt flavor, even in the palest malts.

It is important to understand a little of the chemistry behind this, because it's such a big player in beer flavor, appearance, and aroma. Collectively, the chemistry of caramelization is known as Maillard chemistry, or sometimes as "non-enzymatic browning." This describes all commonly encountered browning during cooking, including the char on your burger, the caramelly golden goodness of sautéed onions, and the roastiness of coffee and chocolate.

The specifics are very complex, but here's what you need to know. If you take some form of sugar or carbohydrate, combine it with some

MALT TYPE AND BEER COLOR

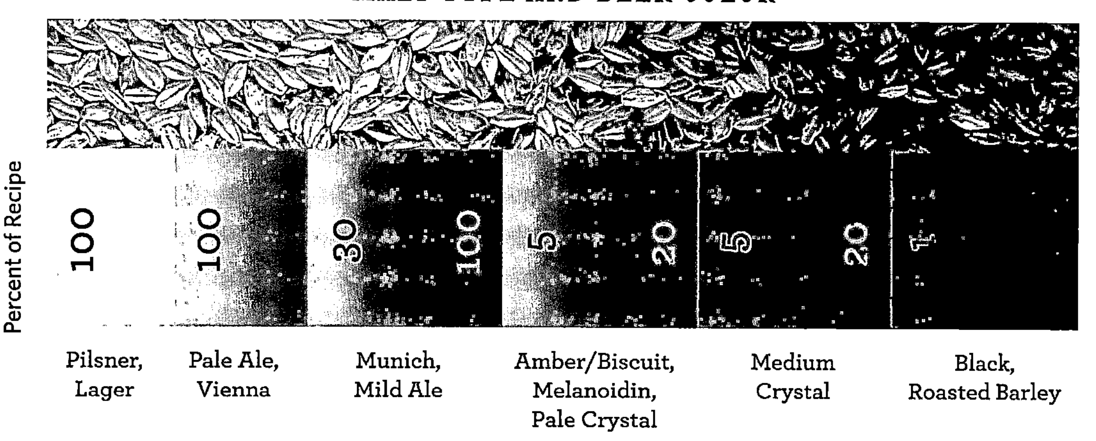

This chart gives a rough idea of the amount of color contributed by varying amounts of different malt types in beer recipes.

---

nitrogen-bearing material (typically derived from protein), and add heat in the presence of moisture, you get a host of browned flavors, aromas, and color. The color components are known as melanoidins, and they are large molecules with either a reddish or yellowish cast and no discernible aroma. Flavor and aroma come from small, ring-shaped molecules called heterocyclics, which contain elements such as sulfur, nitrogen, or oxygen in their hydrocarbon rings. These are very potent odorants, with thresholds in the low parts-per-billion range.

Every different combination of sugars, starches, and the myriad sorts of nitrogenous materials will produce slightly different end products. What's more, each slight difference in time, temperature, pH, moisture level, and other variables will create a different flavor profile. It's possible to produce two different malts of similar color but with different flavors simply by varying the moisture content during kilning. Roast it dry, and you get the sharp toastiness of a malt called "biscuit" or "amber." Roast it moist, and you get melanoidin malt, famous for its toffeelike richness. When you start combining malts in a beer recipe, the same principle applies. There are many ways of producing a brown beer. Large amounts of a modestly colored malt will give a dramatically different flavor than a pinch of a deeply roasted malt. Pay attention to all of this, because in terms of understanding the malt profile of beers, it's the only thing that matters.

Grain color is expressed either in degrees Lovibond (United States) or EBC (European Brewery Convention) units. EBC units = 1.97 Lovibond.

Malt Types

MALT KILNING results in a wide range of colors, from below 2 degrees Lovibond for the palest Pilsner malt to over 500 degrees Lovibond for the deepest-roast black malt. This range gives the brewer a huge color palette from which to choose. Maltsters and brewers organize the various shades of malt into several categories according to how they're made or used, as follows:

Base Malts. These are kilned lightly enough that they can serve as the entire brew if called for. Even in the darkest beers — stout, for example — base malt will be most of the grain bill. Pilsner, pale, Vienna, and Munich are included, although the darker ones may serve as color malts rather than base malts in certain beers.

COLOR: 1.5 to 15 degrees Lovibond

PILSNER: the palest malt available

PALE ALE MALT: classic for pale ales, but many other uses

VIENNA MALT: continental malt produces amber beer like Oktoberfest

MILD ALE MALT: classic as base for dark British ales

MUNICH MALT: will brew deep amber beer; sweet and caramelly, hints of toast

"Kilned" or "Color" Malts. These are used in small amounts, perhaps up to about 20 percent of a recipe. The biscuit/amber and melanoidin malts fall into this group, as does brown malt.

COLOR: 15 to 200 degrees Lovibond 

AROMATIC/MELANOIDIN/DARK MUNICH: brown and amber beers, sweet and caramelly

AMBER/BISCUIT: sharp, brown, toasty flavor

BROWN MALT: classic for porter; smooth to sharp roastiness

PALE CHOCOLATE: various uses; medium-sharp roastiness

Crystal or Caramel Malt. This is a special type of process in which the wet malt is "stewed" at around 150°F (66°C). The result is a glassy, crunchy texture and a heavy, sweet, caramelly flavor that is noticeable even in small amounts — and can easily be overdone. Fat, raisiny, or other dried fruit aromas can be a giveaway.

COLOR: 10 to 180 degrees Lovibond 

(All manufacturers make a range of colors. No common terminology except numbers)

Roasted Malts and Grains. These include chocolate and various shades of black malts. They really do have very similar aromas and flavors to coffee, chocolate, and other highly roasted foods. Typical use is 10 percent or less of the grist.

COLOR: 350 to 600 degrees Lovibond 

CHOCOLATE: sharp roastiness for darker beers

BLACK: classic for modern porters and stouts

RÖSTMALZ: German black malt, sometimes dehusked for smoother flavor

ROAST BARLEY: roasted, unmalted barley is classic in Irish stouts

Adjunct Grains

WHILE BARLEY MALT is by far the most dominant grain in most classic beer styles, brewers since ancient times have recognized the brewing value of alternative, or adjunct, grains. There are many reasons for using adjunct grains. Wheat beers, oatmeal stouts, and rye beers all call for specific grains in addition to malt. In the case of American-style industrial lager, corn, rice, or various forms of sugar are added to lighten the flavor; this usually results in lightening the cost as well. In the old days it was economic, as some grains required better

SENSORY VOCABULARY: MALT

TYPE: aroma; in darker types possibly bitter taste

DESCRIPTORS: grassy, grainy, malty, bready, caramel, toffee, nutty, toasty, roasty, coffee, chocolate, espresso, burned; also (crystal malt) raisins, prunes, dried fruit

THRESHOLD IN BEER: various chemicals (heterocyclics) at low parts-per-billion (ppb) ratios

APPROPRIATENESS: always, but highly variable by style

SOURCE: Maillard browning (caramelization) during malt kilning; also Maillard browning during decoctions, wort boiling; also from certain types of caramelized brewing sugars

soil and yielded less than others. In parts of long-ago England, the poor folk who couldn't afford the premium stuff were called "grouters," after a thick, cheap oat ale.

The wheat is like a rich man,
That's sleek and well to do,
The oats are like a pack of girls,
Laughing and dancing too,
The rye is like a miser,
That's sulky, lean and small,
But the free and bearded barley
Is the monarch of them all.

—A. T.

In today's beers, adjuncts are about texture more than flavor. All tend to be less assertive in aroma than barley malt. Wheat, oats, and rye all add creamy texture and great head retention to beers, and are often called to that task even in beers for which these qualities are not openly acknowledged. Some claim to be able to detect a lemony spritziness from wheat, but I've never found this myself. Corn and rice always thin out a beer. Their paucity of protein means they contribute fermentable sugars, but not a great deal else. Nonetheless, it is possible to detect a delicately husky rice "bite" in Budweiser and a subtle creamy corniness in many beers such as Miller Genuine Draft that use corn as a primary adjunct.

Malted specialty grains such as wheat can sometimes be added directly to the mash without special cooking procedures, but their lack of husk sometimes requires that extra filtering material such as rice hulls be added to aid runoff of the mash. Oats and rye can be treated similarly if used in small quantities — less than about 10 percent. If used in more than minimal quantities (more than 10 percent), unmalted grains all need a cooking procedure to gelatinize their starches. I'll discuss this more shortly.

The Art of the Recipe

Before a drop is brewed, the brewer must decide what's going in the beer. How strong will it be? What will be the color? Bitterness? Primary flavors? Balance? Sneaky, subtle background elements?

Most brewers decide on these and other characteristics first, and then determine how much of what ingredients will cause the desired beer to materialize. Parameters like gravity, the amount of sugars and other solids in the unfermented wort, come first. One, two, or as many as a dozen or more malts can be combined into a brew. Calculating gravity is easy. Each malt has a certain potential yield, and each brewhouse and mash procedure has a certain efficiency, which, after some experience, is usually well understood by the brewer. So it's just a matter of totaling things up. Color calculation is not so straightforward, as color does not add up in a linear fashion, and there are some differences in the way malts of different colors are measured. But there are formulas that approximate this in order to come up with something in the ballpark.

Hops are in a similar situation. The brewer must consider both aroma and bitterness, which work at cross-purposes. To extract bitterness, hops must be vigorously boiled, and this drives off the volatile aromatic oils, so hops are usually added in multiple additions as the boil progresses. Each variety has a certain amount of bittering substance, which varies by region and year. Fortunately, each hop shipment contains an analysis that indicates its bittering potential. So the brewer has to decide how much of which hop added, and when, will add what amount of bitterness and aroma to the beer. This can be done manually, but increasingly it is worked out with computer programs.

Balance is very much a subjective quality and doesn't lend itself particularly well to numerical calculation. A measure called a BU to GU ratio (Bittering Units to Gravity Units) can be helpful; it's a numeric expression reflecting that at any given balance level, the amount of hop bitterness needed increases with the gravity of the beer. What will be an appropriate balance varies widely by drinker and beer style. But even in the maltiest doppelbock or Scotch ale, there is some anchoring hop bitterness; and even in the most tongue-slappingly hoppy double IPA, there is — or at least there should be — some rich maltiness to back it up.

We normally think of balance as being simply about the play of hop bitterness against the sweetness of malt, but there are many other elements involved. Dark malt, for example, may come down on the bitter side of the equation and side with the hops. If a deft touch is applied, you can end up with a three-way balance of toasty malt, hop bitterness, and sweet malt, which makes for a very lively experience as you drink. In specialty beers, the balance can be altogether different. Acidic beers depend on sour against sweet, as hops are usually subdued. Things like smoke, chiles, fruit, herbs, and spices can all come into play.

Brewers use the same kinds of techniques that chefs — or any other kind of artist — use: contrast, harmony, layering, surprise. The best brewers have that twinkle in the eye and the

INGREDIENT TASTING

Conducting this type of tasting is how brewers familiarize themselves with the flavors of brewing ingredients. It's nothing more than laying out a number of different types of malts, hops, and waters and letting everybody taste or smell as appropriate. You can sample them all at once or taste one category per session. All the ingredients can be found at your local homebrew shop (or through mail order if you must). Here's how to do it.

Malt

Pick up a pound each of Pilsner, pale, Munich, biscuit, a couple of crystal malts of different shades, and a black malt. Lay these out and let everybody smell, then taste. If you're feeling ambitious, fill some coffee cups with some of the paler types crushed coarsely, and pour over 170°F (77°C) water to cover. Note the aromas and sweetness that develop in the next few minutes. You are brewing!

Hops

Purchase several different hop varieties in small quantities. Recommended varieties are Saaz, Hallertau, Kent Goldings, and Cascades, which will give you a sense for their use in Czech, German, English, and American craft beer, respectively. Whole hops are preferred, but pellets are okay. Lay them out on plates (the pros use purple paper, as it enhances the hops' green colors), and rub a small amount of each, in turn, between your palms to liberate the aromas; then cup your hands and smell. Premoistened hand wipes are definitely recommended for this. Don't bother tasting hops.

Water

Buy bottles of several different water types and taste. Distilled water is just pure wetness; Evian is a hard, alkaline water with a little tooth to it and a minerally body; plain carbonated water like Perrier demonstrates the powerful effects of carbonation with its familiar bubbly texture but a true acidity that affects beer's flavor. Also, dose part of the distilled water with a little table salt. Measure ⅛ teaspoon, and then use one-eighth of that in a quart, which should get you into the 85 ppm range. It should taste rich and full, but not all that salty.

ability to reach right out and give us an experience, not just a glass of beer.

If you do it right, brewing is about ideas. A big impression can be made with brute force, but sometimes a whisper speaks louder than a shout. In the end, all great beers tell a story.

Mashing and Runoff

At the core of brewing is a magical porridge-making process called "mashing." Crushed malt is mixed with hot liquor (apprentices were fined tuppence if they called it "water") and this mash is allowed to stand. In just a few minutes, enzymes present in the malt convert starch from the grains into sugars. The resulting sweet liquid — called "wort" — can then be drained off.

The quality of the crush is crucial. Too coarse, and the mash gives up little of its sugar; too fine, and the husks that are supposed to serve as a filter bed are useless and you get what is, for all practical purposes, vegetable concrete. A full-size malt mill has up to six rollers and can weigh several thousand pounds, so this is something brewers take very seriously.

There are several enzyme systems in the mash that serve different functions. Each has a preferred temperature range and other optima, including pH, mineral ions, concentration, and more. Each is most active at a specific temperature; below that, they don't work, and just a bit higher they are destroyed by heat, ending their activity.

Some enzymes break down complex gummy carbohydrates such as glucan and pentosan in the mash. Others break down proteins into smaller parts of varying lengths — the smallest are critical for yeast nutrition. It's also important to break up large proteins, as they can contribute to haze and instability in the finished beer.

The main event is the conversion of starch into sugar. Starches are polymers of sugars, meaning they are large molecules strung together from a number of smaller molecules of glucose. In the mash, enzymes liberate maltose, a two-unit sugar, plus some longer ones of varying degrees of fermentability. The genius of the enzyme system in malt is that there are two enzymes working at slightly different temperatures. One enzyme creates highly fermentable sugars, the other, less so. The beauty of this is that the brewer can adjust the fermentability of the wort by varying the mash temperature.

At 145°F (63°C), a highly fermentable wort is produced, and this will ferment into a dry, crisp beer. At 155°F (68°C), the wort will have a good proportion of unfermentable sugars, resulting in a sweet, rich beer. In practice, most

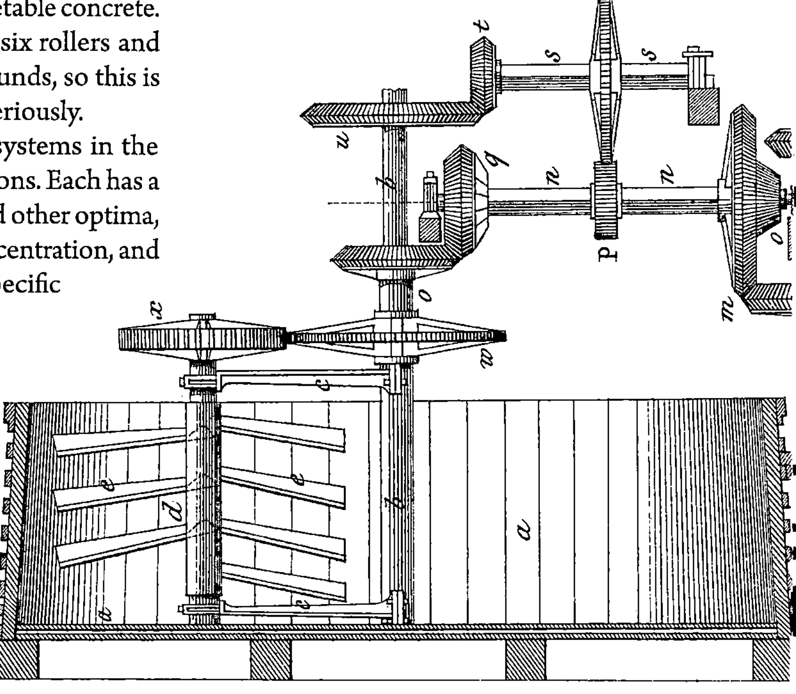

Nineteenth-Century Mash Tun

beers are mashed somewhere between these extremes. This is a dramatic simplification of what actually happens, but it gives you an idea of the importance of the decisions the brewer makes in the brewhouse.

Once the mash has done its work, the temperature is raised, ending enzyme activity and locking the ratio of fermentable to unfermentable sugars, a step called "mashing-out."

There are a number of different mash procedures in use today. Most basic is a single infusion in which hot water is mixed with the grain and allowed to stand for about an hour. A variation of this is called a "step infusion" or "upward step mash." In English-style beers, there may be just a couple of steps, but in some rustic methods, as used in Finnish *sahti*, multiple small steps are used, from room temperature to nearly boiling. Most complex of all are the traditional German decoction mashes. In this method, about a third of the mash is removed from the tun, raised through a series of steps, and boiled briefly before being returned to the tun to create a temperature rise. Decoctions come in one-, two-, or three-step versions, the most complex of which takes more than 6 hours to execute. These are rare now, for reasons of time and energy use, but their ability to add layers of rich caramelly flavor to beer still has value.

At the end of the mashing process, you need to separate the sweet wort from the matrix of husks and chunks known as "spent grain." Most

SENSE AND NONSENSE IN BEER ADVERTISING CLAIMS

Beer advertisers often use the following terms and concepts to sell their beer. Here's my take on it all.

Water

You hear descriptions such as "sky blue," "Rocky Mountain," etc. Brewers need great water, and there was a time when they had to brew with the local water as it was. Nearly all modern breweries treat the water to make it suitable for the type of beer they're brewing. **Verdict:** Won't hold water.

Fire-Brewed

Kettles that use direct-flame heating do caramelize the wort more heavily than those with steam systems, and this can produce a different-tasting beer. However, there may be problems with this, as it creates the potential for oxidation issues later on. **Verdict:** Depends.

Beechwood-Aged

At one time, most American breweries aged their lagers in "chip tanks" with a pile of wooden slats in the bottom. These are stripped of any wood character before going into the tanks and do not impart any wood flavor to the beer. Their real purpose is to provide additional surface area for the yeast to settle on and this may have benefits for the conditioning of the beer. Anheuser-Busch has found it is worth the considerable trouble for their yeast and their beers, but few breweries feel the same these days. **Verdict:** Nice nod to tradition, but not what it sounds like.

Krauesened

This is the process of adding some freshly fermenting beer to another batch nearing the end of maturation. The idea is that the lively yeast will hasten the reduction of unwanted "green" flavors such as acetaldehyde and diacetyl from the beer. It's an old method, and it really works. **Verdict:** Usually a good thing, but doesn't work for everybody.

Reinheitsgebot

This time-worn Bavarian law forbids anything other than hops, malt, water, and yeast in lager beer. As far as I'm concerned, most beers on the planet

breweries use a lauter tun, a vessel with a perforated bottom, although sometimes the mash tun itself also serves this purpose. As the sweet wort is run off into the kettle, more hot water is added to the top of the mash, a process called "lautering." When enough wort is collected, it is run off into the kettle. The whole runoff takes about an hour.

Hops

ONCE IN THE BREW KETTLE, the wort is brought quickly up to a boil and the first load of hops is added.

Let's pause for a moment and consider what this unique plant has given to the beer world. A climbing vine in the nettle family and closely related to marijuana, hops have been cultivated since ancient times, although they didn't regularly find their way into beer until about a thousand years ago. The parts useful in brewing are the cones, and despite the fact that many brewers call them flowers, they're actually catkins or, botanically, strobiles.

Hops are cultivated between 35-degree and 55-degree latitudes in both the Southern and Northern hemispheres, as they need specific summertime day lengths to trigger cone production. They are large, showy plants and make nice ornamentals, despite their vulnerability to pests and diseases. In the Old World, the most prized varieties are tied to very specific

would probably be improved by this limitation, but there are many legitimate instances in which beer can be improved by sugar, herbs, spices, and other forbidden ingredients. **Verdict:** Maybe.

Draft in a Bottle

This is an indirect slam against pasteurization, which its detractors say affects the beer negatively, although the beer literature says the differences are slight. "Bottled draft" beers are often filtered in some special way (see below) and then kept refrigerated right through the point of sale, which is generally better for beer. **Verdict:** You be the judge.

Cold-Filtered

This is specifically a Miller product claim, but the technology is licensed from the Japanese brewer Sapporo. The idea is to remove yeast and spoilage bacteria while not stripping away proteins, color, and other valuable properties. **Verdict:** Subtle, very subtle.

Brewed Longer

Although there are many parts of the brewing and fermenting process that may benefit from a little more time, this term always reminds me of marketing guys trying to fathom what the guys in the rubber boots are doing and then turning it into something the consumer can see as a benefit. I've spent too much time in ad agencies — and breweries — to believe otherwise. **Verdict:** Nonsense.

Craft-Brewed

While this should properly refer to small, independent breweries making highly flavorful and creative beers, the term is unenforceable, and maybe even a little difficult to agree upon. However, there are clear instances in which large industrial breweries slap on the craft-brewed label in the hope that a little microbrew mojo will rub off on them. **Verdict:** Read the fine print. Know your brewery.

Will Get You Hot Chicks

It's staggering that in this day and age, there are still enough people vulnerable to this fantasy that breweries feel justified in spending billions repeating the message, especially when the supposed love potion is bland, mainstream beer. **Verdict:** You really need me to tell you?

SENSORY VOCABULARY: CHEESY (ISOVALERIC ACID)

TYPE: aroma

DESCRIPTORS: stinky cheese; stinky feet

THRESHOLD IN BEER: 0.7 ppm for isovaleric acid

APPROPRIATENESS: never

SOURCE: Formation of organic acids during improper storage of hops. Also may be one of the many aromas of a bacterial infection. Rare in commercial beer, but occasionally encountered.

locations: the Saaz gets its spicy character from the orange soil in western Bohemia; the herbal Hallertau grows in its namesake district in northern Bavaria; and in a region just a short jump southeast of London, the East Kent Golding develops its twangy green spiciness, prized for two centuries for the finest pale ales. Worldwide, there are easily more than a hundred varieties of hops; brewers in the United States probably have access to about a third of those.

America grows its share of hops, nowadays near Yakima, Washington, and elsewhere in the Northwest. Classic European varieties such as those just mentioned don't taste the same out of their homelands, but have their own desirable brewing qualities.

Inside the hop cone there is a small internal stem, or strig, holding the leafy parts of the cone together. All around the strig are tiny golden globules of the pungent waxy substance lupulin. This contains the bitter resins and aromatic oils so valued in beer. The bitter resins can be divided into alpha and beta acids, the former being the more important of the two and the measure used to describe a hop's bittering power. Alpha acid content for hops range from around 2 percent for the least bitter aroma hops up to nearly 20 percent for high-alpha types.

SENSORY VOCABULARY: HOP BITTERNESS

TYPE: taste

DESCRIPTORS: bitter, hoppy

THRESHOLD IN BEER: 5 to 7 ppm (5 to 7 International Bitterness Units or IBU)

APPROPRIATENESS: always to some extent; may be up to 100-plus IBU in some extreme beers

SOURCE: isomerized hop alpha acids; should be clean, pleasant, without harsh, woody, or astringent character

ALSO IN THE LUPULIN are dozens of aromatic oils, each with its own character. Every variety and location produces hops with a unique mix. Floral to resiny, minty to spicy, hop aroma is a great tool for adding personality to beer. The characteristics seem to fall into national groups. German hops tend to be herbal, sometimes almost minty, while English hops are spicy to fruity, with a healthy dose of fresh green grassiness. The celebrated Saaz hop has a clean, refined spiciness that's quite distinctive. American hops are all over the map, but the most characteristic varieties veer off into the piney and resiny. There are some beer styles — American and English pale ale come to mind — in which the only meaningful difference is the choice of hops. Aroma hops are a powerful tool.

There is a group of European hops historically called "noble," usually used for aroma in lager beers. These are the Saaz plus the German Hallertauer Mittelfrüh, Tettnanger, and Spalt. There is a chemically defined requirement for this exclusive club, but as new aroma varieties have been developed, the rules have been extensively gerrymandered to limit the group to the original clique. No doubt these are all great hops, but I don't know if they are the only varieties truly deserving of the name these days.

In addition to aroma hops, there are high-alpha varieties that have been developed in

This old botanical print details the showy beauty of all parts of the hop plant.

the past hundred years with ever-increasing amounts of bitterness. These are sold by alpha acid pounds and so tend to be more of a commodity item. However, some crafty American brewers have seized on the rustic, grapefruity charms of varieties such as Chinook and Columbus and have used them to create bigger-than-life pale ales and other beers.

There are also dual-use hops that combine moderate alpha acid levels with pleasant aromatic qualities. Breeding programs worldwide are always working on new varieties, seeking better aromas, higher alpha acid, better agricultural characteristics, and other qualities. Newer hop varieties like Simcoe, Ahtanum, Glacier, and Amarillo are well worth seeking out.

AS NOTED above, hops are usually added in stages. In order to extract bitter substances, a vigorous boil is essential. In a process called "isomerization," hop alpha acids are rearranged chemically into a form that is more bitter and more soluble in wort. The longer the boil time, the more bitterness, but after about 2 hours this is subject to diminishing returns and may cause other problems (see page 53). Vigorous boiling drives off volatile oils, so if hop aroma is desired, more hops must be added toward the end of the boil.

Brewers may also make one or more "flavor additions" of 15- or 30-minute boil times, which add both bitterness and aroma. Hops may also be added after the boil has ended. Special devices called "hop backs" or "hop percolators" can be loaded with hops and the hot wort run through them on its way to the chiller. Hops may also be used after fermentation, in conditioning tanks or even in serving casks, a technique called "dry hopping" and often used in English cask ales and American craft beers in which hops are front and center.

SENSORY VOCABULARY: HOP AROMA

TYPE: aroma

DESCRIPTORS: hoppy, spicy, herbal, floral (rose, geranium, orange blossom), lavender, piney, resiny, citrus (lemon, lemongrass, grapefruit), ribes/black-currant leaf/cat pee

THRESHOLD IN BEER: There are hundreds of different oils; for some, thresholds well below 1 ppb; for others it may be 100 times that.

APPROPRIATENESS: style dependent; should be absent in some; absolutely critical to other styles

SOURCE: Aromatic oils from hops; technically, terpenes, sesquiterpenes, ketones, and alcohols. Extracted during boil, post-boil, or post-fermentation techniques such as dry hopping. Also may be added as solvent-extracted pure or blended oils.

Q: WHAT DIFFERENTIATES LIGHT, LOW-CARB, AND DRY BEER?

A: Brewers have a number of tools at their disposal to affect the caloric and alcoholic content of their beer. These techniques find their way into certain classes of products that can be confusing to the public, and even to beer aficionados. Here's a summary of these products.

Light Beer

This starts with a low-gravity recipe, and then fungus-derived enzymes are used in the mash to convert any remaining starches into sugars. This means there are no residual carbohydrates in the beer, as they all have been fermented into alcohol. Light beer is lower in alcohol than regular beer.

Low-Carb Beer

This is made in a similar manner to light beer, but the starting gravity is such that the alcohol content is about what a normal beer would be. All the carbohydrates have been turned into alcohol, and there are none remaining in the beer. In Europe, these are primarily aimed at diabetics, but in the United States they are aimed at dieters.

Dry Beer

Again, the process is similar, but this time the brewer starts with a normal-strength wort. But because the same extreme methods are used to turn all carbohydrates into fermentable sugars, which then are fermented into alcohol, dry beer is a little higher in alcohol than regular beer.

A Rolling Boil

Once the kettle is full, it is brought to a vigorous boil. This accomplishes a number of things. First, it sterilizes the wort, which prevents the beer from being taken over by bacteria and wild yeast. Second, as noted previously, boiling isomerizes the hops, which makes them both bitter and soluble. And third, it coagulates excess protein with help from the tannins (polyphenols) present in the vegetative parts of the hops. This produces flakes of protein very much like egg drop soup, known as the "hot break," which removes long-chain proteins that would otherwise come back to cause instability or the phenomenon of chill haze, the harmless but unsightly cloudiness that can appear when beer is served cold. The boil also puts an end to any enzyme activity remaining from the mash and locks in the ratio of fermentable to non-fermentable sugars. Direct-firing of kettles may also add some caramelization.

Another important thing that happens during the boil is the creation and expulsion of a chemical called DMS (dimethyl sulfide). A precursor, s-methyl methionine, is present in malt, and at temperatures above 140°F (60°C), it is turned into DMS, which usually has an aroma of creamed corn. It's a very volatile chemical, so it can be expelled rapidly during the boil, but as soon as the boil stops, DMS starts to build, making it important to get the wort chilled as quickly as possible.

Once the goals of boiling are met, the wort is cooled as rapidly as possible. In addition to the DMS and oxidation problems noted above, the beer may also be subject to microbial contamination if cooled too slowly. Typically a counterflow heat exchanger is used. Through a series of thin plates, hot wort flows in one direction and cold water in the other. The wort emerges at fermentation temperatures. This sudden chilling precipitates protein and some lipids (fats). These are usually removed by running the wort into a settling tank in a way that creates a whirlpool, which concentrates the cold break and any remaining hop particles into a shallow pile, allowing the wort to be drained into the fermenters and leaving the crud behind.

Yeast and the Magic of Fermentation

Brewers make wort, not beer. Yeast makes beer. The specific biochemical pathways are amazingly complex, but here are the basics: Yeast metabolizes sugars and creates ethanol, carbon dioxide, and many other chemicals in much smaller amounts.

Yeast is a single-celled fungus that has been cultivated since ancient times for both brewing and baking. In the brewing world, there are two main families of yeast responsible for ale and lager fermentations. Ale, or top-fermenting, yeast is a species called *Saccharomyces cerevisiae.*

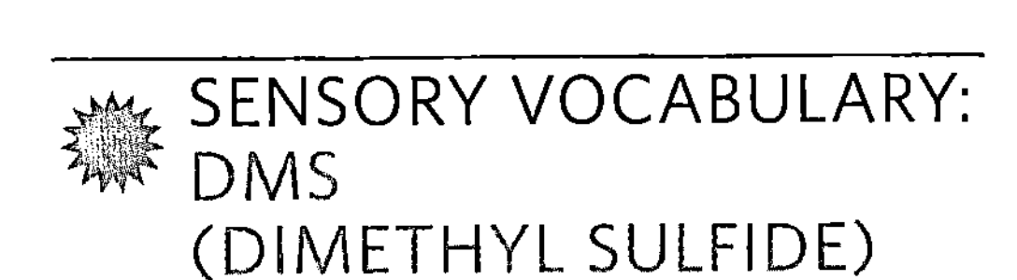

SENSORY VOCABULARY: DMS (DIMETHYL SULFIDE)

TYPE: aroma

DESCRIPTORS: creamed corn, cabbage, vegetal, green beans, canned asparagus; in dark beers, more like tomato juice

THRESHOLD IN BEER: 30 to 50 ppb

APPROPRIATENESS: usually not appropriate, but acceptable in small amounts in lagers

SOURCE: created in boil from SMM (s-methyl methionine), a precursor found in grain, and usually symptomatic of brewhouse problems; may also be a symptom of infection, especially when found in large amounts

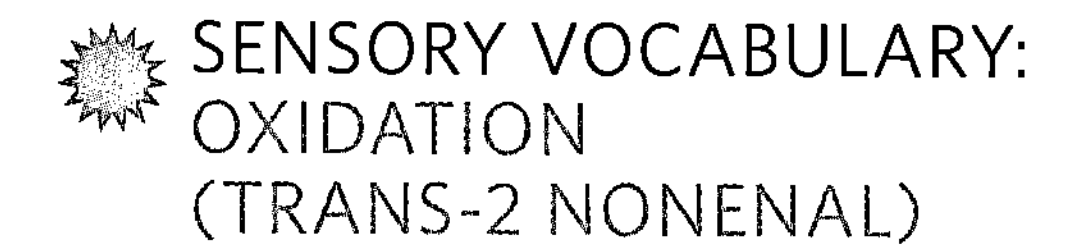

SENSORY VOCABULARY: OXIDATION (TRANS-2 NONENAL)

TYPE: aroma/flavor

DESCRIPTORS: papery, stale, cardboardy, shoe box

THRESHOLD IN BEER: 0.05 ppb (trans-2 nonenal)

APPROPRIATENESS: never; symptomatic of overboiling or poor brewhouse technique; also common in stale beer, and increases as beer ages

SOURCE: created by oxidation of malt components during mashing, boiling, or other brewhouse activities where contact with air is possible

Recent evidence conclusively shows that lager yeast is a second, close-related species, *Saccharomyces pastorianus*. There is considerably more genetic variation among the ale yeast strains, as you can easily detect even in a cursory survey of ales. Other yeasts and even bacteria are involved in some specialty beers, but the vast majority of beers are fermented with these two species.

Yeast cells are fantastic little chemical factories. They must find food, metabolize it into energy, synthesize proteins and many other molecules necessary for life, rid themselves of waste, and create more yeast. Think of them as little sacks of goo with membranes porous enough to allow some molecules through but not others. Inside, all this chemistry is going on in various structures as well as in free-floating reactions. For each goal, many steps are required, and some of the intermediate products are aromatically potent enough themselves to be minor aroma and flavor components of beer. The higher the temperature, the faster all the chemistry happens. And because the yeast is not always efficient in the way it does its work, some of the intermediates leak out of the cells and into the beer.

At low temperatures, relatively fewer of these by-products are created, and at higher temperatures, more are created. This explains the main flavor difference between ales and lagers. Lagers, fermented at 40 to 45°F (4 to 7°C) and conditioned at near freezing, have a relatively clean, pure flavor without fruity or spicy aromatics. Ales, normally fermented well above 55°F (13°C), have loads going on, with fruity, spicy esters and higher alcohols and phenolic compounds, among others.

One important chemical produced by yeast — even at low temperatures — is diacetyl. This familiar buttery compound is one step in an elaborate protein synthesis. Its precursors have relatively little flavor, but diacetyl is so buttery that it is used in theater popcorn and butterscotch candies. At warmer temperatures, yeast will reabsorb it and turn it into something flavorless. This step — a few-day elevation of temperatures during conditioning — is called a "diacetyl rest." This is common practice in lagers and is often employed in ale fermentations.

YEAST IS VERY SENSITIVE to temperature variations, and it will often produce markedly different beers at slightly different temperatures. It is also sensitive

SENSORY VOCABULARY: BUTTERY (DIACETYL)

TYPE: aroma/flavor (called vicinal diketones, or VDKs, including a related chemical called pentanedione)

DESCRIPTORS: buttery, theater popcorn; in larger amounts, butterscotch

THRESHOLD IN BEER: around 0.10 ppm, but variable

APPROPRIATENESS: sometimes pleasant at very low levels in English-style ales

SOURCE: Leaks out of yeast cells during amino acid synthesis. In larger amounts it may be a sign of stressed or mutated yeast. In very high amounts, it may be a sign of bacterial contamination and is especially common in dirty (infected) draft lines.

TERROIR IN BEER

Terroir is a term used to describe the sum total of the effect of a region on a wine or other traditional product. Climate, soil, moisture, geology, micronutrients, and more may be involved. Terroir isn't just jumping out of the glass in beer, though, as it does with wine. You have to know what you're looking for:

Heirloom Malts

Certain classic English varieties are very difficult to cultivate but have flavors that normal commodity malts can't match. First among them is Maris Otter, long prized for its complex, slightly nutty flavor. Other varieties to look for are Halcyon and Golden Promise. In the Czech Republic, a strain called Hana is valued in production of undermodified malts for classic Pilsners. Klages, once widespread in the American Northwest, is a rare malt now that it has largely been replaced with Harrington, a malt with better agronomic characteristics.

Noble Hops

The clean spiciness of the Saaz only comes through if the hops are grown in the bright orange "cinnamonic" soil of the traditional Czech growing region of the Goldbach Valley, and this is also true of the other noble varieties grown elsewhere. As with wine, climate, soil, and many other factors play a role in the subtlety and refined character of the hops from the traditional growing areas.

Water

As noted elsewhere, water chemistry is now under the control of the brewmaster, but characteristic water types do sometimes shine through. One of the most famous brewing waters is the mineral-rich borehole water from Burton-on-Trent, England, which adds a crisp dryness and plastery nose to many Burton beers. Dortmund Export beers, now rare, relied on a water with a mix of sulfate, carbonate, and salt for a unique, minerally flavor.

Wild Yeast

In the wild-fermented-style lambic, brewers depend to some extent on the local microflora to inoculate the beer and begin fermentation. Because the old cherry orchards in the area just south of Brussels that harbored the yeast are long gone, the situation has changed somewhat. It is now believed that many of the microorganisms are resident in the barrels, but exposure of the cooling wort to the night air of the region is still practiced. Brewers elsewhere have attempted to create their own wild-fermented beers, with varying degrees of success.

to physical parameters like tank depth and geometry. Yeast needs a proper nutrient mix and adequate number of cells per unit of beer (which varies with the strength of the beer). Yeast also needs oxygen to create more yeast, a process that happens before fermentation begins in the beer. This, it should be noted, is the only acceptable time in the brewing process for oxygen to be in contact with beer.

There are hundreds of brewing strains stored in yeast banks around the world. Larger brewers usually have their own proprietary strains; smaller brewers can order from dozens of strains available through commercial brewer's yeast suppliers. Often, if one can read between the lines, the particular pedigrees of specific strains can be gleaned from the catalog descriptions. For a fairly comprehensive list and description of the types of brewer's yeast, have a look online at one of these Web sites: Wyeast (www.wyeast.com) or White Labs (www.whitelabs.com).

A MEASURED AMOUNT of healthy yeast is added to the oxygenated wort in a carefully sanitized fermenting vessel. The yeast takes in the oxygen and begins to make more yeast by "budding" off new cells. This takes several hours, and during this time there is very little actual fermenting going on. But at a point, all the available oxygen is used up and the yeast turns its attention to the sweet wort. First, because it's easier, the yeast eats the small amount of available glucose (a single sugar), and then it begins to metabolize the maltose. This tiny, ravenous beast can throw a thick, rocky head on the surface of the fermenting beer more than a foot high and generate enough heat that tanks need to be cooled to avoid runaway temperatures.

This violent process takes between a day and a week, depending on the temperature, wort strength, yeast vigor, and other factors. Although it's a somewhat questionable term, many call this the "primary fermentation." When the maltose is used up, the yeast will turn to the next longest sugar, maltotriose. At this point, things slow way down.

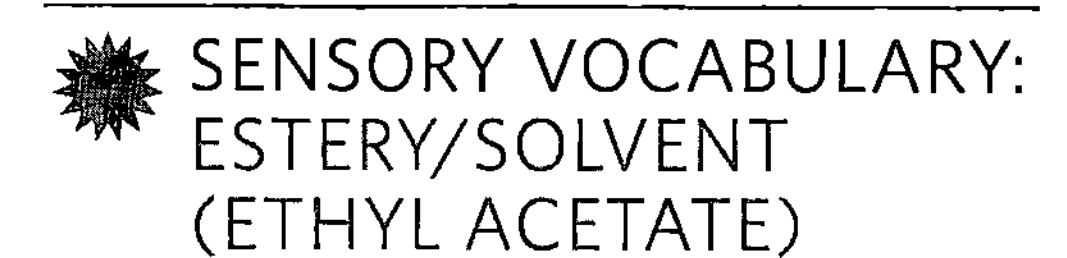

SENSORY VOCABULARY: ESTERY/SOLVENT (ETHYL ACETATE)

TYPE: aroma

DESCRIPTORS: fruity at low quantities, but in larger quantities it comes across as nail polish remover or solvent; sometimes more evident as an eye-watering sensation rather than an actual aroma.

THRESHOLD IN BEER: 18 ppm

APPROPRIATENESS: In small amounts, it is an important contributor to fruity aromas in beer. In larger amounts it may be a sign of too-high fermentation temperature, improper wort aeration, or other yeast stress. Often found in very high-alcohol beers.

SOURCE: Formed during fatty acid synthesis and then leaks out of yeast cells. Very high amounts may be a result of bacterial contamination (especially vinegar-forming *Acetobacter*).

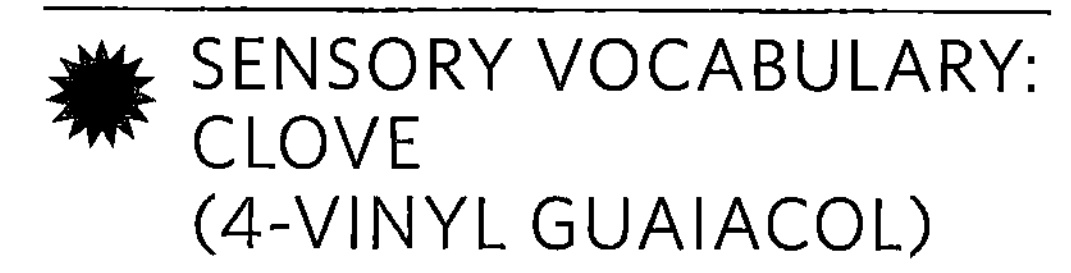

SENSORY VOCABULARY: CLOVE (4-VINYL GUAIACOL)

TYPE: aroma

DESCRIPTORS: clove, phenolic

THRESHOLD IN BEER: around 1 ppb

APPROPRIATENESS: at detectable levels only in German weizens

SOURCE: formed during fermentation from precursor, ferulic acid (interestingly, also a precursor to vanillin), formed during malt kilning

A few beer types require very specialized yeasts to create the appropriate flavor profile. Bavarian *Weissbier,* a.k.a. hefeweizen, uses a unique *Torulaspora delbrueckii* yeast that produces a clove aroma, along with banana and bubble-gum fruitiness. The Belgian farmhouse ale saison employs a unique strain thought to be related to red-wine yeast. It's most notable for being able to thrive at temperatures up to 90°F (32°C), which is very high compared to normal ale yeast. It's a low ester and a high phenol producer, giving a unique black-pepper spiciness that is a cornerstone of the style. It is one of the great delights of Belgian beer that many styles rely on highly individualistic yeast strains.

Then there are beer styles that rely on different species of yeast and even bacteria for their unique taste and aroma profiles. All of these listed below are dreaded contaminants in most breweries; brewers bold enough to bring them under their roofs need to take extraordinary measures to prevent their escape and the fouling up of the whole place. Here are a few of them:

Brettanomyces: slow-growing yeast that may be endemic to oak wood. Plays a role in lambic, some saisons, and traditional English old ales. Has barnyard or horsey aromas. Metabolizes maltose. Can be used alone to (slowly) ferment a beer. Also seeing use among adventurous brewers in North America.

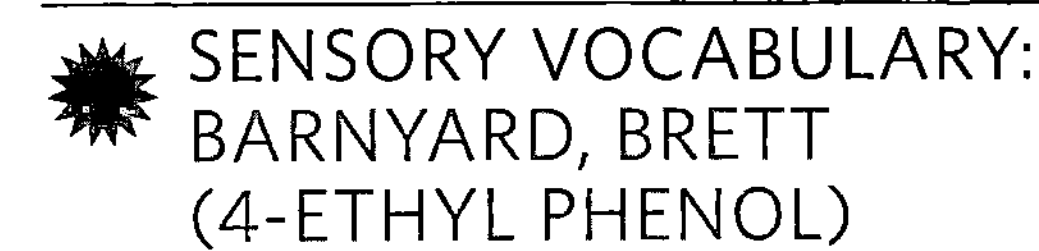

SENSORY VOCABULARY: BARNYARD, BRETT (4-ETHYL PHENOL)

TYPE: aroma

DESCRIPTORS: horsey, horse blanket, barnyard, woody

THRESHOLD IN BEER: around 420 ppb

APPROPRIATENESS: commonly found only in *Brettanomyces*-affected beers

SOURCE: produced by *Brettanomyces* yeast; usually accompanied by 4-ethyl guaiacol

***Pichia* and *Candida*:** film-forming yeast similar to those in sherry; minor player in lambic, but also occurs as spoilage organism.

***Lactobacillus* and *Pediococcus*:** related genera that do the job of souring lambic and Berliner Weisse. Depending on the species, can also create a lot of diacetyl (buttery) and goaty, sweat socks–reminiscent aromas.

***Acetobacteria*:** transforms alcohol into acetic acid, but requires oxygen in order to do so. Adds vinegar or pickle aromas, but may also create a fair amount of ethyl acetate (see page 56). Common in oak-aged beers and important to the aromas of lambics and especially Flanders-style red/brown ales.

SENSORY VOCABULARY: GOATY (CAPRYLIC, CAPROIC, CAPRIC ACIDS)

TYPE: aroma

DESCRIPTORS: goaty, animal, sweat socks, sweaty

THRESHOLD IN BEER: 8 to 15 ppm, depending on specific chemical

APPROPRIATENESS: generally not pleasant; sub-threshold may add earthy complexity

SOURCE: part of a large family of organic acids with animal aromas common in many foods and beverages

AFTER THE EARLY STAGES of fermentation, the beer begins a process of maturation or conditioning. During this time, raw "green" flavors are mellowed by the yeast's continued metabolic activities. Errant molecules are roped back into the cell and changed into something less obnoxious. During this time, yeast and other particles in the beer slowly settle out. Stronger beers take much longer to condition than everyday ones. Normal English-style ales might not need even two weeks until they're ready to drink, while a barley wine might take six months or more. Because everything is moving in slow motion at near-freezing temperatures, conditioning a lager takes much longer. Four to six weeks is average, but a big doppelbock may take six months or more.

SENSORY VOCABULARY: ESTERY/BANANA (ISOAMYL ACETATE)

TYPE: aroma

DESCRIPTORS: banana, circus peanuts

THRESHOLD IN BEER: 1.2 ppm

APPROPRIATENESS: In small amounts, it is an important contributor to fruity aromas in beer. In larger amounts it may be a sign of too-high fermentation temperature, improper wort aeration, or other yeast stress. Often found in very high-alcohol beers.

SOURCE: Formed during fatty acid synthesis and then leaks out of yeast cells. Common, and desirable if not out of control, in Bavarian weizens.

SENSORY VOCABULARY: OTHER ESTERS

TYPE: aroma

ETHYL HEXANOATE (also known as ethyl caproate)

THRESHOLD IN BEER: 0.17 to 0.21 ppm

DESCRIPTORS: ripe apple, hints of aniseed

PHENYLETHYL ACETATE

THRESHOLD IN BEER: 3.8 ppm

DESCRIPTORS: flowery, roses, honey, sweet

GIVEN ENOUGH TIME, beer will usually clear itself just fine. But because brewing is a commercial activity, sometimes it is necessary to speed things up a bit. A process called "fining" is often used, in which some gelatinous or other substance is put into the beer to pull down yeast and other flotsam. Isinglass, the dried swim bladders of certain fish, is the traditional English fining, but gelatin and special plastic microspheres (PVPP/Polyclar) are also used.

Filtration is a more powerful tool, but it can be too effective. In theory, a filter can be set to remove the finest particulates and bacteria. However, in practice, if a filter is set too tight, it can remove color, hop bitterness, and body- and head-forming proteins from the beer. The so-called cold-filtration process that Miller licensed from Sapporo seeks to avoid these problems, but it is an expensive and complex process suitable only for megabreweries. Another solution for larger breweries is a centrifuge, which spins out particulate matter and may be used as a prefilter.

It should be noted that filtration will not speed up beer's maturation. Too-early filtration can lead to "green" beer aromas, especially of acetaldehyde and possibly diacetyl as well.

In many beers, the yeast is not removed at all. If some yeast is left in the beer when it is put into the bottle or cask along with a small amount of sugar and left to ferment, the additional carbon dioxide produced will be trapped, providing natural carbonation. Live yeast in the bottle or cask actually scavenges the dreaded oxygen and provides a protective effect. Products that are naturally carbonated in the serving cask or bottle are called "real ale." This is the traditional method for English ales, but many Belgian ales and American craft beers are bottle-conditioned too.

Real-ale casks are delivered to the pub still fermenting. It is the publican's duty to manage this process and determine when the beer is fit to serve. This is a challenging process, but aficionados feel the challenges and short shelf life are worth the extraordinary texture and subtle flavors of real ale. For more on real ale, see chapter 6.

At the opposite end of the spectrum is pasteurization. In this process, the finished beer is heated for a short time at temperatures high enough to kill any remaining yeast and bacteria, typically 2 to 3 minutes at 140°F (60°C). Some studies have shown that "cooked" flavors of pasteurized beer can be detected by expert panels, but they clearly pose no problem for

SENSORY VOCABULARY: ALCOHOL

TYPE: aroma, sensation (warming as you swallow)

ETHANOL/ETHYL ALCOHOL)

DESCRIPTORS: alcoholic, sweet, warming

THRESHOLD IN BEER: around 6 percent

APPROPRIATENESS: in normal-strength beers, usually not detectable

SOURCE: the main product of yeast fermentation (with carbon dioxide)

SENSORY VOCABULARY: HIGHER ALCOHOLS/ FUSELS

TYPE: aroma

APPROPRIATENESS: in normal-strength beers, usually not detectable, but adds to the overall character of beer; elevated in higher-temperature fermentations

SOURCE: yeast metabolism

Compound	Threshold
2-PHENYLETHANOL DESCRIPTOR: roses	45 to 50 ppm
N-PROPANOL DESCRIPTOR: alcohol	600 ppm
ISOBUTANOL DESCRIPTOR: alcohol	80 to 100 ppm
ISOAMYL ALCOHOL DESCRIPTOR: alcohol	50 to 60 ppm

SENSORY VOCABULARY: OTHER ORGANIC ACIDS

TYPE: aroma

BUTYRIC ACID

DESCRIPTORS: rancid butter, often a marker for *Lactobacillus*

THRESHOLD IN BEER: 2.2 ppm

SOURCE: develops in spent grain

ISOVALERIC ACID

DESCRIPTOR: cheesy; see above.

SENSORY VOCABULARY: ACETALDEHYDE

TYPE: aroma

DESCRIPTORS: green apple, apple skin, green leaves

THRESHOLD IN BEER: around 10 ppm

APPROPRIATENESS: should never be detectable

SOURCE: formed in the metabolic process as the yeast rids itself of waste carbon dioxide from precursor pyruvate. Most commonly a symptom of too-young, "green" beer. Most acetaldehyde is eventually taken up by the yeast and converted to ethanol.

the millions of consumers who consume pasteurized beer regularly. Flash-pasteurization before packaging is generally regarded as being kinder to beer flavor. In this method, the beer is heated to 161 to 165°F (71.5 to 74°C) for 15 to 30 seconds. Either method will get a greatly improved shelf life over filtered, unpasteurized beer. Almost all keg beer sold in the United States is unpasteurized, which is the reason it should always be kept below 38°F (3°C).

A similar debate rages over carbonation. In most breweries, carbon dioxide gas is dissolved in beer, either in-tank during conditioning or post-filtration just before bottling. Or the tanks can simply be closed toward the end of fermentation and fitted with a bleeder valve that allows carbonation to safely build to the desired level. Proponents of the latter method claim a finer bead and tighter head, but it's a very fine point and not generally agreed upon.

Packaging and Beyond

In a brewpub, packaging can be as simple as just racking the beer over to a serving tank. But for most breweries packaging can be the most challenging aspect of production. It is telling that of the three-volume set of books published by the Master Brewers Association of the Americas, the packaging volume is by far the largest. The equipment for bottling is large, complex, and expensive. Operation is a high skill. Poorly packaged beer can suffer from a number of problems that customers can actually taste in the glass.

The most important potential problem is oxygen. Too much and the beer can develop stale, cardboardy flavors (see oxidation, page 54). There is no generally agreed-on low limit for oxygen in the bottle. It's always bad to some degree, and brewers can become obsessed about ways to get the numbers down. Sierra Nevada just switched from twist-off to regular bottle caps with a special lining because they felt that the pry-off caps kept the oxygen out a little better.

Although it is rare, incompletely rinsed sanitizers can produce a Band-Aid aroma of chlorophenol. This is not uncommon at bars and restaurants, as the sanitizers for glassware or growlers are chlorinated or brominated, either of which can produce chlorophenolic flavors.

The other most common packaging problem is really a marketing choice. Clear or green bottles offer no protection from the wavelengths of blue light that cause beer to become skunked (see Sensory Vocabulary, page 61). Brown bottles provide excellent protection from the sunlight or fluorescent tubes that typically cause skunking. But as an English

CLEANING AND SANITIZING

Cleaning and sanitation are of supreme importance in brewing beer. The late homebrewer and scientist Dr. George Fix used to say, "You can't sanitize dirt," which will give you an idea of the relationship between the two. Special chemicals and, in larger breweries, mechanized spray-down cleaning equipment are available to do the job, but it is the ever-vigilant eye of the detail-obsessed brewer that really makes cleanliness happen. And there's always some elbow grease involved.

Poorly sanitized equipment can be a safe harbor for quite a number of offensive bugs that can get into beer at various stages, along with unwanted flavors, aromas, and more. Bacteria and wild yeast often produce large and unpleasant amounts of aroma chemicals that culture yeast makes in merely modest quantities. *Lactobacillus* and *Pediococcus* are the most notorious, but there are many others in the gang.

SENSORY VOCABULARY: AUTOLYSED

TYPE: aroma, flavor

DESCRIPTORS: autolysed, muddy, soy sauce, Marmite, umami

THRESHOLD IN BEER: varies

APPROPRIATENESS: generally not pleasant; acceptable in older, stronger beers

SOURCE: various lipids and amino acids, the results of the death and disruption of yeast cells

SENSORY VOCABULARY: MUSTY/MOLDY (TRICHLOROANISOLE)

TYPE: aroma

DESCRIPTORS: moldy, corked

THRESHOLD: less than 0.1 ppt (parts per trillion!)

SOURCE: In cork-finished bottles, may be a result of tainted corks or mold-tainted malt. Moldy aromas may migrate through plastic hoses in wet brewery locations. Amazingly potent odorant! Generally tolerated as rustic earthiness in corked bottles.

Other musty/moldy compounds that can taint beer include geosmin (earthy, beetlike), 2-ethyl fenchol (earthy, with patchouli top notes), and many others; usually they are formed in damp locations and imparted to the beer through plastic or wood, or via contaminated packaging materials.

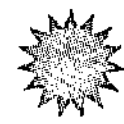

SENSORY VOCABULARY: CHLOROPHENOL

TYPE: aroma

DESCRIPTORS: Band-Aid, adhesive tape, disinfectant

THRESHOLD IN BEER: less than 0.5 ppb

APPROPRIATENESS: should never be detectable

SOURCE: commonly a reaction of residual chlorine-containing sanitizers to phenolic compounds in beer, but may also result from yeast problems. Also can happen at point of service if chlorine or bromine sanitizers are incompletely rinsed.

SENSORY VOCABULARY: SOLVENTY-STALE (FURFURAL ETHYL ETHER)

TYPE: aroma

DESCRIPTORS: stale-solventy, chemical

THRESHOLD IN BEER: 6 ppb

APPROPRIATENESS: never

SOURCE: Develops during aging from precursors formed during malt kilning and in combination with sugars and amino acids in the boil; a pretty consistent marker chemical for beer staleness. As with most stale flavors, FEE develops faster at higher temperatures.

Brown is the only color of glass that can protect beer from the skunky aromas caused by blue light interacting with certain hop compounds. Cans and ceramic bottles offer good protection. Green and clear bottles offer no protection.

brewmaster holding his beautiful clear bottles full of skunky beer explained, "Yeah, but they look bloody great, don't they?"

It should be pointed out that Miller uses a specially processed hop-bittering extract called Tetra Hop that has the offending precursor removed. As an interesting side benefit, Tetra Hop actually improves the foam stability of beer in which it's used, and other brewers are looking at it specifically for its foam-enhancing properties.

AS BEER GETS OLDER, its flavor changes (for more on this, see chapter 6). Lighter beers change fastest, and higher temperatures accelerate the process.

First, hop aromas begin to dull, and there is the sense that the beer is just tired out. Papery or cardboardy oxidation aromas start to become evident. The beer might display a waxy, appley, or honeylike sweet aroma that's different from fresh malt. Hop bitterness also decreases. When they are extremely stale, pale, filtered beers start to throw a little haze or have "snowflakes," both of which develop from proteins coming out of solution.

SENSORY VOCABULARY: SKUNKY (METHYL OR ISOPENTYL MERCAPTAN)

TYPE: aroma

DESCRIPTORS: skunky, rubbery

THRESHOLD IN BEER: 0.05 ppb

APPROPRIATENESS: never

SOURCE: Formed by a reaction of a precursor in hop-bittering compounds (isohumulones) to blue light. May happen in a matter of seconds, even in a fluorescent-lit cooler case. Brown bottles are good, but not perfect, protection.

SENSORY VOCABULARY: SULFUR

TYPE: aroma

DESCRIPTORS: sulfidic: rotten eggs, sewer gas; sulfitic, burned matches

THRESHOLD IN BEER: hydrogen sulfide, below 1 ppb; sulfur dioxide, 25 ppm

APPROPRIATENESS: occasional whiff in a lager acceptable

SOURCE: metabolic by-products of yeast; most commonly a symptom of too-young "green" beer; certain lager strains are known for this. Stressed or mutated yeast may produce these chemicals. Large amounts of hydrogen sulfide can be indicative of bacterial infection, especially of *Zymomonas.*

In stronger beer, the changes are not all negative. In fact, some connoisseurs take the trouble to age certain beers like fine wine. Hop flavors mellow and become fruity. Spicy aromas fade in favor of rich maltiness, and the body thins out and becomes dry. Additionally, oxidation aromas akin to sherry often manifest themselves as a sort of leathery aroma that can be quite pleasant in the right context. Very old beers display tastes of umami (see chapter 2), a result of broken-down proteins, and sometimes display aromas of soy sauce that have similar origins.

WHEN THE BEER leaves the brewery, it is subject to a host of woes. Time and temperature are the enemy, but so are vibration, indifference, and laziness. It is difficult enough with beer served in its home country, but the challenges multiply when beer is shipped across the globe. So great are the challenges that it really makes one grateful for all the beer in great condition that actually ends up in the glass.

Probably the greatest problem is mishandling at the point of service. Tap lines are subject to exactly the same sanitation and infection issues as breweries, especially the buttery/hazy contamination of *Lactobacillus* and *Pediococcus.* A regular and rigorous program of line cleaning can prevent this, but not all bars and restaurants go by the book in this regard. At a minimum, a good cleaning every other week should prevent major problems. The most fanatical publicans clean their lines weekly.

It might be worth your while to take a tour of a brewery to see how all this brewing actually happens. There are a lot of technical details covered in this chapter, but as I've tried to make clear, these kinds of decisions are the heart and soul of brewing and really are what makes one beer different from another. Think about these decisions as you sip and your beer will tell you a story.

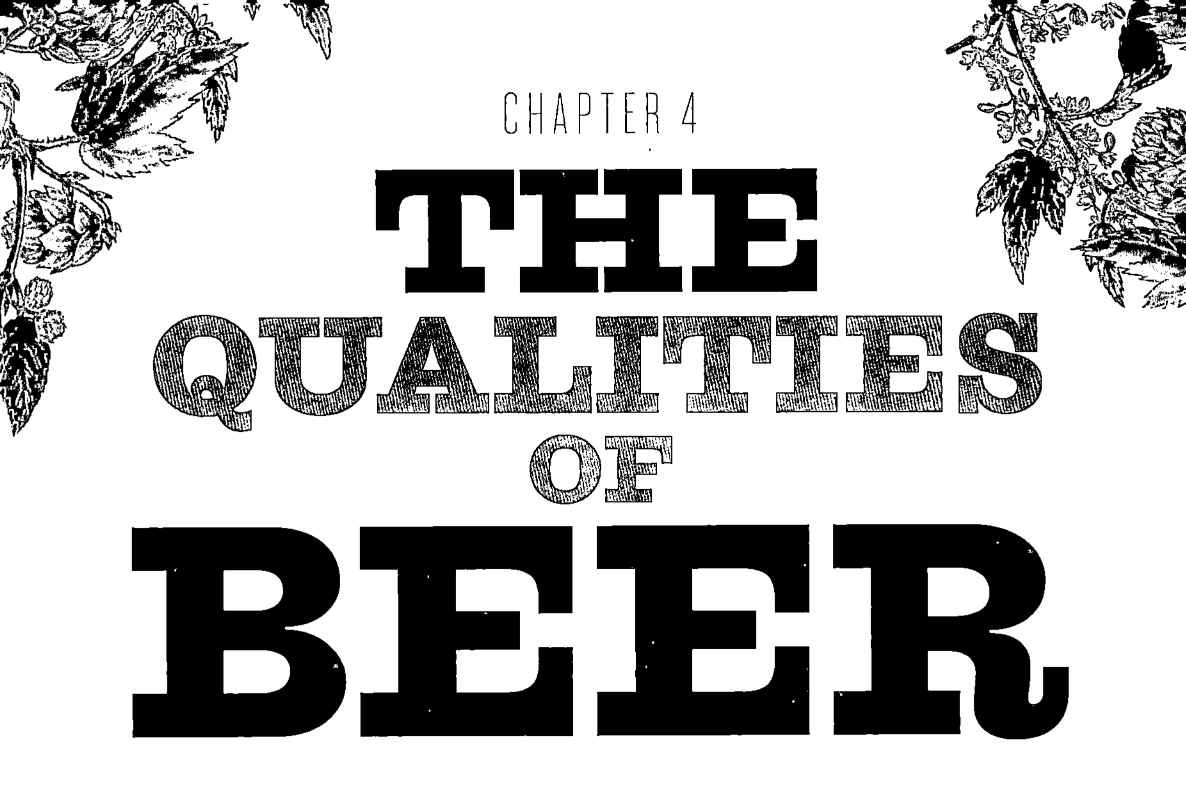

CHAPTER 4

THE QUALITIES OF BEER

MORE than any other drink, beer is a kaleidoscope of colors, flavors, strengths, balance, and other attributes. We have already seen the huge range of flavors and aromas contributed by ingredients and the brewing process. In this chapter, we'll see how those add up and present themselves in a finished beer.

So what kind of variables are we talking about here? First comes strength, both in terms of alcohol and in the even more important measure of gravity, which is the amount of dissolved solids (mostly sugars) in the unfermented wort. More malt brings more alcohol, along with a host of malty, caramel, toasty, and roasty flavors, depending on the recipe. More malt requires more hops, and that ramps up flavor even more. You can see how this adds up.

Beer is a whole rainbow of color. No other beverage goes from palest straw to inky black, surely offering something for every taste, mood, and moment. We have already seen how different malt types contribute to a rich mix of flavors in beer. Here, we will look at the way color is measured and described.

Bitterness may be minimal or quite confrontational, and when you layer on floral, spicy, herbal hop aromas, you have another dramatic way that beers can vary from one another.

Because there are so many variables and brewers have a need to be able to tightly control them, it is important to have objective measures that can be expressed numerically. Numbers aren't everything, but words are just not as specific or objective as a numerical system. For reasons of consistency, economics, quality control, judging, and even matters such as taxation, numbers are essential.

I don't think you need to run out and buy an ultraviolet spectrophotometer to determine the bitterness value of every beer you drink (although they're pretty cheap on eBay), but it is important to be fluent in the numerical language of beer. After working with these measurements for a while, one develops a pretty good idea of what a 1.065 gravity, a 44 IBU bitterness, or an 8 degree SRM color actually drinks like. Practice makes perfect, but nobody ever complains about practice with beer.

Gravity

This is the density of wort or unfermented beer and is simply a way of saying how much sugar and other dissolved solids are contained in the beer. There are two main numerical systems used to describe this in beer. First is degrees Plato, which is expressed as a percentage by weight of the dissolved solids. A 10 degrees Plato wort contains 10 percent solids; a 12 degrees Plato wort contains 12 percent, and so on. Older books may mention a scale called Balling, which was the standard of the day until Professor Plato fixed it up. Plato is used by all German brewers and by lager brewers worldwide, but it is not the only scale. The Czechs still use the Balling scale, as he was one of their own. If you've heard the term *Brix* in connection with wine, it's just about the same scale as Plato, but that term is almost never used in brewing.

The British use a scale called original gravity (OG). This is the specific gravity relative to water — the ratio of the weight of the wort to the weight of the same amount of pure water.

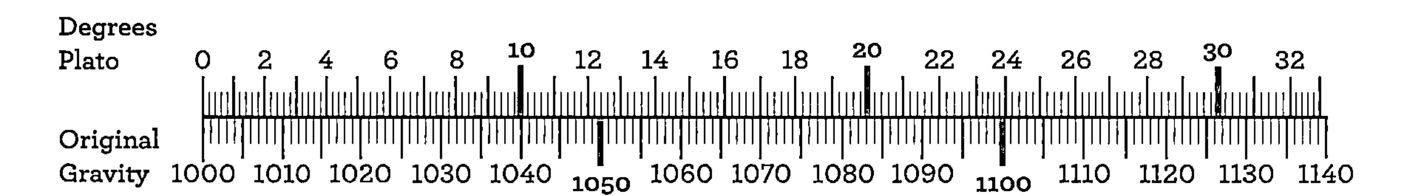

Original Gravity and Degrees Plato
This chart shows the relationship between these two different systems used to express wort density.

DRINKABILITY: WHAT IS IT?

Large brewers know that their drinkers value drinkability above almost everything else, and they have done a lot of research in the area. Despite this, it's still a difficult quality to define precisely. In the words of August Busch III, "You stop drinking because you know it's time to stop but you don't want to: That's drinkability." This quest is one thing driving the very low hop bitterness levels in mainstream beers. Anything that has taste will fatigue the palate; and so malt is removed and replaced with corn or rice. Smoothness and freedom from aftertaste also count, all of which add up to the fact that water is highly drinkable.

The drinkability attribute plays an important role in serious beer as well. There is no question that the hop bombs emanating from the West Coast are, for most people — even craft-beer lovers — not all that great as session beers, and are perhaps meant to titillate more than beguile. There is something quite remarkable about a beer of ordinary strength with enough personality and depth to keep you interested, but with enough subtlety to keep you charmed right to the bottom of the third pint.

Our 10 and 12 degrees Plato worts would have original gravities of 1.040 and 1.049, respectively, meaning they are 1.040 and 1.049 times as heavy as pure water. Often the decimal point is omitted as a matter of convenience. English ale drinkers still look for the gravity on the tap handles as a way of gauging how strong (and how expensive) a particular beer is. Because so much of the early homebrewing literature was English, many American homebrewers still think in terms of original gravity, and this is also common among brewpub and other small-scale brewers.

It figures that the Belgians would have an oddball scale of their own: Belgian degrees, sometimes called *"degré Régie"* in the old books. Used mostly in reference to abbey-style beers, to determine this scale, just remove the "1.0" from the specific gravity. For example, a 1.050 beer becomes a Belgian 5 degrees beer, a 1.080 beer becomes 8 degrees, and so on. Be aware that for many Belgian beers these numerical designations were based on recipes from decades ago, and as beers change over time, they may no longer represent the gravities they once did.

GRAVITY IS MEASURED in various ways. The simplest is with a hydrometer, which is a floating tube, usually of glass, with weights at the bottom and a thin glass tube at the top with a scale inside. The higher it floats, the higher the number that appears at the liquid line, which is how the instrument is read. Liquids, like all materials, expand and contract according to temperature, which means the density of liquids changes with temperature. As a consequence, hydrometers are always

Hydrometer
This simple tool floats at different levels depending on the density of the liquid, giving brewers a rough idea of potential strength of their beers when fermented.

calibrated for a particular temperature. Higher or lower than this, corrections must be made.

In 1785 a brewing scientist named Richardson was the first to publish the results of brewing experiments with a hydrometer. He fairly well turned the brewing world on its head, but that is a story that belongs in the porter section (see chapter 9).

An instrument called a refractometer uses the refractive, or light-bending, power of sugar to make an accurate measurement of gravity. A drop is placed inside, the lid is closed, and the gravity is read on a scale through the eyepiece. However, once the beer is fermented, the alcohol's higher refractive power distorts the measurements, so the refractometer is mostly a brewhouse, not a cellar, tool. High-precision measurements are made with a special vessel called a pyncnometer that has a known and very accurate volume. It is weighed empty, then filled, the weight of the bottle subtracted, and then the weight of that volume is converted into a gravity number. This is a laboratory procedure and is used only in labs and larger breweries. The guy on the floor in the rubber boots rarely needs such precision.

Gravity is a rough measure of the amount of alcohol that may end up in the finished beer. A good rule of thumb is that a 1.050 beer will be in the neighborhood of 5 percent; a 1.060 beer will be around 6 percent, and so on. However, this is a very rough measure, as differing worts have varying degrees of fermentability, and yeast further complicates the picture.

Alcohol and Attenuation

Ethyl alcohol (ethanol) is the main product of fermentation. There are two ways of expressing the amount of alcohol: percent by volume and percent by weight. The former is the current international standard, and that includes the United States. But between 1933 and 1990, the United States used the alcohol-by-weight standard. After the disaster of Prohibition, American brewers were eager to showcase their products as temperate beverages, so they chose the measurement system that gave the lowest numbers. A 3.2 percent beer by weight is actually a 4 percent beer by volume. Canada and the rest of the world stayed with the percent-by-volume measurement, and this is perhaps responsible for the legend that imported beer was so radically, mind-bendingly strong compared to domestic brew.

Not every wort of the same gravity will yield a beer with the same alcohol content. The degree to which sugars in the wort are converted into alcohol is affected by the brewing process, sugar and adjuncts used, yeast strains, fermentation temperature, and other variables. The brewer has a lot of control over these processes in the brewhouse, where a hotter mash will produce a less fermentable wort and a cooler mash a more fermentable one.

Now we need to deal with the slightly confusing concept of attenuation and the different ways it may be measured and expressed. Most often, the brewer divides the finishing by the starting gravity and subtracts that number from 100 to come up with the apparent attenuation. This gives useful information, but it is not a reflection of the true situation. Because alcohol is lighter than water, any alcohol present makes the terminal gravity readings appear lower than they actually are. With some very fermentable beers, it's possible to get higher than 100 percent apparent attenuation. To get "real attenuation," actual alcohol content must be measured. This is normally done by distilling the alcohol out of a small sample, so it's a bit of a cumbersome procedure and usually done only by larger breweries. All but the largest craft breweries usually get along fine working with apparent attenuation.

Alcohol Strength by Beer Style

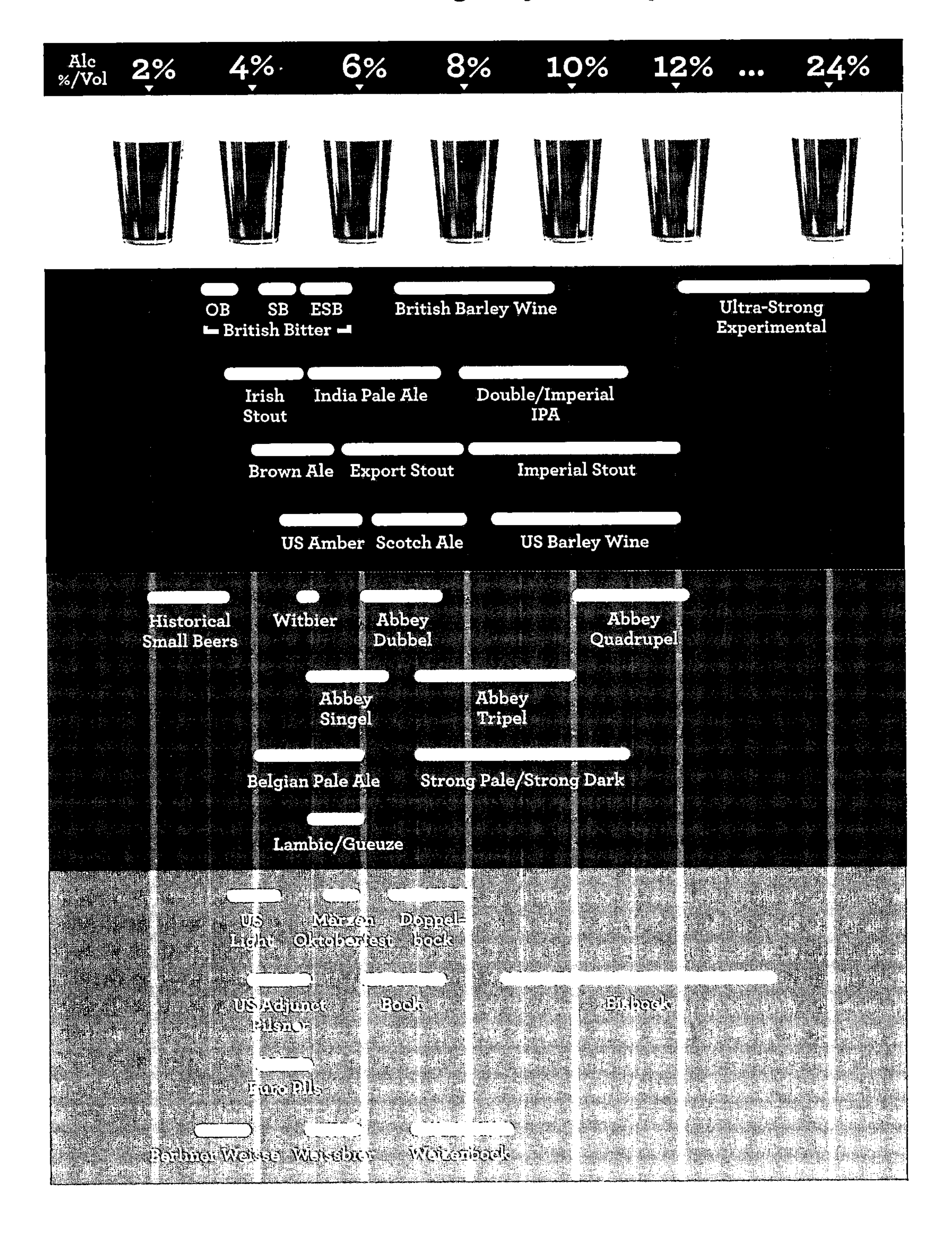

Beer Color Scale

Beer colors as delineated on the American beer color scale, SRM.

Less-attenuated beers are heavier, sweeter, and have less alcohol than highly attenuated beers made from the same gravity wort. Highly attenuated beers have more of their extract turned into alcohol, and this end of the scale encompasses low-carb, dry, and light beers.

Beer Color

Because we are such visual creatures, we are very sensitive to small differences in appearance, way out of proportion to the flavors. So getting color right is of extreme importance to brewers. Despite many years of experimentation to create a more detailed view of beer color, the current measurement scale is a single numerical scale of light and dark. Because beer is a reddish liquid, it is most opaque to blue light, so that color gives the most sensitive readings and is the type of light used for measuring beer color. Technically speaking, beer color is 10 times the optical density (absorbance) in a 1 centimeter sample cuvette, as measured by a 430 nanometer blue light, typically in a spectrophotometer. This is the American Society of Brewing Chemists (ASBC) color standard, called the Standard Reference Method or degrees SRM. The ASBC is the organization that oversees analytical standards for brewing in the United States.

Originally, beer color was determined by using a set of colored glasses devised by Joseph Lovibond in the late nineteenth century. A device like a stereoscope was held up to the light, beer samples were poured into a sample holder on one side, and then the operator would slide in different-colored glasses until a good match was found. Happily, when the spectrophotometric method was developed, the colors matched almost perfectly — which is why you still see beer color described as degrees Lovibond, and nobody gets too bent out of shape about it.

Beer Color and Beer Styles I: Light Beers

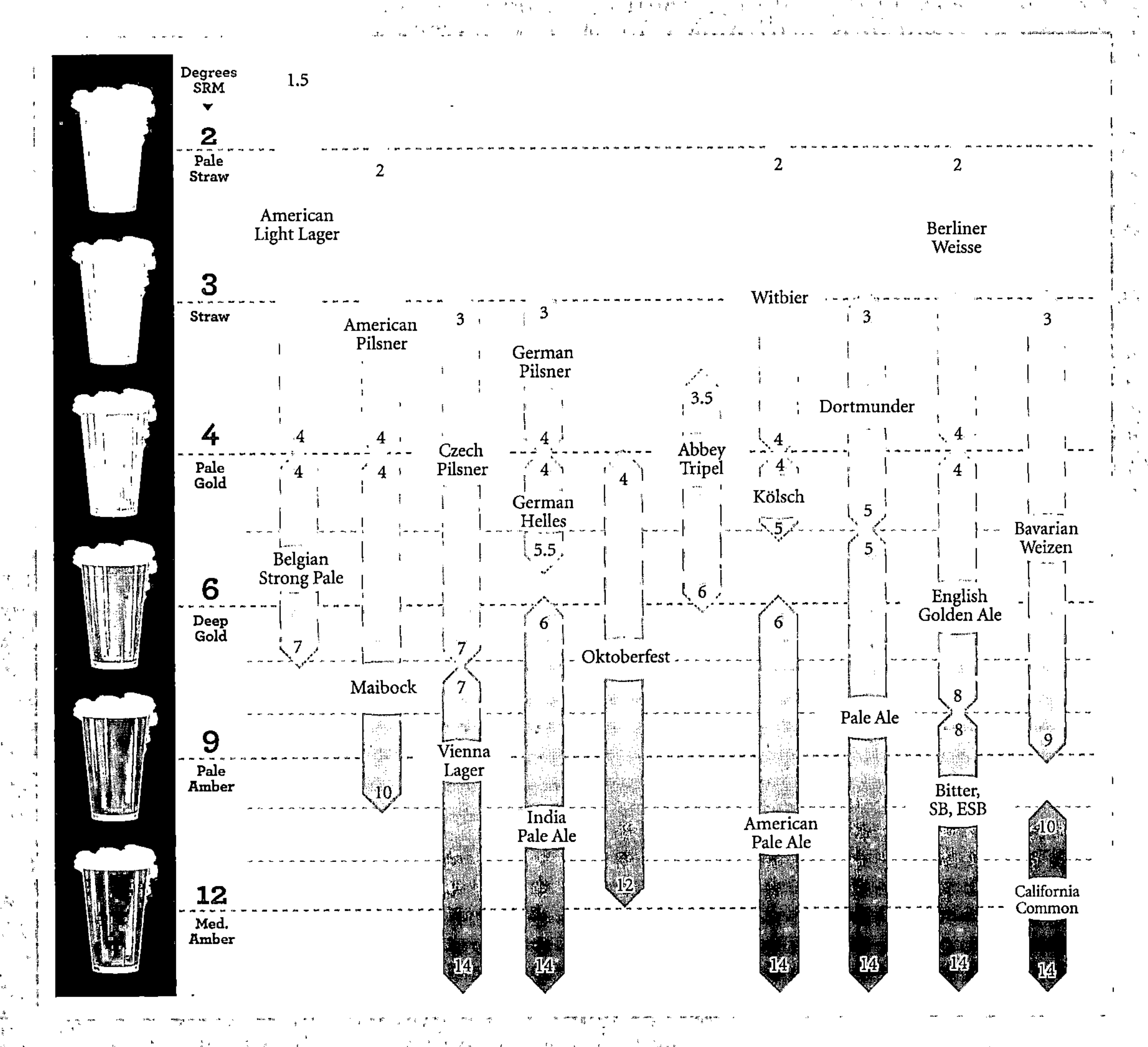

Arrows indicate the range of colors for commonly encountered beer styles.

The Europeans use a different scale, EBC (European Brewery Convention, the European equivalent of the ASBC), which after recent efforts to coordinate with their brewing cousins on this side of the ocean now reads approximately double (SRM × 1.97 = EBC) the American degrees SRM scale.

There is no generally agreed-upon verbal description of a color scale for beer. In the chart above, I have picked the most common and neutral terms available and paired them with sample pints that approximate the colors named.

Beer color varies a little between red and yellow. A method called "tristimulus" measures beer color in the same red, green, and blue wavelengths that the eye is most sensitive to, but this is only rarely used in brewing.

Beer Color and Beer Styles II: Medium and Dark Beers

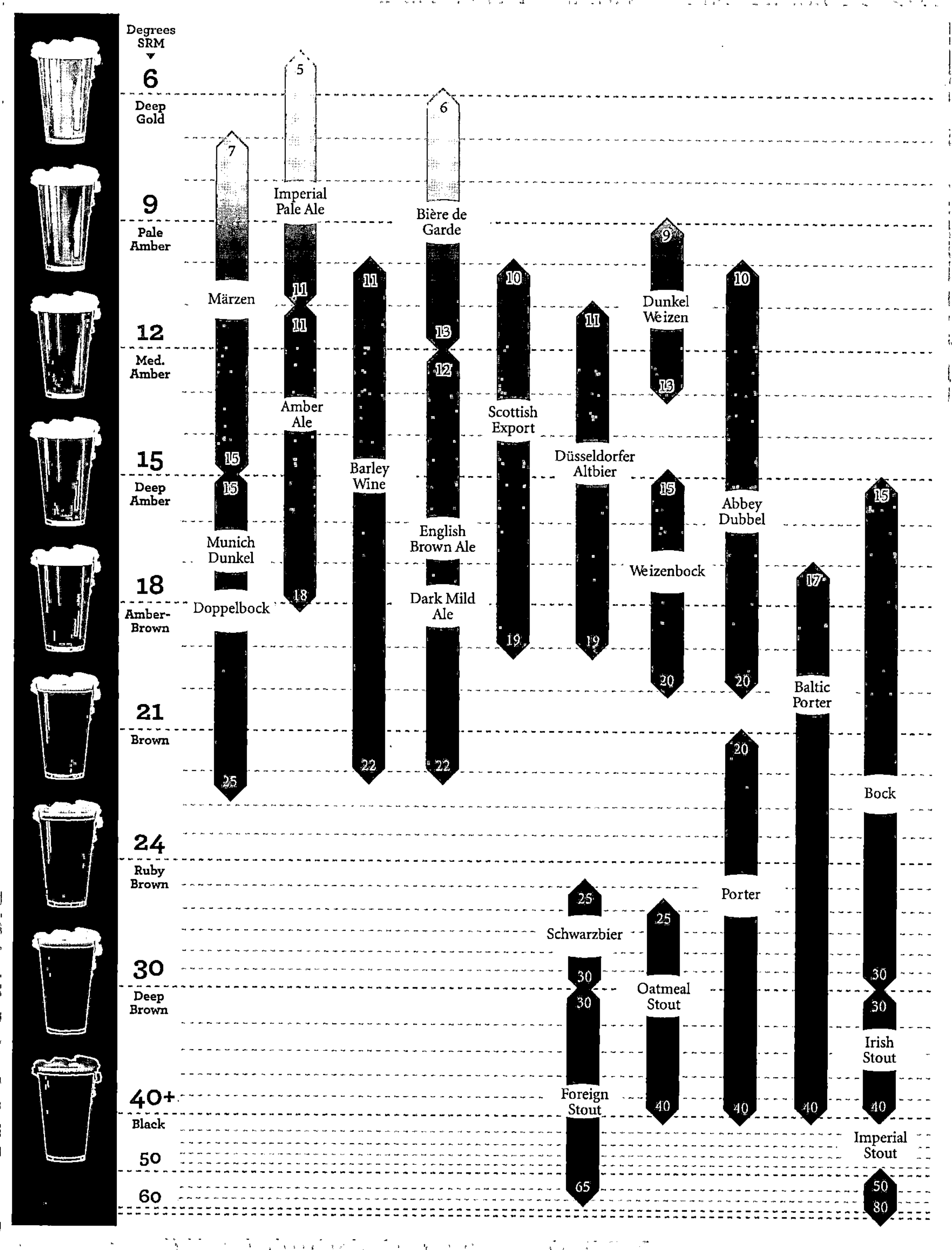

Arrows indicate the range of colors for commonly encountered beer styles.

Bitterness by Beer Style

Bitterness is an important aspect of beer style. This chart shows some of the more common styles, measured in IBUs (internatonal bitterness units).

Hops, Bitterness, and Balance

ALTHOUGH HOPS CONTRIBUTE quite a complex aroma to beer, the only measurement routinely made is of a simple scale of bitterness. This is a measure of the bitter alpha acids from the hops, isomerized and dissolved during the boil. International bitterness units, or IBUs, are the parts per million (ppm or mg/L) of iso-alpha acids in the finished beer. The laboratory analysis is done with reagent chemicals and an ultraviolet spectrophotometer. It's not too difficult to do, but the equipment is fairly expensive. Most small brewers calculate their IBUs during the recipe-formulation process and get an outside laboratory to do a proper analysis when they need accurate numbers.

Beers range from about 5 IBU to well over 100 IBU. The human threshold is about 6 IBU and 6 IBU is also about the limit of human discrimination between levels of bitterness.

Hop bitterness is absolutely critical to balance malt sweetness, even in the maltiest beer styles. The interplay between taste elements is very important for drinkability. Few beers are perfectly balanced; there's usually a tilt to one side or another. With malt, the paler types are perceived as purely malty, but as a result of caramelization during kilning, flavors and aromas such as caramel, nutty, malty, and all the various types of roastiness may also be present in a beer. Some of these malt flavors can be very sweet and cloying, and need hops to balance them, but roasty malt flavors often come down on the bitter side of the equation.

Bitterness from hops cuts sweetness and adds a refreshing quality. As discussed in the last chapter, the method commonly used for

Relative Bitterness

Bitterness tastes stronger in a weaker beer, so it's really the ratio of bitterness to original gravity that matters. The chart shows international bitterness units against gravity units — the two most significant digits of the original gravity (1050 = 50 gravity units).

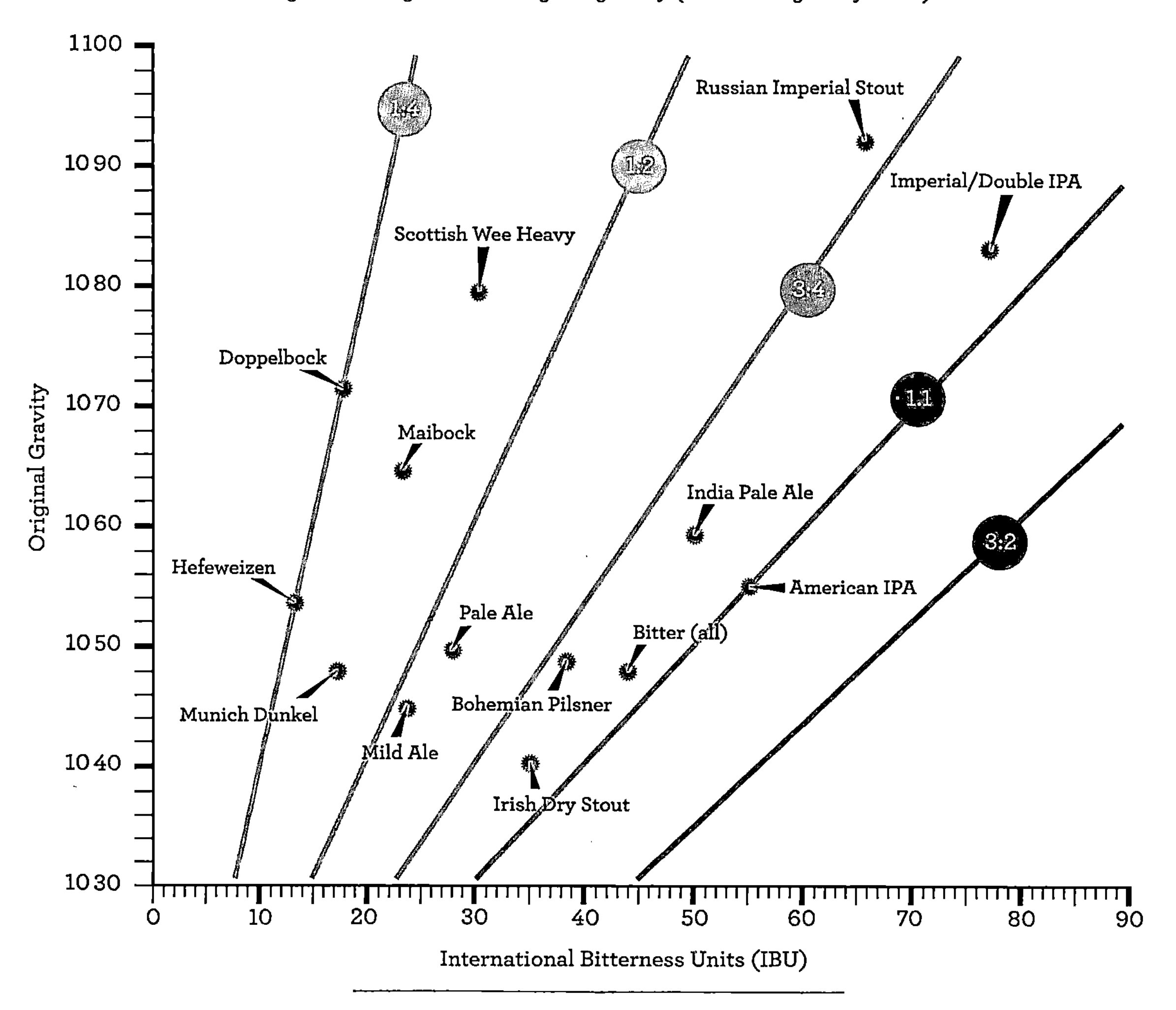

measuring beer balance, at least as it applies to sweet malt versus hop bitterness, is the BU to GU (bitterness units to gravity units) ratio. (The BU is just the IBUs we've been talking about.) Fifty IBU, for example, may be quite a lot of bitterness, but it sure tastes different in a big malty barley wine than it does in an English bitter. The GU is the wort's original gravity with the 1.0 removed: 1.050 OG becomes 50 GU. If you plot some familiar beer styles showing BU against GU, the differences pop into focus.

It is important to keep in mind that this BU to GU ratio only expresses the sweet malt versus bitter hops balance vector, and although this is the major sensory player in beer, there are many others: toast, roast, fruit, smoke, acid, carbonation, and more.

As for hop bitterness, once in the beer it's all pretty much the same. Hops express their considerable individuality through their aromas.

Haze and Beer Clarity

SINCE ANCIENT TIMES, people have praised the virtues of luminously clear beer. Today, clarity is a desirable aspect of almost all beer styles regardless of their origin. The important exceptions are noted below.

A perfectly clear beer requires expertise and vigilance on the part of the brewer. Malting, brewhouse procedures, fermentation, conditioning, filtration, and packaging all play a role. And this can all be for naught if the beer gets mishandled down the chain of distribution, as most beers of normal strength will throw a haze if they get old enough or are mistreated.

SOURCES OF HAZE IN BEER

Chill Haze. This is the result of malt-derived proteins precipitating in the beer when chilled. It is often seen in unfiltered (or lightly filtered) craft beers, where it is felt that the cosmetic downside is a worthy trade-off for the added complexity of an unfiltered beer. Chill haze is totally flavorless and vanishes as soon as the beer warms up a bit.

Yeast. This may either be deliberate, as in the case of hefeweizen (see at right), or a consequence of a sloppy pour or shaken bottle of a sedimented, bottle-conditioned beer. In the hefeweizen, yeast may also contribute a slight bready yeastiness. In an aged bottle-conditioned beer, the yeast sometimes imparts a slightly muddy taste and should be avoided if possible. Wheat beer kegs are often stored and shipped upside down, then turned over for serving, dispersing the yeast in the beer.

Starch Haze. In certain archaic traditions, the brewing process is conducted so as to leave a fine opalescent "shine" to the beer. See witbier on page 74.

HAZE AS AN INDICATOR OF FLAWED BEER

Old or Mishandled Beer. A haze, often accompanied by small "snowflakes" of precipitated protein, is a common feature of seriously old beers, especially in pale imported lagers. Multiple cycles of cooling and warming accelerate the process.

Infection. Many beer-spoilage organisms will throw a haze. Dirty tap lines, a breeding place for *Lactobacillus* and *Pediococcus* bacteria, are an all-too-common culprit.

PURPOSEFULLY HAZY OR CLOUDY BEERS

Most barley-malt-based beers are designed to be served crystal clear, but a common feature of many wheat beers is a certain cloudiness. This goes back to the Middle Ages, when beers were divided into two classes, red and white. In addition to their paler color, the reference to "white" likely refers to their haziness.

Hefeweizen. The word *hefe* means "yeast," and indeed yeast is added to the bottles of this spritzy German wheat beer. Part of the pageant of serving this beer from the bottle is the dollop of dregs swirled atop the thick creamy head. If you really must have your *Weissbier* clear, ask for a Kristal.

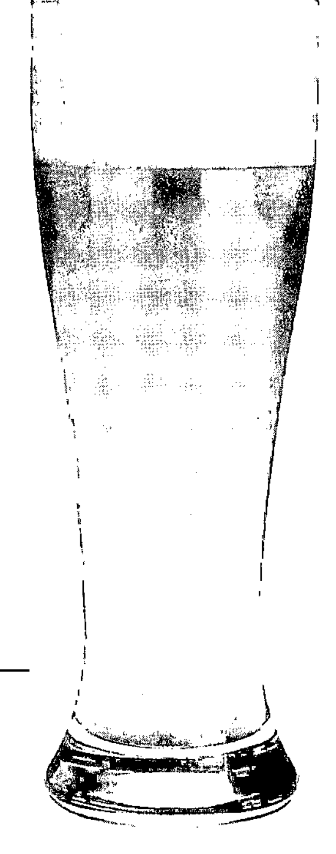

Hefeweizen is a wheat beer with "hefe," or yeast, which gives a cloudy appearance.

Berliner Weisse. This sour wheat beer may show a haze from the protein-rich wheat that makes up 50 to 60 percent of the recipe. In the photo above, it's dosed with the traditional green woodruff syrup, although raspberry is also popular.

Witbier/Belgian White Ale. This ancient style has a starchy sheen, a result of turbid mashing techniques — or a handful of flour tossed into the kettle.

Kellerbier. This little-known specialty is usually a pale German lager, served in its *bierkeller* directly from the aging tanks, without filtration. At least one bottled version is imported into the United States, and a few craft brewers have tried their hand at it, naturally.

Evaluating Clarity

UNLESS THE STYLE specifies haze of some sort, all beers should be bright and clear when served. With pale beers, it's easy. In darker beers, haze may be masked by the color. As a rule, if you can't see it with the naked eye, it's not a problem, but some aficionados when evaluating dark beers for clarity use a small flashlight and observe the beam as it illuminates the suspended haze. When you look for clarity remember to wipe the glass first, so you're not mistaking condensation for haze. And also, allow craft beer to warm to the higher end of appropriate serving temperatures, as chill haze may disappear.

Carbonation and Beer Foam

THE FOAMY, EFFERVESCENT NATURE of beer has fascinated us since the very beginnings of our long love affair with it. Beer is the only beverage with real foam, a result of beer's unique protein structure. It's not just the drinker that takes foam seriously. It is one of the most technically complex and well-studied aspects of

FILTRATION: DREAM OR NIGHTMARE?

This is a very complex topic for which there is no simple answer. On the plus side, filtration is a fast and efficient way of removing yeast and other material that might otherwise contribute to instability and shorten the shelf life of certain beers. Bright, fresh beer at affordable prices is the benefit. Filtration is often used to speed up what happens naturally.

Like so many aspects of brewing, proper filtration requires a wise and experienced brewmaster. Well-filtered beer can indeed be a thing of beauty. The downside is that overfiltered beer may sometimes be stripped of color, body, head retention, and flavor, leading the drinker into bland land.

POURING FOR GREAT FOAM

To get the best head on a beer, pour boldly down the center of an absolutely clean glass. It will foam up, but this is good. Really. Allow it to settle and then repeat until you have a full glass. By delaying gratification and allowing a large amount of foam to build up and then shrink, you have created a dense, creamy foam, filled with tiny, long-lasting bubbles. As a side benefit, you have knocked some of the excess gas out of the beer, and the result will be more like the smooth creaminess of draft beer.

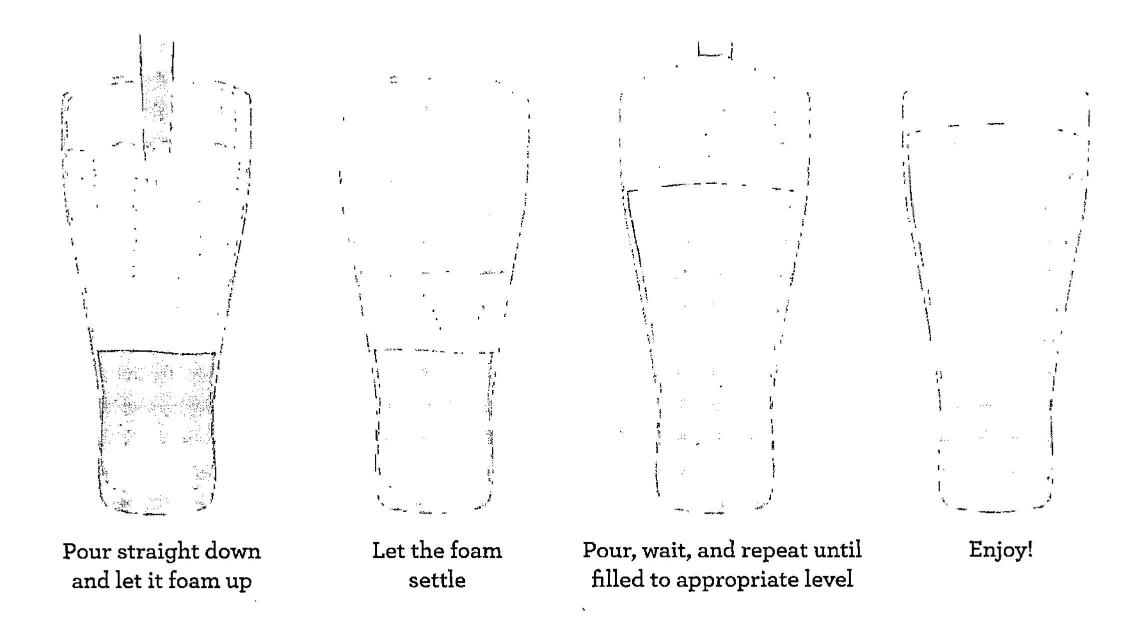

Pour straight down and let it foam up — Let the foam settle — Pour, wait, and repeat until filled to appropriate level — Enjoy!

brewing, and its proper management starts with decisions made way out in the farm fields.

Foam is all about beer body. Proteins in beer form what is called a "colloid," a loose protein net that ties the whole beer together. You can actually taste or, rather, feel this as a fullness on the palate. It is very similar in structure to a thin sort of Jell-O. This colloidal state affects the surface tension of the beer, which in turn is crucial for the formation and retention of foam. It's a Goldilocks thing: Beer foam requires proteins that are "just right" in length; those that are either too short or too long won't do. Hops and yeast also play a role. Like I said, it's a complex topic.

Wheat has the right kind of proteins to form a great head, and this is one of the desirable characteristics of any wheat beer. In fact, wheat and other grains such as oats and rye are sometimes collectively called "head grains" and quietly find their way into recipes in which a little help with the head might be needed: Kölsch and English bitter come to mind.

Some substances in the serving environment are deleterious to beer foam. Either detergent or oil will kill a head pretty quickly — a testimonial for beer-clean glassware.

OF COURSE, there would be no foam if there weren't carbonation in beer. Carbon dioxide is highly soluble in water-based liquids, and a good deal of it can dissolve in a cold beer. Compare it to nitrogen, which

SELECTED BEER STYLES AND CARBONATION LEVELS

HIGHLY CARBONATED BEER STYLES

Style	Volumes CO_2
Belgian strong golden	3.5–4
Belgian abbey	2.7–3.5
Belgian gueuze	3–4.5
Bavarian hefeweizen	3.5–4.5
Berliner Weisse	3.2–3.6
American industrial lager and light	2.5–2.7
Normal lager range	2.2–2.7
Normal ale range	1.5–2.5

LIGHTLY CARBONATED BEER STYLES

Style	Volumes CO_2
British cask ale	0.8–1.5
Straight lambic	0.5–2.5
Barley wines	1.3–2.3
Imperial Stout	1.5–2.3
Super-high-gravity ales	0–1.3

Pressure and Temperature as Related to CO_2 Volumes

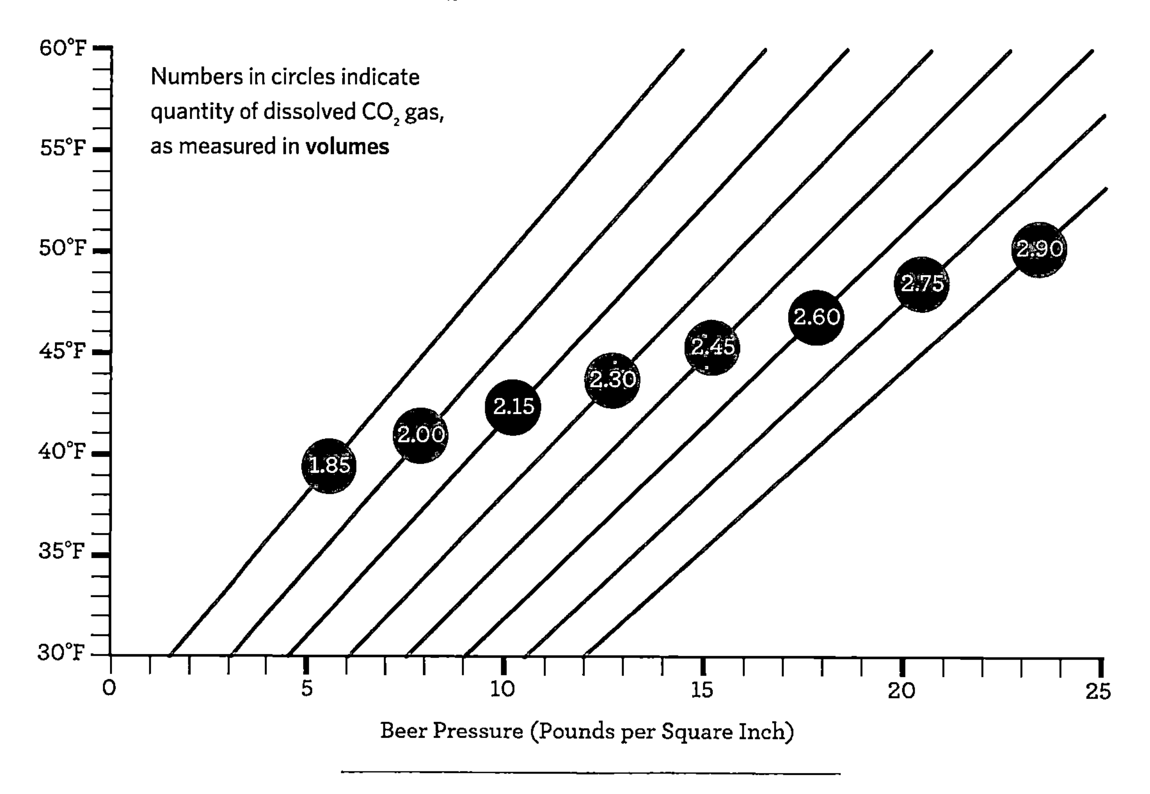

As anyone who has ever opened a warm beer knows, the pressure of beer's carbonation increases with temperature. Brewers use CO_2 "volume" to express the absolute amount of CO_2 gas dissolved in beer.

CARBONATION: NATURAL VERSUS ARTIFICIAL

For many, forced carbonation is the tool of the devil himself, and because of the crusading nature of the Campaign for Real Ale's (CAMRA) battle to preserve traditional ales, the debate takes on an ideological rather than a scientific tenor. There is little theoretical or sensory science to support the position that one is better than the other. In terms of physics, gas in equilibrium must be the same no matter how it got there. Opponents often conflate forced carbonation with other woes: adjunct lagers, serving at improper (too cold) temperatures, pasteurization, overfiltration. Although it is true that these things do change the taste of beer, well-brewed, unfiltered, *living* ale does just fine with forced carbonation.

has minimal solubility. On those draft cans of stout, as soon as you pop the top, the nitrogen leaves the beer, which is what it's designed to do. Open a regular beer, and it doesn't gush out, even though there's a tremendous amount of dissolved gas in there (as evidenced by what happens if you shake the can before opening).

The delicate veil of Brussels lace clinging to the glass is a sign of a well-made beer and a clean glass.

Brewers discuss carbonation in terms of volumes, which is an absolute measure not affected by pressure or temperature. However, as you can see from the graph on the facing page, the three are related; the higher the temperature, the more pressure at any given volume.

Not all beer styles are carbonated to the same degree. Beers such as cask ales are only lightly carbonated, as beer was ages ago. Wooden casks in the old days could stand only so much pressure. It doesn't hurt that British ale tastes great this way, never mind the fact that a highly carbonated beer served at cellar temperature would be asking for trouble. Because we like 'em c-c-c-cold and because the carbonation adds to the crisp, refreshing quality, American industrial-style beers are highly carbonated. The chart on the facing page lists a few more of the beer styles that fall outside the normal range of carbonation.

Color, clarity, carbonation, and much more — the range of qualities that beer displays is truly dazzling. I think that's one of the things that makes our relationship to beer so compelling. No matter how schooled you think you are, there is always more to discover. Beer has a language all its own, and it gives up its secrets only if you approach it the right way. Treat it with respect and gaze deeply into its amber, bubbling depths. If you listen very carefully, it will speak volumes to you.

CHAPTER 5

TASTING, JUDGING, AND EVALUATION

IT SHOULD be clear by now that this is not a book about the uncritical guzzling of beer (not that this practice is without its pleasures). This chapter is about the various ways and settings in which we taste and the goals of such encounters. I hope in every case there is some pleasure in it, but that may be far from the expressed purpose. No matter the situation, the chemistry of the beer remains the same, and we all bring our own unique physiology and psychology to every interaction.

Depending on the occasion, your relationship to the beer will be very different. In a casual, fun, educational tasting, you are the beer's friend, trying to size him up; but, like any friend, be gracious and tolerant of faults; try to pick out the best and don't dwell on — or at least publicly acknowledge — the shortcomings.

In a competition, it's your job to give him a merciless grilling, stacking him up against the other beers and possibly some idealized notion of the style. You and your tablemates might disagree, which can spark a debate of near-metaphysical import over intention, purity of concept, historical details, and a quality I like to call "wonderfulness" — a summation of artistic and technical brilliance in liquid form.

In serious quality-control settings, great care is taken to remove any notion of like or dislike. The taster's job is to describe, without editorializing, in highly standardized language. In the simplest and most accurate of all these tests — the triangle — the taster's job is simply to pick which two of three samples are identical.

You, as a taster, will be tested too. In the casual settings, knowing details like starting gravity, IBUs, or what color pants the brewer wore while brewing will get you big-time beer-geek cred. But that's nothing compared to the study and work needed to pass the Beer Judge Certification Program (BJCP, the sanctioning organization for homebrew competitions) exam and move up through the ranks, or to achieve the industry standing that gets you a seat at the World Beer Cup (WBC). In industry quality-control settings, it is common practice to calibrate judges, so that their strengths and weaknesses can be factored into evaluations of the sample beers.

The Tasting Environment

No matter what the purpose of the tasting, the environment is critical. As long as the room is reasonably comfortable, this is as much of a list of what *not* to do.

Limit Distractions. Generally, the job is to get rid of distractions, as tasting takes intense concentration. You don't want to break the samplers out of their reverie. As you go from casual to structured, this becomes more important. Too many rules would be overly restrictive for a social tasting, but in the most critical tests, judges are put into small booths, and it is just them and a few cups of beer.

So anything not essential to the occasion must go. You want to separate your group from the Junior Miss Hemisphere Pageant going on in the ballroom next to you. It is quite reasonable to request that cell phones be turned off or set to vibrate. Do everything you can to make it easy to keep everyone's attention. Music is okay for very casual events, but it should not be so loud as to impede conversation.

Consider Lighting. Good light is always welcome. The ideal, rarely achieved, is natural, north light. Lighting is not always under your control at hired locations, but it is something to consider, especially for competitions.

Provide Water. No matter what the event, unlimited amounts of drinking water should be available. It does not need to be bottled, but there can sometimes be a distracting amount of chlorine in municipal tap water. Raw or softened well water rarely makes the grade. So I guess what I'm saying is that unless you have access to great mountain tap water, stick to bottled.

TASTING RECORD

DATE

TASTED BY

BEER

AGE OF BEER

TYPE/STYLE

PACKAGE

LOCATION

ALCOHOL/GRAVITY

AROMA

APPEARANCE

BODY & TEXTURE

AFTERTASTE

OVERALL IMPRESSIONS

SPECIFIC OFF-FLAVORS AND AROMA

- O Acetaldehyde
- O Acetic
- O Acidic (Vinegar)
- O Alcoholic
- O Astringent/Harsh
- O Barnyard
- O Earthy/Corked
- O Cheesy
- O Chlorophenol (bandage)
- O Diacetyl (buttery)
- O DMS (creamed corn)
- O Estery/Solventy
- O Goaty/Sweaty
- O Metallic
- O Phenolic
- O Oxidized
- O Skunked
- O Sulfuric/Sulfidic
- O Yeasty/Autolysed
- O Other

To download a printable version, go to http://tastingbeer.org.

Dump It. Might as well come out and say it: dump buckets. Painful as it is to throw away beer, you have to make it easy for people at any kind of tasting to throw it away or else you just cultivate chaos.

Jot It Down. For casual tastings, a listing of beers makes it easy for people to take notes and look for the beers in a store later on. Supply paper and have some extra pencils available, and make sure they are mechanical, not wood; I have more than once had the thought, "Man, this is a cedary beer," only to realize a split second later that I'm holding a pencil and the glass in the same hand. Like I said, details count.

Keep Score. Judging depends heavily on score sheets, which have been structured to put the proper emphasis on various attributes of the beer, from appearance to aftertaste. The sheets are like a road map, guiding the judges as they consider every dimension and put it all into perspective. Even novice tasters can benefit from this kind of discipline, and it's a lot of fun to run through a few beers on the tasting sheet opposite (or on score sheets downloaded from the BJCP or WBC Web sites).

Eliminate Unwanted Odors. Wayward aromas can be devastating. Grandma's perfume can stink up a whole city block; bless her, but there are times when it's gotta go. A little perfume is okay in casual or even educational settings, but there is no conceivable reason you would want it if you are judging a competition, and it's absolutely forbidden in professional taste panels. Even scented hand lotion can interfere as you hold the cup up to your nose. And ladies, lipstick can ruin a beer's head. The other most common olfactory contaminant is the kitchen. Make sure you know in advance where it is relative to the tasting, and how well the vent fans work. This is generally not a problem, but when it's bad, it really stinks.

We once made the mistake of holding a judge-certification exam in a house where several cats lived. This was not a problem except for the one individual who was spastically

TASTING TYPES AND THEIR REQUIREMENTS

	Aroma Free	No Smoking	Quiet	Drinking Water	Dump Buckets	Notepaper	Score Sheets	Beer List	Style Guidelines	Non-Wood Pencils	Crackers or Bread
Casual Tasting	Y	Y	-	Y	Y	-	N	Y	-	OK	-
Structured	Y	Y	-	Y	Y	-	N	Y	OK	Y	-
Educational Presentation	Y	Y	-	Y	Y	Y	N	Y	OK	Y	OK
Casual Competition	Y	Y	N	Y	Y	Y	N	N*	N	Y	OK
Competition	Y	Y	Y	Y	Y	Y	Y	N*	OK	Y	Y
Sensory Panel	Y	Y	Y	Y	Y	-	Y	N	OK	Y	N

** Judges get "pull sheets" in categories for which it is important to know what special ingredients, such as fruit or spices, may have been used and should be expressed in the beer.*

allergic to cats, and it was a total washout for him. I have some allergies myself, and because ingredients in beer sometimes trigger them, I try to remember to take an antihistamine before any serious tasting or judging.

Provide a Palate Cleanser. People have varying opinions on the usefulness of bread or crackers. Generally, when there is a chance that judges may get fatigued or when the beers presented are different enough from each other to require a palate cleanser, it is a welcome addition. Plain water, crackers, saltines, or French bread are preferred. Anything else is too much. Avoid fatty crackers (most are), as the fat will ruin the beer's head if it gets into the beer. All bets are off when it comes to beer and food events, though.

Consider the Glass. Tasting glasses are usually a bit of a disappointment. In an ideal world, all beer would be evaluated in stemmed white-wine glasses. These present beer beautifully, the inward taper holding aromas below the rim, and the stem keeping our sticky fingers from heating it up. In fact, there is an ISO (International Organization for Standardization) standard tasting glass, a diminutive stemmed tulip.

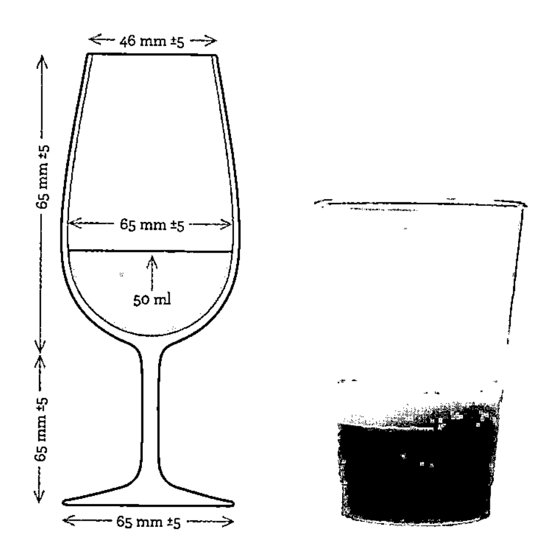

ISO Standard Tasting Glass and Plastic Judging Cup
Research by the International Organization for Standardization led them to this glass for tasting wine and other beverages. Note the incurved rim and where the fill line is. For beer, a similar geometry works great, even at a somewhat larger size. Crystal-clear 10-ounce cups will also work for most tasting purposes.

For a small number of judges with a limited number of beers in a controlled setting, using proper tasting glasses can be possible. But the logistics of a large competition like the World Beer Cup are hairy enough already, so just about all homebrew and commercial beer gets judged in plastic cups. The hard, crystal-clear cups of about 10-ounce capacity are the best. Plastic aromas usually aren't a problem these days, but do check. Avoid the milky translucent cups, as they can make it difficult to tell if a beer is sparkling clear. Opaque or colored cups won't do.

No matter the glass type, it should never be filled more than one-third full. You need all that headspace to develop the proper aroma. Two to 3 ounces is about all that is needed to give a beer a very thorough judging.

Tasting Types

Tastings fall into a wide range of possible formats, ranging from completely spur-of-the-moment thrashes to carefully planned and staged educational events. They may be large or small, formal or informal. The following list is by no means complete, but it should give you an idea of what's out there.

Reception-Style Tasting. Like a beer festival, these tastings are often mostly for enjoyment, with education as a secondary goal. In the most common format, there are 10 to 15 beers of either widely varying types or examples more narrowly chosen from a style or region, or to illustrate a specific point. Bottled beers are usually placed in bus tubs with some (but not massive amounts of) ice. Attendees usually circulate and try beers at their own pace. With smaller groups, you can get away with people pouring their own; larger groups require pourers. There may be a program to suggest a particular tasting order or to suggest things to look for in the beers. A handout with some detail on the beers is very helpful. There may be some spoken introduction.

In many settings, it is important to match the beers to your audience. If you have wine drinkers in the crowd, serving a fruit lambic may be a way to entice them over to our side, or at least to get them to admit that beer is not all yellow and fizzy. I love to hear them say, "I *like* this. It doesn't taste like beer!" With a general audience, it's also not a bad idea to have some yellow, fizzy beers. By that, I mean something that mainstream drinkers would recognize as beer. It's okay to push them a little, as that is what they are there for. A high-class Euro Pilsner or an American wheat beer will work fine in this role. I have found that stronger, darker beers are often well received by women of my mother's age. Doppelbock feeds a sweet tooth, and the bigger, richer stouts also have their chocolaty charms. It is often the case that you can push people a lot further than you might have thought. The only area you have to be a little careful with is very hoppy beers. Just like chile heat, bitterness in beer takes some getting used to, so use a sensitive touch unless you have a well-seasoned audience.

Casual Competitions. These are not widely held, but they can be a fun way of engaging the beer providers as well as the attendees, and the results can be meaningful. The key feature is that scoring is done by whoever attends the event and not by highly trained judges under controlled conditions. In a way, it's more of a real-world way of evaluating a beer, as it is more of a social situation in which people are enjoying and talking about the beers. The Chicago Beer Society has been holding one such event for over thirty years. The current format is to have around a dozen draft beers, identified only by style. Attendees have a scorecard with room for notes and a tear-off portion to record their first, second, and third favorite beers; about 90 minutes is allotted to sample the beers in any order. After the ballots are collected, the identifying tap handles are installed and dinner is served. This type of tasting can be done with bottled beer, but it's best for a smaller number of guests because the beers have to be poured out of sight of the attendees, which means a lot of pouring and schlepping.

Educational Programs. These are usually presented in lecture or classroom settings. The object will be to present beers that illustrate styles, history, flavors, or some other specific aspect of beer. Two- to 3-ounce samples are presented in a specific order. You often have to urge people to offer up descriptions to the rest of the class —nobody wants to get it wrong — but keep at them. It's important that people get comfortable discussing what they are perceiving. They are usually better at it than they expect to be.

SPIKING BEERS

When discussing flavors, and especially off-flavors, it's usually impossible to find beers that display specific aromas or other features, so it becomes necessary to add small amounts of individual chemicals to the beer in a process called "spiking," which can give you the equivalent of years of experience in the field in just a single session. There are dozens of beer flavor and aroma chemicals that can be spiked into beer, but just a half dozen that are really important, and those are the ones we use for the introductory courses.

Clean, neutral, consistent beers work best as a spiking base. Non-light beers are better, as light beers don't have enough "beer" aroma and are easily overwhelmed by the spiking chemicals. One 12-ounce beer will serve six to eight tasters.

There are a couple of ways to do the spikes. A company called FlavorActiv makes premeasured single-dose shots designed to be added to a 12-ounce beer. Alternatively, food-grade versions of the pure chemicals can be purchased and diluted into stock solutions, which can then be squirted into the beers in appropriate quantities. A dispensing pipette (the kind that has a dial to set the amount that is picked up with a push of the button) is the best tool for the dosing. A capacity of 1,000 microliters (1 ml) is the most useful size.

A word of warning: Some of these spiking chemicals are not pleasant and will stink up your freezer pretty strongly. And in their pure form, they may actually be flammable or otherwise dangerous. Any work with pure flavor chemicals should be done in a very well-ventilated space. It's also a good idea to do your spiking in a wide plastic tub or tray so any spills or drops can be contained. Many, such as DMS, are not stable and will deteriorate within a matter of months. All keep best in the freezer as long as you have something to contain them. A metal box with a tight, waterproof gasket is advisable.

Once you have done the math and mixed up the stock solutions, it's a simple matter to put on a fresh tip and adjust the pipette to the desired amount of spike. If you're using twist-

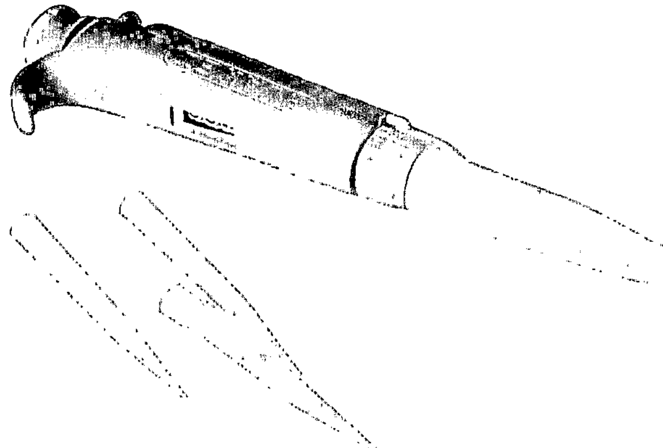

Spiking Pipette with Disposable Tips
An acurate pipette is best used to spike mainstream premium beer.

COMMON SPIKING CHEMICALS

Chemical	Descriptor	Threshold	Sample Concentration
Ethyl Acetate	Solvent/Ester	18 ppm	144 ppm (8x)
Acetaldehyde	Green Apple, Leafy	10 ppm	40 ppm (4x)
Isoamyl Acetate	Banana/Ester	1.2 ppm	5 ppm (4x)
Diacetyl	Buttery	0.10 ppm	0.40 ppm (4x)
DMS	Creamed Corn	40 ppb	160 ppb (4x)
Trans-2 Nonenal	Papery	0.10 ppb	0.80 ppb (8x)
Hop Iso Extract	Bitter	5 ppm (IBU*)	25 ppm (5x) + base beer

**International Bitterness Units*

For more on these individual aroma chemicals and their origins, see chapter 3.

off beers, then just carefully twist off the cap. Don't use a bottle opener, because you're going to screw it back on when you're done spiking. With the beer open, gently push the sampling button down until it stops, then dip it into the stock solution, and release the button to draw a sample into the tip. Move over to the beer and again gently push the sampling button, which will squirt the spike into the beer. Set the pipette down and tightly twist the cap back on. As an alternative, a homebrewing capper and fresh crowns can be used.

It is also important to present tasters with a "control," or unspiked, beer so they can go back and forth and compare against the spiked samples. The control beer is just the base beer minus any spiking chemicals.

We generally find that for most audiences, spikes between four and eight times the threshold values seem to work best to introduce people to these aromas. It is also possible to do a rough calibration by mixing up a series of spikes at ½x, 1x, 2x, 4x, and 8x thresholds and have people work their way up until they can detect the spiked sample. In this sort of an exercise it is especially important to have the control beer for people to compare against, or even present them with a pair of unmarked samples, one spiked, the other a control. Obviously this isn't the simplest thing to do, but it is manageable for a small group. As we all differ in our sensitivities to various aromas, it makes sense for serious beer judges to get themselves calibrated.

Some off-flavors are easier to present as real beers than as artificially spiked-up samples. Skunkiness, the smelly effect that light has on hops in beer, is simple enough. Just take a Corona or Heineken (or any beer in a clear or green bottle) and expose it to daylight for a few minutes, and voilà, skunk! Note that Miller products won't work (the chemical that causes skunkiness has been removed from their hop extract). The clove-tinged aromas that yeast adds to weizens can be simulated with a chemical called eugenol, but I find it simple enough (and more accurate) to just buy some hefeweizen and use that. Overaged beer is hard to simulate, but not that difficult to lay your hands on. It's a little indelicate, but you can ask at your liquor store if they have any out-of-date beer they're planning on sending back to the distributor. If you have time for advance planning, you can buy some imported Pilsner and store it in your attic or other warm place to prematurely age it.

Judging and Competitions

Competitions are an important tool in pushing forward the art and science of brewing. For most brewers, having an unbiased panel of their peers bestow a medal for a well-brewed beer is a soul-tickling thrill. These guys build their reputations — and sometimes get their raises — on these awards. It's as serious as beer gets.

There are many ways to select the winners, and every competition is different, but there are similarities in all approaches, as follows:

- Judges are carefully vetted and often tested and trained.
- Usually, judging is highly structured, by means of score sheets and a specific methodology.
- Conditions are controlled in terms of lighting, aromas, noise, and other distractions.
- Beers are always presented blind, which means judges have to evaluate just what's in the glass and nothing else.
- Judging is structured so that judges don't unduly influence each other.
- Beers are presented in flights, usually of eight to fifteen beers all in the same style category.

BEERS MAY BE JUDGED either in the absolute or against some agreed-upon notion of what a particular style should be. The former is called "hedonic" judging, and judges simply score the beer based on how good it tastes to them. This is a perfectly legitimate means of rating beers as long as beers of similar styles are being compared. The bias is that no matter how sophisticated they are, those who judge these contests tend to give higher scores to bigger, more flavorful beers such as barley wines. As long as apples are compared to apples, there's no problem with this method.

The other approach is style-based judging. Each beer is judged on how well it expresses the essential character of the style category in which it is entered. The style guidelines are similar to the ones in the back of this book, and a copy is present right at the table; judges will usually confer to make sure they all understand the style before actually judging. An enormous amount of work has been put into the guidelines to match historical styles with modern commercial practice and to structure the process to ensure a thorough, balanced evaluation.

In larger competitions, more than one round will be needed to winnow down large categories to a number that can be judged in a single, final round. Typically the senior judges from the preliminary round will get together and quickly rejudge the best from the former flights to determine medal status.

In addition to bragging rights, breweries know winning medals is a powerful sales tool.

Great American Beer Festival and World Beer Cup. These two competitions are run by the Brewers Association, which is the trade association for America's craft brewers. They are identical except that the former is open only to American brewers and the latter is a worldwide competition. The GABF (Great American Beer Festival) judging has been going on since 1981 and in 2007 drew 2,793 entries in 75 categories. The World Beer Cup began in 1996 and operates in even years only.

These are style-based competitions, and an extensive set of style guidelines (available at www.beertown.org) is updated every year based on feedback from judges and brewers. The categories in these competitions tend to reflect current commercial practice in the United States and abroad. All the judging takes place within three days. The scoring is not based on points; each flight is judged as if it were a best of show. Beers are brought to the table all at once, and then the judges go through them one by one and make notes and add appropriate comments on a specially designed judging sheet. Most judges go through and smell all beers before tasting any, making a few notes if necessary. The first pass is done without discussion, to prevent judges from unduly influencing each other. Once everybody has had a chance

HOW DO YOU BECOME A BEER JUDGE?

Judging beer is by far the best way to hone your skills as a critical taster. Whether you're a brewer or not, you can participate in the Beer Judge Certification Program (BJCP). You study, take a test, and become recognized as a judge. Higher ranks are attainable with higher test scores and experience points. The BJCP itself (www.bjcp.org) is your best portal to all of this, but equally important is your local homebrew club. The American Homebrewers Association (www.beertown.org) or local homebrew shop can help you get in touch. Many clubs run study sessions, and these invariably include lots of beer tasting, so they're as fun as they are educational.

If you want to dip your toes into judging gradually, sign on as a steward and be involved with all the behind-the-scenes work involved in getting judges their beers in the proper order and condition. There are often opportunities to taste along and get a sense of what the judging process is all about. Your help is always welcome.

The BJCP program allows judges to climb in ranks with experience, knowledge, and effort.

to form opinions about the beers, the discussion begins.

The most obviously problematic or out-of-style beers get kicked out first. Then it comes down to small problems with flavor or style or beers that just don't come together. The field narrows to a handful of beers. At that point, they are pretty much all in the style, so the judges must focus on less-tangible attributes: deliciousness, memorability, and the ability to create a positive impression. It's not easy, and with a contentious group, this can drag on. A flight usually takes between 60 and 90 minutes to taste.

Professional judges are preferred, although some exceptionally skilled homebrewers and journalists are included. It's a hot ticket: there is a waiting list, and many judges are on a rotation.

BJCP/AHA-Sanctioned Homebrew Competitions. There are many of these at local, regional, and national levels, and competitions are a valued part of the homebrew-club experience. Like the GABF, these are style-based competitions. The BJCP (Beer Judge Certification Program) guidelines (available at www.bjcp.org) are similar to those of the GABF but are more focused on historical or "classic" versions of the styles, less influenced by current commercial practice, and get revamped only every five years or so. The National Homebrew Competition, run by the AHA (American Homebrewers Association), is the biggest beer competition in the world. There were 5,644 entries in 2008! Entered beers go through a two-round process. The first round is split up and the beers are judged in multiple locations. Beers that make the cut are sent by their brewers to the second round, always held during June in conjunction with the National Homebrewers Conference.

Judging is very structured, using a 50-point scale, with a certain number of points allotted for appearance, aroma, flavor, body, and overall. Whether the competition is large or small, winners are determined for each category, and then all the category gold medalists face off in one final best-of-show round. As in the GABF, contending beers are lined up in front of the judges, and after a period of contemplation, elimination begins. Sorting out the last few is complicated by the fact that they are all different styles. Judges may have to weigh the sheer power of a barley wine against the delicate beauty of a witbier.

BJCP/AHA-sanctioned competitions happen on a local level as well, from small competitions with fewer than a hundred entries to the gigantic madhouse (and I mean that in the best sense) that is Houston's Dixie Cup. In addition, there are a number of different regional circuits that tally up the points from a season's worth of competition, just like NASCAR does. It's a rare club that doesn't hold a competition.

SUGGESTIONS FOR TASTING TYPES

- **By style:** IPA, weiss, etc.
- **By country or brewing tradition**
- **Craft versus traditional producers of classic styles**
- **Vertical:** same beer, different years
- **By ingredient:** hops, malt, etc.
- **By season:** summer beers, etc.
- **A variety of yeast types:** lager, ale, weiss, Belgian
- **A comparison of tradition**
- **Similar ales and lagers:** brown ale and Munich lager, for example
- **With food:** cheese, chocolate, etc. (for details, see chapter 7)

Mondiale de la Bière. This exciting beer festival in Montreal has a competition associated with it. As competitions go, it's a little unusual. Instead of a single style, each flight is a mix of different styles. Additionally, all the judges at the table will be judging different beers. Organizers believe this cuts down on discussion biases. If you're used to style-based judging, it can be a little disorienting at first, but when you get comfortable, it works just fine. The unusual feature of this system is that you are asked to guess which style the beer fits into, and then to rate it based on how much pleasure it gives as an example of this style. Definitely unconventional, but in my experience, the great beers still do very well here.

Beverage Testing Institute. This Chicago-based company is exactly what the name says, and started out as a wine-evaluation program that expanded into beer and spirits in 1994. The company runs judging panels frequently and sorts beers by styles. However, this is a hedonic system, meaning judges are asked to evaluate the beers on a 14-point scale by how much they like them. Naturally this gives some disparities from style to style, but because all the ranking is within each style, it doesn't matter. BTI (Beer Tasting Institute) medals are based on achieving certain scores, which trigger bronze, silver, and gold medals. The company has been criticized by some for being too free with the awards, but this point-based medal system is widely used in other food and wine competitions. Scores and reviews are published at Tastings.com and in *All About Beer Magazine.*

Non-competitive Evaluation and Taste Panels

Breweries have a need for highly structured systems for evaluating products, and although much of the work can now be accomplished with sophisticated analytical equipment, there is still much about beer that only a human being can reveal. Breweries may need to simply monitor their current beers for consistency, or check that the same beer brewed at different breweries all tastes the same; or they may be looking to evaluate improvements to the beer, or to try keeping it consistent even though materials, equipment, or brewing techniques have changed. And of course, when new products are created, those have to be tasted, too. Taste panels are usually selected from tested and trained brewery personnel, but when it comes to things like new products, it is important to use regular consumers as well.

There are many types of protocols. The most sensitive are those in which panelists are presented with beers that differ only in one respect, that is, as a set of three with one odd beer. An example of this technique is called a "duo-trio," in which a reference sample is presented first, and then the panelist is asked to identify which of the next two beers is the same and which is different. In the "triangle," three beers are presented simultaneously, and the panelist has to pick the odd beer. And in a "paired comparison," the taster is asked which of the two beers is higher in one specific attribute — bitterness, for example.

Subjects may be presented with a series of beers and asked to rate any difference in specific attributes, often on a scale of 1 to 5 or 1 to 10. Other scales use a (−) to 0 to (+) system, with +7 or −7 as the extremes and 0 as neutral. Subjects might be asked simply to rank a series of beers, usually six or less, in order of some characteristic or preference.

With all these approaches, there is a certain amount of statistical work that needs to be done to determine the validity and reliability of the results, as there is some chance that tasters will pick the right beer simply by chance.

In addition to statistics, there is a whole raft of psychological effects that need to be accounted for in any evaluation in which big money is at stake. It is well known that the order in which samples are presented affects the way they are evaluated, with the most honest appraisals going to the middle of the pack. Strong contrasts from beer to beer have an effect, which is why less intense beers are evaluated first. Beers that are all fairly similar tend to mesmerize the panelists into seeing them as more similar than they really are. Individual judges use the scale differently, too, with some using the extremes and others sticking to the middle of the scale. Sometimes, the lowest and highest scores on any panel are tossed to smooth out the data. And of course, we are all susceptible to suggestion, either from prior expectations such as brand names or packaging or from the opinions of other tasters, which is why those things are eliminated or avoided as much as possible in serious settings.

Presenting Beer for Judging or Evaluation

ANY TIME A BEER is evaluated in a serious way, every effort must be made to ensure that the beer arrives at the taster's lips in the best possible condition and with minimal distractions.

The first consideration is proper temperature. This is devilishly hard to manage, especially because the creator of the universe chose not to bless us with 50-degree ice. As a general rule, 40°F (4°C) for lagers and 50 to 55°F (10 to 13°C) for ales is about where you would like to end up, with stronger beers warmer than weak ones. The usual approach is to pull refrigerated beers out of the cooler an hour or so in advance of the competition and let them warm to their ideal serving temperature, or actually a little below, as the beers will warm a few degrees just by contact with the cup. This is one of the finer points of competition stewarding. An infrared thermometer is a useful tool for a competition organizer or head steward because with it he or she can take a beer's temperature just by pointing at it — much less messy than probe-type thermometers.

Judges should be aware of beer temperature. Too-cold beers will lack aroma, and some will throw a forgivable chill haze. Beers that are obviously a little too cold may be warmed up in the hands before rechecking the aroma.

Beer should always be poured just before tasting. Pour the beer right down the middle of the glass, wait for the foam to settle, and if needed, pour a little more, but never more than one-third full.

Some judges like to carry a small flashlight or a laser pointer with them. This can help to evaluate haziness, especially in darker beers. It should be aimed either up through the bottom or through the side of the glass; if you can see the beam, that's the haze lighting up. This is the hyper-geek approach for all those boys who love their toys. My favorite tool for competitions is pretty low-tech — a grease pencil. It's useful for writing entry numbers on beers that I want to keep on the table and come back to, so I don't have to keep them in order to remember which is which.

Organizers should be *organized.* Tasters should know what to expect. Plenty of information means the tasters and the beers will both get the best out of the experience.

Lighter beers should go first, which means less hoppy, less roasty, and lower alcohol beers go first. A dozen beers per flight is considered a good maximum, although this is sometimes pushed a little. Make sure the tasters have adequate breaks and reasonable creature comforts.

Finally, it's important to understand the limits. Formal tasting can be quite fatiguing, even if the amount of alcohol consumed isn't all that great. Twelve to fifteen beers is about max in a session before a break is needed. In casual settings where people are drinking as much as tasting, be aware of overconsumption. Limit sample sizes, give people something else to do, have water available, and encourage discussion.

How to Taste

THE BEER'S ON the table. The conditions are perfect. The stars are aligned. Now what?

SMELL

It's best to smell the beer before anything else, as there are aromas — especially sulfur-based ones — that are so volatile they may linger for only a minute or so before wafting away forever. Smelling is best accomplished by quick sniffs — think about how a bloodhound does it. A long draw of air will only dry out your nose and saturate your receptors. Give it a few moments to sink in, as some aromas take a while to register. Be especially aware of any little memory flashbacks you have, as these can be valuable clues to identifying aromas. Try to linger on these memories, walk around in them, and use them to help you figure out what is triggering the flashback. Where are you? Is that toast? Roses? Wax lips? This is spooky stuff, but when it clicks, it's amazing.

Write your notes about the aroma. If you're not getting much, try swirling the beer in the glass. If the beer seems overly cold for the style, cup it in your hands as you swirl to help warm it up and release aroma. A useful trick if you need to freshen your senses is to smell the back of your own hand. This gives you something else to smell, so you can come back to the beer fresh. Of course, just waiting a minute or so will accomplish the same resetting, so keep coming back to the aroma as you go through the rest of the tasting process.

LOOK AND SIP

When you think you have gotten all the aroma the beer has to offer, take a good look at the beer and make notes about color, clarity, head character, and retention. Then you can move on to tasting. Take a sip, and let the liquid linger on your tongue and warm up on the bottom of your mouth. Pay attention to basic tastes such as sweetness and acidity, and wait a few beats for the bitterness, as it builds more slowly than other tastes.

There are also mouthfeel sensations to be aware of: body, carbonation, astringency, oiliness. Give special attention to the aftertaste. Is it quick or long? Smooth or harsh? Hoppy, malty, roasty? All of the above or something else? Again, take notes.

TASTE WITH YOUR NOSE

Now take another sip, and this time, try to get some of the aromas to volatilize up into your nasal cavity where the receptors are. Wine tasters use a technique called "aspiration," in which you hold a small amount of the liquid in the bottom of your mouth, against the sides of the tongue, and allow it to warm up. Then, put the tip of your tongue behind your two top front teeth and draw air in through your mouth, slowly, letting it gurgle through the liquid. This releases aromatics, and with a little shallow in-and-out breathing, you can get it up into your nose for a nice concentrated shot of aroma. Because in beer judging we normally swallow the sample, you can also swallow and then slowly expel a little breath through your nose, which has a similar effect. There's no best way. Just be aware that the object is to get the aroma molecules up in the top of your nose where they can trigger olfactory neurons. Figure out what works best for you. It's obvious when it's working right. At this point, expand or revise your aroma comments if you feel so moved.

Look for anything sticking out awkwardly. Are there off-flavors such as diacetyl or DMS? Is there any harshness or astringency, especially on the finish? Are there any papery or woody notes of oxidation, or unwanted acidity?

ANALYZE AND SCORE

Finally, do a little higher-level analysis. If the beer is being judged by style, how well does it fit in terms of overall intensity, bitterness, malt character, and the overlay of fermentation? If it is a lager, is it free of fruity, estery aromas? How is the balance? Do all the parts seem to fit together? Is this a beer you would drink a pint of? Or two? Take to a desert island? Will you remember this beer in a year . . . in a good way?

Once you've written all your notes and scored the beer (if appropriate), then you can discuss with the other judges. Those discussions are best when the most experienced judges make an effort not to dominate the discussion, as even new judges have useful contributions to make, and everybody misses a thing or two.

A Sampling of Tasting Events

SOCIAL TASTINGS ARE ONE of the great joys of being a beer fancier. Setting forth in a room full of beer enthusiasts to seek out and share new beer discoveries is just like being in church for me, but a whole lot more fun. And in my experience, they're even more enjoyable when you get involved and help organize them. For over 20 years, I've been involved with the Chicago Beer Society, an all-volunteer, non-profit group that puts on about half a dozen beer-tasting events a year. Over the years we've explored a number of different formats and have learned quite a lot about what works and what doesn't.

The simplest events are just social get-togethers with a little structured beer focus. You can either ask people to bring things, share the cost, or just take turns doing events. The important thing is to have an idea, and don't try to drink in the whole beer world at one whack. Preparing people with an introductory talk, reading from an authoritative book, or working with a set of tasting notes will help everyone get the most out of each event. Try to limit the number of different beers to 10 or so, as it gets overwhelming beyond that. Nice glassware adds to the experience, and often you

can ask people to rinse and reuse the same glass (or two) all evening.

You don't have to organize your own events. Most brewpubs and many packaging breweries regularly hold brewmaster dinners, which can be great places to meet the brewers as well as fellow beer fans, and they are a great way to get to know a particular brewery's beers and what makes them tick. Although there are few beer-appreciation groups right now, they are worth seeking out. Many homebrew clubs have beer-tasting events of various kinds and never seem to mind nonbrewers in their midst.

At the Chicago Beer Society we prefer to have food at our events. First, we believe it is the responsible thing to do, as food slows down alcohol absorption and gives people some other diversion besides beer. Second, it does make the occasion more social and highlights beer at its best — as part of a gastronomic experience. You can also hold the tasting in a private room at a restaurant; the cost of the food includes the room as part of the deal.

BEER DINNERS, LUNCHES, AND BRUNCHES

These are pretty straightforward events that even a smaller club can organize. Once you have a concept, the next step is to contact a restaurant with a private room sized to accommodate your expected group and talk about what you'd like to do and what the costs would be (make sure you include tax and tip in your calculations). Then contact your local breweries and possibly beer distributors to see if they would be willing to donate beer, possibly in exchange for complimentary tickets to the event. They all have budgets for sampling, and these events can be an easy way for them to get their beers in front of potentially passionate customers.

You do need to check out the local laws regarding donation of beer. In many states direct donation of beer is illegal, and in that case the beer may need to be paid for. However, brewers might be willing to pay for tickets or offer a monetary donation to offset the cost of the beer. I can't advise you on specifics, but your local brewers and distributors will know what is allowable.

If all this looks good, put a flier together and place it in local beer hot spots, then put the same information (and a downloadable PDF of the flier) on the Web. There are a lot of logistics, of course, the most difficult of which will be the transportation of the beer. At this point, our club has a pretty sizable collection of draft equipment; you may need to borrow some from the restaurant, local breweries, distributors, or homebrewers.

CASUAL TASTINGS can take lots of different forms. We hold competitive tastings, dinners, and more. We've held a *Weissbier* brunch; an Indian buffet and IPA-fest called "A Hop to India"; a beer and cheese event with 25 different pairings; and a high-end Belgian dinner with Belgian-inspired beers. If you live near a body of water, you can move the whole affair to a boat and have a brews cruise. We tossed in a Chicago blues band and a roast pig and ended up with our Blues & Brews Cruise. Capital-F fun!

If your group is wary of taking on too much responsibility, you might look into partnering with a local group of brewers or your state craft brewers guild. They don't yet exist in every state, but these trade groups are usually happy to have some enthusiastic volunteers to help take care of the details, and will often share the proceeds of a successful event in exchange for the organizing manpower.

(opposite) Beer and Food
Events that combine beer and food give people the most pleasurable way to enjoy either.

To give you some ideas for events, here are some great ones I've been involved in:

Night of the Living Ales. This is a scaled-down replacement for Real Ale Fest, the event that was run for several years by Ray Daniels with the help of the CBS (Chicago Beer Society). We usually have around 40 firkins of real ale set up. This takes an especially accommodating host space, as the beers have to be set up by Tuesday for a Saturday event, and it also takes a certain skill level to make sure the beers are in prime condition when it comes time to tap them. We find it best to hold this when the weather is guaranteed to be cool (early March in Chicago), so that we can control the beer temperature by opening windows or lowering the thermostat. There are real-ale cooling systems, varying in complexity from ice blankets to circulating glycol, but these are expensive and very labor-intensive, and should be avoided unless absolutely necessary. We serve by gravity, which means we need only simple plastic taps and not hand pumps, which are expensive and add nothing to the beer in this situation. We have simple but substantial appetizers for this event, plus some artisanal cheeses accompanied by representatives of the cheese merchant, and a pile of sausage we refer to as "alottagoddammeat," a term our Hungarian butcher spit back at us in response to a request for $500 worth of deli trays.

Festival of Barrel-Aged Beers. This is technically an Illinois Craft Brewers Guild event, but members of CBS do much of the legwork. It is just what it sounds like, a walk-around tasting of this very specialized type of beer from all over the country. As part of this event we also conduct a professional judging, which ups the ante for those who enter.

The Brewpub Shootout. For this event we send invitations to all the breweries and brewpubs from our area. Each has to bring a small-portion dish and a specific beer to pair with it, as well as the equipment and staff to serve it. Packaging breweries have to find a restaurant partner. Nick Floyd once brought White Castle hamburgers to complement his Alpha King Ale; it was a surprisingly good pair. Breweries are welcome to bring additional beers beyond the one designated as the pairing beer. We set up in what used to be an old grade-school gym that is now part of an Irish-American cultural center, and people walk around and sample; at the end of the afternoon, everybody votes on best beer, best food, and best pairing. The club schedules and sets up the structure of the event and provides trophies, ice, and disposables. The breweries provide the heavy lifting, which makes it quite manageable to run. We don't directly pay for the beer and food, but allocate a certain portion of the ticket sales to go back to the breweries to help defray costs. It's a great way for breweries to push their limits and experiment with new dishes while getting exposed to a very enthusiastic bunch of potential customers. At this point, there is quite a rivalry between many of the breweries to take home the gold.

Making the Most of Beer Festivals

FESTIVALS HOLD A LOT OF ALLURE. Acres of beers lined up for your tasting pleasure, a whole year's worth of pub crawling in just a few hours, being elbow to elbow with a teeming mess of beer fans: nirvana!

But festivals can sometimes be a little overwhelming, with large crowds, too much choice, and uncomfortable conditions. A good strategy and a little self-restraint can go a long way to making the event more enjoyable. Here are some tips.

Know your limits — of alcohol, heat, sun, being on your feet, and dealing with crowds. Be aware that brewers sometimes trot out their biggest, baddest beers for these events. This is great, of course, but you have to be respectful of high-alcohol beers.

Go when the crowds are lightest. Get there when it starts, or if it's a longer fest, pick a slow day. Know when to quit — I never mind missing the chaotic last hour. Some festivals will have a "private session," which may cost more but will be much less rowdy. These are well worth the money as far as I'm concerned.

Do your research. Find out who's making great beer before you get there. BeerAdvocate.com and RateBeer.com aren't the final word but can be very helpful.

Don't be afraid to dump. There's just no point to drinking a beer you don't like. You won't offend anybody.

Have a purpose. Focus on something, such as beers you haven't had before, a particular style, breweries you have never heard of, or finding the perfect session beer. Take notes. Discuss.

Talk to the brewers. Some festivals have brewery personnel stationed with their beers. This is a great opportunity to find out more about their beers, how they brewed them, how they think of them, what inspired them, and maybe even a few recipe secrets.

Volunteer. Events are often more fun when you are on the other side of the taps. You usually are working with other interesting beer fans or pro brewers and have the opportunity to spread the word of good beer to the crowd. It gives you a sense of purpose and is often rewarded by perks such as a private tasting, an after-event party, or swag such as T-shirts.

Check out the "extra" events. Many festivals have a dinner, tour, or other event within a few days of the festival. Sometimes these are open to the public; sometimes they are limited to brewers and those involved in the fest, which is another great reason to volunteer.

Hydrate. Eat. Make sure your body is well cared for.

Make sure you have a ride home when you need one.

FROM THE MOST FORMAL JUDGING to the simple joy of a fresh, delicious brew in a sun-dappled beer garden, the range of tasting experiences varies almost as much as beer itself. Once the beer is in the glass, it's up to you to decide what your relationship to it will be: advocate or critic, stranger or best buddy. Like any worthy pursuit, the beer-tasting experience is only as good as you make it. Summon all your senses and experience and dive into it wholeheartedly. You'll find the experience that unfolds between you and your beer to be truly enlightening.

CHAPTER 6

PRESENTING BEER

BEER is a fussy beverage. It doesn't like to be too warm or too cold. It shies away from the sun. It cares about the size, shape, and cleanliness of the glass it is served in and really responds to a great pour. In the whole constellation of different beers, every one is a prima donna, demanding just the right touch to bring out its best.

Beer has a generous spirit, so if you make any kind of effort at all, it will reward you with a rich and memorable experience. Sure, you can just grab a bottle and gulp it down — and there are beers made for this — but most beers need to be treated with a little more respect if you want them to reveal their inner souls.

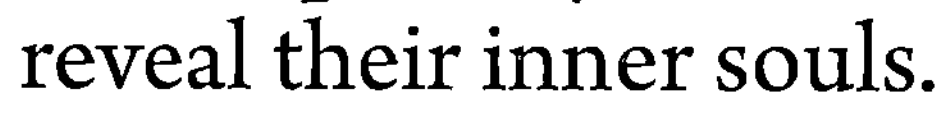

CHECKLIST FOR A WELL-SERVED BEER

- [■] Beer at proper temperature
- [■] Correct glass for beer and occasion
- [■] Good pour with a tight, long-lasting head
- [■] Squeaky-clean, well-rinsed glassware
- [■] Proper expectations of drinker

A LUMINOUSLY BEAUTIFUL BEER suited to the mood and moment, of proper age and condition, with a creamy, long-lasting head, bursting with aroma, can be a delight to every sense. It is an experience that has moved people since the very beginning of beer, and it is every bit as exciting today. It's worth the small effort required to do it right. In this chapter I will cover all the aspects of beer's presentation with the goal of making you, with a little practice, a master beer server.

Temperature

NOTHING AFFECTS the beer in the glass more than the serving temperature. Flavor, aroma, texture, carbonation, and even clarity may change with temperature. It's not always easy to hit the nail on the head, especially when a large number of beers will be served. But it's always worth putting some effort into it.

To some degree, beer-serving temperatures are determined by tradition, but they do follow a certain logical pattern: stronger beers warmer than weak; dark beers warmer than light. Lager beers are fermented cooler than ales and should be served cooler as well. American industrial beers have been formulated to taste best at lip-numbingly cold temperatures, but no specialty beer should ever be served at anything approaching these temperatures.

The proper range for serving beer is between 38 and 55°F (3 to 13°C), the specific temperature being very much dependent on the style. Too cold, and aromas just sit in the beer; if they don't become airborne they are not of much use to us. Too warm and, well, we all know what warm beer tastes like. In practice it's very difficult to get it perfect. Come close and you'll have a great experience.

Ideally, a retail establishment serving specialty beers should be able to control the temperatures in at least a couple of sections and serve beers at temperatures appropriate to each style. This is harder than it sounds. Probably the best recommendation is to have one area at 35°F (2°C) for domestic and specialty lagers,

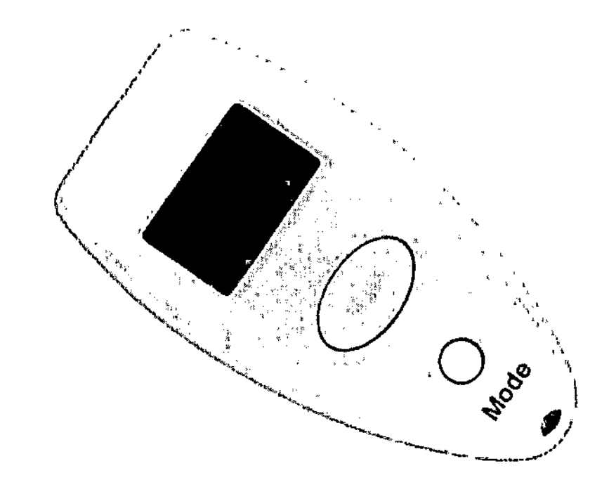

Infrared Thermometer
Although a little geeky, this type of thermometer will take a beer's temperature without touching it. Just point and shoot.

Suggested Serving Temperature

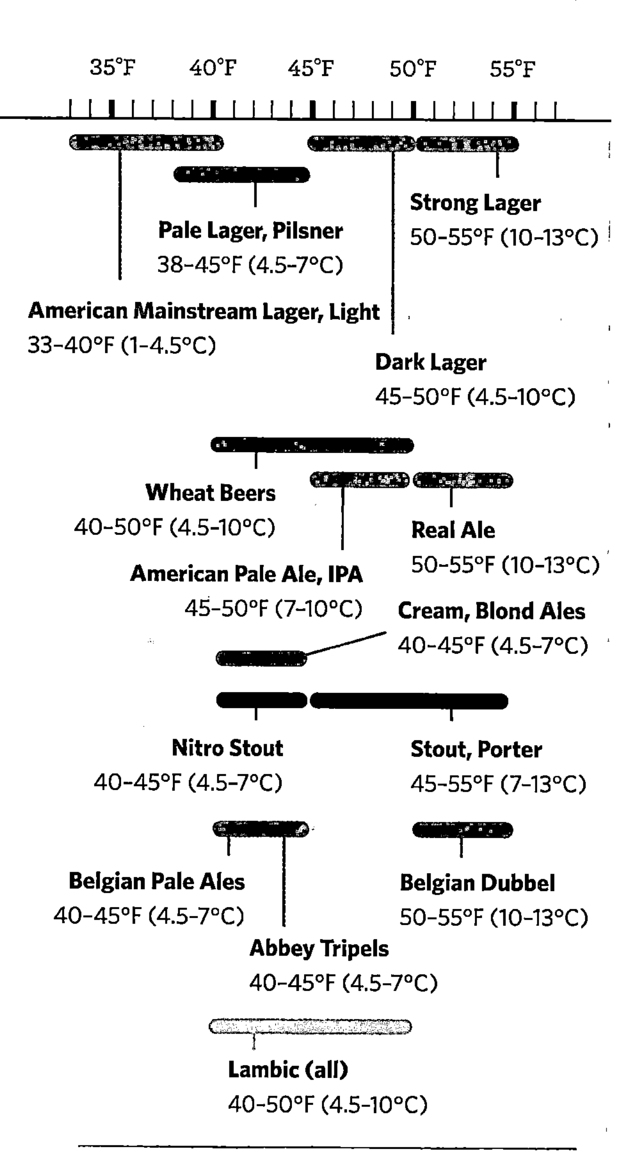

NOTE: These are temperatures in the glass. Be aware that most of the major draft equipment companies recommend a 38°F (3°C) storage temperature for all beer types (except real ale), as higher temperatures may cause foaming.

and another at perhaps 45°F (7°C) for specialty ales, maybe a tad warmer if you're concentrating on English-style ales. This is true for both draft and bottled products.

Real (cask) ale requires its own temperature control, unless you have a deep, dark cellar with a very constant temperature of 50 to 55°F (10 to 13°C). Most bars in the United States that serve real ale typically limit the selection to one or two at a time, so it doesn't take up too much space.

Bottles and Draft

DRAFT AND BOTTLED forms of beer both date back to the beginnings of our fascination with the golden elixir; perhaps the arguments over the merits of each do too. The technology has changed, of course, but the discussion goes on. Which is best? There's no simple answer. Both can be perfectly wonderful storage vessels for beer, and each has its potential for trouble.

Most draft beer today is unpasteurized and must be kept chilled for maximum storage life. Most people feel the taste and texture are a bit better than the equivalent bottled product.

BOTTLED BEER

Bottled beer comes in a number of forms, and you may not be able to tell exactly how it's packaged by looking at the label. Which one will be better is very much dependent on beer type and how it will be enjoyed.

A bottle is good when it's not too new,
I'm fond of one, but I dote upon two.

—Anonymous

FORMS OF BOTTLED BEER

Bottled, then pasteurized.
This is the most common bottled beer type. Many feel pasteurization dulls the flavor of beer, but this is a fairly subtle effect.

Flash-pasteurized, then aseptically bottled.
Practitioners feel this shorter but hotter form of pasteurization is gentler on the beer.

Micro- (cold) filtered, then aseptically packaged.
This is supposed to give "real draft" flavor in a bottled product; not heat-pasteurized.

Bottle-conditioned.
Beer with live yeast and some sugars remaining to ferment is sealed into the bottle. Yeast produces carbon dioxide, which gives the beer its carbonation. Yeast provides oxygen scavenging and other protective effects. Considered "real ale."

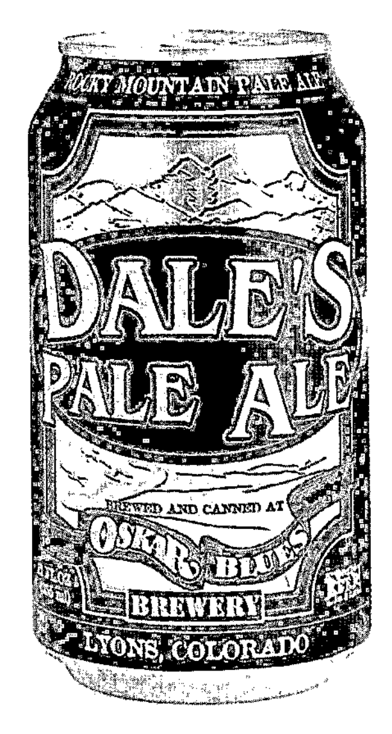

Canned Craft Beer
Normally associated with mainstream lagers, canned beer has proved popular for the few craft breweries that choose to produce it.

Brewers and consumers like the stability that pasteurization brings to mainstream beers. Bottle-conditioned beers really should be poured into a glass. It's not harmful, or even unpleasant, but not everybody appreciates the slight earthiness that often comes with the slug of yeast in the bottom of the bottle. And not all bottles are created equal. Brown bottles offer reasonably good protection from the blue light that causes skunkiness.

CANNED BEER

Canned beer can be thought of as pretty much the same thing as bottled. We see it mostly from larger breweries in pasteurized or cold-filtered form, but there are a few craft breweries having great success with it. Just like with the big guys, their customers appreciate the benefits of the light weight, unbreakability, quick chilling, and eco-friendliness of canned beer.

Chances are the local brewpub sells beer to go in "growlers." Today, these are usually half-gallon glass jugs, but the term is an old one originally meaning a small metal bucket that was used for the same purpose. This is fresh draft beer with a short shelf life. As one pub brewer tells people, "It's like milk" — best when kept under refrigeration and consumed within a few days.

DRAFT BEER

A draft-beer system consists of a pressurized container of beer connected by a beer line to some form of serving tap, plus a bottle of high-pressure dispensing gas, dropped through a regulator and hooked up to the beer keg through the same fitting as the liquid connection.

Carbon dioxide, because it is the gas that the yeast creates to provide carbonation, is the most common dispensing gas. Carbon dioxide has the added advantage of liquefying under just a few hundred pounds of pressure in the storage cylinders. This means each cylinder can contain a large amount of gas relative to its volume.

Nitrogen, or a mix of nitrogen and carbon dioxide, is often used to dispense English- or Irish-style beers, especially stouts. Because nitrogen has a very low solubility in beer, the gas can be forced in, but as soon as the pressure is released, the nitrogen fairly well jumps out of the beer, releasing a huge number of tiny bubbles and leaving the beer very lightly carbonated and creamy textured. It should be noted that this "nitro" serving method is meant to be an easier-to-implement facsimile of the traditional real-ale cask method (see page 102). And while nitro beer can be a fine thing on its own terms for a stout or an IPA, it in no way matches the subtlety of the real (ale) thing.

Nitrogen can also be used to supply the additional pressure needed to bring beer up to the serving point through very long lines. If sufficient pure carbon dioxide were to be used, the beers might be overcarbonated, as up to 30 or 40 psi might be required to get the job done.

If you want to set up a home draft system, kits of varying completeness can be found at beverage-service companies and at most homebrewing suppliers. Unlike commercial installations, home systems are easy to set up, and smaller, one-sixth barrel kegs make it possible to have variety too. Having fresh draft beer at home is a true luxury.

Draft beer today is almost universally packaged in straight-sided stainless steel kegs. The version most popular in the United States is the Sankey. American Sankeys are based on the old 31-gallon barrel, originally derived from an English ale (as opposed to beer) barrel of 31 U.S. gallons (117 liters). Full barrel kegs don't exist anymore. At 300-plus pounds, they'd be pretty tough to handle, although the old guys back in the day managed somehow. Half (15.5 gallons), quarter (7.75 gallons), and sixth (5 gallons, usually in the tall "soda keg" form) barrels are the current market forms.

The older, barrel-shaped kegs of my youth are called Hoff-Stevens. For various reasons these are mostly obsolete now, although they birthed the whole craft-brew industry. A few small breweries continue to use them for their cheapness and availability. Because they lack handles, a wet, cold, Hoff-Stevens keg can be a challenge to wrangle off a truck and into a cellar. Doing so gives you real respect for the pros that used to sling these things around.

KEG THEFT

American brewers estimate that stolen kegs cost the industry well over $50 million a year. With the price of metals such as stainless steel escalating, criminals find the easy pickings of loose kegs irresistible. And who pays for this? You do. There are legislative and public-awareness efforts under way to combat this, but the situation will remain problematic as long as the cost of the deposit continues to be just a fraction of the keg's true value. Each keg costs a brewer as much as $150, and the price continues to rise as the price of stainless does. And homebrewers, please get your kegs from legitimate sources. A deposit is not a purchase price.

SOME LARGE, HIGH-VOLUME BEER venues don't use carbon dioxide, but rely on nitrogen or sometimes compressed air. The latter is damaging to beer in the long run, but in places like stadiums where the kegs empty very quickly and won't be stored with air pressure, this may be less of a problem. Experts believe that in practice, these systems result in a lot of less-than-perfect draft beer and shouldn't be used.

SEND IT BACK!

No one expects you to drink a bad beer, so when you get one that's problematic you should feel well within your rights to return it and ask for another — *without* an argument. Send it back when you encounter the following:

Dirty glasses. Large areas on the inside of the glass where mats of bubbles cling are a sure giveaway. Another telltale sign is lipstick on the rim. This is just inexcusable laziness.

Cloudiness in beers normally expected to be crystal clear, such as Pilsners. Note that many micro- and especially brewpub beers will have a little haze, especially when cold.

Off-aromas. Butteriness, spoiled milk, or cheesy, animal-like aromas all indicate some problem. It could be the beer, but more likely it is a symptom of a sick tap line.

Sourness. In anything but the rare Belgian styles, for which it is appropriate, sourness can be a symptom of dirty lines, and it is often accompanied by the off-aromas described above.

Beer lines connecting keg to tap can be just a few feet to well over a hundred. This has dramatic consequences for the way the draft lines are designed, installed, and cleaned. Because long lines can hold a fair amount of beer and often snake through uncooled parts of a premise cellar, it is usually necessary to install them in insulated runs, chilled either with cold air or refrigerated glycol. As lines become longer, there is more beer sitting in them overnight, and if the lines are not scrupulously clean, they can develop infections, typically the buttery sour tang of *Lactobacillus* or *Pediococcus* bacteria.

When beer runs through plastic lines, a minute film of protein sticks to the sides of the tubing, and this can be very difficult to remove. Beer lines are most often cleaned by pumping hot caustic cleaning solution through them. There are now sophisticated machines that force small foam balls through the tubing, which are supposed to do a better job of scrubbing the tubing walls. A good beer bar will clean their tap lines every two weeks; a great one will do it more often than that.

Dirty lines cause great consternation for those in the brewing world. The drinkers aren't necessarily aware of all the things that can go wrong with a beer after it leaves the brewery. All they know is that they're holding a bad beer from a particular brewery, and guess who they blame? Well-informed beer mavens look for patterns. Too many buttery beers at a bar might mean the establishment is not taking beer-line cleaning seriously.

ODE TO THE BARREL

The barrel is one of the barbarians' finest gifts to humanity. Invented around the year 0 CE, the wooden barrel has had a useful technological life of 2,000 years — so far. It is a testament to the cleverness of these forest folks that, save for the introduction of metal hoops a couple of centuries ago, the barrel continues in its original form and purpose even today. It is now only rarely used for beer, having been replaced by the metal keg after World War II, but wooden barrels are indispensable for all aged spirits and a good portion of all wines. In today's craft scene, barrel-aged beers are an exciting addition to the luxurious end of the beer world.

Cask (Real) Ale

THE BRITISH BEER preservation society the Campaign for Real Ale (CAMRA) (see page 24)defines real ale as "a natural product brewed using traditional ingredients and left to mature in the cask (container) from which it is served in the pub through a process called secondary fermentation."

A hundred years ago, this was the norm for British beers. Brewed quickly, and rushed out to the pubs while still fermenting, real ale requires skilled and motivated cellar staff to make sure the beers arrive in the customers' glasses in perfect, bright, delicious condition. This is a very old way of doing things, and it has clashed pretty dramatically with business realities of the past few decades.

Not-quite-finished beers are racked into casks and bunged, then sent off to the pubs. Each has two openings: one on the head, into which the tap is inserted, and another at the broadest point around the middle, which is on top when the cask is sitting on its side ready for service. Into this is inserted a bung with a hole called a "shive." Once in the pub's cellar, the condition of the beer is assessed by the cellarmaster and a porous reed peg called a "spile" is inserted; this peg allows excess carbon dioxide to vent. When this venting slows down and the beer is deemed in prime condition, the soft spile is removed and a solid wooden peg called a hard spile is gently driven in, allowing pressure to remain in the cask.

A PERIOD OF TIME, usually just a few days, is allowed for the beer to rest and drop free of yeast and other solids. Sometimes

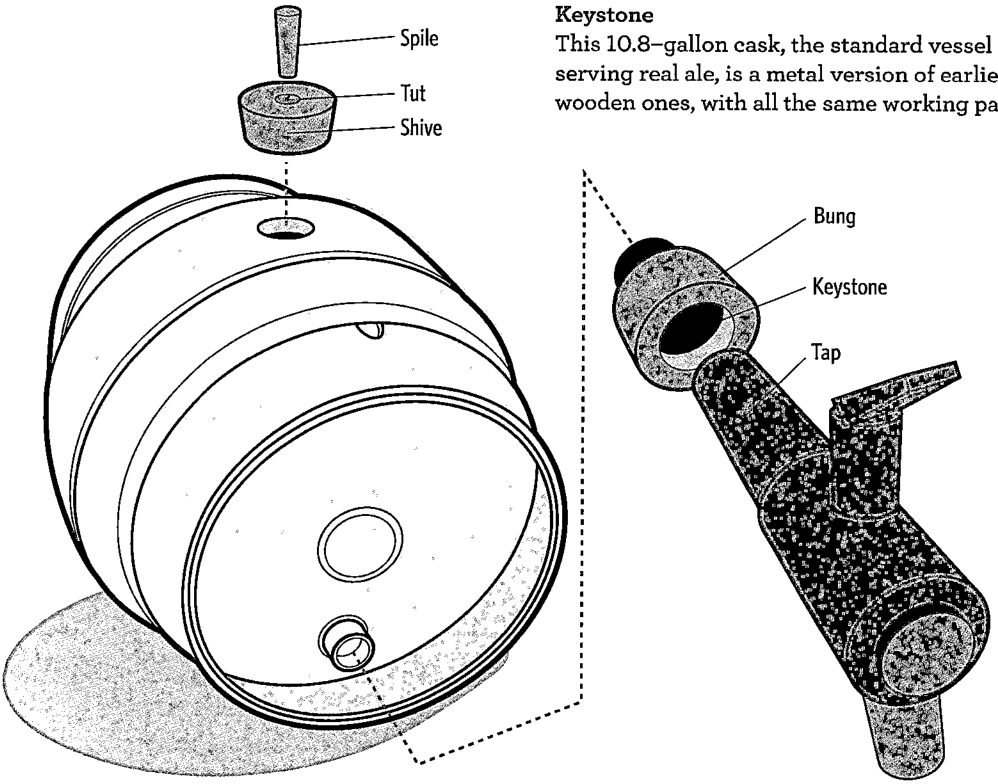

Keystone
This 10.8–gallon cask, the standard vessel for serving real ale, is a metal version of earlier wooden ones, with all the same working parts.

a fining agent, isinglass, is added, which speeds up the settling process. When the beer is ready to serve, a plastic tap is pounded into the bung with a brisk whack. An inner wooden plug in the bung, the keystone, gives way and allows the tap to seat. If done correctly, very little beer escapes, but a timid hand with the mallet may only partially seat the tap and release a gusher of beer. The hard spile must temporarily be removed to allow air to enter to displace the beer being served, but it is usually placed back in the hole when the pub closes for the night. Beer served this way has a very limited shelf life, as the carbonation dissipates and the deleterious effects of oxygen take hold. Once the cask has been tapped, the ale must be consumed within a few days. Seasoned aficionados can tell how long a cask has been on tap and may even prefer the somewhat softened flavor a little oxygen may impart. But at a certain point it all goes wrong and the cask ale will turn flat, lifeless, and perhaps even sour.

In most pubs, the beer is stored in the cellar, which necessitates some means of transporting the beer up to bar level. Because the use of carbon dioxide pressure is frowned upon (it actually disqualifies the beer from being classified as real ale), hand pumps are used. These are the large and showy but simple devices that operate much like a bicycle pump, with a cylinder, a plunger, and valves at either end. When the pump is pulled down, beer is drawn up through the line and out the spout into the glass. Sometimes a small plastic restrictor known as a sparkler is screwed onto the end of the spout. This forces the beer through a small orifice, releasing some carbon dioxide and helping to create a dense, creamy foam. Like so many things about British beer, the use of sparklers varies by region; the practice is much more popular in the north. It should be noted that hand pumps, although a highly visible part of the regalia of real ale, actually add nothing to the flavor or texture of the beer (with the exception of the sparkler); they are simply a means of elevating the beer up to the bar level from the cellar. For festivals and other situations where the casks are on the same level as the drinkers, simple gravity taps can be used to no ill effect.

WARM AND FLAT?

Contrary to the oft-repeated first impression of American tourists, British ales should be served at cool cellar temperatures of 50 to 55°F (10 to 13°C), and with a lively, but not excessive, carbonation. The proper amount of head is subject to vigorous debate in the United Kingdom, and this standard varies by region — more head being appropriate in the north. Although the royally approved pint glass now has a fill line about an inch below the rim, just a few years ago the rim of the glass was the full measure, which led to endless gamesmanship from patrons, wary of any foam, who would down half the glass and then call for a "top up"!

CAMRA HOLDS ON to the old ways with a death grip. The transition from a mainstream product to a specialty one has been painful and continues still. But if it weren't for the tenacity of CAMRA, real ale might be only a memory. Sometimes, however, this conservatism is less than helpful. One problem is that in the traditional method, the beer is exposed to air when the cask is broached. In 1995, CAMRA did a detailed study of the use of cask breathers, devices that replace air with a gentle blanket of carbon dioxide, which give casks a longer life in the pub. Blind tests showed that cask breathers did no harm to beer. CAMRA, however, chose to ignore its own research and rule in favor of tradition, disallowing their use.

The Beer Glass

SPECIALIZED BEER-DRINKING VESSELS have been a treasured part of beer culture for thousands of years. They come in many sizes, forms, and materials, yet the goals have always been the same: deliver the beer to the lips in great form, in a pleasing, even celebratory way. They must fit the hand and suit the brew; if they dazzle the eye, so much the better.

Until the past 150 years or so, the beer glass was more commonly made of some other material. Glass was a rare and expensive material, and its production depended on highly skilled artisans. Only the wealthy could afford glass. Regular folks drank from clay, metal, or even tar-coated leather vessels known as blackjacks. It wasn't until machine-made glassware became available in the second half of the nineteenth century that it became possible for everyone to enjoy the beer-enhancing qualities of glass drinking vessels.

Beer glasses range from a few ounces up to a full liter. Typically, the beer will be matched to the glass, with the strongest ones calling for the smallest glasses, for obvious reasons.

CONTEMPORARY BEER-DRINKING glasses often have shapes very similar to earlier ones. The geometry of the glass affects the way beer looks, smells, and tastes, so it's not surprising that certain forms have withstood the test of time.

Clear glass is nearly always best, although subtly tinted colors can also be attractive (see the Pasglass, page 107). Deeply colored beer glasses are rare. Designs such as faceting can add to the optical effects of the beer itself.

How the glass feels in the hand is also important. An outward taper or various types of ridges or bump-outs can keep the glass from slipping out of the hand. For larger vessels, a handle is almost mandatory. Stems can accomplish a similar effect as a handle, as they allow one to hold the glass without transferring too much heat from the hand to the beer.

From an aroma standpoint, nothing helps a beer so much as having a narrower top than middle. A wineglass is the classic example, although there are many beer glasses that share this feature. When served filled to the brim, this feature doesn't add anything, but as soon as the beer drops an inch or two below the rim, the inward taper holds the aroma inside the glass instead of letting it drift out into the room. The effects are obvious, even dramatic. Try a side-by-side comparison of a standard "shaker" pint and any red-wine glass. Fill both half full and try to give an honest appraisal of the aroma. I won't tell you what to find. But it can be striking.

An outward taper, as in a classic Pilsner glass, has an effect on foam. The tapering shape serves as a wedge and gives the head on the top of the beer some additional support. An inward taper seems to force a head in on itself as the glass is filled. This has the effect of concentrating the foam, which results in a denser, creamier head.

Beer foam has been prized since ancient times. Soap or oils inside the glass can degrade the delicate colloidal structure. Foam forms at nucleation sites, microscopic rough patches formed by dirt or scratches that can also serve as a pretty dramatic indicator of sloppy cleaning and can be cause for a good scolding of bar staff. Nucleation sites are sometimes added intentionally to cause a small stream of fine bubbles to be continually released, replenishing the head and releasing aroma at the same time — the Chimay goblet has a small Chimay logo etched with a laser into the bottom of the bowl for this purpose.

Foam has an especially dramatic effect on the way hop flavor manifests itself in beer. Because of their electrical and chemical nature, bitter hop compounds preferentially migrate to the head. The result is that the foam may taste quite a bit more bitter than the beer itself. Be aware of this if you are serving beer that is pushing your audience's hop comfort level.

HOW MUCH FOAM is the proper amount? Most people feel that an inch is about right, although this is a culturally determined preference. The amount is also related to the level of carbonation. Many of the Belgian beers have loads of carbonation, and it's virtually impossible to pour a beer like Duvel without creating a big, fluffy head. For this reason, many of these beer glasses have a capacity about twice the size of the serving portion.

With the right beer, properly poured, you can create a rich, creamy head. To do so, pour the beer right down the middle of the straight-up glass. Trickling down the side is for sissies and will result in a too-gassy beer with little aroma and a poor, quickly dissipating head. A vigorous pour will create a lot of foam, and this is good because when it settles down, the head will be dense and long-lived. It's also important, especially with bottled beer, to release some of the carbonation. Too much fizz masks things like hop aroma and fills you up quickly. So pour and let the beer settle as many times as you need to in order to fill the glass. There are places in Europe where drinkers are suspicious if the beer arrives too quickly, because they understand what is needed to create a great head on a beer and are willing to delay gratification for a minute or two for the sake of a better experience.

With highly carbonated beers such as Belgian ales or Bavarian weizens, it may be beneficial to rinse the glass with clean water before filling. This breaks the surface tension and allows these ultra-fizzy beers to be poured without troublesome amounts of foam.

Practical qualities such as cost, stackability, and ease of cleaning play a huge role in deciding what glasses are used in eating and drinking establishments. Unfortunately, we seem to have gotten stuck with the worst possible beer glass: the shaker pint. Not only is the word *pint* a source of confusion — most hold only 14 ounces, some only 12 — these do absolutely nothing for the aroma or presentation of beer.

The final aspect of a glass is the rim. These may turn inward or flare outward (called "everted" by glassware experts). The shape of the rim changes the part of the mouth into which the beer is delivered, and it seems to distribute the liquid more widely across the mouth, not just to the center of the tongue. This changes the way flavors are perceived in the mouth.

(*continued on page 110*)

Nor wanting is the brown October, drawn,
Mature and perfect, from his dark retreat
Of thirty years, and now his honest front
Flames in the light refulgent, not afraid
E'en with the vineyard's best produce to vie.

— James Thomson, from his poem "Autumn"

HISTORICAL BEER-DRINKING VESSELS

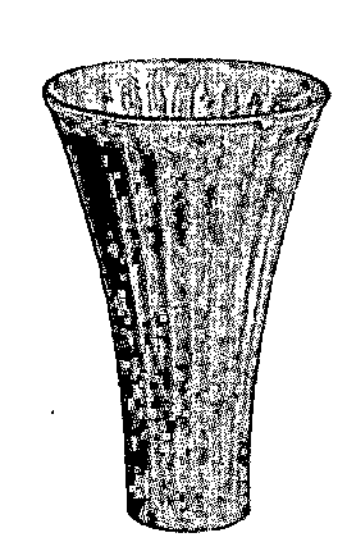

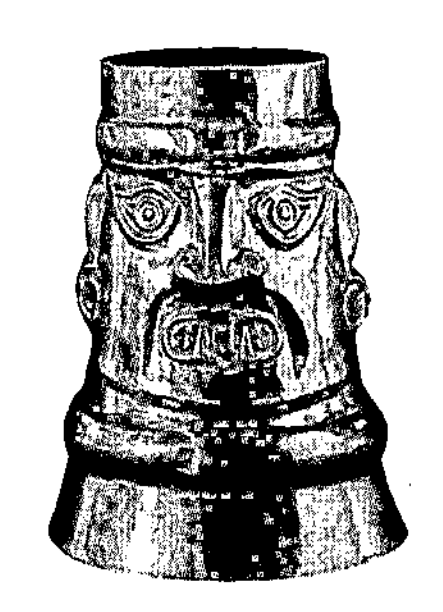

◂ The Golden Tumbler of Lady Puabi

Northern Iraq, c. 2400 BCE

Found in a royal burial at the Mesopotamian city of Ur in northern Iraq and dating to 2400 BCE, this expensive vessel shows the status ancient people placed on their drinks.

▴ Golden chicha vessel

Siccan culture, northern Peru, 1000–1476

A corn-based beer called "chicha" was central to both ritual and daily life of people responsible for the sophisticated ancient cultures of northern Peru.

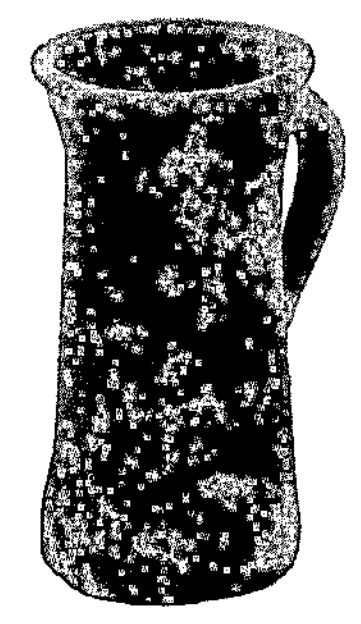

◂ Medieval ceramic drinking jug

London, c. 1271-1350

Medieval drinking vessels used by ordinary folks were largely utilitarian.

"Beaker Culture" beaker ▸

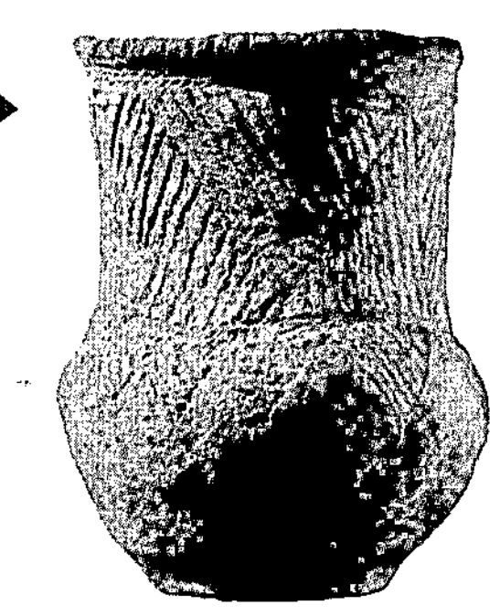

Great Britain, c. fourth millennium BCE

Bell-shaped beakers are found all over Europe. The corded decorations suggest a connection of these people to the hemp plant.

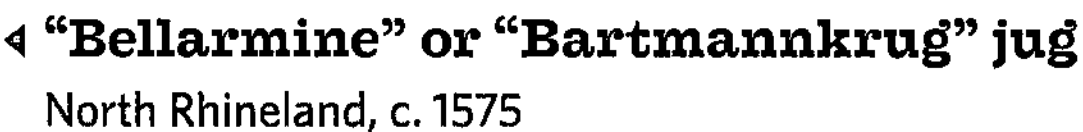

◂ "Bellarmine" or "Bartmannkrug" jug

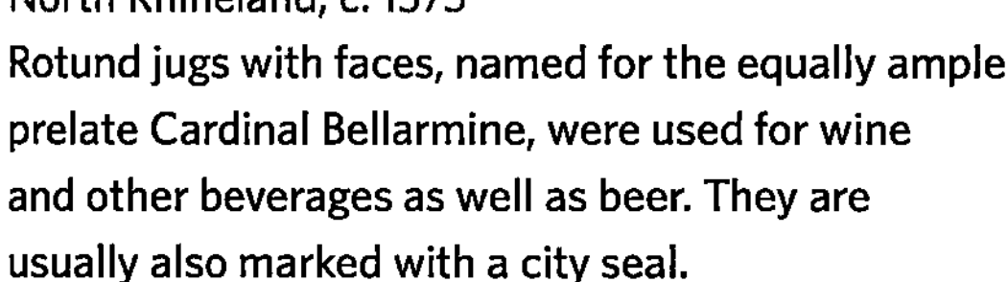

North Rhineland, c. 1575

Rotund jugs with faces, named for the equally ample prelate Cardinal Bellarmine, were used for wine and other beverages as well as beer. They are usually also marked with a city seal.

Leather "blackjack" or "Bombard" ▸

London, England, sixteenth century

Pitch-lined leather tankards like this could have withstood the rough-and-tumble conditions of earlier times. They were made from easily available materials and were unlikely to serve as a weapon in bar fights. Their use continued into the nineteenth century.

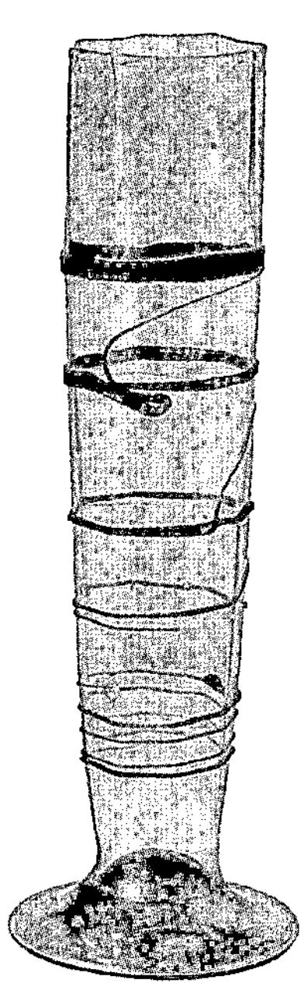

"Pasglass" ▸

Northern Europe, seventeenth century

The tall, tapered form of this glass is the direct ancestor of the modern Pilsner glass. Like so many glasses, this was meant for communal use and passed from drinker to drinker. The rings are part of a drinking game in which each drinker is expected to drink *exactly* to the line, no more, no less. The green cast is typical of the so-called forest glass and comes from iron and other impurities in the glass. Reproductions of these and other old styles are still made by artisans in the Czech Republic.

◂ **Sterling silver pint tankard**

London, c. 1704–5, Philip Rollos (the elder)

◂ **Chased silver tankard, London**

c. 1670–75, Jacob Bodendick

Gentlemen (and ladies) drank their ale from luxurious mugs ranging from the simple to the ostentatious.

Beer steins ▸

Germany and Austria, c. 1830–1900

These lidded vessels come in a variety of sizes, materials, and personalities, and are great for drinking outdoors.

▴

"Schnitt"

United States, c. 1900

These stubby little tumblers are designed to hold a small amount of beer, which used to be delivered automatically as a chaser to whiskey. Versions with logos are highly sought after by breweriana collectors.

English "Dwarf Ale" glasses ▸

c. 1780–1820

These delicate little glasses were designed to hold just a few ounces and were used to sip the strong "October" beers brewed on the country estates of the landed gentry. Although the size and proportion varied, they were decorated in many ways, with the engraved hops and barley design being one of the most common.

MODERN CLASSIC GLASSWARE

Shaker Pint Glass 

- Standard in United States
- **Not recommended** for stronger or more exotic specialty brews

This is called a shaker glass because of its original use in combination with a slightly larger metal cup as a cocktail shaker. It was never designed for drinking anything, much less a beer. These were not used for beer until the 1980s, when they started getting filled with craft beers. They were appreciated for their relatively large serving size, but they're not particularly attractive or flattering to the flavor and aroma of beer.

English Tulip Pint 

Another twentieth-century glass. This one has found a home especially for Irish stouts.

"Nonick" Pint 

- English ales since early 1960s
- Low-gravity session beers
- Bump keeps rim from chipping and makes it easier to hold for stand-up drinking

Snifter 

- Popularized in the twentieth century for brandy
- Good for barley wines and Imperial Stouts

Another not particularly ancient form, but with its deep, incurved rim and small stature, it is ideal for serving strong ales.

Stemmed Tulip or Poco Grande (Libbey) ⑤

- Inward taper holds aroma
- Outward flare supports the head and fits the lips

In many ways, this is the best of all worlds. Tulips like this are rare in history, but start to show up in the late nineteenth century.

Tapered Pilsner Glass 

- Narrow shape shows off pale color
- Outward-tapered shape supports head
- Footed design adds elegance and stability

The Pilsner glass we know today appeared in a similar form in the late Middle Ages, but it really didn't find wide acceptance until the 1930s, when its dramatically angular form reflected the Art Deco spirit of the age.

Weissbier "Vase" 

- Large size holds foam
- Inward taper concentrates foam

The *Weissbier* vase seems to have evolved from the late medieval footed-beaker forms, but it probably didn't develop its modern curvaceous style until the twentieth century.

"Bolleke" Goblet 

- Inward taper concentrates head and aroma
- Smaller size is great for strong beers
- Famous in Antwerp, Belgium

Bolleke translates from the Dutch as "little ball," the meaning of which I will leave to you to derive.

Pokal

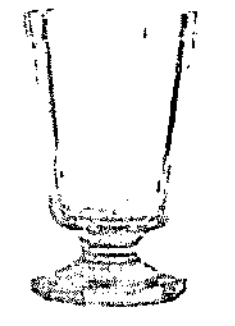

- Classic for bock
- Small size for stronger beer
- Outward taper supports head
- Short stem

The original pokals were often large and decorated in quite showy ways and fitted with removable (not hinged) lids. By the nineteenth century, they were most often associated with bock beers.

Updated Pokal

- Inward taper concentrates head
- Good general-purpose glass for high-class beers such as Belgian-style Tripel, Maibock, and Imperial IPA.
- Stem keeps hand from warming beer

English Dimpled Pint

- Appeared c. 1948
- Used for mild ale and bitter.

This is a shortened, wider, handled version of the lens-cut "pillar" pale ale glasses that became popular around 1840 or so in England. They're quaint and comfortable, even if they're not antiques. The lens design makes a beautiful play of light on an amber-colored beer.

Bavarian Seidel

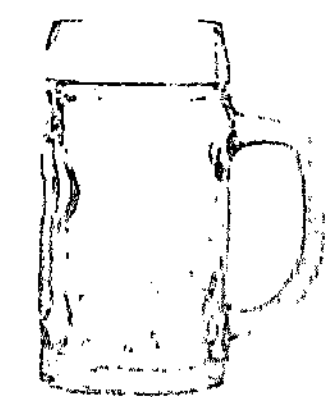

- Big glass for small beer, such as Pilsner, helles, and Oktoberfest

This seidel is just a glass version of the simple stoneware krugs that were used for centuries as drinking mugs. The optic circles first appeared in the mid-nineteenth century when machines for cutting and polishing glass became available; later, they were molded in.

A PROPER WEISSBIER POUR

Highly carbonated Bavarian weizens have their own special ritual of pouring and presentation. First is a tall, gracefully tapered "vase" glass with a fair amount of headroom above its half-liter capacity. The unique, traditional method of pouring will amaze and astound your friends. First, rinse a very clean glass with clean water. Then, uncap the bottle and invert the glass over it. With the glass in one hand and the bottle in the other, invert both and hold at a steep diagonal angle. As the glass fills, keep the neck of the bottle just above the level of liquid in the glass. If you do it right, you'll get a full glass with foam right up to the rim. If you do it wrong, well, you may find yourself mopping beer off the table. The final step is to take the near-empty bottle and roll it back and forth on the table, then pick it up and dribble the yeast in a circular motion on top of the foam, where it will melt through and create a cascade of cloudiness through the beer.

A slice of lemon may be added, or not. Most of my beer-geek friends turn up their noses at it, but I think it makes a nice presentation. If you like lemon, I say go for it without shame.

(*continued from page 105*)

The effects are complex, and I can't say there are simple rules about rim shapes that are universally true. I do personally find an everted rim (and a thinner edge) pleasant to drink from, as it matches the natural curve of the lip.

Much of the supposed benefits of the geometry of the myriad of highly specialized wineglasses derive from the pseudoscience of the tongue map, and it turns out this doesn't really work the way we were all taught in grade school (see chapter 2).

BECAUSE IT IS THE YEAST that provides the carbonation, bottle-conditioned beers have a slug of it on the bottom. As mentioned above, the yeast in wheat beers is meant to be served with the beer. In most other beer types the yeast mars the appearance and may sometimes contribute muddy flavors. So it's helpful if you can pour a whole bottle in one go and leave the yeast in the bottle. If you are serving small portions, especially from large bottles, it is usually best to decant the beer into a pitcher. From there you can pour at will.

Proprietary Glassware

THE BELGIANS ARE MAD for custom-made glasses emblazoned with the brewery's logo. There are bars in Belgium where, if all the logo glasses of the beer you want are being used, you have to have something else and wait for an appropriate glass to be returned. I like the showiness of the presentation and what it says about how we should respect the beers. But I

can't tell you that they all have been scientifically designed to perfectly show off the sensory properties of specific beers, and some are better than others. Many American craft breweries have been creating their own glasses as well.

Storing and Aging Beer

BEER IS A VERY DELICATE PRODUCT. As such, it is never a fixed thing, but constantly evolving. Every day during fermentation and conditioning it's a little different, and at a certain point it's deemed ready for shipment. But the beer keeps changing, and for most beers, after they leave the brewery the changes are not positive. Flavors fade, the death grip of oxidation takes over, and the subtle protein structure that gives beer much of its body and head-forming qualities simply falls apart. The more delicate the beer, the quicker these changes will degrade the drinking experience. In severely overaged beers, the collapsed proteins actually appear as little flakes that make it look like egg drop soup. A beer should not resemble a snow globe.

Heat is the enemy. All chemistry speeds up as the temperature rises. With beer, repeated cycles of ups and downs in temperature also have a negative effect, especially for the proteins, which is the reason why once cold, beer should be kept cold. One or two trips in and out of the fridge won't kill a beer, but steady temperatures are always preferred over wild swings, even if that means a slightly higher average temperature.

The first thing to go is that nice fresh flavor, especially the hop aroma. Malt flavor dulls a bit and takes on a kind of sweet honey or waxy aroma. In ales, fruitiness gradually fades as esters oxidize into less-fragrant higher alcohols. Bitterness declines, losing maybe half its punch in five or six months — which is way beyond the "best by" date of most normal beers, though this kind of time frame is relevant to stronger beers and those that are designed to accommodate a little aging.

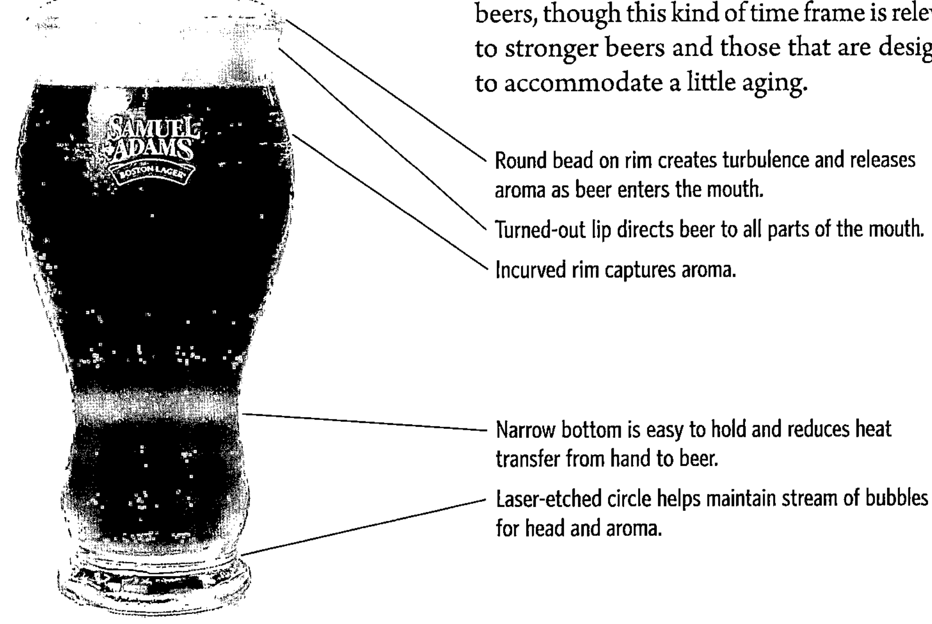

Boston Beer Company's Jim Koch spent two years on a mission to make a glass that would really enhance the taste experience for its Samuel Adams Boston Lager.

That said, beers with less than 6 or 7 percent alcohol are never meant to age. Most are intended to be consumed as soon as they leave the brewery. Brewers of mainstream beers so completely control the conditions under which their products are sold that this is rarely a problem.

Most beers use some kind of date coding on the package, although this is not always designed to be read by the drinking public. There is no standard format. A typical date code marks the date of bottling and will show the day, month, and year, plus perhaps some other information like a specific brewery or bottling line. Fortunately, there is a wealth of information on the Web, so the chances are good you'll be able to find the decoders for your favorite beers.

Freshness is a particular problem for imported beers, especially of the pale lager type. These beers command a premium here, but those who have tasted the same beers in their homelands know that they are in no way the same thing, even the beers that are not brewed with a special recipe designed for the American taste. Yes, for many large brands, the recipe is customized for Americans, usually with less body and less hop bitterness.

Importers swear to me that a high-volume beer like Heineken can reach store shelves in as little as three weeks, which may be possible, but judging by the taste, this is just a dream for many brands, especially the lower-volume ones. The beer has a long journey: from brewery to docks to a ship across the ocean to the docks here, then through customs and off to the distributor's warehouse, and finally to the shelves in the store, with every leg of this voyage promising conditions that are less than ideal.

Some stronger beers can handle a little age. It was the custom in eighteenth-century England to brew an extra-strong "double" beer to celebrate the birth of a son, and then to drink it when he reached majority at eighteen. During the early to mid-nineteenth century, porters and strong ales were commonly aged for as long as a year before being deemed fit to drink. And even today, certain strong and wood-aged beers get this type of treatment.

YOU CAN do this yourself if you have reasonable cellar conditions. The ideal is a cool basement without too much moisture. These are common enough in the East and Midwest; folks in the South and West either rent wine storage lockers or rig a setback thermometer on a refrigerator or chest freezer to create a cool environment. I have an unadorned basement room in Chicago and I can report that it ages both beer and wine admirably. So there's no need to rig up fancy temperature- and humidity-controlled vaults.

Ideally, we are talking about temperatures in the 55 to 65°F (13 to 18°C) range, although higher temperatures in the summer seem not to cause any real trouble. Again, daily temperature swings should be avoided if at all possible.

So which beers are best for aging? Ales are, primarily, with bottle-conditioned ones preferred, as the yeast provides a bit of a protective effect. These "live" beers undergo more complex changes and age more gracefully than filtered or pasteurized ones. There is rarely a need to age lagers, as these are normally brought to their peak of flavor at the brewery.

You should be looking at beers upward of 7 percent alcohol; bigger beers will age even longer. Belgian Dubbels will lose a little of their sweet edge, dry out, and become a little more complex and elegant in a year or two. In beers with *Brettanomyces,* such as Orval or Goose Island Matilda (which Orval inspired), the wild yeast continues to evolve fascinating barnyard overtones over the course of a year or two.

Sour Belgian-style beers are somewhat the exception to the strength rule. Many of these beers will age for quite some time, yet they rarely exceed 6 percent alcohol. Many, such as lambic, are aged for several years at the brewery, but the boisterous little party of microflora in the bottle will keep the beer evolving for quite some time. You have to like bold, sour beers to undertake this, as they get more acidic as they age.

Some beers *need* some aging. The classic Bigfoot barley wine from Sierra Nevada Brewing is, in my highly personal opinion, a little overwhelming when it is young. Sierra Nevada owner Ken Grossman likes it "on the fresher side, up to a year old." But he also says, "I have tasted some Bigfoot up to ten years old and have found it quite enjoyable, although a totally different beer." I buy a six-pack every year and usually don't crack one of the bottles until five years later.

As beer ages it dries out, becoming less sweet and more vinous. Somewhat counterintuitively, aged beer may become more sweetly malty on the nose as the fragile hoppy and fruity aromas dissipate. As aging progresses, rich leathery, nutty, or sherrylike oxidation adds another layer of flavor.

Yeast contributes rich, meaty flavors through a process called "autolysis," the same process that gives champagne its toasty aromas (autolysed yeast rarely manifests this toastiness in beer). The meatiness comes from the breakdown products of the yeast such as glutamic acid, often manifesting as umami. In very old beers, sometimes soy sauce flavor notes are present, and if they get too strong they cease to be charming.

Cork-finished beers destined for more than a few months of aging should be laid on their sides just like wine to keep the corks from drying out and leaking carbonation.

AGED BEERS provide a great opportunity for a fun and educational vertical tasting, although this may require some serious advance planning. The idea is simply to compare the same beer from different years to try to understand how the beer has changed as it has aged, but also to see if you can determine variations between the beers as they were brewed. Sometimes there's a lot more variation than you'd expect. If you have a large circle of beer-aficionado friends, it may not be all that difficult to gather a representative sampling of some of the more widely available big beers such as Bigfoot, Rogue's Old Crustacean, and

AGING TIME FOR VARIOUS BEER TYPES

Beer Type	Percentage Alcohol	Maximum Aging Time
Belgian abbey Dubbel	6.5-7.5	1-3 years
Belgian abbey Tripel/strong golden	7.5-9.5	1-4 years
English or American strong/old ale	7-9	1-5 years
Belgian strong dark ales	8.5-11	2-12 years
Imperial pale/brown/red, etc.	7.5-10	1-7 years
Barley wine & Imperial Stout	8.5-12	3-20 years
Ultra-strong ales	16-26	5-100 years

J. W. Lees Harvest Ale, as it seems that many beer maniacs have these little nuggets squirreled away. A number of bars have started vertical collections of stronger beers. Washington, D.C.'s Brickskeller and the Stuffed Sandwich in Los Angeles's San Gabriel Valley are famous for this. These older beers can be fairly expensive, but with a group it can be easily worth the money to get the benefit of such a long perspective.

Like any art, beer needs a proper context to be truly compelling. The effects of a thoughtful presentation are not smoke and mirrors; the details really do affect the quality of our beer experience, sometimes in very dramatic ways. The brewers who make great beer for us put their hearts and souls into it. Let's honor that artistry by doing all we can to bring it to the table in a way that allows it to really shine.

NOTES ON SELECTED VINTAGES OF THOMAS HARDY'S ALE, FALL, 1997

With the help of some of my beer-experienced friends, I ran through a lineup of this legendary English barley wine for *All About Beer* magazine. The beers showed a surprising amount of variation.

1995: Medium amber color, just a hint of carbonation. Even balance of sweet and bitter. Caramelly, with Madeira-like overtones, finishing with a lingering leathery sharpness. Mellow and well integrated.

1994: Deep reddish amber, with the barest suggestion of carbonation. Pure, malty joy, with nicely oxidized (like port) notes. Hints of peachy fruitiness, sugary (but not syrupy) middle and lightly bitter finish. Enjoyably complex.

1993: Big fruity nose with light carbonation. Sweet and spicy with touches of cinnamon or star anise. Quite nutty; reminiscent of liquid pecan pie. Low bitterness with hints of cocoa on the finish.

1992: Dead flat, but with tones of apricot fruitiness, and plenty of alcohol showing. Evenly balanced, with a sherrylike sharpness up front and firm, bitter middle and smooth finish.

1991: Reddish color, quite fizzy. Hot, almost peppery notes, just a little raspy. Huge taste, loads of bitterness all the way through. Even at six years old, it tastes like it could use some more age.

1990: Solid amber, a touch of carbonation. Nice sherrylike aromas of toasted nuts melding to a round bitterness and a firm, bittersweet, almost chocolaty finish. Deliciously complex, and at its peak right now.

1987: A bonanza of dried-fruit aromas: raisins and prunes. Fairly sweet, incredibly rich with loads of nuts and burnt sugar, finishing moderately bitter, but very dry.

1986: Mahogany color, with no evident carbonation. A solventy hot nose with loads of raisins and black cherry fruit. Gooey sweet malty middle, without a lot of oxidation and just a dab of hop bitterness. Ages slowly — tastes like another ten years in the bottle wouldn't hurt it.

BEER AND FOOD

BECAUSE it is nearly a food itself, beer's range of flavors, aromas, colors, and textures complement many kinds of fare, giving us plenty to choose from when seeking resonance. From a cheery golden Pilsner to a brooding Imperial Stout; from a comforting, malty Scotch ale to a bracingly hoppy India pale ale, beer is hands-down the most varied beverage on earth. So whether it's a rustic handmade sausage or the loftiest tall-food masterpiece, there's a beer that's made for it.

THE GRAIN-BASED NATURE of beer delivers a large vocabulary of bready, toasty, and roasty flavors that resonate with many kinds of food. Hops add herbal, citrus, resiny, or pinelike aromas. Yeast adds soft or strident fruitiness and spiciness ranging from the enveloping warmth of cinnamon and cloves to the crisp austerity of black pepper.

And then there are beers that actually do have spices in them, from hearty wassails to delicate wits, plus many other possibilities: fruit, nuts, coffee, chocolate, and the vanilla-soaked wonderfulness of a used bourbon barrel. Are you getting hungry yet?

BEER AND FOOD transform each other. Contrasting elements balance and sometimes blend into one another, like matter and antimatter, into a powerful, singular experience. These effects are often quite stunning and are at the core of a well-chosen match. To find combinations that really work and create memorable experiences, you will need to pay attention to the effect each partner has on the other. Bitterness in beer can overwhelm delicate flavors, but it can also be just what is needed to balance rich or creamy foods, even the sweetest desserts. Carbonation, roastiness, sweetness, smoke, and alcohol also come into play as contrast elements in beer. In food, sweetness, fat, the savory flavor of umami, and chile heat are all potential pairing elements.

Beer's lively carbonation tackles problems that make wine shrink in horror. Carbon dioxide bubbles literally scrub out your palate, which is sometimes helpful with intense or rich foods — cheese, for example. Fortunately, there is a range available in carbonation as well, from the slight tingle of British cask (real) ales to zippy *Weissbiers* and Belgian Tripels.

Another tool we have to work with is our own familiarity with certain flavor combinations that normally have nothing to do with beer. A grilled cheese sandwich is an iconic combination of gooey cheese and the toastiness of grilled bread. When you pair a soft, creamy cheese like a Camembert or Münster with a toasty brown ale, you are simply conjuring this familiar sensation in an entirely new context. These familiarity-based pairs can be striking and memorable, as well as a lot of fun.

Sommeliers, if you can get a beer or two in them, will grudgingly admit that wine has a long list of blind spots with food — more than just the asparagus conundrum — voids that beer happily fills. Various experts have thrown up their hands trying to pair wine with soup, salads, vegetables, mushrooms, cheese, dessert, and every spicy cuisine ever created. The wine world has done a very good job of convincing people that it is the only acceptable beverage for fine dining. And I have to say I do love a nice Langhe Rosso with a great steak. But with everything else, it is time for beer to take its place at the head of the table.

A cauldron of fat Beef and stoop of ale
On the huzzing mob shall more prevail,
Than if you give them with the nicest art,
Ragouts of Peacock's brains, or Filbert tart.

— William King

Getting Started

I AM SORRY TO TELL YOU that there is no "red wine with meat" rule as far as beer goes. Pairing beer and food is really all about common sense and taking a few things into consideration. There is nothing difficult or mysterious about the process. Follow a few basic rules, pay attention, and it is hard to go wrong. Don't be too consumed with finding perfection — there is no such thing. But every now and then you will have a truly transcendent moment, which is what we are all in this for.

If you're not doing this already, start paying attention to the beers and foods you enjoy now: the crisp bitterness of a pale ale cutting the boldness of a grilled hamburger; the smoky silkiness of a stout balancing the creamy tang of smoked salmon; the bittersweet edge of a barley wine cutting through the sweetness of crème brûlée. Memorable pairs are there for the taking. All it takes is a little focus. To paraphrase an Eastern mystic, "Beer here now."

For those new to this pursuit, it can be a bit overwhelming. The guidelines presented here should give you a framework for thinking about beer and food and let you get down to the very important business of finding great beer and food matches. As you practice, you will develop an intuitive grasp of the ideas here and develop your own repertoire of no-fail pairings to amaze and astound your friends. Of course, it helps to keep notes on your beer and food odyssey.

Three basic principles should be considered. Each one is important, but there is no particular order for the pairing process. Start with either a specific beer or food, and then seek a suitable partner according to the following guidelines.

Match Strength with Strength. Delicate dishes work best with delicate beers, and strongly flavored foods demand assertive beers — no surprise there. Intensity of flavor is not any single thing, but a sum of the taste experience. In beer, it may involve alcoholic strength, malt character, hop bitterness, sweetness, richness, roastiness, and more. In food, richness

FOODS IN ORDER OF INCREASING INTENSITY

FOODS IN ORDER OF INCREASING INTENSITY
Sushi, poached fish, fresh mozzarella cheese, pretzels
Sautéed white fish, chèvre, grilled vegetables
Roasted chicken, spinach salad, pizza, fried fish, Gouda or Gruyère cheese
Grilled pork chops, salmon, or portobello mushrooms; roast turkey; crab cakes
Hamburger, barbecued chicken, *Schweinshaxe* (ham hocks), kielbasa, authentic English Cheddar cheese, pâté
Fajitas, *guylás*, gumbo, soppressata, apple strudel, chocolate chip cookies, Münster cheese
Smoke-roasted prime rib, cheesecake, pecan pie, aged Gouda cheese
Grilled lamb, *chevapchichi* (uncased pork and beef sausage), blue cheese, carrot cake
Barbecued ribs, Texas mesquite-smoked brisket, Stilton cheese, chocolate mousse
Chocolate lava cakes, chocolate truffles

(or fat), sweetness, cooking methods (such as roasting, grilling, or frying), and spicing all play a role.

Find Harmonies. Combinations often work best when they share some common flavor or aroma elements. The nutty flavors of an English-style brown ale and a handmade Cheddar cheese; the deep, roasted flavors of Imperial Stout and chocolate truffles; the clean, caramelly flavors of an Oktoberfest lager and roasted pork are all examples of this, but there are many more. It's important to consider both the food ingredients and the method of preparation. Often, it is the roasted, caramelized, or grilled flavors of certain cooking methods that are the keys to the resonant elements of the pair. Spices, herbs, glazes, and other seasonings can be layered onto the dish to reinforce a beer-pairing choice. Familiarity with ingredients and preparation techniques, a memory for flavors, and a willingness to be constantly surprised will all serve you well here.

Consider the Contrast Elements. Sweetness, bitterness, carbonation, heat (spice), and richness — certain qualities of food and beer interact with each other in specific, predictable ways. Taking advantage of these interactions ensures that the food and beer will balance each other, with neither one hogging the limelight. These are specific interactions, different from the notion of the matching of intensity mentioned above. One has to parse these out to find flavors that will enhance one another.

Sweet and fatty-rich foods can be matched by various elements in beer: hop bitterness, sweetness, roasted/toasted malt, or alcohol. Carbonation is also effective at cutting richness.

FOOD AND BEER INTERACTIONS

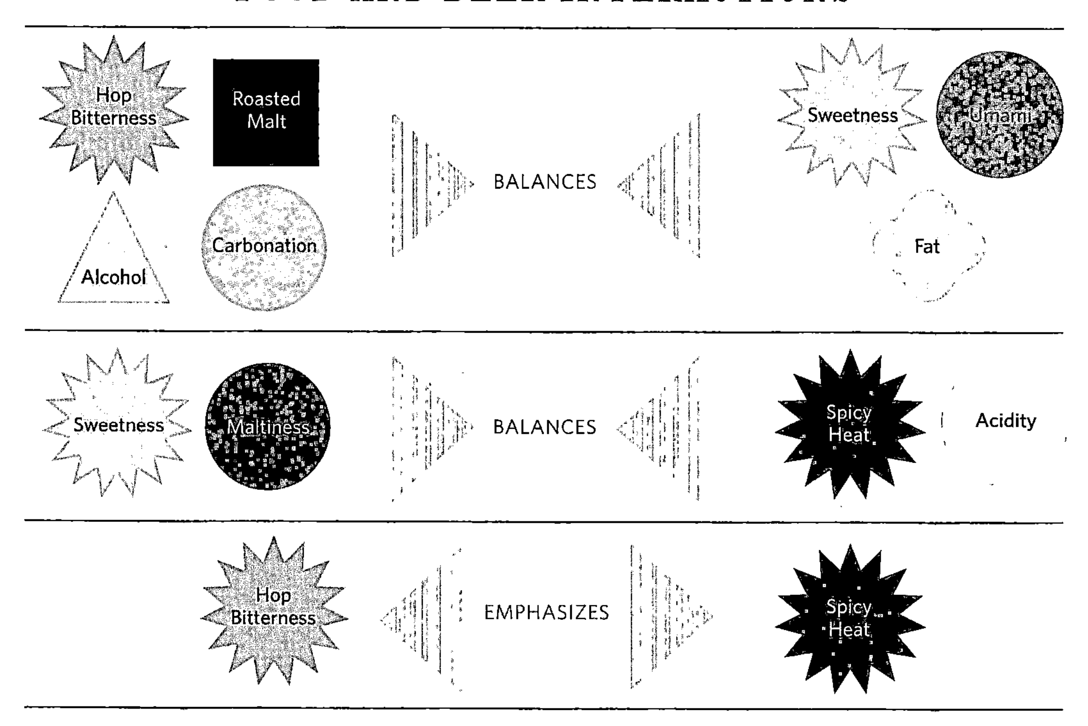

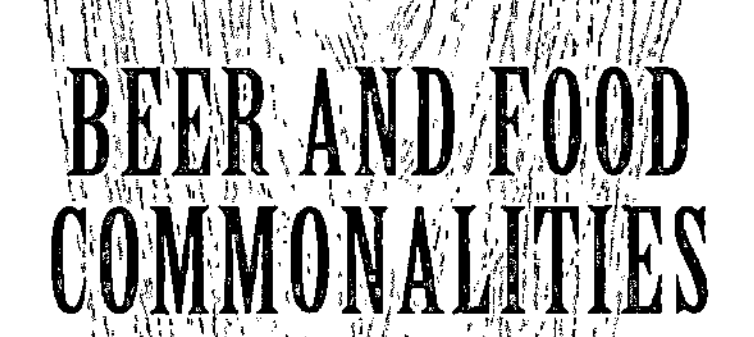

BEER AND FOOD COMMONALITIES

Here are some of the foods that share specific beer flavor and aroma profiles.

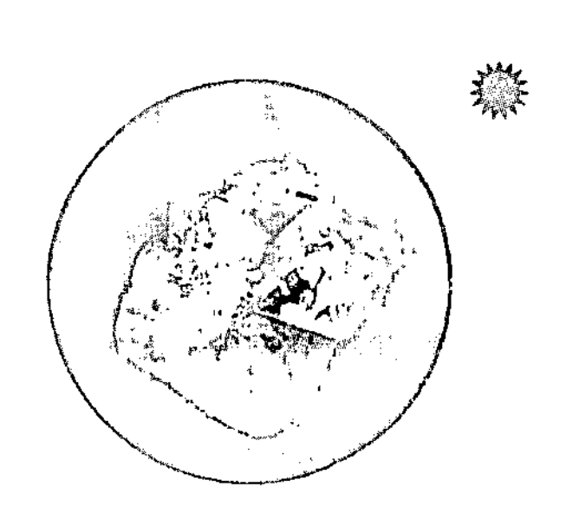

Herby hop aromas
blue cheese, herb rub, salad dressing

Citric hop aromas
citrus fruit, pepper, vinegar

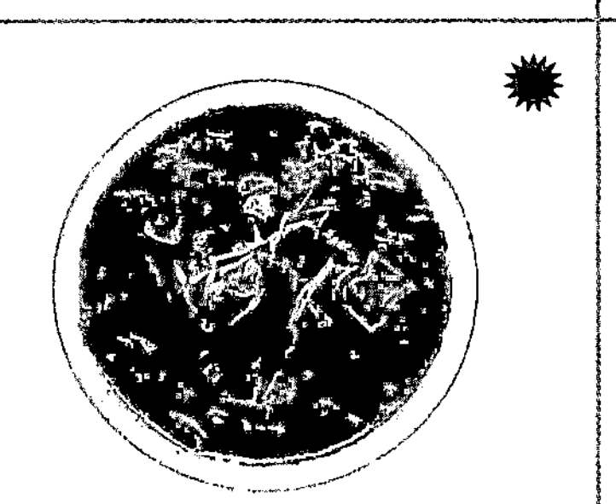

Spicy yeast character
spicy dishes, such as Indian, Cajun, etc.

Peppery or earthy yeast character
earthy cheese, mushrooms

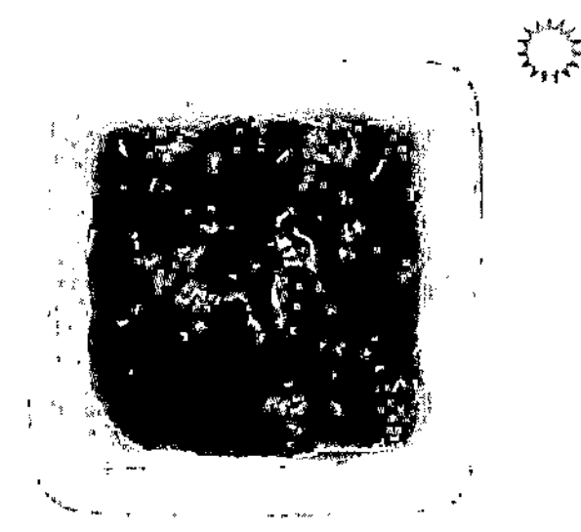

Fruity yeast character
wine- or fruit-based dressings, chutney

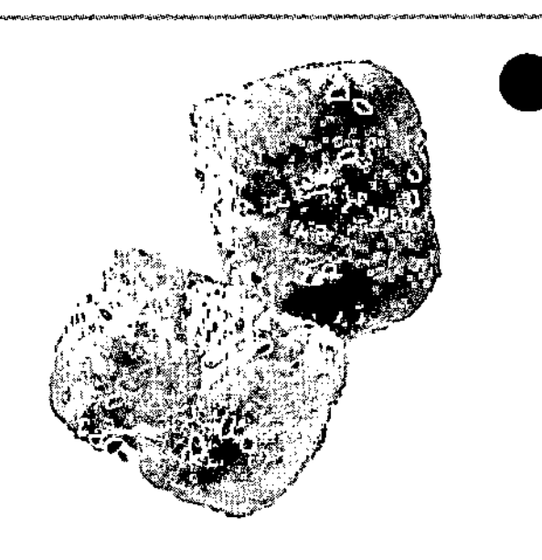

Nutty malt flavors
bread or crust, nutty cheese, aged sausage

Barrel-aged, vanilla, coconut aromas
many dessert items containing vanilla

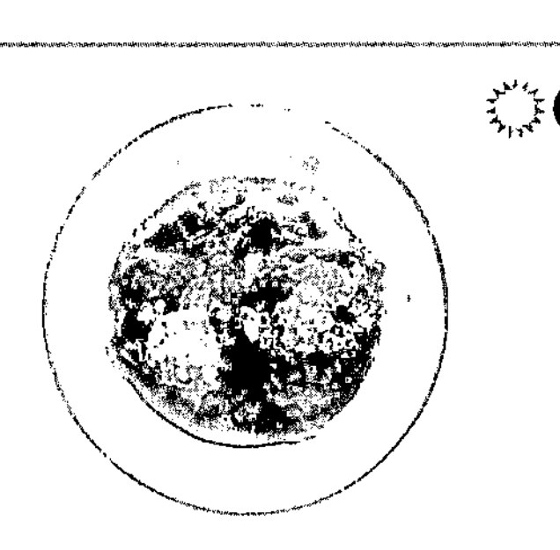

Honeyish malt or yeast character
light caramelization, fruit, honey

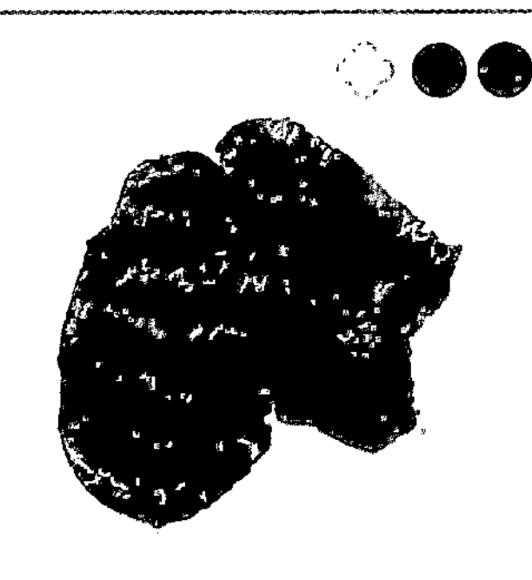

Toasted malt flavors
grilled or roasted meats, toasted nuts, aged cheese

Roasted malt flavors
well-aged, meaty cheese; roasted or smoked meats; chocolate; coffee

Caramel malt flavors
sautéed or caramelized flavors of meat, onions, vegetables; barbecue sauce; aged cheese; caramel in desserts

FAMILIARITY-BASED PAIRINGS

Soft Camembert cheese + a toasty brown ale = liquid grilled cheese sandwich

Burrata* cheese + a fruity hefeweizen = peaches and cream

Meaty, aged Gouda + Imperial Stout = roasted or grilled meat

**Burrata is fresh buffalo mozzarella stuffed with cream and curds.*

Umami is the rich, savory basic taste found in fatty fish, aged cheese, meat, ripe or cooked tomatoes, and many other dishes, as well as occasionally in well-aged beer. Umami can be balanced by the same things in beer as are used to balance sweetness, but because umami is less intense in character than the sweet taste, it can get by with a lower level of matching intensity.

Spicy (chile) heat is another specific interaction. Hoppy beer will make hot food taste hotter. If you're the kind of hothead that would just as soon have capsicum injected directly into your veins, this won't bother you, so have at it. For the rest of us, a more balanced approach with some maltiness is always welcome. If you're leaning to a hoppy beer with spicy food, make sure it has plenty of malt as well.

The principles outlined above are the primary considerations. Here are a few additional thoughts about enjoying beer and food together.

Look to classic cuisines. The cuisines of beer-drinking countries offer many great beer and food combinations. Beer and cheese from the same region or even the same monastery may be an obvious choice, as is bratwurst with pale lager, but who would have thought to put stout together with oysters? Classic matches are tried and true and are a great starting point for further exploration. The Belgians have a near-obsession with beer and food and a highly evolved *cuisine de la bière*. Learning about how they do things will give you lots of ideas for pairings.

Make use of familiar patterns. The flavor combinations in certain dishes are so familiar to most people that they constitute a common ground on which to build. If you can re-create or even evoke these recognizable flavor pairs in the new and different context of beer, you're halfway to acceptance.

Practice makes perfect. Not every pairing works as expected, and this can be fun if you can appreciate the unexpected. If it's not so great, make a note of it and move on. Build on the things that work and keep seeking out those magic combinations.

Consider seasonality. Go lighter in the summer and heavier in the winter; the beers and foods of a given season pair very naturally and suit the mood.

Contrast and complement. All beer and food combinations should involve both of these principles. Some pairings will be more dependent on the contrasts, others on complementary flavors, but all should strive for some kind of balance. A creamy bock against the salty tang of ham, IPA with carrot cake, or a crisp pale ale with a steak all work mainly on contrast. The chart (see page 118) shows the important contrasting elements. But even with contrasts, it's important that the beer and food are of somewhat similar intensity or one will overwhelm the other.

When in doubt, go Belgian. If you are going to a dinner and you need a beer that would go with just about anything, I'd suggest a Belgian-style abbey Dubbel or Tripel. These have enough substance to stand up to just about anything but do not have any overly aggressive malt or hop flavors that will overwhelm most foods. Plus, the big bottles make a nice presentation.

Remember, the above suggestions are just that — not absolute rules. Beer gastronomy was founded on creativity and experimentation. We hope you follow that spirit on your beer and food journey.

BEER WITH SALADS AND APPETIZERS

Crisp, refreshing beers are the best way to start a meal. Lighter wheat beer can be a perfect match for simple salads, but when the salads and appetizers get more complex with stronger flavors, the intensity of the beers will need to increase.

There is no simple rule with appetizers because they are such a disparate group. A simple shrimp cocktail is a very different beast from a cheese-stuffed fried jalapeño pepper, so the same rules about matching intensity, finding affinities, and dealing with contrasts apply. A character-filled blond ale might be great with seared ahi tuna. A hoppy American pale ale can balance succulent appetizers such as cheese tartlets and bruschetta. Spicy saison is the perfect counterpoint to tangy New Orleans–style shrimp. A full-flavored red ale or amber lager can be an ideal mate to smoked fish — or you might choose to present it with a light-bodied, smoky-roasty stout. Apertifs should present a fantastic experience without wearing out the palate. Look for beers that are light in body and are not ferociously bitter.

BEERS FOR LIGHT APPETIZERS

All-malt Pilsner
Belgian-style saison
Hefeweizen
Witbier

BEERS FOR HEARTY APPETIZERS

India pale ale
Fruit beer
Red rye ale
Belgian pale ale

Salads can match well with moderately bitter beers, especially if a link is made with the use of bitter greens such as arugula or radicchio. This bitterness is usually balanced by sweet elements in the dressing or a garnish such as sugar-glazed nuts or crumbled blue cheese, either of which will stand up to a fairly hoppy beer. The same goes for tomatoes, as ripe ones have a lot of umami, which can handle a moderate amount of bitterness. Aged cheese is another source of umami likely to be found sprinkled on top of salads. All of this means that a lighter-bodied beer with a fair amount of hops can fare well with salads. Hoppy saisons and lighter IPAs both fill the bill.

BEER WITH MAIN COURSES

There's a beer to suit every main dish, as long as you remember the rules: match intensity, find resonances, create contrasts. You also need to think about the following three aspects of each dish.

Like appetizers, main courses combine a main ingredient, cooking method, sauce, and garnishes, each with its own contribution to the overall intensity and character of the dish. First, consider the main ingredient. Lamb, for example, is a heavier taste on the palate than chicken, so its intensity begins to build at a higher level.

Second is the method of cooking. Poaching adds little of its own flavor, but roasting, sautéing, frying, grilling, and smoking give progressively more intense flavors. Because the chemistry of browning is basically the same in food as it is in the kilning of malt, it's a great place to look for affinities, such as these common beer flavors: bready, nutty, caramelly, toasty, roasty. Different foods and methods of preparation result in varying amounts of fat, which demand a certain intensity in the beery elements used to balance it (see Food and Beer Interactions chart, page 118).

The third thing to consider is any seasoning, sauce, or other element added to the dish. These dramatically change the character of the dish and may contain herbs, spices, fat, sugar, acidity, chile heat, or all of the preceding. Seasonings and sauces present lots of opportunities for finding affinities, but may also mean lots of complications as far as matching beer. Remember, there is no perfect match. Usually the best approach is to pick out the more intense flavor elements, whatever they are, and match to those.

Barbecued ribs are a good example of this. Pork ribs by themselves have only a moderately intense flavor. But when you pile on a spicy rub, a load of smoke and browning of the meat from heat, some chile spice, and a final caramelly layer of sweet and tangy sauce, you have quite a mouthful. The sweet caramel aspect of the meat and sauce are the primary element, which provides a link to the caramelly malt flavors in beer. Because of their sweetness and richness, a beer that is dry on the palate is helpful in balancing, and a moderately high alcohol level and high carbonation will further help cut down this richness. Although several other beer styles may fit here, I like a Belgian-style Dubbel. In addition to all the other characteristics, Dubbel also matches the dish pretty well in terms of overall intensity.

For lighter items such as grilled fish, a Dortmunder-style lager is a treat. For roasted chicken, a malty amber lager or pale ale can be great. For grilled steak or roast beef, a hearty porter or stout is an excellent choice. Remember that for spicy dishes, very hoppy beers may add fuel to the chile fire, which some may prefer. For most palates, rich malty beers such as Märzen, Munich dunkel, or Scottish ale do a great job of putting out the fire.

BEER WITH DESSERT

Dessert works beautifully with beer. In case you missed that, let me reiterate: beer is fantastic with dessert! At first thought, this might seem to be an odd fit, but when you think about the rich, sweet, caramelly, and roasty flavors that can be commonly found in both beer and food, it makes perfect sense. Not just any beer will do. The sweetness and richness of dessert demand rich, full-flavored beers. For the most part, don't even think about beers of less than 6 percent alcohol to pair with dessert, and the

"sweet spot" is probably higher than that. We tend to think about sugar as being a fairly bland flavor, and it is true that it is not complex, but on your tongue it explodes and takes over, which is why it needs a strongly flavored beer to balance it. The same is true for fat.

Fortunately, there are plenty of choices in dessert beers. You might pair a fruity dessert such as apple pie or apricot tart with a strong-but-crisp Belgian-style Tripel. Bread pudding or a sugary pecan pie might play off something with similar qualities. The caramelly bittersweet charms of an old ale fills the role beautifully.

The sweeter the dessert, the better it will work with hop bitterness. Strong, highly hopped beers such as double IPA are ideal partners for supersweet items such as cheesecake, crème brûlée, or carrot cake. This is a dramatic beer and food interaction, with each partner changing the way the other tastes. No matter how sweet the dessert, a hoppy beer will knock the sweetness right out of it. Likewise, even the most aggressively bitter beer can be totally tamed by a nice, sweet dessert. Spice and citrus qualities in many beers work well with desserts that highlight similar flavors.

CHOCOLATE LOVES A DARK BEER. Milk chocolate is beautiful with Belgian-inspired strong dark ales or any strong beer without too much black roasty character. The purest, most intense expressions of chocolate, such as flourless chocolate cake or truffles, really do well with a huge black beer, such as inky Imperial Stout. Desserts with less chocolate — chocolate chip cookies and peanut butter cups come to mind — can do well with less roasty brews, such as gutsy brown ales, Scotch ales, or old ales. Don't forget about white chocolate. It can be great with strong pale beers and sometimes even with fruit beers.

Fruit beers have an obvious affinity with fruit desserts. The acidity of a kriek or frambozen can cut the sweetness and creamy richness of something like a cherry cheesecake or raspberry tart. Fruit beers are often best with lighter desserts. More intense examples can be magic with chocolate, especially if there is a fruit component such as raspberry coulis in the dish.

Recently, a number of barrel-aged beers have become available. These are big, flavorful beers that offer sophisticated tones of bourbon, vanilla, and sherry, and are absolutely delightful with any rich dessert. There are also specialty beers with coffee, chocolate, hazelnuts, and many other ingredients that offer obvious possibilities for pairing.

BEER AND CHEESE

As Brooklyn Brewery's Garrett Oliver is fond of telling audiences, cheese is grass processed through a cow and modified by microbes. Beer is also grass processed through a microbe — yeast. So it is not surprising to find a wide range of common flavors from which to draw when seeking pairing possibilities.

The herbal, hoppy nose of an IPA blends nicely with the complex aroma of blue cheese, while the bitterness cleanses the palate. The

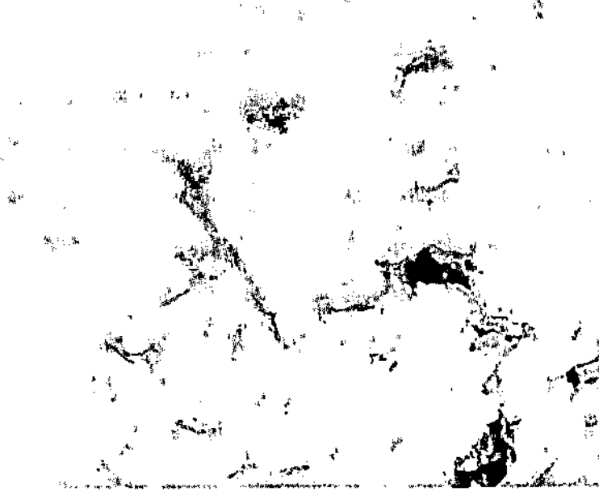

fruity aromas of hefeweizen make a nice match with the milky simplicity of fresh mozzarella. Fruit beers are excellent with delicate ripened cheese such as Brie or triple-cream types. Stout and Cheddar make another great pair, as does smoked beer with a smoked cheese. The meaty richness of salty, well-aged cheeses works best with strong, dark beers such as Imperial Stout. This meat-plus-roast is a great example of a familiarity-based pair; when they come together in a beer-food pair, there is already a sense that they fit together.

Cheese is a tough dish to match with beverages. Its intense, pungent, earthy, salty, and creamy aspects often overwhelm lesser beverages — although I'm not naming any names. Beer, with its mix of carbonation, hop bitterness, and roasty elements, can handle the mouth-coating richness of cheese just beautifully, if you observe the usual pairing guidelines previously noted.

Like beer, cheese comes in a wide range of intensities, from delicate to magnificently pungent. So the choice of beer partner depends first on matching intensity. I find that putting together pairings gets easier as the flavors get more intense. It's almost impossible to screw up a combination of a barley wine or Imperial Stout with a huge, well-aged cheese such as a Stilton.

BEER AND CHEESE PAIRING SUGGESTIONS

Stoudt's Weizen
with burrata (fresh mozzarella stuffed with curds and cream)

Dogfish Head 90 Minute IPA
with Golden Ridge Blue (a creamy, sophisticated blue with mushroomy overtones)

Flossmoor Station Pullman Brown
with ColoRouge Camembert (a deliciously gooey washed-rind cheese)

Orval Trappist Ale ▸
with Hillman Farmhouse (an ash-ripened goat cheese)

Lindemans Framboise
with Redwood Hills Fresh Chèvre (an earthy, creamy fresh goat cheese)

Saint Arnold Fancy Lawnmower Beer (Kölsch)
with Fair Oaks Farms Triple Cream Butter Käse (a simple but indulgently creamy butter cheese)

As with mainstream beer, Americans have gotten used to the rubbery, plastic-wrapped grocery-store varieties of cheese. What passes in chain stores for Cheddar, Münster, Jack, Swiss, and all the rest are but limp imitations of the genuine thing. *Real* cheese is flavorful, funky, varied, sublime, and authentic. And some of the best stuff comes from some of the smallest producers, whether they are staunch traditionalists or bomb-throwing renegades. In other words, great cheese has a lot in common with craft beer.

It is well worth seeking out high-quality cheese. It's a delight to the senses and a joy to pair with great beer. Grocery stores usually have few cheeses of real interest, so you are much better off at a specialty grocery or gourmet store or, if you're lucky enough to have one nearby, a specialty cheese shop.

Like craft brewing, there is an artisanal cheese movement in the United States, and some of the resulting cheeses are the equal of anything found in Europe. They are well worth the effort and expense. In my experience, the cheesemonger behind the counter usually knows his or her stuff, and it is a good idea to ask for recommendations (and perhaps a taste) as you are making your decision. Quite often these folks will have good suggestions for pairing beers.

Okocim Palone Smoked Schwarzbier
with Roth Käse Vintage Van Gogh Gouda (a rich and nutty six-month Gouda)

Rogue Ale's Shakespeare Stout
with Rogue Creamery's Smokey Blue (an explosive dry-textured blue with a nice smokiness)

◂ **Samuel Smith's India Ale**
with Neal's Yard Montgomery Cheddar (a dry, fine-textured mild Cheddar)

Three Floyds Dark Tripel
with St. George (a dry, artisanal, aged cow's milk cheese)

Two Brothers Dog Days Dortmunder
with Canasta Pardo (a sheep's milk cheese with a delicate dusting of cinnamon)

Einbecker Mai-Ur-Bock
with Meister Family Dairy Horseradish White Cheddar (every bit as zippy as you might imagine)

Schlenkerla Rauchbier Märzen
with Carr Valley Applewood Smoked Cheddar (an American-style Cheddar with a delicious bacony twang)

CHEESE IS a great place to start off on a beer and food journey (desserts work well, too). Great cheese is not too hard to find, doesn't need extensive preparation just before serving, and because it is one thing and not a mix of ingredients, seasonings, and cooking methods, it's a little easier to pair. As a subject of study, though, cheese is every bit as complex as beer, so I advise getting a good introductory text to help you understand the world of cheese.

Anchor Old Foghorn Barley Wine and Point Reyes Farmstead Cheese Company Original Blue

NO-BRAINER, NO-FAIL BEER AND CHEESE PAIRINGS

An earthy saison + **A creamy bloomy-rind cheese**

- Brasserie Dupont Moinette
- North Coast Le Merle
- Southampton Saison

+

- Sweet Grass Green Hill semi-ripened
- MouCo Camembert
- French Coulommiers

A toasty, deep brown ale + **A nutty, firm sheep's or cow's milk**

- Dogfish Head Indian Brown
- Unibroue Chambly Noire

+

- Ossau Iraty
- Compte St. Antoine

A big, hoppy pale ale + **A rich creamy blue or Gorgonzola**

- Sierra Nevada Celebration
- Bell's Two Hearted
- Victory Hop Devil

+

- Green Mountain Farm Goredawnzola
- Rogue Creamery Rogue River Blue
- Maytag Blue

A big or Imperial Stout + **A meaty, well-aged Gouda**

- North Coast Old Rasputin
- Deschutes Abyss

+

- 4-year Dutch Gouda
- Roth Käse Vintage Van Gogh

Barley wine + **Stilton or other intense, aged blue**

- Anchor Old Foghorn
- Three Floyds Behemoth
- Brooklyn Monster

+

- Colton Bassett Stilton
- Jasper Hill Bayley Hazen Blue

The simplest way to hold a casual tasting is to gather a few friends together with four or five different types of cheese and have everybody bring some beers, then lay them all out and have at it. For a casual tasting, an ounce of each cheese per person is a good place to start; double that if they're big eaters. If you want bread or crackers, keep it really simple. Fine cheese tastes best at room temperature, so don't forget to let it warm before serving. Talk about what works and what doesn't. Sure, you are going to find some great pairs, but ultimately it is the process that is most meaningful. Oh, and don't forget to have fun.

Staging a Beer Dinner

BEER AND FOOD EVENTS may take many forms, but most typical is a multicourse dinner with a specific beer — or sometimes two — paired with each course. Ambitious dinners also attempt to include beer as an ingredient in each food course. These events are a good way to encounter beer and food together and are also a great way to get to know the folks behind the scenes at your favorite brewery and to meet others who share your fan-club status. Most brewpubs and many packaging breweries regularly conduct brewmaster dinners.

You can do your own, as you would do any other kind of dinner party, but with some thought put into which beers to serve with the courses. There are menus all over the Internet, and beer-specific cookbooks are another great resource; look for books by Garrett Oliver and Lucy Saunders.

Beer-centric cuisines such as Belgian or German are can't-miss options, but it is possible to get a lot more exotic with what you serve: India pale ales with Indian cuisine, Thai food with German lagers, Mexican with Oktoberfest, barbecue with Belgian ales — possibilities abound.

LIKE ANY gastronomic experience, the proper setting and preparation can make the difference between an ordinary experience and an extraordinary one. Here are a few things

Southampton Saison and Pavé d'Affinois (a soft, creamy ripened cow's milk cheese)

PAIRINGS FROM A RECENT CHICAGO BEER SOCIETY'S BREWPUB SHOOTOUT

Wild Onion Brewpub

- **Harissa-spiced beef** with fig jam and couscous
- **Abbey Tripel**

TASTING NOTES:
The Tripel cut the richness and soothed the spicy heat, while echoing the figgy fruitiness.

Goose Island Clybourn Brewpub

- **Whole applewood-smoked hog** with McIntosh apples
- **Doppelbock**

TASTING NOTES:
Toasty and caramelly beer flavors keyed in nicely with the caramelized pork.

Prairie Rock Brewpub, Elgin

- **Thai chicken lollipop** with spicy Asian sauce and baby greens
- **Double IPA**

TASTING NOTES:
Hoppy contrast to the richness of the dish, but with enough malt to balance the heat.

Rock Bottom Brewery & Restaurant

- **Beer-braised brisket** with watercress and Asiago cheese in mini flatbread sandwiches
- **Dry-hopped American brown ale**/winter warmer

TASTING NOTES:
The rich, beefy taste resonated with the toasty beer, which had enough bitter crispness to cut the considerable richness.

to consider when planning your beer and food extravaganza.

Beer or food first? There's no rule here. In many situations, this question may answer itself. For a dinner featuring one brewery's beers, the selections are a given. Just sort them out by intensity and start looking for food pairs. Assign the lightest beers to the appetizers and save the heaviest for dessert. What's left should fit nicely in the middle of the meal, so pick dishes that will showcase the beers you have to work with.

Taste from low to high intensity. Alcohol, hops, roastiness, and sweetness can all beat up your palate, so it only makes sense to put the more delicate beers at the start of the tasting. This dictates a lighter- to stronger-flavored food progression as well, following the classic pattern.

Don't overdo it. Tasting too many beers can lead to palate overload. When planning a dinner, try to limit the number of beers to six to eight tasting portions. This means a maximum of about 4 ounces a pour; somewhat less for strong beers. And always encourage the use of public transportation, especially in a public tasting.

Present the beer in its best light. Serving temperature, proper and clean glassware, decent light, and a setting free from smoke or other distracting aromas should all be considered when preparing for any beer and food pairing event.

Thai chicken lollipop with Stone Ruination Double IPA

Cooking with Beer

Because of its wide range of properties, beer makes an excellent companion in the kitchen. It may be used like other cooking liquids, but it does require a few considerations. Match the intensity of the beer to the dish, just as if you were pairing a beer and any other food. Bitterness in beer requires special attention. In general, low-bitterness beers are best for cooking. It is advisable not to reduce beer, as even a slightly bitter beer may become too bitter for the dish. Small amounts of bitterness may be balanced by a touch of sweetness, salt, or acidity. As always, taste as you cook.

Mushroom and cheese tartlets and two kinds of bruschetta with Wolaver's American Pale Ale

Lighten up a batter. Beer adds lightness to batter used for deep-frying items like fish and chicken.
BEER SUGGESTIONS: pale or amber lightly hopped lager or ale.

Deglaze the pan. A quick sauce for sautéed or roasted items can be made by using beer to deglaze the pan. Do not reduce the beer, as it may become excessively bitter.
BEER SUGGESTIONS: either delicate or intense, to match the nature of the dish, but low-bitterness beers preferred.

Dressings and marinades. Beer can make a great addition to salad dressings and marinades for grilled meat or barbecue. Acidic beers can substitute for vinegar in dressings.
BEER SUGGESTIONS: pale, low-bitterness beers for dressings; heartier amber or brown beers for marinades.

Steaming or poaching liquid. Although mussels steamed in wheat beer is a classic, other great combinations are possible.
BEER SUGGESTIONS: witbier, *Weissbier*, other delicate, lightly hopped brews.

DISHES PREPARED WITH BEER

Roast pork loin with apples and cherry ale

Pork shanks with dunkel lager or schwarzbier

Duck glazed with doppelbock

Roast salmon with witbier cream sauce

Grilled steak marinated in red ale and green peppercorns

Roast chicken with dried apricots and weizenbock sauce

Steamed scallops in witbier

Gingerbread brown ale cake

Chocolate Imperial Stout truffles, dusted with powdered black malt

Barley wine–walnut ice cream

Replace or augment stock in soups and sauces. Many beers can add richness to hearty soups or meat gravy. Don't make cheese soup without it!

BEER SUGGESTIONS: sweet stout, doppelbock, Scotch ale.

Make dessert more luxurious. Strong, rich beers may be substituted for other liquids in cakes and pastries. Fruit beers add a complexity to fruit compote or sauce. Or, make beer the star — drop a scoop of ice cream into a glass of Imperial Stout and voilà, dessert!

BEER SUGGESTIONS: sweet stout, doppelbock, fruit beer.

WE'RE EATING AND DRINKING all the time, so it takes just a little adjustment in behavior to start paying closer attention to the flavors, textures, and other sensations as you go. A little effort leads to big rewards, and pretty soon you'll develop the kind of repertoire that means always having the perfect sip ready for the next forkful. Like the great dance team of Fred and Ginger, beer and food are lively, supple partners that seem to have been made for each other. A beer and food match is always a great interaction, whether supporting, cajoling, caressing, or raising each other to lofty new heights. Beer and food just swing together.

ANATOMY OF A STYLE

THERE are those in the brewing community who chafe at the notion of beer styles. Beer is art, they say, and any attempt to limit it to preordained categories diminishes its greatness; styles are nothing more than a crutch for unimaginative minds.

But styles are a reality. They exist in history, in the marketplace, and in some places have the force of law behind them. Brewers brew by them, consumers buy by them, and competitions are judged by them. Styles honor the past and give order to the present. They help people wrap their heads around beer.

I LOVE CREATIVE BEERS that break all the boundaries. Just the same, rebellion is a little empty without something to rebel against; styles provide that kind of structure in wild abundance. The notion of styles adds a depth and dimension to the wide world of beer. Studying them brings into focus the less-obvious aspects of beer, such as balance, cultural taste, changing fashions, and notions of ourselves.

It's a bit like religion. You can choose to believe or not to believe, but the landscape is richer and more profound when all manner of unsupported ideas are tolerated. So I say: Bring 'em on!

JUST WHAT IS A STYLE? It's a collection of qualities that combine to form a single, identifiable whole. That one thing may turn out to be many when you start looking closely, but it doesn't matter. Styles are all about consensus.

First and most obvious among these qualities are the objectively measurable attributes: color, gravity, alcoholic strength, bitterness, attenuation, and others. A beer style can almost be defined by these alone. On top of that are subjective sensory characteristics: aroma, flavor, texture, and mouthfeel, which complete the picture of what's in the glass — and what's in or out of the style box.

But this only scratches the surface. Sensory characteristics can't tell us the full story or explain how the style came into use, through whom, and for what purpose. At a deeper, richer level are technological, geographic, and cultural foundations that gave rise to the more obvious points of the style. Understanding them and also seeing beer styles in their proper historical context are essential to grasping the bigger themes and essence of a style, and allow both brewer and drinker to celebrate them at a higher level.

Styles are indispensable for brewers and drinkers to share some common ground about what a particular beer is going to taste like. A style is marketing shorthand. What's easier to understand, "American pale ale" or "an amber-colored, top-fermented ale of 5 to 6.5 percent alcohol and crisp bitterness with the resin and citrus overtones of American hops?" Sure, that may be written in tiny type on the back of the label. But does anybody really read labels? Studies have shown that shoppers spend no more than a couple of seconds on an initial scan of packages on the shelf, so communication has to be nearly instantaneous. Styles really help with that.

Historically, many styles develop spontaneously and only later get the name by which they become famous. Dark brown ales were brewed in London for a generation before the name "porter" was applied to them sometime around 1725. "Stout" was a term used generically for strong beer in England as early as the late seventeenth century, but it didn't find common use until a generation later, when it came exclusively to mean a strong porter. Münchener beers were simply the local brew until they became popular elsewhere and then took on the city's name.

Other beers are the product of invention, not evolution. Pilsner dates quite precisely to 1842, when the city fathers decided to build and brew a pale beer, then a new idea in the lager world. Bill Owens, the creative force behind one of the first latter-day U.S. brewpubs, lays claim to the invention of the "amber" designation: "I had a dark and light, and what was I gonna call that middle one? *Amber*."

STYLES GO THROUGH CHANGES, generation by generation. What seems to be constant is that no one wants to drink his or her father's beer. It seems that each generation has to find its own way, even if it ends up pretty close to home. Newness has its own appeal, and tradition, while nice at times, doesn't always rule. For instance, amber beer has been going through a metamorphosis recently; every time the World Beer Cup style guidelines are revised, it gets a little more hop-centric.

Whatever the other influences on the formation of a style — and there are many — it must be satisfying to the senses. All the parts must come together to produce a whole that looks, tastes, smells, and feels great. In the range of all possible beers, not everything is going to work. There are differences in what turns people on, of course, and this is one thing you can learn by studying foodways such as beer. But having brewed quite a number of extinct historical beers and found them all quite delicious, I have the feeling that, despite our differences, we all have a lot in common about what we like in a beer. All it takes is a reasonably open mind.

Different beers serve different needs: hydration, nutrition in the form of "liquid bread," a dinner companion, an everyday session beer for special occasions, and luxury goods for the high end of the market. Beers that suit all these purposes date back to Sumeria, where weak, strong, extra-quality, and even diet beer all existed side by side. Beer is a part of culture, so it must take on forms to suit the many tasks it is called on to perform.

You have to look at human activities in the broadest possible context to fully understand beer styles. There are places on the globe where barley grows well, places better suited to other grains, and of course, places where grains just don't do well at all. This affects who will be making beer and from what. There is a line that

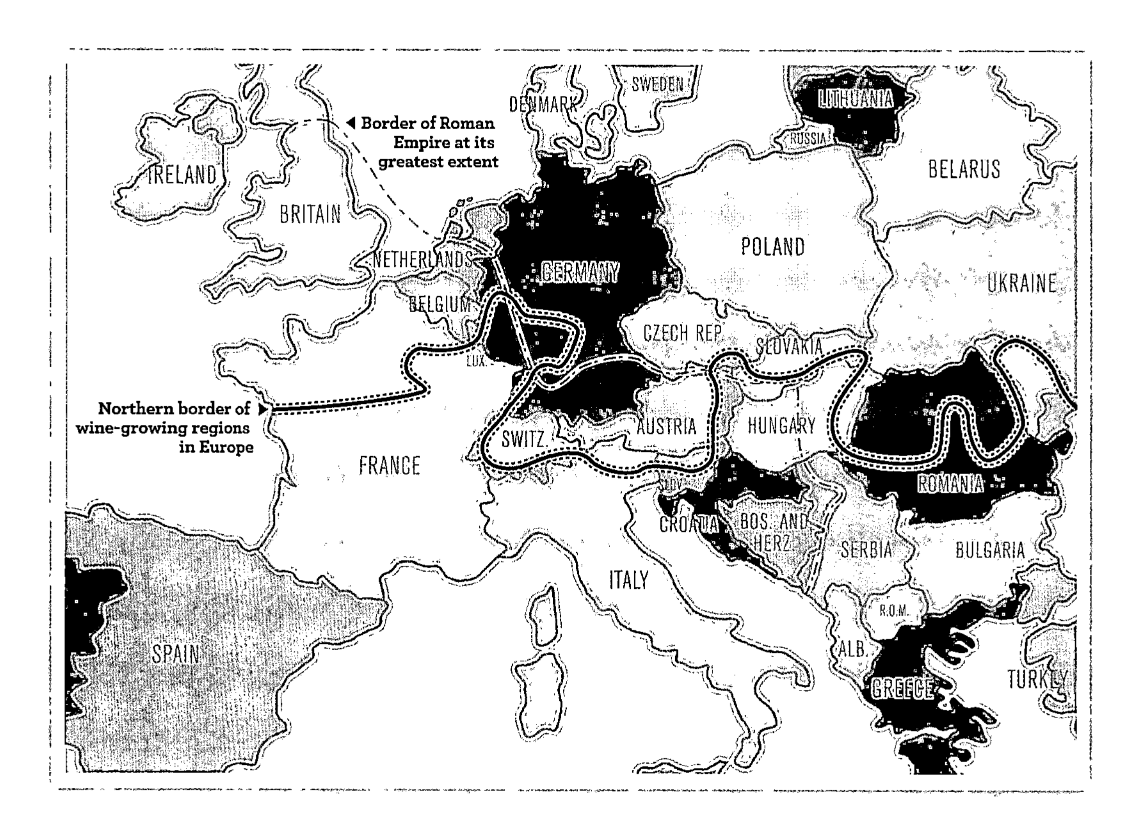

The Grape Line

This indicates the northern extent of grape cultivation in Europe, and approximates the extent of the old Roman Empire (Britain excepted). Above the line, they were definitely beer drinkers.

cuts across Europe, north of which wine grapes don't grow, and this roughly corresponds to the northern boundary of the old Roman Empire. For reasons of agriculture as well as cultural patrimony, the lands south of that line have always preferred grape to grain. The Greeks, and the Romans after them, saw wine as civilizing and beer as a barbarian's drink, an attitude that has infected Western thought since those days. Happily, this is changing. Former beer deserts such as Italy have recently blossomed with some very exciting artisanal beers, but these are delightful experiments more than any kind of deep cultural shift.

BARLEY AND, to a lesser extent, wheat have always been the preferred grains for beer, but a passable brew can be coaxed out of hardier grains like rye and oats, which will endure harsher climates and soils. So in England, the Low Countries, and Scandinavia, even all the way up to the Baltic Sea, oat and sometimes rye beers used to be commonplace. Wheat requires a specific climate and very good soil, and there's always competition from the bakers for raw material. So in various times and places you find wheat beers more tightly regulated than barley beers, sometimes banned in difficult years, or assigned to a royal monopoly, as in eighteenth-century Bavaria.

Hops have an even narrower range of conditions under which they will produce cones. In England, for example, they do stupendously well in the south but less so farther north. The rate of hopping in English beer tends to follow this tilt. And when you get to Scotland there are no local hops at all. I'll leave it to you to decide whether the Scots are thrifty, but one thing that's fact is that they have never enjoyed giving money to the English. No surprise, then, that Scottish beers tend to be very malty. Hops are a compact, high-value crop, which means that they may be economically shipped great distances. Following the trail of hops is another way to make sense of beer styles.

In addition to climate, one must also consider geology. The underlying bedrock of a region has a big influence on the chemistry of the local water. As it flows through rivers, lakes, and aquifers, it dissolves minerals. These affect the hardness and acid-alkaline balance, both of which have a strong influence in the brewing process. It wasn't until about the dawn of the twentieth century that water chemistry was understood well enough to be manipulated, so brewers in a given place had to brew a beer that worked well with the local water.

Although it's a complicated subject, the most important vector to understand is that hard, alkaline water is best for dark, malty beers. Hoppy beers require either hard and acidic (gypsum) water or soft water. The brown beers of London, Dublin, and Munich were all created in cities with chalky, hard water. The crisp hoppy brews from Plzeň and Burton-on-Trent, long famous for bitingly bitter pale ales, each took full advantage of the local water.

As any farmer can tell you, weather is unpredictable. Beer crops are subject to this uncertainty, and as I write this, the beer industry is starting to feel the effects of both a global realignment of cereal crops and a severe short-term hop shortage. Supply is tight and prices are way up. The net effect of bad years is that brewers look for substitutes. Sugar was forbidden in beer in England prior to around 1825, when a couple of inadequate barley crops led first to the temporary, and then to the permanent (in 1847), allowance of the use of sugar and other adjuncts for brewing.

Climate plays out in a seasonal cycle, too. Refrigeration and other changes made brewing a year-round venture; just a little more than a hundred years ago, this was not the case. First of all, the demand for agricultural labor meant that in many places, workers were not available for brewing in the summer. And then there's the heat. With no means to limit fermentation temperature, and a very high count of airborne bacteria and wild yeast, the heat of summer produced beers that soured very quickly, so only the vital, thirst-quenching, small beers continued to be brewed. Storage conditions were not great either, and by summer, last fall's malt — and especially the hops — were pretty tired out.

Common practice was to brew moderately strong beers at the end of the brewing season — March or maybe April — that could last all through the season and then be consumed in the fall before the newly brewed beer was ready. This cycle was similar in many parts of Europe. England's most prized beer in the old days was a strong "October" beer, and similar, but slightly lower-quality, "March" beer was also made. For at least a couple of centuries, the French brewed and enjoyed *bière de mars*. Of course Märzen, although fading, still exists in Germany and was the original model for Oktoberfest beers, which today seem to get lighter every year. The Germans in Saxony had *erntebier* (harvest beer), with many similarities to modern-day altbier.

Bock beer is another brew with old and fascinating seasonal connections. Born in Einbeck, this strong beer migrated south, was corrupted from *einbeckisches* to *einpockisches*

THE YEAR IN BEER

New Year's. Pop a Belgian-style Tripel as an alternative to the same boring old champagne when the year changes. The next day, nourish your soul and your head with a nice yeasty weizenbock.

The last twelve interminable days of January. Nothing makes the time fly like a vertical tasting of your favorite barley wine or Imperial Stout. Take care to avoid the tasting becoming a horizontal one.

Valentine's Day. Loads of choices! Try a Belgian strong dark ale with milk chocolate, or an Imperial Stout with something really hot and sinful like lava cake with a touch of spicy ancho chile inside. If your sweetie wants to walk on the pale side, how about a Belgian strong golden ale with a white chocolate version of Black Forest cake? Who says beer guys and gals can't be romantic when it counts?

Lent. Personally, I don't have a lot of experience with self-denial. I'd go with a bock or doppelbock, the proven remedy for mortification of the flesh. And they do taste great at this time of year.

Easter and more pagan expressions of the vernal equinox. Easter beers used to be big business in Scandinavia and elsewhere in northern Europe. We'll have to be content with something pale and slightly strong, provided we can crack open the maibock a little early. Open up a bottle of raspberry lambic when Aunt Ruth comes to brunch.

The first really nice day of spring. Even though I sometimes do it, I think there is something wrong with drinking *Weissbier* indoors. So I am greatly relieved to be rid of my guilt when it's finally nice enough to sit outside in some makeshift beer garden and enjoy a dunkel weizen in the chilly sunshine.

May. Go for a maibock, if there's any left from Easter.

June. Let's just call it India Pale Ale month.

Seasonal Beer Labels
Over the ages, beer has been brewed to suit the seasons. Once waning, this tradition is thankfully coming back.

Fourth of July. Let the national frenzy take hold and honor honest-to-God, U. S. of A., lawn-mowing beers, both great and small. There are many to choose from: pre-Prohibition Pilsners, steam beer, cream ale, American wheat ale, and craft-brewed malt liquor.

St. Swithin's Day, July 15. Yes, there really is one, and its history involves an interesting story about great torrents of water. I recommend a light beer.

Dog days. Still hot. Time to break out the big thirst-quenching guns: witbier, English summer ale, classic German Pilsner, hefeweizen — in large glasses, please.

Back to school, or whatever. Still warm and sunny but change is in the air. It's the perfect time for a nice saison, but many beers suit the season: British bitter, Irish stout, schwarzbier, gueuze. Wait till the end of September and you can taste them all and much more at the Great American Beer Festival in Denver.

Oktoberfest. You really need a suggestion here?

Halloween. Pumpkin beer is a natural at this time, but see if you can score one of its scarier variants: pumpkin barley wine, pumpkin weizenbock, or pumpkin Imperial Porter. Better 'n pie!

Turkey time. Try a Tripel with the succulent bird, roasted to perfection — but toss a pint of Scotch ale into the bottom of the pan when you start roasting. The Tripel will go nicely with pecan pie, but for pumpkin pie, a strong brown ale will be better.

Christmas Eve. I hear the old man is partial to drinking Imperial Pale Ale with his chocolate chip cookies.

The Holidays. The English had their wassail and many other hot compounded drinks that can make you the life of the party if you don't burn the house down. There are many festive beers inspired by the rich, spicy flavors of Jolly Old England. But honestly, at this time of year just enjoy all the big celebratory beers available and give yourself incentive for some serious New Year's resolutions.

bier, and eventually was shortened to *bockbier.* The word *bock* is the German word for male goat, prancing symbol of priapic fertility whose natural season is spring. Religious observants like monks, looking for a loophole to the denial of Lenten fasting, studied the rules and decided that God somehow overlooked banning beer along with meat, and so took full advantage. To show their gratitude, the monks at Paulaner — then a monastery, not a commercial brewery — cooked up an extra-strong version of bock in 1773 and named it Salvator. This name served as a generic name for the style for a couple of centuries, until they decided to take their trademark back. Such jumbled mythology highlights the enormous task facing beer-style researchers.

We still can follow the flow of seasons with our beers. A beer that can be tossed down to quench thirst in the heat of summer fails to satisfy in the dreary gloom of February. The promise of spring creates a different mood than the breezy desiccation of fall and demands a different sort of beer.

Technology and Beer Styles

Technology has a huge influence on beer. But while progress in, say, aviation, where the level of technology is clearly in line with the quality of the product, the effect of technology on beer is more complicated and doesn't always result in more delicious beer. A knowledgeable guy with little more than a bucket and a pinch of yeast can brew beer good enough to make you weep, but it takes technology to be able to do this consistently and, especially, economically. Every new technology brings with it changes that may not have been on the mind of its inventor, and so influences the styles for which it is employed.

Malt can be dried just by spreading it out on the attic floor, but more commonly, heated kilns were used. In the early days, malt kilns were direct fired, so the hot combustion gasses passed over the malt and gave it a smoky aroma. By 1700, improvements had been made to kilning technology such that most European beer was no longer smoky. However, the rustic touch of smoke is still enjoyed today in Bamberg and northern Bavaria, and in the ancient homebrews of Gotland, in Sweden. A century ago smoke-touched beers were more widespread, with beers such as *grätzer* and *lichtenhainer* thriving in northern Germany and even Strasbourg, France.

Smoke wasn't the only issue in early malt kilning. It's fairly easy, with simple equipment, to make amber- to brown-colored malt. Getting it really light or dark poses more of a challenge. The problem with black malt is not so much with roasting, but with keeping it from catching fire as it reaches perfection. A guy named Daniel Wheeler came along in 1817 with a drum roaster fitted with a water spray and patented the device. Even today, it is called black patent malt. Black malt changed porter forever. Just a generation before, a brewer named Richardson had written a book detailing his observations on brewing aided by a hydrometer. Surprise! All that brown malt is making the beer nice and dark, but it has a lot less fermentable extract than pale malt, and so the brewery accountants were climbing all over themselves to get the brewmasters to use more pale and less brown, since the cost was not that different. Although it was not strictly legal, the government seemed to look the other way as porter and stout were colored by caramelized sugar, at least until Wheeler came along with his patent. Books covering the tumultuous period of change in these popular beers often lamented the fact that you couldn't get "real" porter anymore.

SIMILARLY, IT TOOK sophisticated indirect kilns with good temperature control to produce malt light enough to brew what could truly be called pale beers. While air-dried "white" malt had long been available in England and on the Continent, it wasn't until the mid-nineteenth century that very pale, or Pilsner, malt was produced in any serious quantities.

Caramel-crystal malt, the intensely rich malt used in many modern beers, wasn't created until about 1870, so it played little role in the creation of most of the classic European beer styles. It found an early role in the creation of low-gravity English bitters, where its chewy, caramelly character lends heft to what are very low-gravity beers. Crystal eventually found its way into many classic styles, but it had little to do with the beginnings of most of them.

Malt Roaster, c. 1850
Patterned after the revolutionary device patented by Daniel Wheeler in 1817, roasters like this made black malt possible and ushered in a new era of very dark beers.

A very challenging task in early breweries was the big job of heating water, mash, and wort. Metal vessels are still among the most expensive parts of the brewhouse, and if you go back in time far enough they simply don't exist. Wood will hold water just fine, but you can't put a flame to it. In the earliest times, heated rocks were dropped into the mash or boil to raise the temperature. Later on, a brewer with a small kettle could remove some of the mash, boil it, and return it to the rest of the batch for a temperature step-up. This process, known as decoction, figures heavily in traditional German and Czech styles of lagers, where it adds a unique and delicious caramel touch.

INSTRUMENTS OTHER THAN the hydrometer had their influences. Brewers had long been able to control mashing temperatures by eye, either by carefully proportioning boiling water with cold and making allowances for the seasonal temperatures, or by observing the way water behaves as it is heated. At a certain point as the water heats, the blanket of mist clears, but before the surface starts to roil from the heat there is a brief moment when a calm, glassy surface lets the brewer see his reflection. This is at about 170°F (77°C), which is in the neighborhood of the right point to make the mash. Even with a lifetime of practice, this technique must have been approximate, so it's hard to say how much fine control there was over the fermentability of the wort. Temperature affects every part of the brewing process, so being able to fine-tune it at every stage is critical if you want to make beer consistently and efficiently. Using temperature measurements also allowed brewers to discuss the most critical parts of the brewing process using a common language.

Old-Time Technique
Bottling in the nineteenth century was sometimes a primitive affair.

When brewers understood how temperature affected the brewing process, they developed a keen interest in controlling it. This led to temperature control of fermenters, usually accomplished by passing cold water through pipes suspended in the tanks. Refrigeration technology finally reached the point where it was ready to be useful for brewing in the 1870s. Now it was possible to brew a beer all year long instead of during just the coolest six months. And eventually, beers were brewed that were designed to be consumed ice-cold. These crisp, pale, highly carbonated beers were American adjunct Pilsners.

Louis Pasteur had an effect as well. While the nature of yeast was discovered by others, Pasteur figured out in his 1871 *Études sur Bière* what caused the "diseases" of beer and worked out practical methods for avoiding them. He also figured out a method for rendering beer and other products microbiologically stable by heating — or pasteurizing — them by way of a specified time and temperature regimen. Pasteurization greatly increased the shelf life of bottled beer, and it was this, in conjunction with refrigeration, that made a massive distribution network possible and brought beer to places like the southern United States, where beer previously had been scarce.

Draft beer had always been modestly carbonated, as the wooden kegs could hold only limited amounts of pressure. Bottles handmade of glass or clay existed, but these were as unreliable as the kegs. It wasn't until about the last third of the nineteenth century that machine-made bottles capable of holding serious pressure came on the market. This led to new, highly carbonated beers. Gueuze, a blended and bottled form of lambic, came into being shortly thereafter. Berliner Weisse enjoyed a huge popularity in the nineteenth century in its very heavy stoneware bottles. In Scotland (mainly as an export to America), Australia, and the United States, sparkling ales were all the rage. And let's not forget modern industrial lager.

Perhaps the biggest change all this technology brought was that beers were no longer so closely tied to the materials and conditions at their points of origin. There were plenty of cultural reasons why certain beer styles stayed in particular areas, but by 1900 or so, there were few technological ones. With certain styles — Pilsners, for example — being brewed internationally and slowly morphing into something very different, the pure and authentic expression of a style often depended on the bullheaded intransigence of the original brewers. I'm all for creativity, but it's a lousy way to preserve tradition. The power to make anything anywhere changes the tradition equation dramatically. Today, with tinkering of the classics like Oktoberfest and Bohemian Pilsner by the geniuses in the marketing departments, it falls to passionate and historically informed brewers elsewhere to preserve a style in its truest form. Like animals in a zoo, the styles may eventually be released back into their wild habitat, but for now, the task is simply to save the species.

Laws, Taxes, and Beer Styles

THE GOVERNMENT HAS had its sticky hands on our beer since the earliest days, and our desire for beer is so strong that we usually let them get away with it. The famous stone stela upon which is chiseled the 2225 BCE Code of Hammurabi, the world's first written laws, includes a regulation about how tavern owners should charge for beer. In medieval Europe, beer tax made up as much as half the municipal revenue in places like Bruges. Before the advent of hopped beer, tax was in the form of the *Gruitrecht*, which was the right to sell a highly marked-up seasoning mixture to the local brewers, who were forced to use it. Later, when hopped beer came about, the tax was levied on malt and hops. The *Reinheitsgebot*, the much-vaunted Bavarian beer "purity" law, was created mainly as a tax-enforcement law, forcing the brewers to use the taxed ingredients.

When brewers are taxed on malt, there are often additional laws specifying how much must be used for beers selling at specific prices to ensure that drinkers get the strength of beer they're paying for. These regulations were common in northern Europe for hundreds of years. When the hop tax is high, brewers are cautious about their hop use. The repeal of the hop duty in 1862 coincided with a greater popularity of the highly hopped pale ales.

British brewers today are taxed on their original gravity, which means there is constant pressure to keep the beers as weak as possible, and of course this fits with the British style of session drinking. In addition, there is a price differential between stronger and weaker beers in the brewer's range, which keeps up the demand for the weaker products.

The Belgians had a unique system for taxing the volume of the mash tun, the vessel used to hold the soupy porridge in which malt's starches are converted to fermentable sugars. Because the tax was on the size of the vessel regardless of how much malt was in it, this law encouraged brewers to fill the tuns to the brim and above, and this affected the beers. The government allowed the use of a second tun for unmalted grains. Taxed at less than the full volume, brewers were eager to fill that one, too, leading to the classic recipes for both witbier and lambic, which use unmalted wheat in wild abundance.

TAXATION OF ALCOHOL is newer, dating to the end of the nineteenth century. Typically there will be tiers based on alcohol content with progressively higher tax rates, as with the class I, II, and III system used in parts of Scandinavia. Everywhere it is done, beers get realigned to the very highest end of the lowest class into which they can reasonably fit. Many beers in Germany that had been table strength (4 to 5 percent alcohol by volume) were dropped into the schenkbier, or small beer, category when it was created in about 1890, bringing them more into the 2 to 3 percent alcohol range.

There is often a beer versus spirits battle that ultimately affects beer styles. In most times and places, the government will tax beer at a lower rate to discourage the use of spirits. When the Belgian government banned the on-premise sale of gin in 1919, it inadvertently created a market for strong beer to fill the hole in the marketplace.

War affects beer in profound ways. It can create shortages of ingredients and equipment, and the resulting beer is not very good. This wouldn't be such a problem if people didn't get so damned used to it. It seems the affected beers never bounce back well from such catastrophes. And for the soldiers, war is such a transformative event; the beers they shared with their mates become a part of lifelong patterns. Canned beer was the beneficiary of such male bonding during World War II.

Brewers and governments sometimes work together when it comes to appellations. These are protected categories of products that limit how and by whom the beer may be brewed and labeled as a particular style. Trappist ales, for example, are not a style at all, but adhere to a set of rules governing what is a true monastic brewery and what is not, and thus, who is allowed to use the *Trappiste* designation (see chapter 12). Lambic has its own set of rules. In Germany, many styles have upper and lower limits on the gravity of the wort, and brewers of Oktoberfest beer must be located within the city limits of Munich. America is largely free of these types of rules, although a few lunatic states (Texas comes to mind) have some strange and outmoded laws regarding what a beer or ale must be.

Pressures of the Beer Business

CONTROLLING COSTS and being competitive in the market influence much of what happens on the brewhouse floor. American brewers first started using adjuncts to thin the body of the beer and dilute the protein to levels that could be manageable in packaged beer, but eventually they caught on that adjuncts such as corn and rice are cheaper than barley malt. American brewers after World War II went through an orgy of product cheapening as the inexpensive beer segment exploded. Today, the cheapest bargain beers contain up to half adjuncts, the maximum allowed by law.

Competitive pressures push brewers to seek out products with the largest possible audience. This means inoffensive, easy-to-drink products; sometimes in this process, more character-filled beers don't survive. It is thanks to a miracle of luck and the resourcefulness and tenacity of Fritz Maytag that steam beer survives today. Anchor Brewing was just one of dozens of old breweries teetering on the edge in the later part of the twentieth century, and it just happened that they had a historically unique product that the cycles of the market had pretty much left behind.

Long arcs of cultural attitudes also affect what we eat and drink. We are now enjoying the civilized benefits of a pendulum swing back to the pleasures of more specialized and authentic foods and drinks. For more than a century, this immigrant nation tried to find ways to become one people. Finding common language in mass-market, "modern" products was one way to do this: Campbell's Soup, Wonder Bread, American cheese. They're still on the shelves, but the bright, soulless rationality of these industrial icons no longer holds so much appeal. Many of us would rather have our bread unsliced, our cheese moldy, our coffee freshly roasted, and our beer dark and maybe just a little bit hazy. Irrationality can be a beautiful thing, and I hope we can keep pushing the pendulum for a long, long time.

A FEW NOTES ON THE FOLLOWING STYLES AND SUGGESTED BEERS

Once you start dividing the beer world into styles, there are decisions to be made. Large brewing competitions slice the style pie into very thin slivers to reduce the number of beers in a category to manageable size. Many styles that warrant separate categories in competitions are minor variants of each other that share common history, brewing ingredients, and more. In this book, I have treated certain styles — pale ale and bitter, for example — as a close-knit family rather than as a bunch of individual entities. My aim is to clearly describe the styles and to elucidate the relationships among them.

Styles themselves are moving targets, changing with market tastes and economic pressures. There is a tug-of-war between current and historical styles, with some beers like Oktoberfest rapidly morphing into something different, even as some small brewers dig up and re-brew historically inspired examples for the market. I have generally taken the conservative approach and cast a wide net, keeping the classic historical point of view in mind when defining styles and setting parameters.

I have chosen a mix of European classics and American craft-brewed beers as examples, the latter almost always being a little more in-your-face than their European inspirations. I've tried to pick beers that are widely available, and from different regions. Smaller, local craft breweries and brewpubs often make dazzling examples of many styles, so please take the time to seek them out.

I've picked these beers to illustrate specific aspects of beer styles. There are many terrific beers that bend the rules a little. And, never forget that there are a huge number of excellent beers that have nothing to do with any particular style. Sometimes these can be the most fun of all.

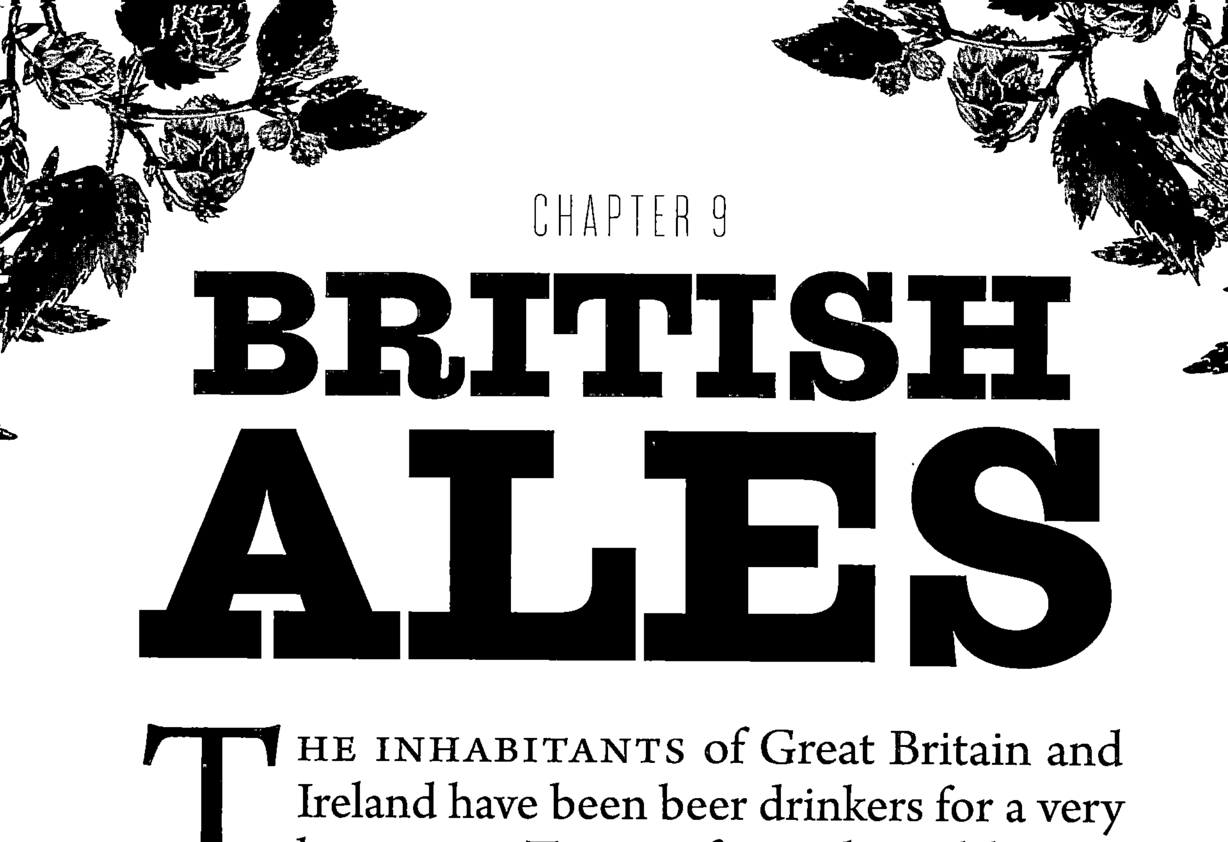

CHAPTER 9

BRITISH ALES

THE INHABITANTS of Great Britain and Ireland have been beer drinkers for a very long time. Traces of cereals and honey, a common ancient mixture, have been found in Scotland on potsherds dating to about 3000 BCE. Elsewhere in Scotland, there is more evidence that the original Pict inhabitants enjoyed beer spiked with such things as heather, meadowsweet, sweet gale (a.k.a. bog myrtle), cranberries, and a dangerous psychotropic herb called henbane. Scholars believe it is entirely possible that these brewing traditions originated in place and may not have been transferred from regions to the east.

They talk about their foreign wines — Champagne and bright Moselle —
And think because they're from abroad, that we must like them well,
And of their wholesome qualities they tell a wondrous tale;
But sour or sweet, they cannot beat a glass of old English Ale.
D'ye think my eye would be as bright, my heart as light and gay,
If I and "old John Barleycorn" did not shake hands each day?
No, no; and though teetotalers at malt and hops may rail,
At them I'll laugh and gaily quaff of old English ale.

— J. Caxton, from the song "A Glass of Old English Ale"

IN ADVANCE OF THE ROMANS, there was no great Celtic invasion, as is often suggested. But over time the Gallic tribes later identified as the Celts did seep into Britain, and with them came a long-established beer tradition. The Greeks and Romans had plenty of encounters with the Celts in the east, as well as in France and Italy. Classical writers record their fondness for drinking and their shockingly indiscriminate beverage choices, befitting the "barbarian" moniker. Imported Italian wine was a luxury product. Beer made of wheat and frequently boosted with honey, usually called "cerevesia," was considered the premium stuff, likely because of its greater strength. A barley beer called "korma" or "curmi" was the brew of the masses. Pliny the Elder said the Gauls had "many types" of beer made "in many ways," but we are left to our own imaginations to try to determine what he meant.

Starting in 55 BCE, Julius Caesar introduced Roman culture onto this already complex scene. He notes that in Kent (Cantium) people lived as the Gauls did, but farther north was a culture less familiar to him and much more beer-oriented. Beer was immensely popular among troops hired to protect the Roman frontier, as these were not Italian but Germanic auxiliaries. These troops may have actually helped bolster Britain's beer-drinking proclivities in the face of the Roman wine culture to which other barbarian tribes largely succumbed.

There is a large amount of documentary and archaeological evidence for beer and brewing in Roman Britain. As always, details about the beer are scant, but it is known that barley, wheat, and spelt (a kind of grain intermediate between the two) were used, and that dedicated malting and kilning facilities existed.

Ireland was never conquered by the Romans and maintained its native brewing traditions, melding them with early Christianity as they moved into the monastic age. St. Brigid, in particular, had some fantastic powers, turning water into beer for the benefit of the ill and multiplying beer for an Easter celebration at a time when grain was short.

Beer in the Dark Ages

The Romans finally left the British Isles in the fifth century. At that time, there was a lot of raiding into England by the Picts from Scotland and the Scots, who were the original inhabitants of Ireland. After appealing to Rome for help and receiving none, Briton leaders turned to Anglo-Saxon mercenaries, who eventually decided they liked the place just fine and stayed, against the wishes of their hosts. King Arthur's mythic success at Badon Hill was a rare victory in an ultimately unsuccessful effort to drive them out.

With the Anglo-Saxons came yet another wave of beer drinkers, as well as a tradition of communal drinking in mead halls. The saga *Beowulf* mentions four types of beverage: *win* and *medo,* clearly wine and mead; *beor,* which despite its seeming similarity to the word *beer* probably refers to another honey beverage; and *ealu,* which is the early form of the present English word *ale* and indicated a beverage made from grain.

Documents in the early Middle Ages mention "clear ale," "Welsh ale," which was sweet and may have included honey, "double-brewed ale," and "mild ale," the meaning of which is unclear in context; but later on, the term "mild" referred to a beer that was relatively fresh and had not undergone an extended aging period.

Hops show up in English herbariums in connection with drink as early as the ninth or tenth century. Hops, of course, don't become widespread in English brewing until about 1500, but by the fourteenth century, there was a distinction being drawn between unhopped ale and hopped beer. By the early fifteenth century hopped beer had established a significant beachhead in Kent and elsewhere in southeast England.

By the tenth century, taverns start to become an important locus of Anglo-Saxon beer culture. Outside of the monasteries, beer production was a domestic activity, primarily performed by women; this would remain so for several hundred years, until brewing increased in scale and prestige enough to become thoroughly commercialized and mainly an affair of men. The early women brewers were called brewsters or alewives. Brewing at home was a legitimate way to bring in a little extra money and was especially helpful for women who were widowed or otherwise in difficult circumstances. Just as in ancient Sumeria, where women were also the brewers and tavern-keepers, alewives with beer available for sale would hang a broom or a small bush — an ale-stake — above the door. The practice may have its roots in the use of twisted or braided twigs to entrap yeast and preserve it between batches.

Her ale, if new, looks like a misty morning, all thick; well, if her ale be strong, her fire good, her face fair, and the town great or rich, she shall seldom sit without chirping birds to bear her company, and at the next churching or christening, she is sure to be rid of two or three dozen cakes and ale by gossiping neighbors.

— Donald Lupton, *London and the Country Carbonadoed,* 1632

Even in late medieval times, recipes show the use of some proportion of wheat. There were also oat beers that were made cheaply and sold to a poor class of clientele called "grouters," after the grain and spice mix that was used to season it. Such beers are actually related to the great family of white beers that spread along the North Sea coast of Europe and had their last refuge in late nineteenth-century Devon and Cornwall.

Seeth grains in more water, while graines be yet hot,
And stirre them in copper as poredge in pot,
Such heating with straw, to make offal good store,
Both pleseth and easeth, what would you have more?

— Thomas Tusser, "Pointes of Good Huswiferie," 1557

For centuries, possibly as far back as the Norman Conquest, the English have had some form of price control on their ale. A legal device known as the Assize of Bread and Ale fixed the price for specific measures of beer based on the prevailing price of malt; it also specified how much malt was to be used for single and double beer and, therefore, how strong each type of beer could be. The assize was retooled to increase revenue several times, but it stood in place until 1643, when it was replaced with a stepped system that greatly increased the tax on strong, expensive beers and was a forerunner of the current excise system.

For nearly a thousand years in England, beer has been sold only in measures certified by royal gaugers. The old documents are full of violators being put to the pillory or ducking stool for tampering with the measures, selling in uncertified measures, and other crimes. For Americans accustomed to buying beer by the glass, the seeming fixation on a full measure seems obsessive until you realize how deeply ingrained it is in the English culture.

Toward the Modern Era

THE SIXTEENTH AND SEVENTEENTH centuries saw the development of the roots of modern British beer styles. As is so often the case with a conquering army, the old unhopped ale didn't vanish outright, but was transformed, little by little, into a hopped beer. Even a small amount of hops gave the beer a good deal more stability, and when combined with a lot of alcohol, beers could be aged for a year or sometimes much longer.

During this time, country estates became larger and more efficiently run, and a brewery was always needed for smooth functioning of the enterprise, as beer was a specified part of wages for employees. Country estate or "house" breweries typically produced three strengths of beer: "small beer" of around 2 percent alcohol, to which everyone had nearly unlimited access; "table beer," which we would recognize as normal strength at between 5 and 6 percent; and "March" or "October" beers of 8 to 10 percent, named for the months in which they were brewed. It was a point of etiquette that there was no special grade of small beer for the family; everybody drank the same small beer. There were stronger beers as well. A "double beer" of 10 or more percent alcohol was sometimes brewed and laid down to mature for special occasions.

The domestic-scale recipe given by Elizabethan chronicler William Harrison (*The Description of England,* 1577) is a barley-malt beer with 5 or 6 percent each of wheat and oats, showing those grains still in use in mainstream beers of the time. Elsewhere called "headcorne," they were likely used to enhance the beer's head, a task to which wheat is still applied in English beers. This recipe also makes use of about three-quarters of a pound per barrel of hops, a reasonable quantity by modern standards. Harrison likely got the recipe from his wife — she was the brewer in the family.

BY THE TIME industrialization began, the strong amber beers of the countryside had the reputation of being superior to commercially brewed beers. Landowners didn't have the same economic pressure as common brewers and so could use more malt and hops and likely a better grade, too. Plus, they were homebrewers and could brew whatever pleased them. They paid less tax than public brewers, which gave them further advantage.

Another important feature of the era was the distinction between "mild" or "running" ales and aged "stale" beers, whose long residence in wooden barrels or tuns allowed them not only to ferment very thoroughly, but also, more importantly, to pick up earthy aromas and tangy, even acidic flavors from the microorganisms that lived in the wood. Such beers rightfully deserved the term "old" ales, as the aging really did impart unique flavors to them. This formerly universal practice with strong beers is now a rarity in Britain. It should be noted that Guinness still blends a small portion of this stale, aged beer into every stout it makes.

Even with the tremendous advances in technology and the breathtaking increases in the scale of industrialization, the eighteenth century was a challenging time for beer in England. Coffee and tea were replacing small beer for all but the poorest folk, and gin roared into popularity with such force as to upset the social fabric due to high levels of consumption. As with Prohibition in the United States, attempts to restrict alcohol led to rampant bootlegging and all the problems that come with pervasive criminality. Many brewers at that time began adding medicinal materials for added zip, such as *Cocculus indicus* (a bitter berry from Southeast Asia containing a potent, dangerous stimulant) and bitter bean (a bitter spice from the Philippines containing strychnine), which were toxic or narcotic. It wasn't until the early nineteenth century that this mess was cleaned up.

DESPITE, OR PERHAPS BECAUSE OF, this turmoil, brewing became concentrated in the hands of fewer but larger operations, and this consolidation continues to this day. London was at this time the undisputed brewing center of the kingdom. By 1701, London's 194 common brewers made twice as much beer between them (on average, about 5,000 barrels each) as the 574 common brewers elsewhere in the country; but it should be noted that public brewing was at that time concentrated in the south.

In late seventeenth-century London, a beer called "amber" or "twopenny" was the last remaining vestige of unhopped ale. It did have a modest charge of hops, but much less than the new, hoppy chestnut brown ales that would soon be called "porter."

The old books abound with paeans to the fine strong beers of the day, and although the nicknames were numerous, the plainer description tended to be "brown" or "nut-brown" ale. Despite the difficulties of the eighteenth century, this era exemplifies for many the classic period for beer in Jolly Old England. There has been a great deal of nostalgia for that time laced through British beer culture ever since.

The stronger beere is divided into two parts (viz.) mild and stale; the first may ease a man of drought, but the latter is like water cast into a Smith's forge, and breeds more heart-burnings, and as rust eates into Iron so overstale Beere gnawes aulet holes in the entrales, or else my skill failes, and what I have written of it is to be held as a Jest.

— **John Taylor, *The Water Poet*, c. 1630**

Hogarth, *Gin Lane* (left) and *Beer Street* (right)
The English social critic's view of the disastrous impact of the unlicensed production and sale of spirits in the eighteenth century. Beer has long been viewed as a beverage of moderation.

Then came porter. Like industrialization, porter's story will be told elsewhere (see page 161), but for now it is enough to say that this was a phenomenon unlike anything the beer world had ever seen. Cheap, potent, flavorful, and largely wholesome, porter suited the mood of the moment and spawned the whole family of black beers — including stout — that lives on to this day.

An Exporting Nation

EXPORTATION HAS PLAYED an important role in Britain's beer since the late fifteenth century. By that time British brewers had learned the art of hopped beer well enough to export it back to Holland, from whence it had originally come. As the empire grew, so did opportunities to sell all kinds of goods — including beer — around the world. And to the benefit of beer, cargo space on outbound ships was cheaper than inbound, and heavy items were often needed to place low in the hold to stabilize the ship. So, wherever there were Englishmen, there were casks and bottles of mellow old English beer. This was most famously the case in India, where there was a large contingent of soldiers, traders, and administrators. English beer was being shipped to them as early as the 1630s. At first it was just a trickle, then, as demand increased, a flood. Initially strong amber-colored or brownish ales were shipped, but when the porter phenomenon struck, stronger versions of that were sent as well.

THE REALLY FAMOUS PART of the export story starts in the middle of the eighteenth century, with pale and eventually India Pale Ale. In the early 1780s, a London brewer named Hodgson started exporting

The English beer is famous in the Netherlands and Lower Germany, which is made of barley and hops, for England yields plenty of hops, howsoever they also use Flemish hops. The cities of Lower Germany upon the seas forbid the public selling of English beer, to satisfy their own brewers, yet privately they swallow it like nectar. But in the Netherlands great and incredible quantity there is spent.

— Fynes Moryson, *Itinerary*, 1617

---

casks of an amber-colored, highly hopped October beer. This was a strong beer, designed for long keeping. It suited the six-month sea voyage and arrived in superb condition. There is no evidence that a special recipe for the India export market was developed at this time. After forty years of booming success his son, now running the brewery, got greedy and lost the good graces of the East India Company, the powerful monopoly that controlled trade in Britain's Asian exploits.

Meanwhile, the brewers up north in Burton-on-Trent had been renowned since the thirteenth century for strong ales made possible by a unique type of hard well water. A canal project had opened up a reliable route to the sea from Burton just a little before 1800, and brewers of Burton had vastly increased the amount of the sweet, dark beer they were shipping up the Baltic Sea all the way to Russia. The Russian connection collapsed due to the imposition of a high tariff in 1822, just as the kerfuffle over Hodgson left the Indian market wide open, and Burton's Allsopp brewery was quick to capitalize on this opportunity.

The paler, hoppy beer Hodgson had been selling was very different from the Burton beers of the day. These sweet, dark beers may have been as little as 50 percent attenuated, so some work was needed to develop a paler, crisper beer that would convincingly replace the London beer. The gypsum-laden water of Burton was actually better suited than London's to a pale, hoppy beer; the first recipe supposedly was worked out in a teacup.

THE NEW INDIA-BOUND Burton pale ales were hopped more highly than those destined for domestic use, following the general rule of increasing hops for beers that are meant to keep longer. There is a famous story in the Bass marketing literature that barrels of India Pale Ale were recovered from a foundered ship bound for India, and the salvaged beer found wild popularity with the English drinking public. Although there are some historical problems with this tale, it's certain that at some point the public did catch on to this India ale, and the paler and crisper beer was received with great acclaim. Like porter before it, the new beer spread like wildfire and by the middle of the nineteenth century, pale and India Pale Ales had replaced porter as the fashionable beer in England.

British beers of the mid-nineteenth century were pretty strong by later standards. George Amsinck's very detailed brewing notes give gravities in 1868 that range from 5 percent alcohol by volume for a single stout, mild, or running ale to a massive 13.8 percent "London Ale," with many beers in the 5.5 to 7 percent range, far higher than today's English brews. Amsinck, as an intimate of the brewing industry, saw where beer was going and didn't like it. He was a vocal critic of British brewers and wrote in *Practical Brewings* (1868) that the brewers instituted "a system of low class brewing, shilling Ales and upwards at any price, allowing enormous discounts . . . these expenses must have been, in a vast number of instances, unproductive of any profit."

The Roots of Modern Styles

In 1880, THE MALT TAX was abolished and replaced by a system that taxed beer based on the original gravity of the wort, which roughly corresponds to alcohol content. This graduated system stands to this day and had the effect of applying pressure to brew weaker and weaker beer, a trend that accelerated for the next half century.

In late Victorian England, most styles of beer came in a number of different intensities. The strength of both pale and dark beers was indicated by one or more Xs, topping out at "XXXX." The term *bitter* as a beer style designation shows up as a consumer slang for the new pale ales and IPAs at mid-century. In the south especially, the "K" designation was used to identify a range of pale, dry, and somewhat less-bitter beers than proper pale ale. Like the X beers, these formed a range, starting at about 1.045 OG (11 degrees Plato) for single-K (also known as AK) beers, up to about 1.090 OG (24 degrees Plato) for "KKKK." Over time, the once-separate threads of pale ale, bitter, and K-style beers have become hopelessly entangled due to a century and a half of common parlance, regional differences, overeager marketers, and the normal drift of any cultural product. By late in the nineteenth century, porter was on its last legs. The really dark end of the beer spectrum was now occupied by its descendant, stout, proudly brewed with plenty of black patent malt (or black roasted barley in Ireland), with no apologies for abandoning the old ways of brown malt and yearlong fermentations. What edged in to take porter's place was called "mild." The term is a very old one, referring to beer that has not undergone a

OLD ENGLISH NAMES FOR STRONG BEER

Stingo
Huffcap
Nipitatum
Clamber-skull
Dragon's milk
Mad-dog
Lift-leg
Angel's food
Stride-wide

"Pillar" Ale Glasses
These crystal glasses were popular, as they showed off the luminous optical effects of the new paler style of beer in the midnineteenth century.

souring due to long storage in wooden vessels and is sold relatively fresh from the brewery. But in the late nineteenth century, mild was a beer brewed from a malt slightly darker than pale ale malt, with a dash of black malt for color, and thinned out with sugar added to the kettle. In London, they were usually colored a ruby brown, but elsewhere there were pale milds. All were lightly hopped compared to the pale ales of the day. Like most beers, mild came in a variety of strengths, but it topped out at about 1070 OG (17 degrees Plato) in 1871 and dropped over the next century.

THE GREAT WAR was hard on English beer. All the usual shortages, rationing, and pressure for war production meant that beer gravity fell and pub hours shortened, while prices increased, ratcheting ever tighter as the war progressed. By 1918, the government required that half of all beer be no stronger than 1.030, which meant an alcohol content of less than 3 percent. Breweries, beers, and tax levels never returned to their prewar conditions. On top of it all, beer was starting to be seen as an old-fashioned drink, lacking the modern sparkle of cocktails and classiness of wine. All the stress just added to the pressures for consolidation and as a result, many breweries closed.

Late in the 1930s there was an increase in beer consumption, but war was again on the horizon in Europe. The Second World War had similar effects as the first: Thinner beer at higher prices, and this time it was personal. German bombs were destroying pubs and breweries. When the war was over, there was an immense amount of recovery to be done, limiting brewing progress for more than a decade. By 1950, there were one-third fewer breweries in England than there had been in the year 1940.

All of the classic styles were pretty much in place by 1900, and while they have ebbed and flowed for the past century, it's not likely that the twentieth century added much to any of them. Quite the opposite. English beers are weaker, less bitter, more adjunct filled, and less varied than they were in 1900. There's plenty of blame to go around, but these effects are a result of much larger social forces that have played out similarly in many other countries.

Real Ale, Rescued

RESPECT FOR BEER and its long, colorful past had became so compromised that by the 1960s, England's traditional living drink, real ale, was about to be replaced by inert keg beer delivered by tanker truck and squirted into large serving tanks in pub cellars. Real ale is discussed in detail in chapter 6, but essentially the beer is still fermenting when it hits the pub, and the small amount of continued fermentation carbonates the beer right there before the yeast settles out. This means the cask has not been pasteurized or filtered, and this lack of processing results in a more complex and subtle beer. Scientifically, the jury seems to be out on the specific benefits of natural carbonation per se, but because it comes along with the natural process, that makes it a good thing.

An organization called the Campaign for Real Ale (CAMRA) formed in 1972 to actively lobby in support of cask ale tradition. It's easy to see why the forces of modern business are against real ale. It's fusty, complex, and inefficient. Casks are inconsistent and require a subtle skill to handle in order to get a great beer into the glass. The shelf life is limited, too. After a few days, the beer is too flat and lifeless — perhaps too sour as well — to sell. But it's also easy to see why it is so prized by those who take the time to open themselves to its charms. Subtle and silky, a great real ale has a sense of life about it and a depth that makes for pint after fascinating pint. There's nothing else like it on planet beer.

CAMRA did manage to stop the annihilation of real ale, but as for gassy keg beers, there are plenty of those out there these days. Lager is big business in Britain, and it's growing. Real ale has been saved, but it is now a specialty beer no longer resembling anything mainstream, and my guess is that it never again will. That's not all bad. As long as there is a viable marketplace of people who know the difference and are willing to make the effort to get it, there is money to be made, and real ale will survive.

The Taste of Ale

ALL OF THE STYLES described here are fermented with top-fermenting strains of yeast that have long been associated with English, Scottish, or Irish ales. Because they are fermented between room and cellar temperatures, they tend to display a good deal fruitier and spicier personality than lagers. The strains vary widely but tend to be less ebullient than their Belgian cousins. A lot of the magic of British yeast lies in its ability to magnify and augment the flavors of the malt, hops, and other ingredients in the brew. Some accentuate a creamy maltiness, while others emphasize the woodiness of certain malts or the crisp, green best of hops.

Between about 1700 and 1847, British ale was by law an all-malt product. After that time, the use of sugar or other adjuncts was allowed, and British brewers have been using them ever since. Adjuncts may be good or bad. In small amounts, grains like wheat or oats add luscious, creamy texture and improve head retention. Sugar or grits of corn or rice thin out the body and make for a lighter, less filling (i.e., more drinkable) beer. This may or may not be a good thing, but because most adjuncts are cheaper than barley malt, there is always the temptation on the part of the guys in finance to add more than the brewmaster thinks is necessary for a great beer. It's certainly something to pay attention to when you taste an English ale.

The malt itself leans toward the crisp and brisk with hints of toast, even in the pale beers. Generally the kind of creamy caramelness so often found in German dark lagers is not a big player here. An exception is the category of strong Scottish ales, in which those lush malt flavors are the star attraction.

All members of the pale ale family prominently feature hops. English hops have a family resemblance in the form of a rich, green spiciness. In reality, English brewers use a good deal of imported hops, but they avoid using them in a way that would overstep the bounds of tradition in terms of the aroma; in other words, no overtly American hop varieties such as Cascade. In the past, darker beers like porter and stout were plenty hoppy, but not so much these days. Of all these dark beers, only the Irish stouts retain anything like their original bitterness.

In the United States, we seldom get English ales served properly. There are rare specialty casks that make it across the ocean, and many survive the crossing with some life in them. The draft kegs of Bass and other big sellers are generally too gassy and served too cold. If you have control over it, 50 to 55°F (10 to 13°C) is about right. Take your fork and whip your beer around briskly to get rid of some of the gas and you will be starting to get close. Your best bet might be to search out an American craft brewery that makes the traditional styles in the classic manner and buy one of those on cask.

Ale must have these properties: it must be fresshe and cleare, it must not be ropy nor smoky, nor it must have no werte nor tayle.

— Andrew Boorde, *A Compendious Regiment or a Dyetary of Helth*, 1542

Pale Ale and Bitter

As NOTED EARLIER, these constitute a mingled family of closely related ales with a somewhat confusing nomenclature. The "pale ale" name is more typically applied to bottled beer representing the strong end of the range, but there are plenty of draft versions. "Bitter" may encompass all strengths, and while the term usually refers to draft beer, packaged versions exist. The designations "Ordinary," "Best or Special," and "Extra Special Bitter" (ESB) are applied to beers of increasing strength, although this is by no means universal, and many breweries offer just two, not three.

The family of top-fermenting beers reached their present form largely after World War I, although there has been some drift since then. In terms of flavor, these beers are built on a base of a lightly kilned malt called "pale ale" that brings a nutty quality and often just a hint of a toasty edge. For the most part, these are adjunct beers, which gives them a crisp, drinkable quality. It's not coincidence that the style name is "bitter." Hops are always a key player, sometimes dramatically so. English-style hops are mandatory, at least as far as aroma goes.

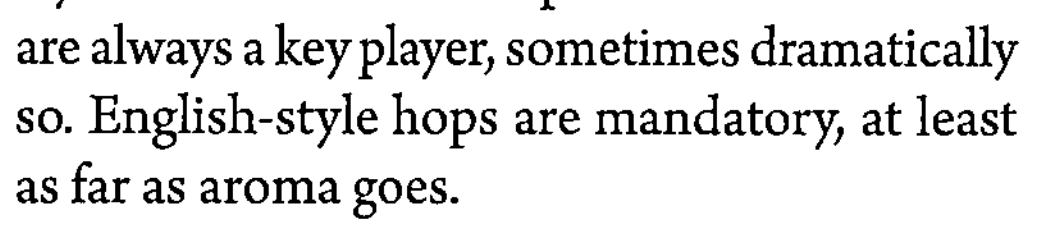

Classic Bitter

ORIGIN: Developed 1850–1950 as draft pale ale, this grew lighter in gravity and body over time. It comes in a range of imprecise substyles, as noted earlier. Usually these are brewed with adjuncts in addition to the malt to lighten the body and improve drinkability. By far it is best when served from the cask as real ale. Despite their low gravity and adjunct recipes, the best of these beers can be seductively complex and appealing.

LOCATION: Britain, especially England; credible traditional versions also made by a few U.S. and Canadian craft brewers

FLAVOR: fresh hops plus nutty maltiness, crisp finish

AROMA: hops first, plus nutty/woody malt; spice and fruit also evident

BALANCE: hop or malt balanced; bitter finish

SEASONALITY: year-round

PAIR WITH: wide range of food; roast chicken or pork; classic with curry

SUGGESTED BEERS TO TRY: This style really is a different beer served as a real ale. See if you can locate one at a specialty bar or local brewpub. Coniston Bluebird Bitter, Ridgeway Ivanhoe, Harviestoun Bitter & Twisted, Royal Oak, Anchor Small Beer, Goose Island Honker's Ale, Deschutes Bachelor ESB.

GRAVITY: Ordinary: 1.033-8 (8-9°P); Best/Special: 1.038-40 (9-10°P); ESB: 1.046-60 (10-15°P)

ALCOHOL: Ordinary: 2.4-3%; Best/Special: 3.3-3.8%; ESB: 4.8-5.8%

ATTENUATION/BODY: very dry to medium

COLOR: 8-14°SRM, light-dark amber

BITTERNESS: 25-55 IBU, medium to high

I've tasted hock and claret too, Madeira and Moselle,
But not one of those boshy wines reveal this languid swell;
Of all complaints from A to Z, the fact is very clear,
There's no disease but what's been cured by glorious bitter beer

— MacLaghlan

Classic English Pale Ale

As noted, it's just about impossible to completely differentiate pale ale from the bitter family, but since the contests all do it, we will, too.

On the whole pale ale is a more substantial beer than bitter, but there is *much* overlap. You are more likely to find an all-malt version of a pale ale than a bitter. American brewers love this style and have made it their own. Many American craft-brew examples would fit right in over in England, but others are unquestionably American. For the most part, American versions are stronger and almost always all malt, but the real difference hinges on the hops. Proper English pale ales always display English hop character.

ORIGIN: Descended from amber-colored "October" beers brewed in the English countryside, it was adopted in London well before 1800. A little later this style became strongly associated with the northern city Burton-on-Trent, and eventually all of England, being more or less the national beer. It experienced tremendous downward changes in gravities between 1870 and 1920.

LOCATION: England; credible versions made in the United States and elsewhere

FLAVOR: crisp (it's the water), nutty malt, spicy hops

AROMA: clean malt plus a good dose of spicy/herbal English hops

BALANCE: even or dry/bitter; clean finish

SEASONALITY: year-round

PAIR WITH: wide range of food; meat pies, English cheese

SUGGESTED BEERS TO TRY: As with the bitter range, try to find this on cask, or properly bottle-conditioned. O'Hanlon's Royal Oak, Whitbread Pale Ale, Firestone Walker Double-Barreled Pale Ale, Odell 5 Barrel Pale Ale.

GRAVITY: 1.044–1.056 (11–14°P)

ALCOHOL: 3.8–6.2% by volume

ATTENUATION/BODY: crisp, dry

COLOR: 5–14°SRM, gold to amber

BITTERNESS: 20–50 IBU, medium-high

India Pale Ale

Very much a part of the broader pale ale family, and in fact the styles may overlap a little. In any given brewer's portfolio, the IPA is just about guaranteed to be just a little paler, stronger, and more bitter than their pale, which is in keeping with the history of the style. They can be tricky to recognize; one brewer's pale is another's IPA. And as with pale ale, Americans make much lustier versions that call on the racy, piney, grapefruity aromas of American hops.

ORIGIN: True India Pale Ale evolved from October ales shipped to India by a London brewer, George Hodgson, around 1780. By 1830, Hodgson was out on his ear and Burton-on-Trent brewers had developed a crisper, drier version that became the standard for the style.

LOCATION: England, U.S. craft breweries

FLAVOR: plenty of malt, but dominated by hops; should be some sense of balance even in the bitterest examples

AROMA: spicy English hops in the foreground, plus a nice backup of nutty malt

BALANCE: always hoppy, but to varying degrees

SEASONALITY: year-round

PAIR WITH: strong, spicy food; bold, sweet desserts like carrot cake

SUGGESTED BEERS TO TRY: Burton Bridge Empire IPA, Meantime India Pale Ale, Goose Island India Pale Ale, Summit India Pale Ale, Wild Goose India Pale Ale.

GRAVITY: 1.050–1.070 (12–17°P)

ALCOHOL: 4.5–7.5% by volume

ATTENUATION/BODY: crisp, dry, but may have hints of malty richness

COLOR: 6–14°SRM, gold to amber

BITTERNESS: 40–60 IBU, high

Historical Style

Burton Ale

This darker cousin to IPA was what the Burton brewers were cooking up before the huge phenomenon of India Pale Ale hit them. These were rich, deep-amber, even brown-colored beers with a lot of residual sweetness and often very high original gravities. They were eagerly consumed all the way up to Russia, which was Burton's original export market. Although this style is largely under the radar, a few versions are brewed commercially, and it deserves to be better known. Confusingly, "Burton Ale" was a trade term later applied to pale or India Pale Ales.

English Golden or Summer Ale

It's great to see some new ideas coming out of British brewers after a long, dry century.

ORIGIN: A recent development from smaller UK breweries, this style is basically a lightened-up IPA designed to help fight the tide of lagers in the form of a crisp and quenching beer.

LOCATION: England; also U.S. craft breweries

FLAVOR: bright, clean pale malt; firm hoppy finish

AROMA: clean malt plus spicy hops

BALANCE: even to reasonably hoppy

SEASONALITY: summer

PAIR WITH: a wide range of food; chicken, seafood, spicy cuisine

SUGGESTED BEERS TO TRY: Hopback Summer Lightning, Wychwood Scarecrow Golden Pale Ale, Tomos Watkin's *Cwrw Hâf* ("Summer Ale" in Welsh).

GRAVITY: 1.036–1.048 (9–12°P)

ALCOHOL: 3.6–5% by volume

ATTENUATION/BODY: dry, crisp

COLOR: 4–8°SRM, pale gold-amber

BITTERNESS: 20–28 IBU, medium

Scottish Ales

The beers of Scotland are closely related to their English cousins. Although there are some differences, they all come from the same broad tradition, and as industrialization progressed, the beers became even more similar.

Our standard picture of Scottish ale is of sweetish, lightly hopped, ruby-colored brews, and there are certainly examples that support this. But Scottish beers of today show a lot of variety, and more than a century ago Edinburgh was famous for its dry, minerally pale ales, built on a water similar to Burton's.

Because the climate is cooler up north, Scottish beers are usually fermented at cooler temperatures than English ones. This means Scottish ales display less of the fruit and spice of English ales, which pushes the malt character more into the foreground. Hops were grown in Scotland, but it really is pretty far north for them, and there is currently no commercial production there. Whether it's a matter of the Scots not wanting to give the English their money or some less-charming reason, Scottish ales in general are lightly hopped.

As we're still in the British Isles, the nomenclature is going to be confusing. Scottish beer comes in several strengths historically designated in shillings (60/-, 70/-, and 80/-), which at some vague point in history was the actual price of a barrel of the stuff. This terminology is now falling into disuse. The three price ranges correspond to light, heavy, and export. These designations roughly correspond to the three prices or strength levels of English bitter. At higher alcohol levels is a beer simply called Scotch ale, but this is also known as a "Wee Heavy," or by its shilling designation, 120/- ale. Sheesh.

Medieval Scottish ales must have reeked of smoke from the peat used as fuel to dry the malt. According to the old brewing books, brewers around 1700 clearly enjoyed the clean flavors of malt dried in the newer coal- or coke-fired indirect kilns. They viewed smoke-free beer as real progress, and it stayed that way for close to three hundred years. But recently, as craft-oriented brewers started reevaluating their roots, it seemed completely logical to reintroduce small amounts of peated malt back into Scottish beer, and they did just that. It should be noted that some of the water available to breweries runs through peat and picks up a certain amount of peaty tinge that may find its way into the beers.

Scottish Light Ale (60/-)

ORIGIN: low end of Scottish draft beer range, similar history to English bitter

LOCATION: Scotland

FLAVOR: dry maltiness, with hints of caramel and toast

AROMA: clean maltiness, no evident hop aroma; hints of peat okay

BALANCE: fat and malty, may be a little toasty

SEASONALITY: year-round

PAIR WITH: lighter food; simple cheeses, lighter preparations of salmon and chicken

NOTE: Generally unavailable in the United States. Check your local brewpub.

GRAVITY: 1.030–1.035 (8–9°P)

ALCOHOL: 2.5–3.2% by volume

ATTENUATION/BODY: light and dry

COLOR: 10–25°SRM, amber to ruby brown

BITTERNESS: 25–35 IBU, low

Scottish Heavy (70/-)

ORIGIN: middle of range of Scottish draft beers, similar history to English bitter

LOCATION: Scotland

FLAVOR: soft maltiness, with hints of caramel and toast

AROMA: clean maltiness, no evident hop aroma; hints of peat okay

BALANCE: creamy maltiness balanced by barest hints of hops and a slight roastiness

SEASONALITY: year-round

PAIR WITH: lighter food; simple cheeses, lighter preparations of salmon and chicken

SUGGESTED BEERS TO TRY: Caledonian Amber Ale; other examples are rarely available in the United States. Check your local brewpub.

GRAVITY: 1.035–1.040 (9–10°P)

ALCOHOL: 3.2–4.0% by volume

ATTENUATION/BODY: medium to very light

COLOR: 9–19°SRM, amber to brown

BITTERNESS: 12–20 IBU, low

Scottish Export (80/-)

ORIGIN: top of range of Scottish draft beers, similar history to English bitter

LOCATION: Scotland

FLAVOR: rich toffee/toasty malt flavors despite relatively light body; yeast character subdued; hints of peat okay

AROMA: complex malt; nuances of cocoa; not a lot of evidence of hops

BALANCE: definitely malty, but balanced by toasty elements and a kiss of hops

SEASONALITY: year-round

PAIR WITH: lighter food; moderately intense cheeses, lighter preparations of salmon and pork

SUGGESTED BEERS TO TRY: Belhaven Scottish Ale, McEwan's Export, Odell's 90 Shilling, Samuel Adams Scotch Ale, Three Floyds Robert the Bruce

GRAVITY: 1.040–1.052 (10–12.9°P)

ALCOHOL: 4.0–5.2% by volume

ATTENUATION/BODY: moderately light to slightly full

COLOR: 10–19°SRM, amber to brown

BITTERNESS: 15–30 IBU, low

Scotch Ale/ Wee Heavy

ORIGIN: evolved slowly as top of range of Scottish ale family, perhaps influenced by Burton Ale; a dark barley wine, really

LOCATION: Scotland, U.S. craft breweries

FLAVOR: rich, toffeelike malt flavors go on and on; yeast character subdued; a little portlike

AROMA: huge complex malt, a mix of toffee and soft roastiness; little else, but sometimes a hint of peat

BALANCE: fat and malty, may be a little toasty

SEASONALITY: year-round

PAIR WITH: sticky pudding and other substantial desserts

SUGGESTED BEERS TO TRY: Traquair House Scottish Style Ale, Brasserie de Silly Scotch Silly, AleSmith Wee Heavy, Founders Dirty Bastard.

GRAVITY: 1.072–1.085 (17–20°P)

ALCOHOL: 6.2–8% by volume

ATTENUATION/BODY: full and sweet

COLOR: 10–25°SRM, amber to ruby brown

BITTERNESS: 25–35 IBU, low

English Brown Ale

THE BEGINNINGS OF BROWN ALE are lost in the mists of time. People have been brewing brown beers since the earliest days, but we pick up the story in about 1700, when the descendant of the old unhopped English ale, the amber or twopenny beer, was kicking around London. At the time there were other, more bitter brown beers on the scene, and these became porter. Despite the huge success of porter, lightly hopped dark beers managed to survive alongside their more popular cousins for quite some time. The terms *brown* and *nut brown* had been loosely applied to beer for centuries, but it appears that the word didn't become anything like a style description or a trade term until the end of the nineteenth century.

Brown ale has never been the most popular beer, but there always seem to be customers for a beer that is a little toastier and less hoppy than pale ale. The style is split between the north and south of England. Northern browns are paler and a bit stronger than southern ones, and there is subtle variation from place to place. While some make a case for a southern form of brown ale, at this point it is pretty much indistinguishable from mild ale, and competitions such as the World Beer Cup consider them one and the same.

Let misers turn their riches o'er,
And gaze on bags of gold;
With my wealth they must be poor
When all their treasure's told;
But I have more
True wealth in store,
And joys that never fail
Whilst friendship's shrine
My cot is mine,
And a glass of rich brown ale.

— John Hammond, "A Glass of Rich Brown Ale"

Northern English Brown Ale

LOCATION: northern England, especially Yorkshire, and some U.S. craft breweries

FLAVOR: toasty, nutty, with some caramelly malt; light hopping

AROMA: complex and malty, may be hints of roast, no hop aroma

BALANCE: crisp to very slightly sweet; clean finish

SEASONALITY: year-round

PAIR WITH: roasted meats and a wide range of hearty foods

SUGGESTED BEERS TO TRY: Samuel Smith's Nut Brown Ale, Goose Island Hex Nut Brown Ale

GRAVITY: 1.040–1.052 (10–13°P)

ALCOHOL: 4.2–5.2% by volume

ATTENUATION/BODY: dry to slightly sweet

COLOR: 12–22°SRM, medium to deep amber

BITTERNESS: 20–25 IBU, low to medium

Mild Ale

The original meaning of this name designated a beer that was sold relatively fresh and hadn't undergone long wood aging (see Old Ale, on page 60). By 1880 or so, the everyday ales of London were starting to resemble latter-day milds. Until about 1910, *mild* simply referred to any fresh, unaged beer and not to any particular color, strength, or style. By the time World War I was over, *mild* certainly referred to a low-gravity session beer. Mild was immensely popular in the middle of the twentieth century; by 1960 it represented 61 percent of the English beer market. Although there are rare examples of pale mild, the most enduring form of mild is a dark, ruby-colored beer, and today there are a range of strengths available. By 1980, mild made up just fourteen percent of the English market.

LOCATION: northern England, especially around Birmingham, and some U.S. craft breweries

FLAVOR: slightly roasty with some caramelly malt; light hopping

AROMA: complex and lightly roasty/malty, may be hints of roast, no hop aroma

BALANCE: malty, but with hints of roast and a crisp finish

SEASONALITY: year-round

PAIR WITH: roasted meats and a wide range of hearty foods

SUGGESTED BEERS TO TRY: Orkney Brewery Dark Island, Broughton Black Douglas, Wychwood Hobgoblin Dark English Ale, Goose Island PMD

GRAVITY: 1.040–1.052 (10–13°P)

ALCOHOL: 4.2–5.2% by volume

ATTENUATION/BODY: dry to slightly sweet

COLOR: 12–22°SRM, medium to deep amber

BITTERNESS: 20–25 IBU, low to medium

English Old/ Strong Ale

This term has two meanings. The "old" properly refers to a beer that has been aged in wooden vessels for a year or so, during which time it picks up a piquant acidity and a rich set of aromatics. Beers treated in this manner were called "stale" and were usually blended with fresher beers when sold. There are few beers made this way in England these days, but the style lives on in Flanders (see chapter 12), and Guinness still does this, although the blending component is fairly small.

The other meaning is just as a catchall for anything strong in any shade of amber or brown. Other aspects of the beer, such as hopping, may vary widely, and many breweries' products along these lines don't bear the "strong" or "old" descriptor. It's just barely a style.

ORIGIN: ancient holdover from the days when all strong beers were aged in wood for up to a year

LOCATION: England, U.S. craft breweries

FLAVOR: fat and fruity caramel, a touch of hops; properly "stale" versions have a definite touch of acidity

AROMA: fruity, raisiny malt, and possibly some toasty/ roasty elements; may have some wild yeast character

BALANCE: usually on the sweet side, but may be evenly balanced

SEASONALITY: year-round, but really great in cold weather

PAIR WITH: big, intense dishes such as roast beef and lamb; stands up to rich desserts

SUGGESTED BEERS TO TRY: Gale's Prize Old Ale, Greene King Olde Suffolk Ale, North Coast Old Stock Ale, Pyramid Snow Cap Ale

GRAVITY: 1.060-1.090 (15-22°P)

ALCOHOL: 5-9.5% by volume

ATTENUATION/BODY: medium to full

COLOR: 12-30°SRM, amber to deep brown

BITTERNESS: 30-65 plus IBU, medium to high

English Barley Wine

ORIGIN: Another old one, it is descended from strong "October" ales brewed on country estates. The term was first applied by Bass in 1903 to its No. 1 strong ale. There is much variety within the category.

LOCATION: England, U.S. craft breweries

FLAVOR: loads of complex malt backed up by hops

AROMA: rich, fruity malt and spicy hops

BALANCE: malty or hoppy

SEASONALITY: year-round; best in winter

PAIR WITH: very intense food, but better with dessert; try with Stilton cheese

SUGGESTED BEERS TO TRY: O'Hanlon's Thomas Hardy's Ale, J. W. Lee's Harvest Ale, Anchor Old Foghorn, Lakefront Brewery Beer Line Barley Wine Style Ale

GRAVITY: 1.085-1.120 (20-29°P)

ALCOHOL: 6.8-10% by volume

ATTENUATION/BODY: medium to full

COLOR: 10-22°SRM, amber to brown

BITTERNESS: 40-60 IBU, medium to high

Porter

Think you know what a porter is? Me neither.

Studying the history of porter is like staring into the multidimensional universe of theoretical cosmology, with multiple shifting parallel worlds constantly warping and shifting with the flow of time. The more you try to pin it down, the more it wriggles free and becomes something unexpectedly different. Naturally, this makes for much fun.

Far from being invented (despite the tales about Ralph Harwood and the Bell Brewery in Shoreditch), porter emerged over a generation or more, transforming itself from an assemblage of brown ales into a pedigreed family of chestnut-colored brews that eventually came to be named for the transport workers who were its most visible enthusiasts. There never was a single thing called "porter." By the time the name came to be applied to it, there were many variations in both name and interpretation.

Porter has changed every generation during its nearly three-century history. At first it was a beer made largely from a moderately kilned "brown" malt, which gave it a rich toastiness and full body. When brewers working with a hydrometer discovered how inefficient this was, they switched over to the more extract-rich pale malt, in about 1780. This left them with a problem of how to achieve the former dark brown color, and various preparations of burnt sugar, though largely illegal, were employed. This dramatically changed the taste of the beer.

Brewer and author William Tizard, in 1843, stated: "Scarcely does this our beer-sipping country contain any two brewers, particularly neighbors, whose productions are alike in flavour and quality, and especially in the article porter; even in London, a practised connoisseur can truly discover, without hesitation and by mere taste, the characteristic flavour that distinguishes the management of each of the principal or neighbouring breweries. . . ."

In 1817 a man named Daniel Wheeler invented a roasting kiln for making black malt, which solved the coloring problem, but changed porter once again. Throughout the nineteenth century, stout flourished at the expense of plain old porter, and the gravity, bitterness, and color were largely stripped out of it. By World War I it was barely breathing.

Both the Beer Judge Certification Program (BJCP) and the World Beer Cup style guidelines divide porter into two separate subcategories, "robust" and "mild." I find this a little arbitrary, especially since porter was officially dead in its homeland when Guinness ceased production of its porter in 1974. There doesn't seem to be a clear historical or trade-term logic to these two types of porter. In reality, porters represent a fairly wide range of dark brown beers without any well-defined substyles. Some even encroach on stout territory.

ORIGIN: London, about 1700. Porter is considered the first industrialized beer; stronger versions are called "stout."

LOCATION: England, U.S. craft breweries

FLAVOR: creamy roasty-toasty malt, hoppy or not

AROMA: roasty maltiness; usually little or no hop aroma

BALANCE: malt, hops, roast in various proportions

SEASONALITY: year-round, great in cooler weather

PAIR WITH: roasted and smoked food; barbecue, sausages, chocolate chip cookies

SUGGESTED BEERS TO TRY: Samuel Smith's Taddy Porter, Flag Porter, Deschutes Black Butte Porter, Great Lakes Edmund Fitzgerald Porter

GRAVITY: 1.040–1.065 (10–16°P)

ALCOHOL: 4.0–6.5% by volume

ATTENUATION/BODY: medium

COLOR: 20–50°SRM, brown to black

BITTERNESS: 20–40 IBU plus, low to medium-high

Baltic Porter

ORIGIN: This type of porter is based on beers exported from England up to Russia in the eighteenth century. In many ways, Baltic porter is the true inheritor of the porter mantle, as these have been continuously brewed for probably close to two centuries without interruption. Modern versions are lagers, rather than ales, but because they share history with the English versions, they are included here.

LOCATION: Baltic region, including Poland, Lithuania, and Sweden; also U.S. craft breweries

FLAVOR: creamy roasty-toasty malt, lightly hopped, fairly sweet on finish

AROMA: soft, roasty maltiness; usually no hop aroma

BALANCE: malt, hops, roast in various proportions

SEASONALITY: year-round, great in cooler weather

PAIR WITH: roasted and smoked food; barbecue, prime rib, chocolate cake

SUGGESTED BEERS TO TRY: Baltika Porter, Carnegie Porter, Okocim Palone (slightly smoked), Southampton Imperial Baltic Porter

GRAVITY: 1.060–1.090 (15–22°P)

ALCOHOL: 5.5–9.5% by volume

ATTENUATION/BODY: medium to full

COLOR: 17–30°SRM, brown to deep chestnut

BITTERNESS: 20–40 IBU, low to medium

But all nations know that London is the place where porter was invented; and Jews, Turks, Germans, Negroes, Persians, Chinese, New Zealanders, Esquimaux, Copper Indians, Yankees and Spanish Americans are united in one feeling of respect for the native city of the most universally favourite liquor the world has ever known.

— Charles Knight, *London*, 1843

Stout

The word *stout*, meaning a strong black beer, goes back at least to 1630. The term was applied to the "stout butt beers" that would eventually go on to be named "porter." So all the history that applies to porter is also part of the stout story. Stout forms a widespread and varied family of beers whose members all share a deep, dark, roasty character.

ORIGIN: Stout is the son of porter and largely outstripped it, and it has various substyles from dry to sweet, weak to strong.

LOCATION: England, Ireland, United States, Caribbean, Africa — the world

FLAVOR: always roasty; may have caramel and hops too

AROMA: roasty malt; with or without hop aroma

BALANCE: very dry to very sweet

SEASONALITY: year-round

PAIR WITH: hearty, rich food; steak, meat pies; classic with oysters; stronger versions with chocolate

Irish Dry Stout

Exemplified by Guinness and others, Irish stout is characterized by the use of roasted barley rather than black roasted malt. Originally a tax dodge (unmalted barley was not taxed like malt), this gives the beer a unique, sharp, coffeelike roastiness. Raw, unmalted barley is also used in the modern recipe, which gives the beer a rich, creamy texture even in its low-gravity incarnations.

SUGGESTED BEERS TO TRY: Guinness draft, Beamish, North Coast Old No. 38 Stout, Three Floyds Black Sun Stout

GRAVITY: 1.038–1.048 (9.5–12°P)

ALCOHOL: 3.8–5% by volume

ATTENUATION/BODY: dry

COLOR: 40 plus °SRM, black

BITTERNESS: 30–40 IBU, medium to high

Sweet (London) Stout/Milk Stout

Stout devolved to a rather feeble, soft, sweet, and roasty style in its birthplace. By the beginning of the twentieth century, it was positioned as a drink for invalids and was often sweetened with the addition of the unfermentable milk sugar lactose.

SUGGESTED BEERS TO TRY: Mackeson's XXX Stout, St. Peter's Cream Stout, Samuel Adams Cream Stout

GRAVITY: 1.045–1.056 (11–14°P)

ALCOHOL: 3–6% by volume

ATTENUATION/BODY: sweet, full

COLOR: 40 plus °SRM, black

BITTERNESS: 15–25 IBU, low

Oatmeal Stout

The addition of raw or malted oats to stout seems to be a twentieth-century development. The oats add a very soft, rich creaminess and a hint of cookielike nuttiness.

SUGGESTED BEERS TO TRY: Young's Oatmeal Stout, McAuslan St. Ambroise Oatmeal Stout, Anderson Valley Barney Flats Oatmeal Stout, New Holland The Poet Oatmeal Stout

GRAVITY: 1.038–1.056 (9.5–14°P)

ALCOHOL: 3.8–6% by volume

ATTENUATION/BODY: medium, rich, oaty

COLOR: 25–40°SRM, brown-black

BITTERNESS: 20–40 IBU, low to medium

Irish Foreign/ Extra Stout

These were the strong stouts sold at home as a luxury product, but also exported to the ends of the British Empire. The style found its most ardent supporters in the tropics, and strong stouts are brewed everywhere from Jamaica to Nigeria to Singapore.

SUGGESTED BEERS TO TRY: Guinness Extra Stout (bottled), D&G Dragon Stout, Bell's Double Cream Stout, Pike Pub & Brewery XXXXX Pike Stout

GRAVITY: 1.056–1.075 (14–18°P)

ALCOHOL: 5.5–8% by volume

ATTENUATION/BODY: medium to full

COLOR: 30 plus °SRM, deep black

BITTERNESS: 30–65 IBU, medium to high

Imperial Stout

Stronger still, the "Imperial" designation derives from this style's popularity with the Russian monarchy through most of the eighteenth century.

SUGGESTED BEERS TO TRY: Courage Imperial Stout, Harvey's Le Coq Imperial Extra Stout, Great Divide Oak-Aged Yeti Imperial Stout, North Coast Old Rasputin Imperial Stout, Stone Imperial Stout

GRAVITY: 1.080–1.120 plus (19–29°P)

ALCOHOL: 7–12% by volume

ATTENUATION/BODY: medium to full

COLOR: 35 plus °SRM, black

BITTERNESS: 50–80 IBU, high

CHAPTER 10

THE LAGER FAMILY

THE HISTORY of lager is the tale of the beers that dominate the world, at least from a quantity point of view. When well brewed, lagers can be among the beer world's true delights. The lager family encompasses a variety of different styles: From ghost pale to deep chestnut, from weak to muscular, all share the common characteristic of being fermented cool and stored, or "lagered," at cold temperatures for an extended period of time.

The locus of lager's origin is Bavaria and nearby regions. Lager stayed there until the middle to late nineteenth century, when an incredible fashion for it developed and it spread to the rest of the world.

FOR SUCH A SUCCESSFUL FAMILY of beer, it's a little shocking how poorly its origins are documented. Like most beer styles, there is an oft-repeated, somewhat unsatisfying genesis tale, although there may be some truth to this one. The story goes that brewers in Bavaria were fermenting beer either in natural caves or from cellars dug into the limestone hillsides. As time went on, the yeast they were using became adapted to the cold and emerged as a truly new strain, sometime during the sixteenth century.

What we do know is that earlier on, much of the brewing (and other) action was far to the north of Germany, in Bremen, Hamburg, and other cities of the Hansa trading league. Bavaria was then a rustic backwater, an image that is still cheerfully cultivated today despite the fact that the area is home to BMW and other highly sophisticated enterprises.

Hansa towns were among the first in the world to produce hopped beer, which was shipped widely around the North Sea and Baltic regions. In those days, there were two distinct families of beer: red and white. They were so distinct that each had its own brewer's guild. White beers were hopped, while red beers were still brewed using the old gruit seasoning mix. Gruit was a mixture that included bog myrtle *(Myrica gale)*, yarrow, and sometimes wild rosemary, plus a host of unidentified spices pulled from the culinary kit of the day. Gruit was sold at a high price by the church or other holder of the *Gruitrecht* (Gruit Right), and this constituted an early form of beer tax.

By the late medieval era, northern Bavaria, Nuremberg in particular, was becoming known as a hop-trading center (500 years later it is still at the center of the world hop trade). However, in the south of Bavaria, unhopped red beers still dominated. It's important to keep in mind that there was no German nation as we know it today. Instead, it was a collection of small principalities, each with its own laws, customs, weights, measures, and barrel sizes.

Einbeck was a town famous for its beer as early as the thirteenth and fourteenth centuries. Einbeck was outside church control, which meant its brewers were not under obligation to use gruit. As a hop-trading center, it specialized in hopped beer. A good deal of it was shipped to Bavaria, where it was all the rage. It is clear that this new Einbecker beer was an inspiration to Bavarian brewers. We see this pattern of local brewers copying the imports over and over throughout history, especially when it comes to the introduction of hops. The brewing season in Einbeck was between the end of September and the beginning of May, which meant the beer was generally fermented fairly cool and may have led to the development of cold-adapted yeast.

In 1540, Duke Ludwig the Tenth hired a northern brewmaster from Brunswick, near Einbeck, to go south to Bavaria to bring some of the secrets of brewing back with him. Not long after that, Einbeck suffered a devastating fire, and the struggles of the Reformation cut off trade routes between the north and south of Germany. But signs point to the incorporation of the northern way of brewing in Bavaria before that time: There is a mention in the annals of the Munich town council in 1420 that is interpreted as referring to lager beer. A Munich ordinance of 1487 (the forerunner of the *Reinheitsgebot*) limited brewers to hops, malt, and water — a sure sign that the old, unhopped gruit beers were gone for good. And lastly, an edict in 1533 restricted brewing to between September 29 and April 23, which would have kept the yeast transitioning toward the cool-fermenting lager form. These cold-weather beers were known as *Braunbiers* (brown beers) at the time, and Munich has been famous for them ever since.

As elsewhere, beer in Germany remained at a modest "craft" scale of production until the effects of the Industrial Revolution were felt there. An important force in the modernization of brewing in Germany was Gabriel Sedelmayr Jr., and in Austria-Hungary, Anton Dreher. These two were the *wunderkind* of Germanic brewing. Sedlmayr's family was in the brewing business already (Spaten), as was Dreher's (in Schwecat, near Vienna). They were fast friends, having been sent off to England in 1833 when they were just 22 to see what they could find out about the state of the rapidly industrializing British breweries. They admitted to doing a little industrial espionage, going so far as to make a hollow walking stick with a valve on the bottom that they could surreptitiously fill with fermenting beer when no one was looking, taking it back to their hotel to analyze. It must have been great fun, and they learned enough to come back and create empires of brewing whose legacies remain in Europe today.

It took several hundred years, but Bavarian-style lager eventually displaced most of the other top-fermenting beers elsewhere in Germany and nearby countries. The final stroke was the incorporation of Bavaria into the German union in 1871. By then, there were a number of well-developed regional styles of lager that formed the basis for many of the present classic styles of lager. Pale types dominate the market, but there are many other fascinating and delicious lagers.

Meanwhile in North America, lager beer had burst on the scene along with Germans emigrating here in the decades before the Civil War. America had been largely a spirits-drinking land. Consumption statistics are notoriously difficult to pin down, but in 1810 government reports showed per capita spirits consumption of just over 14 quarts of pure alcohol per year. Beer consumption in that time was estimated at just 5 quarts, somewhere in the neighborhood of a 70 to 1 ratio in terms of servings of alcohol. States like Pennsylvania, New York, and Massachusetts did a fair bit of brewing, but elsewhere either barley was difficult to grow or spirits were so much cheaper that it didn't make sense to brew.

Some of these German-American brewers had business visions big enough to match the

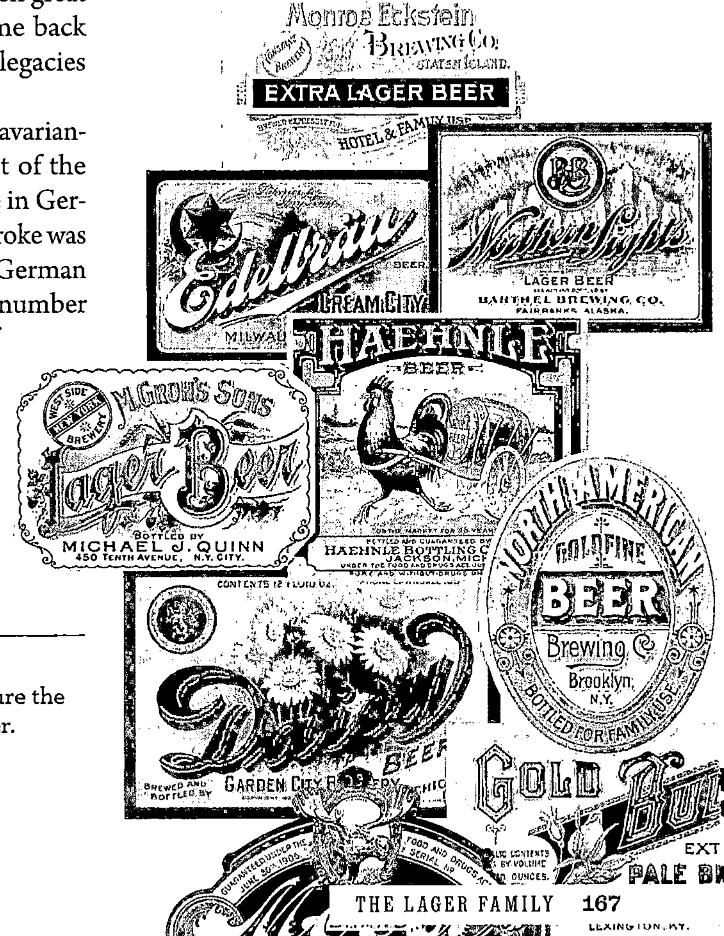

American Beer Labels, 1890–1940
These fine examples of graphic art capture the vitality of the American approach to beer.

national ambitions. Men like Pabst, Busch, and the Uehleins of Schlitz built vast networks of beer distribution by the 1870s, bringing beer to many places like the South, where there had been precious little before. They took advantage of every technological advancement: steam, railroads, refrigeration, pasteurization, and the telegraph. Driven by personalities of baronial proportions and equipped with great organizational skills, these early, large-scale German-American brewers created some of the first national brands in any product category. Even today, maintaining fresh beer in every market is no mean feat; but in the nineteenth century, we're talking about bottled beer in hand-corked bottles in wooden crates traveling thousands of miles in railcars that had to stop every few hours to be reloaded with ice from a stash that had been cut from northern lakes and rivers and laid down at strategic locations the winter before.

EARLY ON, the German-style beer in America was predominantly of the dark Munich type, but there were others. Brewers here took their inspiration from various German cities, so there were beers called Culmbachers, Erlangers, Duesseldorfers, and many others. In the 1870s, Anton Schwartz, a brewing scientist working as editor of *American Brewer*, and others like John Ewald Siebel of the Zymotechnic (later Siebel) Institute, perfected the adjunct cooking method needed to use the body-lightening ingredients rice and corn. At the same time, machine-made bottles and refrigeration allowed brewers to make and sell a beer that was pale, fizzy, and designed to be enjoyed ice-cold. This was the birth of American adjunct beer. By Prohibition, it dominated the market.

AMERICAN CRAFT EXAMPLES OF CLASSIC LAGER STYLES

Deschutes Pilsner (Bend, Oregon)
Victory Prima Pils (Downingtown, Pennsylvania)
Great Lakes Dortmunder Gold (Cleveland, Ohio)
Two Brothers Dog Days Dortmunder (Warrenville, Illinois)
Stoudt's Oktober Fest (Adamstown, Pennsylvania)
New Glarus Uff Da Bock (New Glarus, Wisconsin)
Capitol Dark (Middleton, Wisconsin)
Sprecher Black Bavarian (Glendale, Wisconsin)
Boston Beer Company Samuel Adams Double Bock

. . . and a Few Eccentric American Lagers

Capitol Autumnal Fire, an amber doppelbock (Middleton, Wisconsin)
Dogfish Head Imperial Pilsner (Milton, Delaware)
Rogue Dead Guy, a hopped-up maibock (Newport, Oregon)
Full Sail LTD, a strong golden lager (Hood River, Oregon)

Stein from the Zymotechnic Institute, c. 1910
This brewing school in Chicago is now called the Siebel Institute. Founded in 1872, it is America's oldest such organization.

The Flavor of Lager Beer

Lager beer is fermented cool and conditioned cold, which means the chemistry of yeast metabolism is slowed down. The fruity top notes of esters and other chemicals produced by ale fermentations are found in lager at much lower levels. (In fact, in competitions, any evidence of fruitiness in a lager is cause for banishment from the judging table.) A long fermentation allows plenty of time for these chemicals to be reabsorbed and converted into less odoriferous compounds. This means the flavors in lagers are cleaner, less complex, and more focused on the malt and hops — and almost never anything else. In lagers, brewers ask the raw materials to do the heavy lifting. It's the brewer's job to put them together correctly, and then stay out of the way.

There are hundreds of distinct strains of ale yeast, but only two closely related groups of lager yeast, with some minor variations; this means that yeast-derived flavor and aroma aren't much of a consideration in lager, certainly not to the same extent as in ales.

Balance may be anything from overwhelmingly malty to bracingly hoppy. German- or Czech-character hops are critical for most styles. Brewers of lagers, even craft brewers, tend to stick closely to the rule book, and there is little of the outrageous vamping that goes on in English- and Belgian-inspired ales. I love a well-made classic lager, but I'd like to see Americans loosen up a little and not be so reverential. A dash of creativity could help liven up this category in the marketplace.

Because most traditional Euro-lagers are all malt, it is always worth paying attention to the specific character of the malt. Is the malt bready or does it have hints of honey or light caramel? Toffeelike, deeply caramelly, toasty, roasted? Generally, you won't find a lot of sharp toasted or roasted flavors; *smooth* is the watchword. Dark beers tend to be less bitter than pale ones. Whatever the balance, clean, smooth, pure hop aromas and bitterness are the goal. They're not called "noble" hops for nothing. You may find elegant, herbal, almost minty aromas from German Hallertauers, or perhaps spicier notes from Spalter, Tettnangers, and Saaz. Some of these aroma personalities are very style specific, so get to know your hops.

There should be little fermentation character. Any sign of fruitiness is a sign of a too-warm fermentation. A whiff of sulfur is acceptable, and maybe a dab of DMS (see chapter 5), but any discernable buttery aroma is a sign of trouble. However, make sure it's actually coming from the beer and not the tap line before you complain to the brewer. Harshness could be a number of things, but most likely it has to do with water chemistry. Some Canadian and third-world barleys may contribute a touch of husky, phenolic astringency that's an acceptable part of the style from those places.

Bohemian Pilsner

ORIGIN: This is the original source Pilsner, which spawned thousands of imitators. It was invented in 1842, in the Czech town of Plzeň, in response to pale ale's popularity. The beer became widely known as Pilsner Urquell. *Urquell* means "original." The Bohemian Pilsner style is in flux, as newer management has taken away some of the funky complexity of Pilsner Urquell, and it's getting harder to find a genuinely charming Czech Pilsner. Note that the beers of České Budějovice have for a long time represented a slightly lighter, drier, paler variation of the Czech pale lager.

The real deal, when you find it, will be a shimmering burnished gold, with a complex caramel bouquet just about overshadowed by a fresh, spicy Saaz-hop aroma. There are a lot of pale imitations, so be picky.

LOCATION: Czech Republic, also U.S. craft breweries

FLAVOR: sweet malt, hints of caramel; Saaz hops

AROMA: clean malt plus spicy perfume of Saaz hops

BALANCE: somewhat or very much on the hoppy side; clean bitter finish despite sometimes-aggressive hop rates

SEASONALITY: year-round, but best enjoyed in warm weather

PAIR WITH: wide range of lighter food, such as chicken, salads, salmon, bratwurst

SUGGESTED BEERS TO TRY: Chechvar (Budvar in Europe), BrouCzech Lager, Radegast Premium Czech Lager, Live Oak Pilz, Lagunitas Pils, Summit Pilsner

GRAVITY: 1.044–1.056 (11–14°P)

ALCOHOL: 4–5% by volume

ATTENUATION/BODY: medium

COLOR: 3–7°SRM, pale to deep gold

BITTERNESS: 30–45 IBU, medium

German Pilsner

ORIGIN: northern Germany, and it was based on the success of Czech Pilsner. Northerly versions are more austere.

LOCATION: Germany, elsewhere in Europe

FLAVOR: crisp, smooth malt; herby Hallertau hops

AROMA: clean malt plus good dose of herbal hops

BALANCE: even or dry/bitter; clean finish

SEASONALITY: year-round, but best enjoyed in warm weather

PAIR WITH: wide range of lighter food, such as salads, seafood, bratwurst

SUGGESTED BEERS TO TRY: Jever Pils, Spaten Pils, Harpoon Pilsner, Lagunitas Pilsner, Victory Prima Pils

GRAVITY: 1.044–1.050 (11–12.5°P)

ALCOHOL: 4–5% by volume

ATTENUATION/BODY: crisp and dry

COLOR: 3–4°SRM, straw to pale gold

BITTERNESS: 30–40 IBU, medium

Münchener Helles

ORIGIN: Based on the success of Czech Pilsner, this came out of Munich, Germany. It took the Munich brewers until the 1870s to figure out how to treat Munich water to make a decent pale beer, but even so, it still reflects the local aversion to too much bitterness.

LOCATION: Munich; also U.S. craft breweries

FLAVOR: rich, light caramelly malt, hint of hops

AROMA: clean malt plus good dose of herbal hops

BALANCE: even to malty; rich, soft finish

SEASONALITY: year-round, but best enjoyed in warm weather

PAIR WITH: wide range of lighter food, such as salads and seafood; classic with weisswurst

SUGGESTED BEERS TO TRY: Spaten Premium Lager, Augustiner Lagerbier Hell, Firestone Walker Lager, Rahr & Sons Blonde Lager

GRAVITY: 1.044–1.050 (11–12.5°P)

ALCOHOL: 4.5–5% by volume

ATTENUATION/BODY: crisp, dry

COLOR: 4–5°SRM, pale gold

BITTERNESS: 18–25 IBU, low to medium

Dortmunder Export

ORIGIN: Dortmund, Germany's export beer was the first famous pale lager in Germany. The city's brewers began to industrialize in about 1845, and by 1868, an observer noted that "Dortmunder is to Northwest Germany what Bavaria used to be for the whole country," as far as beer goes. With a shift away from local brewing traditions and raw ingredients, something different was definitely going on here. The "Bavarian process" of lager brewing was adopted in 1865, and the new pale beer was a huge hit. Sadly, after a hundred years of success, Dortmunder Export is now just about dead in its homeland.

Dortmunder was originally a slightly stronger beer designed for export. Fortunately, it is sometimes available in American craft-brewed versions. In terms of balance, it is intermediate between helles and Pilsner, but just a little stronger than either. The city of Dortmund has very unusual water chemistry, including carbonate, sulfate, and chloride, and this was well suited to the production of a moderately hopped pale beer.

LOCATION: formerly Dortmund, but now easier to find from a few U.S. craft breweries

FLAVOR: rich, light caramelly malt, hint of hops

AROMA: clean malt plus soft hops

BALANCE: perfectly even, rich and round, but with a crisp, minerally finish

SEASONALITY: year-round

PAIR WITH: wide range of food: pork; spicy Asian, Cajun, Latin

SUGGESTED BEERS TO TRY: DAB (Dortmunder Actien-Brauerei) Original, Great Lakes Dortmunder Gold, Two Brothers Dog Days Dortmunder Style Lager

GRAVITY: 1.048–1.056 (12–14°P)

ALCOHOL: 5–6% by volume

ATTENUATION/BODY: medium

COLOR: 3–5°SRM, straw to pale gold

BITTERNESS: 23–29 IBU, low to medium

PALE LAGER AROUND THE WORLD

In addition to the classic styles, pale lager has become widespread and assumes a slightly different character in each of its adopted homelands. The following is by no means an exhaustive list.

China and India. These tend toward the rustic, and the local six-row barley usually adds a grassy or sometimes astringent character.

Japan. These form a whole range of products that as a whole are extremely clean and crisp. Rice, as you would expect, is the most common adjunct. All-malt examples exist, and premium products revolve around extreme freedom from harshness, an aesthetic borrowed from sake culture.

Australia. This country has a strong heritage of British-inflected brewing but has embraced lager as its own as well. The beers are in the international style, very much along the lines of the American adjunct Pilsners, but often with a somewhat higher hopping rate. Hops in Tasmania and New Zealand are a little different as well and account for the unique perfume of many beers Down Under.

Poland. These are not far off from Czech beers, except they tend generally to be a little less bitter and maybe just slightly grainier tasting. They come in a wide range of strengths, starting at a conventional 4.5 to 5 percent by volume and moving up to more than 9 percent. I find the ones around 6.5 to 7 percent to be the most interesting. Poland has its own hop-growing region and a variety, Lublin, to go with it. It is said to be related to Saaz.

Canada. Canadian mainstream lagers are very similar to U.S. examples, but up to a half percent stronger in alcohol. The unique Canadian "blue" six-row malt, so named for its colored aleurone (skin) layer, may add a sharp, crisp graininess. Numerous fine craft beers exist, including authentic Pilsners, British-inspired ales from Toronto and points west, and a thrilling Belgian-inspired scene in Quebec.

Mexico and Latin America. Most of these products are of the standard industrial variety, with plenty of adjuncts to thin them down and make them highly thirst-quenching. Standouts do exist, including Bohemia and Negra Modelo from Mexico, and Guatemala's Moza, a bock-style lager. An exciting craft scene is just emerging in many places in Latin America.

KELLERBIER

Many German breweries serve an unfiltered version of their house beers only in their rathskellers. With a slight milky haze, they are very fresh tasting and typically a little more full-bodied than the same beer post-filtration. Kellerbier is the German equivalent of real ale. It makes you realize how much filtration takes away.

Historical Style

American Pre-Prohibition Pilsner

Before World War I, mainstream beers in America had considerably more character than they do today. Gravities were similar, or maybe a touch higher, and judging by the color of the beers in antique ads and photos, the beers were often darker in those days as well. Hop rates were several times what they are today. While all-malt examples did exist, most were adjunct beers, with typically around 20 percent of rice or corn grits in the recipe.

SUGGESTED BEERS TO TRY: Yuengling Traditional Lager, August Schell Firebrick Amber Lager, Saranac Golden Pilsner. Also, keep your eyes open at your local brewpub, as this sometimes shows up as a summer seasonal.

GRAVITY: 1.044–1.060 (11–13°P)

ALCOHOL: 3.5–6.0% by volume

ATTENUATION/BODY: medium

COLOR: 3–5°SRM, straw to pale gold

BITTERNESS: 25–40 IBU, medium

American Adjunct Lager

ORIGIN: Corn and rice adjunct beers date back to 1540 in America. This style as we know it developed in the late nineteenth century, then became ever more delicate as the twentieth century rolled on. This style of beer is the world's best-selling lager. The two main adjuncts used are corn and rice, usually not together. In mainstream brands about 20 percent of the recipe is adjunct; the quantity rises as the price goes down, and sugar is sometimes used as a really cheap adjunct in bargain brands. The upper limit by law, at least in the United States, is 50 percent adjunct.

LOCATION: United States; now international

FLAVOR: Very slightly malty, with a lot of fizz. The barest tickle of bitterness, at least in mainstream U.S. versions; premium or European versions may have a modest bitterness. Corn in the recipe leaves a hint of palate-coating roundness, almost a little sweetness, while rice has a crisper finish, and if used in too large a quantity can add a slight astringency.

AROMA: hints of grainy malt, hops occasionally

BALANCE: dry, with clean, crisp finish

SEASONALITY: year-round, but best enjoyed in warm weather

GRAVITY: 1.040–1.046 (10–11.5°P)

ALCOHOL: 3.8–5% by volume

ATTENUATION/BODY: crisp, dry

COLOR: 2–4°SRM, straw to pale gold

BITTERNESS: 5–14 IBU, very low

Lager Brewery
A typical nineteenth century lager brewey is depicted in this advertising poster, c. 1885.

American Light Lager

ORIGIN: Created in the 1940s as a diet beer for women, light beer was masculinized by Philip Morris, then the parent company of Miller, and their brand "Lite." Light lager now outsells regular lager. Fungally derived enzymes are used to reduce all starches present into fermentable sugars, ensuring that there will be no residual carbohydrates and that the maximum alcohol is produced with a minimum calorie count.

LOCATION: United States mostly, also international

FLAVOR: barest hints of malt, with a lot of fizz

AROMA: slight hints of grainy malt, period

BALANCE: super-dry, with clean, crisp finish

SEASONALITY: year-round, but best enjoyed in warm weather

GRAVITY: 1.024–1.040 (6–10°P)

ALCOHOL: 3.2–4.2% by volume

ATTENUATION/BODY: super-dry

COLOR: 1.5–4°SRM, pale straw to pale gold

BITTERNESS: 5–10 IBU, ultra-low

American Malt Liquor

ORIGIN: Designed as a cheap intoxicant, malt liquor is brewed like other inexpensive industrial beers, with heaping helpings of adjuncts, often just sugar. Malt liquor is very lightly hopped and sometimes sweetened a little at packaging.

LOCATION: United States

FLAVOR: a dab of malt, with a sweetish finish; alcohol evident

AROMA: slight hints of grainy malt, and perhaps a sweetish, alcohol aroma

BALANCE: alcohol versus carbonation and a little sweetness

SEASONALITY: year-round

GRAVITY: 1.050–1.060 (11–15°P)

ALCOHOL: 5–6% by volume

ATTENUATION/BODY: super-dry

COLOR: 2–5°SRM, pale straw to pale gold

BITTERNESS: 12–23 IBU, low

SOME AMERICAN "HERITAGE" BREWERIES AND THEIR OLD-SCHOOL BRANDS

American Brewery	Old-School Brand
Genesee (now High Falls)	Genesee
Joseph Huber (now owned by Minhas Craft Brewery)	Rhinelander, Berghoff
Iron City	Iron City
Point Brewing	Point Special
The Lion Brewery	Stegmaier
August Schell	Schell's, Grain Belt
Yuengling	Yuengling

Oktoberfest, Märzen & Vienna

ORIGIN: It was originally created in Vienna around 1840 by Anton Dreher. Sometime after that, a similar beer was brewed in Munich by his pal Gabriel Sedelmayr Jr. (then in charge of brewing at Spaten). *Märzen* means "March," and this term normally applies to a beer brewed in the late spring to use up the last of the previous fall's hops and malt before brewing ceased for the summer. So the general idea of March beer is probably quite old in Germany, as it is elsewhere. The first Oktoberfest event happened in 1810, probably at least 50 years before the style that now bears its name existed. Early on, the revelers must have been drinking Munich's famous dunkel.

Originally, there may not have been all that great a distinction between these closely related beers, although Vienna brewers used a malt that was slightly paler than the more highly kilned Munich malt. Vienna-style lager has been out of fashion in its birthplace for quite a while, but craft versions are appearing in some of Austria's small, upstart breweries. In Germany, the term *Oktoberfest* applies only to certain beers made by brewers in Munich proper. The Oktoberfest style is a moving target, getting paler and drier in recent years, so much so that some breweries brew an old-fashioned Märzen alongside it for those who enjoy the rich, caramelly experience. There are many great versions brewed as a fall seasonal by American craft brewers.

LOCATION: Germany, Austria, Mexico (thanks to an Austro-Hungarian colonial connection), U.S. craft breweries

FLAVOR: caramel malt, with hints of toast

AROMA: Malt, malt, malt! Brewed primarily from either Munich or Vienna malt. No hops.

BALANCE: malty, barely balanced by hops

SEASONALITY: September through October; also year-round, especially in the United States.

PAIR WITH: Mexican cuisine and other spicy food; chicken, sausage, milder cheeses

SUGGESTED BEERS TO TRY: Ayinger Oktober Fest Märzen, Paulaner Oktoberfest Märzen, Live Oak Oaktoberfest, Summit Oktoberfest, Widmer Oktoberfest

MÄRZEN:
GRAVITY: 1.050–1.060 (12.5–15°P)
ALCOHOL: 5.3–5.9% by volume
ATTENUATION/BODY: medium
COLOR: 7–15°SRM, pale gold to dark amber
BITTERNESS: 18–25 IBU, low to medium

VIENNA:
GRAVITY: 1.050–1.060 (12.5–15°P)
ALCOHOL: 5.3–5.9% by volume
ATTENUATION/BODY: medium
COLOR: 7–15°SRM, pale gold to dark amber
BITTERNESS: 18–25 IBU, low to medium

OKTOBERFEST:
GRAVITY: 1.050–1.060 (12.5–15°P)
ALCOHOL: 5.3–5.9% by volume
ATTENUATION/BODY: medium
COLOR: 4–12°SRM, pale gold to dark amber
BITTERNESS: 18–25 IBU, low to medium

Munich Dunkel

ORIGIN: Descended from ancient "red" beers in southern Germany. Dunkel was the first lager style, probably developing as such in the sixteenth century. Until brewers figured out how to treat the local water, it was considered impossible to brew a pale beer, but it was well suited for malty, brown beer. Originally, the beers were brewed entirely from the amber-colored Munich malt, but more modern recipes are often a mix of Pilsner malt and Munich, with a little black malt added to replace the missing color.

LOCATION: Munich, Germany; also from U.S. craft breweries

FLAVOR: rich caramel malt, roasty overtones

AROMA: full, complex maltiness; no hop aroma

BALANCE: malty, barely balanced by hops and a softly bitter roastiness

SEASONALITY: year-round, great in colder weather

PAIR WITH: hearty, spicy food; barbecue, sausages, roast meat; bread pudding

SUGGESTED BEERS TO TRY: Ayinger Altbairisch Dunkel, Klosterbrauerei Ettal Dunkel, Lakefront East Side Dark

GRAVITY: 1.048–1.056 (12–13.8°P)

ALCOHOL: 3–3.9% by volume

ATTENUATION/BODY: medium

COLOR: 15–25°SRM, ruby to deep brown

BITTERNESS: 16–30 IBU, medium

Historical Style

American Dark/Bock

Most of the immigrating brewers hailed from Bavaria, and they brought the richly malty dunkel recipes with them. Over time, the recipes lightened up in terms of overall strength and with the addition of corn or rice grits. Pilsner came along and overtook the dark style, but it managed to hang on until the 1970s in greatly attenuated form, especially as seasonal bock beers. Most of these have disappeared, but Yuengling and a few other regional heritage breweries still brew the style. An especially light-bodied amber derivative, Shiner Bock, has been a big hit for Texas's Spoetzl brewery.

SUGGESTED BEERS TO TRY: Dixie Blackened Voodoo Lager, Shiner Bock, Yuengling Porter

German Schwarzbier

ORIGIN: Long brewed in certain parts of Germany, especially Augsburg, Kostritz, and Kulmbach, these are Germany's darkest beers. *Schwarz* means "black," but this term is often used in certain regions to denote any dark beer. There seems to have been some connection with the exploding popularity of English porter in the mid-nineteenth century, because the brewer and author Ladislaus von Wagner (1877) calls it *"Englischer Köstritzer."* In those days the beer was brewed with a peculiar mashing regimen called "satz"mashing, which features a long, cold soak of the mash in water, and then a boiling of the hops in thin mash, a step called "roasting" the hops.

LOCATION: Kulmbach, Kostritz; also Japan (black beer); occasionally U.S. craft breweries

FLAVOR: bittersweet, with a clean, soft roastiness

AROMA: full roasty maltiness; little or no hop aroma

BALANCE: roasty-malty, barely balanced by hops

SEASONALITY: year-round, great in colder weather

PAIR WITH: hearty, spicy food, such as barbecue, sausages, roast meat; bread pudding

SUGGESTED BEERS TO TRY: Köstritzer Schwarzbier, Kulmbacher Mönchshoff Schwarzbier, Sapporo Black Lager, Samuel Adams Black Lager, Sprecher Black Bavarian Lager

GRAVITY: 1.044–1.052 (11–13°P)

ALCOHOL: 3–3.9% by volume

ATTENUATION/BODY: medium

COLOR: 25–30°SRM, ruby to deep brown

BITTERNESS: 22–30 IBU, medium

Bock Beer Labels, Early Twentieth Century
Bock was enthusiastically produced by lager brewers everywhere.

Historical Style

German Porter

This little-known style had its heyday in the mid to late nineteenth century, in response to the unprecedented success of English porter. According to contemporary authors, there were two distinct styles: a sweet and malty one and a crisp, highly hopped version, both at 1.071 to 1.075 original gravity (17–19 degrees Plato). Both lager and top-fermented versions existed. Neuzeller Kloster Brau brews a porter that is imported into the United States.

Maibock/ Heller Bock

ORIGIN: Einbeck, southern Germany, claims to be the origin point for bock beer. Even by 1613 it was described in *The Herbal Book of Johannes Theodorus* as "thin, subtle, clear, of bitter taste, with a pleasant acidity on the tongue, and many other good qualities." A Brunswick (near Einbeck) brewmaster brought to Bavaria by Duke Ludwig X helped sort out the details of brewing this stronger style of beer there. By the late eighteenth century, the style seems to have been widespread in southern Germany. Half a century later it was all over Europe, especially in France, where it was consumed with gusto.

LOCATION: southern Germany, France, United States, Thailand

FLAVOR: rich, creamy malt, soft bitter finish

AROMA: loads of malt plus a hint of hops

BALANCE: full, malty body, evenly balanced hops

SEASONALITY: traditional in late spring (May), but now year-round

PAIR WITH: rich or spicy food like Thai; cheesecake, apple strudel

SUGGESTED BEERS TO TRY: Einbecker Mai-Ur-Bock

GRAVITY: 1.066–1.074 (16.5–18.5°P)

ALCOHOL: 6.5–8% by volume

ATTENUATION/BODY: very full, rich

COLOR: 5–11°SRM, gold to amber

BITTERNESS: 12–30 IBU, low

Dark (Dunkel) Bock

ORIGIN: This seems to have been very much the secondary form of bock beer as compared to the amber-colored maibock. Old paintings featuring bock rarely show anything darker than a medium amber. They are rather more important in the minds of American home and craft brewers than they were historically.

LOCATION: southern Germany, U.S. craft breweries

FLAVOR: rich creamy malt; soft, bittersweet finish with hints of cocoa

AROMA: loads of malt plus a hint of soft roast

BALANCE: full, malty body, barely balanced by hops

SEASONALITY: traditional in late spring (May), but now year-round

PAIR WITH: rich or spicy food like stinky cheese (authentic Münster or Taleggio)

SUGGESTED BEERS TO TRY: Einbecker Ur-Bock Dunkel, Weltenburger Kloster Asam-Bock, Anchor Bock Beer, New Glarus Uff-Da Bock, Stegmaier Brewhouse Bock Beer

GRAVITY: 1.066–1.074 (16.5–18°P)

ALCOHOL: 6.5–7.5% by volume

ATTENUATION/BODY: very full, rich

COLOR: 15–30°SRM, amber to dark brown

BITTERNESS: 12–30 IBU, low

Doppelbock

ORIGIN: Created in 1629 as "Salvator" by the monastic Paulaner brewery in Munich. The Salvator name was used generically until the early twentieth century, when Paulaner, by then a secular operation, took steps to protect their name. The "-ator" suffix has stood since then, and most breweries everywhere end their doppelbock names with "-ator." This is still a big beer, but it once was much heavier. In response to changing tastes, its terminal gravity has decreased over the past 150 years, making the beer drier, less sweet, and more alcoholic.

LOCATION: southern Germany, U.S. craft breweries

FLAVOR: massive caramel malt; soft, roasty finish

AROMA: loads of complex malt; no hops evident

BALANCE: malt, barely balanced by hops and a soft roastiness

SEASONALITY: year-round, great in colder weather

PAIR WITH: rich, roasty foods (like duck!); perfect with chocolate cake

SUGGESTED BEERS TO TRY: Ayinger Celebrator, Ettaler Klosterbrauerei Curator, Weihenstephan Korbinian, Leinenkugel's Big Butt Doppelbock, Tommyknocker Butthead Doppelbock

GRAVITY: 1.074–1.080 (18–19.5°P)

ALCOHOL: 6.5–8% by volume

ATTENUATION/BODY: very full, rich

COLOR: 12–30°SRM, deep amber to dark brown

BITTERNESS: 12–30 IBU, low

Rauchbier

Before the advent of direct-fired kilns, all malt was either smoky or air-dried. And while there is evidence in places like Norway of some very primitive indirect kilns, it is clear that many European beers before 1700 had a certain smoky quality from the wood used to kiln the malt. Equally evident from the record is that smoked beers were dropped from production in most places when maltsters figured out how to dry the malt in a smoke-free manner, except in the Franconia region of northern Bavaria. Centered around Bamberg is a pocket of the old-style smoked beer, or rauchbier.

This specialty is in the lager category because most of these beers are lagered (the exception being a wheat beer), and so they share a history and flavor profile with the rest of the Bavarian beer tradition. The only difference is the smoke. Wood, usually beech, is used in the kilns. The beers are brewed from various proportions of smoked and unsmoked malt to achieve the desired smoke level. A number of different beer styles are brewed, including bock and helles, but the most common smoked style is Märzen, whose rich maltiness stands up to the smoke, giving a unique balance to this beer.

Rauchbier can be startling upon the first sip, but hang in there. The beer tastes better and better as your palate grows accustomed to it.

Description: See Märzen, helles, bock, and weizen, then add a layer of dry, hammy smoke. Mmmm, liquid bacon!

SUGGESTED BEERS TO TRY: Any of the Aecht Schlenkerla products; Brauerei Spezial Rauchbier, Midnight Sun Rauchbock, and occasional seasonals at your local brewpub

Historical Style

Steinbier

In medieval days, brewers didn't always have access to metal brewing vessels and so had to make do with wood. This created some obvious problems in heating the mash and wort. The solution was to add heated rocks directly to the liquid, which then gave up their heat quite efficiently. The last holdout of this ancient style was in late nineteenth-century Carinthia, a mountainous southern region of Austria. There they brewed a very low-gravity steinbier using oats and wheat malt.

A Bamberg brewery called Allgauer used to brew a beer called Rauchenfelser, but production has now switched to Privatbrauerei Franz Joseph Sailer. The rocks, a hard type of sandstone called "graywacke," were placed in a metal cage and heated to white-hot, then dunked into the wort. Rapid boiling ensued, and the rocks became encrusted with a thick layer of caramelized wort, which, when dissolved during fermentation, gave the beer a smoky, toffee flavor.

In deference to this antiquated practice, Chuck Skypeck, at his Boscos brewpubs in Memphis, Nashville, and Little Rock, makes a blond ale called Flaming Stone.

CHAPTER 11

CONTINENTAL ALES, WEISSBIERS, AND ALE-LAGER HYBRIDS

EVEN in the great lager fatherland, there is ale. Of course, many hundreds of years ago, all beer was ale, or top-fermented beer, but most of these were swept into obscurity or extinction before the great flood of Bavarian and Bohemian lager that gushed across Europe in the late nineteenth century.

ALL ALES USE YEAST that does its business near the top of the fermenting wort. More importantly, it prefers warmer temperatures than lager, most often between 65 and 73°F (18–23°C), although this varies by style. At these temperatures, yeast produces a great deal more of the fruity aroma molecules called esters and other chemicals that add spicy, fruity complexity to beer. In most cases, the strains of yeast used are critical to the character of the beer. Yeast used for the Rhine Valley ales of Cologne and Düsseldorf are very neutral with a delicate fruitiness, and because they are fermented at the cool end of the ale range and then cold-aged like lagers, their effect is subtle. The same is true for ale-lager hybrids, which are either fermented cool with ale yeast, or at warmer temperatures but with lager yeast. The high-personality yeast used for Bavarian weizen blasts the beer with a whole fruit basket of aroma: banana, bubble gum, and some spicy clovelike notes. There are none of those fruits or spices actually in the beer; this aromatic magic comes solely from the yeast.

Weissbier is the broad term that includes both the various shades and strengths of Bavarian hefeweizen and the tart and tingly Berliner Weisse. Compared to barley malt beers, wheat beers are lighter on the palate, with a citrusy crispness and quenching finish, without the blandness that characterizes beers made with adjuncts such as corn or rice. Pale color and high carbonation levels enhance the refreshing qualities of this style.

All of these beers are session beers, meant to be drunk in reasonably large quantities in the company of other beer lovers. Alt and Kölsch are delicious and are sometimes available in the United States, but to enjoy them to the fullest, you'll have to journey to their hometowns along the Rhine. There the beers are served in the bars and brewpubs from small barrels perched right on the bar tops, slipped into tall, paper-thin shell glasses and brought to your table automatically until you place a coaster on top of your glass to tell them you've had enough.

The word *alt* means "old," in the sense of an old-time style. There are a few altbiers outside of Düsseldorf. Pinkus Müller makes a pale version, and an amber variation (said to be inspired by the once-widespread Broyhan) is brewed by Lindener Gilde in Hanover, the same brewery started by its inventor, Cord Broyhan, in 1546. Dortmund was once famous as an altbier town, gaining world renown for its strong *Adambier* a century ago. Due to consolidation and pilsnerization of the market, the Dortmunder alts are becoming harder to find.

WHAT'S IN A NAME?

Weis, Weiss, and **Weisse** all mean "white" in German and have long been used to describe the pale, hazy beers containing wheat that are found all along the northern tier of Europe.

Weizen means "wheat" in German and refers to the Bavarian or *Süddeutsch* form of *Weissbier.*

Hefe means "yeast" and indicates a *Weissbier* with yeast, by far the most popular form. **Kristal** indicates a crystal-clear weizen.

Kölsch

The word *Kölsch* is an appellation. Only brewers in the city of Cologne (Köln) following certain guidelines may use the name, although that name protection doesn't seem to extend to the United States, where it has become the generic term for the pale, softly hoppy beer that is just barely not a lager. Kölsch is crisp, but not sharp; balanced, but not excessively bitter. There is a delightfully subtle fruitiness in the aroma, and a dryish palate with a hint of creaminess that sometimes comes from the addition of a small proportion of wheat (not all brewers do this). Fresh, seductive, and never fatiguing, it is one of the world's great session beers. Some American craft breweries have recognized this and roll it into their lineup, usually as a summer seasonal.

ORIGIN: Köln (Cologne), Germany; probably late 1800s for present form

LOCATION: Köln, Germany; also U.S. craft breweries

FLAVOR: clean, fresh malt; hops in the background

AROMA: clean malt plus a touch of noble hops, fruit

BALANCE: evenly balanced; soft, bitterish finish

SEASONALITY: year-round, but best enjoyed in warm weather

PAIR WITH: wide range of lighter food, such as chicken, salads, salmon, bratwurst

SUGGESTED BEERS TO TRY: Reissdorf Kölsch, Gaffels Kölsch, Goose Island Summertime, Saint Arnold Fancy Lawnmower Beer

GRAVITY: 1.042–1.048 (10.5–12°P)

ALCOHOL: 4.8–5.3% by volume

ATTENUATION/BODY: low to medium

COLOR: 4–5°SRM, pale to medium gold

BITTERNESS: 18–25 IBU, low to medium

Düsseldorfer Altbier

There is a well-established tradition of brown, top-fermented beers along the Rhine in Lower Saxony. The current Düsseldorfer Alt seems to be descended from an older style called *erntebier* (harvest beer), which was much beloved in the nineteenth century.

The classic alt is a copper-colored all-malt ale of everyday strength. They may be bone dry or softly malty, but all feature a brisk hop bitterness without lots of hop aroma. Like Kölsch, alt is tapped from barrels at the bar into tall, thin glasses.

Imports and American craft beer examples are rare, but when well executed it is a compelling session beer. Twice a year, in the fall and midwinter, breweries make a slightly stronger version called *sticke* that is released without a lot of hubbub as a thank-you to their regular customers. One version is imported here, along with a "Double Sticke" that doesn't exist in its homeland. The Diebel brewery in Issum, up near the Dutch border, focuses on alt and produces a credible Düsseldorf version that is widely available in the United States.

ORIGIN: Düsseldorf, Germany

LOCATION: Düsseldorf, Germany; U.S. craft breweries

FLAVOR: malty but crisp, a punch of noble hops

AROMA: clean toffee malt plus fresh herbal hops

BALANCE: toward the dry and bitter side; clean finish

SEASONALITY: year-round

PAIR WITH: wide range of mid-intensity food, such as roast pork, smoked sausage, or salmon

SUGGESTED BEERS TO TRY: Zum Uerige Sticke Alt, August Schell Schmaltz's Alt, Southampton Publick House Secret Ale

GRAVITY: 1.044–1.048 (11–12°P)

ALCOHOL: 4.3–5% by volume

ATTENUATION/BODY: crisp, dry

COLOR: 11–19°SRM, amber to brown

BITTERNESS: 25–48 IBU, medium to high

American Cream Ale

ORIGIN: nineteenth century; a blend of lager and stock ale

LOCATION: eastern/midwestern U.S. regionals and craft breweries

FLAVOR: smooth, creamy malt, soft bitter finish

AROMA: clean, grainy malt, a hint of hops

BALANCE: a touch of sweetness, clean crisp finish

SEASONALITY: year-round, but best enjoyed in warm weather

PAIR WITH: lighter foods and snacks; craft versions can stand up to somewhat more substantial food

SUGGESTED BEERS TO TRY: Hudepohl-Schoenling Little Kings Cream Ale, New Glarus Spotted Cow, Rogue Honey Cream Ale

GRAVITY: 1.044–1.052 (11–13°P)

ALCOHOL: 4.2–5.6% by volume

ATTENUATION/BODY: dry to medium

COLOR: 2–4°SRM, pale straw to pale gold

BITTERNESS: 10–22 IBU, low to medium

Steam Beer

This term describes a beer style that was brewed around the time of the great influx of settlers into California, Washington, and other western states. Steam beer is said to get its name from the "steam" released when kegs were tapped, a consequence of high carbonation levels. The unique feature of steam beer is that it was an attempt, in those early days, to brew a lager-type beer without access to ice or refrigeration. The high-temperature fermentation gives it a fruity, estery profile compared to a true lager.

Currently, the only well-known steam beer in the United States is Anchor Steam, made by Anchor Brewing Company of San Francisco, which claims the term as an exclusive trademark. The BJCP and World Beer Cup both call the style "California Common," but this poses problems for brewers who are not actually brewing in California.

ORIGIN: western U.S., especially California

LOCATION: San Francisco's Anchor Steam is the last surviving old-time steam beer brewery and holds the trademark on the term, but other craft breweries produce their own versions from time to time.

FLAVOR: malty but crisp, a good helping of the dry-tasting Northern Brewer hops

AROMA: crisp malt with hints of caramel balanced by fresh herbal hops

BALANCE: toward the dry and bitter side; clean finish

SEASONALITY: year-round

PAIR WITH: wide range of mid-intensity food, such as roast pork, smoked sausage, or salmon. Fabulous with coconut-breaded shrimp.

SUGGESTED BEERS TO TRY: Anchor Steam Beer, Flat Earth Element 115, Southampton West Coast Steem Beer

GRAVITY: 1.048–1.056 (12–14°P)

ALCOHOL: 4.3–5.5% by volume

ATTENUATION/BODY: crisp, dry

COLOR: 10–14°SRM, amber

BITTERNESS: 30–45 IBU, medium to high

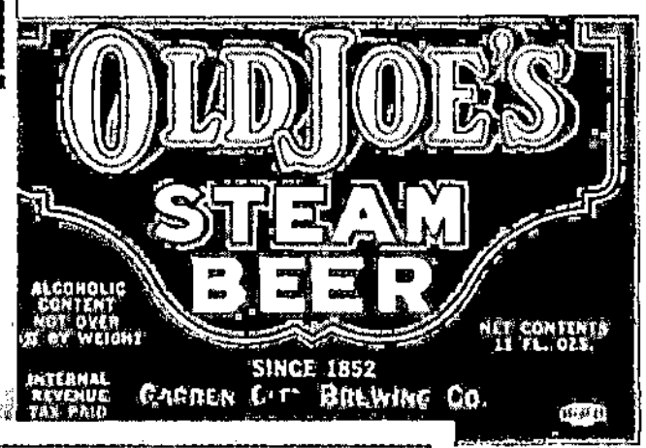

Steam Beer Labels
Steam beer was once widespread across the American West and was a generic term describing warm-fermented lagers. As the last surviving brewer of the style, Anchor now owns the trademark for "Steam."

Historical Style

Sparkling Ale

Let's start with Scottish versions. The 1902 *American Handy Book of the Brewing, Malting and Auxiliary Trades* lists a 1901 version at 18.03 degrees Balling (1.075), with an alcohol content of 8.6 percent by volume. A version of that era by McEwan's comes in at a beefy 21.6 degrees Balling (1.090), and 7.8 percent alcohol by weight (9.6 percent by volume), indicating a high terminal gravity and making it a very sweet beer. Both show moderate amounts of lactic acid, 0.15 and 0.38, respectively (contemporary lambics and Irish stouts both were about 1 percent, by comparison), which indicates some wood aging with its inevitable *Brettanomyces* activity. Hop rates are elusive, but an "X" Scottish ale of similar gravity from mid-century came in at 2.8 to 4 ounces per 5 gallons, which would have put it in the neighborhood of 40 to 60 IBUs.

In America, sparkling ale held a position between cream or "present use" ale and stock ale. Gravities were lower than imported versions, about 14 degrees Plato (1.057), about the same as cream ale. The difference was an extended lagering at 39°F (4°C). Three months is a typical aging time.

SUGGESTED BEERS TO TRY: Cooper's Sparkling Ale, Bell's Sparkling Ale, Rogue Oregon Golden Ale

Weissbier/ Hefeweizen

It is a golden summer afternoon and you are whiling away what's left of the day in a lush and ancient beer garden. Hop vines are curling up the trellis to find a little sunshine. Only quiet conversation and the occasional clink of heavy glassware punctuates the tranquillity. There is but one perfect beverage for this moment, and your lips form the word *Weissbier* as you place your order.

The ritual begins. A half-liter bottle shaped like a bullet appears, along with a very tall, vase-shaped glass. The glass is slipped over the top of the bottle, and the whole thing is inverted. As the beer starts to flow, the bottle is withdrawn, keeping pace with the level of beer in the glass. Then, just before the bottle is completely drained, it is laid on the table and rolled back and forth several times to make sure the yeast on the bottom is well mixed with the remaining foam. This last remnant of meringue-like foam is heaped in a spiral on top of the considerable head already in the glass. This elegant creation is topped with a wedge of fresh lemon, and the ritual is complete, save for the drinking.

By the sixteenth century, wheat beer was solidly established as a regional specialty in Bavaria. The *Reinheitsgebot* has but one loophole, and this allows for the use of wheat in weizens. The Bavarian royal family held exclusive rights to brew wheat beers through a boom and bust cycle that lasted

TO LEMON OR NOT TO LEMON?

There is no clear answer. The slice of lemon that often adorns the rim of the *Weissbier* "vase" goes in and out of fashion. Currently, you're likely to get it in the United States, so if you feel it is an abomination, by all means ask that it not be added when you order. On the other hand, it makes a nice presentation and adds to the spritzy character of the beer. I will say that if you're a male beer geek seeking the respect of your equally geeky friends, you had best leave it off.

nearly 300 years, reaching its greatest popularity during the late seventeenth century. In 1872, the fad nearly spent, Georg Schneider negotiated the rights for himself to brew this royal style, and the Schneider brewery still brews wheat beers in Munich. Wheat beers are now so popular in Bavaria that they account for nearly a quarter of all beers sold.

Wheat beers are at their best when fresh, as they are everyday beers and do not improve with age. They should be served cool, but not ice-cold; 45°F (7°C) is about right. Weizens really should be served in their special vase-shaped glasses — they have the capacity to hold a whole beer and its frothy head. Erdinger, Bavaria's number-one wheat-beer brewer, recommends that the glass be scrupulously clean and wetted first, to keep the head under some control. And the lemon should be cut with a grease-free knife, lest any oil interfere with the spectacular head.

Brewed with 50 to 60 percent malted wheat and the balance of malted barley, these beers are pale to deep gold with a definite yeasty haze. They are lightly hopped, with no apparent hop aroma. The aftertaste should be clean and smooth, with little lingering bitterness. The wheat contributes a firm, creamy texture and a bright, almost citric snap. Carbonation levels are very high, and because of the protein content of wheat, the beer should have a dense, meringuelike head.

Weizens are top-fermented using a special ale yeast that produces something called 4-vinyl guaiacol, giving this style its characteristic clove aroma (see chapter 3). This fermentation character varies in intensity from brewery to brewery and includes banana and bubble gum, plus other fruity notes. For some, these unexpected fermentation characteristics are an acquired taste, but if you get acquainted with them, they're entirely lovable.

ORIGIN: Munich, Germany; originally a monopoly of the royal family; hugely popular in the eighteenth century

LOCATION: all over Bavaria; also U.S. craft breweries

FLAVOR: light graininess with milk-shake texture, not much in the way of hops; highly carbonated

AROMA: fruity (bubble gum, bananas), spicy (cloves)

BALANCE: dry malty/grainy, some richness and creamy texture

SEASONALITY: year-round, traditionally enjoyed in the summer

PAIR WITH: wide range of lighter foods: salads, seafood; classic with weisswurst

SUGGESTED BEERS TO TRY: Schneider Weisse Weizenhell, Erdinger Weissbier, Hacker-Pschorr Hefe Weiss Natürtrub, Sprecher Hefe Weiss. Check your local brewpub in the summer.

GRAVITY: 1.047–1.056 (11.8–14°P)

ALCOHOL: 4.9–5.5% by volume

ATTENUATION/BODY: thick but dry

COLOR: 3–9°SRM, straw to pale amber

BITTERNESS: 10–15 IBU, low

NOTE: Kristal (filtered) versions have the same specs.

Weizen in a nineteenth-century knobby glass

Bavarian Dunkel Weizen

This is the same beer as Bavarian Hefeweizen but with added crystal or other dark malts. It's most often an amber color rather than a true brown, and the emphasis is on caramel rather than toastiness. It may sometimes be a touch sweeter than the standard hefeweizens.

SUGGESTED BEERS TO TRY: Schneider Weisse Original, Franziskaner Hefe-Weisse Dunkel, Ayinger Ur-Weisse, Magic Hat St.Goötz

GRAVITY: 1.048-1.056 (11.8-14°P)

ALCOHOL: 4.8-5.4% by volume

ATTENUATION/BODY: thick but dry

COLOR: 9-13°SRM, pale to medium amber

BITTERNESS: 10-15 IBU, low

Weizenbock and Weizen Doppelbock

Bigger, stronger, and darker than dunkel weizen, this is the perfect winter wheat beer. All the same fruit-bowl aroma, but it also has some deep caramelized malt aromas, and maybe hints of toast as well. Despite the strength, these are very drinkable beers. Schneider also makes an eisbock version that is frozen to remove some water, which brings it up to 12 percent alcohol. It takes a cold day to stand up to that.

ORIGIN: Bavaria, Germany; a stronger, darker version brewed as a luxury product

LOCATION: Bavaria; also U.S. craft breweries

FLAVOR: creamy, caramelly malt; hint of bitterness

AROMA: rich caramel malt plus fruity/spicy yeast

BALANCE: malty and sweet, but highly carbonated

SEASONALITY: year-round, but best in cooler weather

PAIR WITH: hearty food, such as roast pork, beef, smoked ham; big desserts, aged cheese

SUGGESTED BEERS TO TRY: Erdinger Pikantus, Schneider Adventinus

GRAVITY: 1.066-1.08 (16-19.5°P)

ALCOHOL: 6.9-9.3% by volume

ATTENUATION/BODY: medium

COLOR: 15-20°SRM, amber

BITTERNESS: 18-29 IBU, low to medium

Berliner Weisse

Berliner Weisse is a classic, but it is rare outside its homeland. In many ways these beers are right for the times. They are low in alcohol and so may be drunk in quantity as a summer refresher. They have a tart, quenching finish that is slightly sour. Their yeasty sediment earned them the name "white beers." In Germany, they are served with a dash of raspberry syrup or essence of woodruff.

There are just two large brands remaining in Berlin, Kindl and Schultheiss, both now under the same ownership and brewing out of the same brewery. There is a third independent brewery, Berliner Bürgerbräu, that also brews Berliner Weisse, as do many of the local brewpubs.

German brewers brought tart and spritzy Berliner-style wheat beers with them to America during the massive immigration that followed the Civil War. Once a prominent part of the product line of many lager breweries in the United States, wheat beer was killed off as an American style by the ravages of Prohibition. In most places, wheat beer was forgotten for half a century.

ORIGIN: Berlin, part of family of white beers developed in the late Middle Ages

LOCATION: Berlin, and the occasional U.S. craft brewery

FLAVOR: light graininess with sharp, yogurty acidity; highly carbonated

AROMA: bright yogurty tang, a little fruitiness

BALANCE: super-light and dry, with tart, crisp finish

SEASONALITY: a traditional summer beer

PAIR WITH: the lightest salads and seafood, perhaps a mild cheese

SUGGESTED BEERS TO TRY: Bayrischer Bahnhof Berliner Style Weisse, Professor Fritz Briem's 1809 Style Berliner Weisse; also check your local brewpub for summer seasonal versions

GRAVITY: 1.028-1.032 (7-8°P)

ALCOHOL: 2.5-3.5% by volume

ATTENUATION/BODY: tart and dry

COLOR: 2-4°SRM, pale straw to pale gold

BITTERNESS: 3-6 IBU, ultra-low

Historical Style

Broyhan Alt

This was a very famous white beer from Hanover, Germany, said to have been invented by a brewer named Cord Broyhan in 1526. Originally a wheat beer, by the late nineteenth century it had turned into a purely barley-malt beer. It was a modest-gravity beer and was said to have a vinous aroma and a salty-sour taste.

Historical Style

Grätzer/ Grodzisk

Grätzer beer, a low-gravity ale brewed with oak-smoked wheat malt, is a smoked beer that was once quite popular and has now nearly died out. It survives only in the form of a Polish beer, Grodzisk. Such beers were once very popular in northern Europe, Prussia especially, and represent one end of the spectrum that also includes Berliner Weisse and Belgian witbiers. Ranging from 1.028 to 1.032 in gravity, with correspondingly low alcohol at 2 to 2.8 percent by volume, this smoky, highly carbonated beer could have been enjoyed in quantity as an everyday thirst-quencher. *Grätzer* would have been amber in color due to a proportion of well-kilned malt along the lines of "aromatic" or melanoidin types. Perhaps this intriguing beer will be revived for our enjoyment sometime soon.

Historical Style

Gose

This is a white beer once very popular in northern Germany around Jena, Leipzig, and its namesake town, Goslar. Brewed from 40 percent barley malt and 60 percent wheat malt, *gose* is a very pale, top-fermenting beer seasoned with coriander and salt, which enhances body and mouthfeel in this very light beer. At some of the pubs, you could request your preferred level of salt. After a hiatus of thirty years, *gose* is now being brewed by three brewers in Germany, and one example from Bayrischer Bahnhof is currently being imported into the United States.

Historical Style

Lichtenhainer

This is a smoked, top-fermenting beer from northern Germany. Always a relatively low-gravity beer (1.045 [11°P] in 1886; 1.031 [7°P] in 1898), *lichtenhainer* featured a smoky palate from 100 percent barley malt, although up to a third wheat was used in later versions. Like many white beers, it was lightly hopped and had a good smack of acidity.

THE BEERS OF BELGIUM

Ahhh, Belgium! The great adventure land for the beer-curious, the wine lover's beer destination, the foodie's easy pairing resource, the living museum of beer history — Belgium is many things to many people.

The beers of Belgium couldn't be more distinctive, even though brewing in Belgium has similar roots to those of other European countries. The current beer scene is a fascinating mix of ancient folkways and postmodern creativity.

BELGIUM'S OVERLORDS 1477–1830

1477	The Hapsburgs
1526	France
1559	Italy
1570	Spain
1598	Italy
1633	Spain
1713	Austria
1745	France
1748	Austria
1789	Contested between France and Austria
1790	United States of Belgium
1795	France
1815	Holland
1830	Independence!
1915	Germany
1919	Independence
1940	Germany
1945	Independence

Belgium is a small country that never formed a great empire, but it was prosperous from an early age. In the late Middle Ages and Renaissance eras, Flanders (which forms an important portion of modern Belgium) was one of the economic powerhouses of northern Europe. Over the centuries, tiny Belgium has been dominated by all the nearby powers but never was absorbed into them.

Belgium is comprised of a number of smaller regions, each with its own language, culture, and of course, beer specialties.

5,000 Years of Belgian Beer

We'll start the story with the same Iron Age Gauls we — and Caesar — encountered in England. One tribe, the Belgae, was reputedly a warlike mix of Celts and Germans who, it is said, loved beer. The widespread beverage-centered Beaker Culture was present as early as 2800 BCE, so there is a very long tradition of drinking in Belgium. By the eighth or ninth century, monasteries dotted the countryside across northern Europe. With the vacuum created by the collapse of the Roman Empire, power shifted to local lords and ecclesiastical powers based in the abbeys. Brewing was a necessary function for such centers of activity, and because many of the religious orders specified that monks must work to support themselves, the brewing was not left to outsiders. Large amounts of beer were needed for the smooth functioning of the monasteries. As the old saying goes, "Ale is meat and drink and cloth."

A famous medieval document shows the plan for the Monastery of St. Gallin, Switzerland, in about 830 CE. This was never built, but served as an idealized example of the kind of organization and scale that were appropriate for such an institution. The plans show three distinct brewhouses, each dedicated to brewing a different grade of beer. Noble guests got a high-class beer brewed from barley and wheat, while the brothers and poor pilgrims had to make do with lower-quality oat beers. It is estimated that such a brewery complex could have produced 350 to 400 liters of beer per day, which works out to 770 to 880 barrels a year.

One of the earliest written references to specifics of brewing comes from the Abbess Hildegard of Bingen, who in 1067 noted that beer was mainly made from oats. She liked her nuns drinking beer because, she said, it gave them "rosy cheeks." Thirteenth-century documents mention beers made from barley, spelt, and something called *siliginum,* which scholars believe may have been rye. Other documents show that brewers in Liège and Namur paid their taxes in spelt, a brewing grain that is still traditional in those parts of Belgium.

In those early days, there was no hopped beer in Belgium. Bitterness was provided by a mixture called gruit, which contained a secret mix of herbs and spices disguised by its combination with crushed grain. The right to sell gruit, the *Gruitrecht,* was held either by a religious power or a political big shot. In the twelfth century, 5 pounds of gruit were required to brew a barrel of beer (2 kg/hl). It must have been big business back then, as the lavishness of the still-standing *Gruithuis* (gruit house) in Bruges can attest.

IT IS THE BELGIANS who provided us with one of the mythic personifications of beer, King Gambrinus. He may have been an actual person named Jan Primus (Jean I), born around 1250, who ruled as Duke of Brabant, the part of Belgium that now includes Brussels. He was, by contemporary accounts, an all-around great guy: a warrior, great lover, and bon vivant, as politically skilled as he was ambitious. Or, there are other candidates. It may have been the Burgundian John the Fearless (1371–1419), a cupbearer of Charlemagne who bore the name Gambrinus, or simply a corruption of a couple of different Latin phrases: *cambarus,* meaning "cellarer," or *ganae birrinus,* "tavern drinker." Since given his beer-king status by the German chronicler Johannes Turmair in 1519, Gambrinus has served as the jolly, fat-faced symbol of all that is good 'n' beery all across northern Europe. If you want to hoist a tankard in honor of his birthday, it is celebrated on April 11.

King Gambrinus on a German postcard, c. 1900

HOPS FIRST came into Flanders by way of beer imported from Hamburg and Amsterdam, certainly by the beginning of the fourteenth century. In 1364, the Bishop of Liège gave permission for local brewers to use hops, and shortly thereafter levied a tax on hopped beer, a pattern we see whenever hops are introduced.

Throughout the centuries, we get some observations about Belgian beer. The herbalist Johannes Theodorus (1588) states, "The beer of Flanders is a good beer. Above all, the double beer, such as is brewed in Ghent and Bruges, surpasses all the beer of the Netherlands." It is estimated that this double beer would have been in the neighborhood of 1.077 original gravity (19 degrees Plato) and possibly 6 to 7 percent alcohol. He also advises that wheat, spelt, rye, or oats could be used in two- or three-part combinations or singly if needed. Don Alonzo Vasquez, a Spanish sea captain stationed in the Spanish Netherlands around 1617, reports, "Beer, which is brewed on a base of wheat, has a color as clear as linen and it froths forth when one pours it into the jug."

These tantalizing dalliances are always far too brief, but they do give insight into the vibrancy of the Belgian beer scene back then.

By the seventeenth century, brewing had moved well beyond the monasteries. Numerous public brewers existed, and the bourgeoisie in towns had established communal brewhouses similar to the *Zoigl* system in eastern Bavaria, where different individuals took turns brewing for their households. By 1718, there were 621 such breweries in Bruges alone.

About this time we start to see beers we can recognize. In 1698, the *Intendand* of Flanders recorded, "The Flemish use for their beer a sort of barley named winter barley. After having germinated it in water, they add an eighth part short oats, milled without being germinated, and boil the lot for 24 hours. They then barrel the liquid in half-hogsheads where it ferments by means of a certain amount of yeast. Fifteen days later, the beer is fit to drink." It should be noted that this boiling of the mash may be an incorrect impression by a non-brewing observer.

MONASTERIES SAW their political influence wane over the centuries, but they were more influential centers of power in strongly Catholic Belgium than in most European countries. Even so, the monasteries closed in 1797 during the turmoil of the French Revolution and stayed shuttered during the Napoleonic struggles that followed. Most that reopened did so between 1830 and 1840. This created a discontinuity, a 40-year gap that disrupted the orderly flow of traditional monastic brewing. We don't know what was lost, but it is clear that the beers of Trappist monasteries today have more to do with the twentieth century than the eighteenth.

In 1822, the Dutch administrators of Belgium instituted a tax system in which brewers were taxed, per batch, on the capacity of their mash tuns. As G. M. Johnson said in 1916, ". . . the reigning monarch was William I, of anything but blessed memory in brewing circles, for he was signatory to, if not otherwise responsible for, one of the most ridiculous and vexatious Excise laws that ever disgraced the annals of fiscal interference and fiscal stupidity. . . . For the space of some sixty years (1822–1885), the best minds in the Belgian brewing world seem to have concentrated on the problem of getting a quart into a pint pot." This strange system led to many peculiarities of Belgian beers, most importantly the turbid mash procedures that are still used, in modified form, to brew witbier and lambic. When the law was changed to an English-style excise system, consumers complained that the beers were thinner and not as fine as before. Eventually parts of the old processes returned.

The Belgians finally gained their independence in 1830 after 13 changes of overlords. I'm sure there are other reasons for the uniqueness

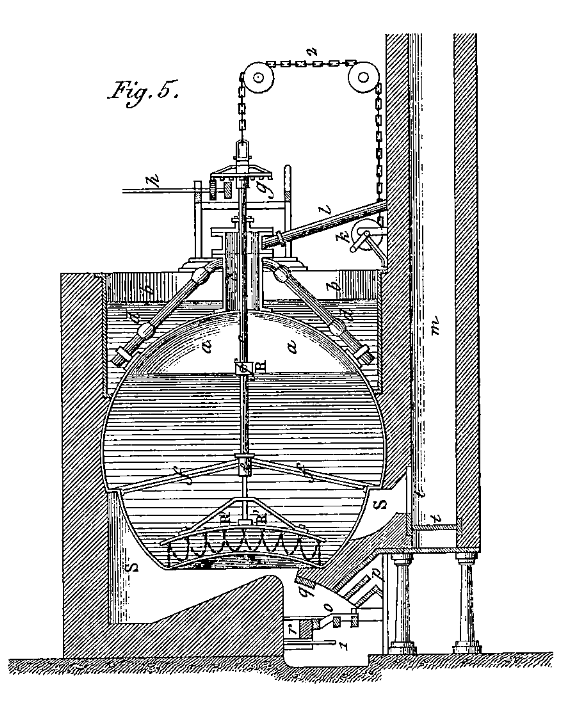

Chain Copper, Belgium, c. 1851
This boiling vessel was fitted with chains that were dragged across the bottom to keep fine particles from sticking and burning.

of Belgian beer culture, but I think one explanation is that as the foreign princes came and went, people tried to hold on to things they felt were truly Belgian. Beer is as pure as it gets in that regard, and taxation aside, foreign potentates usually left it alone, as an adequate supply of beer helps to cool the embers of discontent.

A fairly complete description of the state of Belgian brewing in 1851 was presented by G. Lacambre in his *Traité Complet de la Fabrication des Bières.* "There is not a country," he says, "that brews so many specialties of different natures and varied tastes as Belgium and Holland." According to Lacambre, multigrain was the name of the game: ". . . although a few beers were brewed with barley malt exclusively, in most places they brew with barley, oats, wheat, and spelt concurrently." He points out that even the beers considered

BELGIAN BEER ACCORDING TO G. LACAMBRE, 1851

Bière d'Orge d'Anvers (barley beer of Antwerp). Often brewed with a little wheat or oats, the best ones were all barley malt, around 5 to 6 percent alcohol by volume and aged for at least 6 months. Amber to brown in color; chalk sometimes added to kettle to darken wort. Lightly hopped, but with an emphasis on aroma. Well-aged batches often blended with fresher beer, or sweetened with caramel syrup.

Bière d'Orge des Flandres (barley beer of Flanders, also called *uytzet*). Brewed around Ghent, mainly of amber-colored barley malt with a little wheat and/or oats. Two versions: an ordinary at 3.2 percent alcohol by volume and a double at 4.5 percent. Both were moderately hopped.

Bière Brune des Flandres (Brown Beer of Flanders). A lightly hopped 4 to 5 percent alcohol brown beer brewed from barley malt, sometimes with a little wheat or oats. Color entirely due to a 15 to 20 hour boil.

Bières de Maestricht, Masek, Bois-le-Duc. This was a family of very lightly hopped brown beers brewed in the Dutch parts of Belgium and popular in the interior of Holland, brewed from hard or durum wheat, malted spelt, and low-protein wheat.

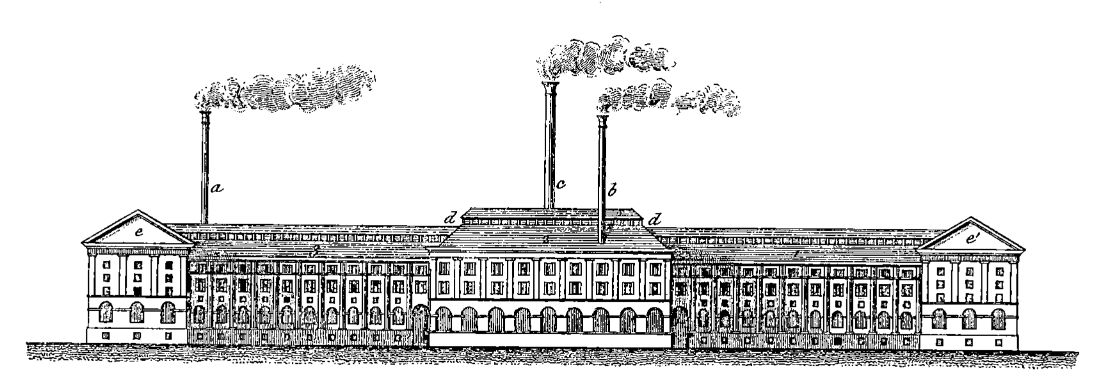

Grande Brasserie, Ghent, 1851
Lacambre's own brewery was a technological marvel, impressive even by today's standards.

barley based, such as *bière d'orge* of Antwerp, contained "a little oats, or sometimes wheat." He notes the antiquity of many of these styles, which our earlier historical references confirm. There is much about Belgian beer that is very old indeed, especially the many adjunct beers broadly in the white-beer family. But despite the remarkable thoroughness of Lacambre's book, there's not a whisper about monastic brewing in it.

FIFTY YEARS LATER, by 1895, an English observer, G. M. Johnson, reported the Belgian brewing scene in a very sorry state. Breweries were small and ill-equipped and the beers were largely weak, sourish, and sold quickly to locals. In 1908, half the beers in Wallonia were 1.020 original gravity (5 degrees Plato) or lower, barely capable of producing 2 percent alcohol. Low import duties were part of the problem. Imported English

Bière d'Orge Wallones (Verviers, Namur, Charleroy) (Wallonian* barley beers). An unruly group, widely variable in taste, color, all between four and five percent alcohol by volume and aged 4 to 6 months before drinking. Versions from Liège and Mons employed hard (high protein) wheat, spelt, oats, and sometimes even buckwheat or broad beans.

Peetermann. A "strongly amber" variant of witbier, with gravities of 1.057 to 1.074 (14 to 18 degrees Plato). Chalk was usually added to darken the wort. The finished beer was poorly attenuated and described as "viscous."

Bières de Diest. Two types, including one called *"gulde bier"* or *"bière de cabaret,"* which was 44 percent malt, 40 percent unmalted wheat, and 16 percent oats, and was described as "unctuous and slightly sweet." The other, known properly as *diest*, was a dark, sweet beer, brewed from 55 percent malt, 30 percent unmalted wheat, and 15 percent oats and available in two strengths: a single at 1.047 to 1.049 (12 to 12.5 degrees Plato) and a double at 1.061 to 1.081 (15 to 19.5 degrees Plato). *Diest* had the reputation of being a nourishing beer, good for nursing mothers.

* *Wallonia is the French-speaking portion of Belgium.*

Bière Brune de Malines (Mechelen). "Very dark" due to a 10 to 12 hour boil, usually with chalk added. One-quarter to one-third of an 18-month-old batch was blended into fresh beer for "a certain taste of old beer," very much along the lines of the Flanders sour beers, although Mechelen is no longer home to that style.

Bière de Hoegaerde. A pale wheat beer that he describes as "of little importance" but "very agreeable in the summertime," with "a certain acidity and refreshing moussy quality." Brewed from 63 percent malt, 21 percent unmalted wheat, and 16 percent oats.

Bières de Lierre, "Cavesse" (Liers). Brewed from 67 percent malt, 13 percent wheat, and 20 percent oats, and available in two strengths. Lacambre describes this as a *"Bière jaune"* (yellow beer) that had a lot in common with beers from Hoegaarde and Leuven.

Bières de Liège. Elsewhere called Liège saison, this style was brewed from barley and spelt malts plus oats and wheat. There were two strengths: a *"bière jeune"* (young beer) and a *"bière de saison,"* by which was meant it was brewed in the proper brewing season of winter.

and Scotch ales, and German lagers, were so cheap that Belgian brewers couldn't brew them at competitive prices, so, imports dominated the premium beer segment.

Naturally the brewers weren't happy about this. Through the Belgian Brewers Guild, the prominent brewer Henri Van Laer organized a "Contest for the Improvement of Belgian Beer" in 1902 and 1903. The object was to create some respectable beers in the 1.044 to 1.057 (11 to 14 degrees Plato) range, with an eye to exports. As brewing details were to be made public, few entered. The next year, secrecy prevailed and there were a flood of entries, a number of which, like Palm Spéciale, Ginder Ale, and Op Ale, still exist. Despite this encouraging development, it would be some time before things improved across the board.

World War I pushed the tailspin even further. The Germans requisitioned all copper brewing equipment and instituted very strict rationing of materials and ingredients. Original gravities fell to 1.010 to 1.015 (3 to 4 degrees Plato), at that point not much more than weak barley tea. Brewers were so desperate for yeast-nourishing nitrogen that malt rootlets — normally used for animal feed — were added to the mash.

Once the war was over, matters took several years to improve. But in 1919, the Belgian government banned the sale of gin in taverns and cafés. This opened up a market for stronger beers aimed at drinkers used to their fiery *jenever* (juniper-flavored liqueur). Gradually, Belgian brewers got their footings and the quality of their beer improved. Many of the old styles were dead, but many others lived on. There was also a new hybrid class of beers that melded Belgian and English traditions. Duvel, for example, was first, brewed in 1923 (as a dark beer) using a strain of yeast from the Scottish brewery McEwan's.

Trappist beers as we know them started to show up at that time. Although Scourmont (Chimay) had been brewing and selling to the public since 1862. Orval got its brewery going in 1931, and registered its image of a fish with a ring in its mouth in 1934. Westmalle registered the name *Trappistenbier* in 1933 and a year later created the first pale Tripel, a beer that would become iconic for the style and widely copied.

The Bavarians had gotten involved in some brewery ventures in the second half of the nineteenth century. The dark Munich style of beer was well-known in Belgium, but never became all that popular there because it was considered impossible to brew in Belgian breweries, as they were not set up to conduct the *Dictmaisch* (thick-mash) decoctions necessary at the time. G.M. Johnson in 1895 reported that of the 2,700 breweries then in Belgium, only 25 were dedicated to bottom fermentation. Still, one can see similarities between those dark Münchener and bock beers and some of the rich, luscious flavors that eventually found their way into Dubbels. The first Pilsner brewed in Belgium was Alken Cristal in 1928. Like everywhere else, Pilsner currently dominates the Belgian marketplace.

World War II was another disaster for Belgium, but this one was not as disruptive to brewing in the long run, probably because the brewing industry this time was in a pretty good state prior to the conflict. There were problems, to be sure, but after the war, things picked up more or less where they left off. Pilsner kept growing at the expense of the local everyday beers such as *peetermann* and white beer, until they disappeared. Belgian brewers eventually found a market for their luxurious beers, and today exports make up a growing 50 percent of their capacity.

---

opposite: Belgian Beer Labels, Midtwentieth Century
Belgian beer styles were just as daunting a generation or two ago.

The Uniqueness of Belgian Beer

ALTHOUGH THERE ARE specific styles (presented here at length), the Belgians favor an artisanal approach to brewing, meaning the brewer is considered an artist and has no sense of duty to conform to preexisting styles. More than half of all Belgian beers do not fit into any style, and the styles they do have tend to be interpreted rather casually. This makes it difficult to get a handle on things, but who doesn't like this kind of adventure?

There's a huge variety of strengths, colors, textures, and brewing methods; hundreds of distinctive yeasts and other microorganisms; fermentation in barrels; blended beers; sugar, honey, and caramel syrup in addition to malt; unmalted grains, like oats, wheat, spelt, and occasionally buckwheat; a whole basket of fruit; every conceivable kind of spice, including grains of paradise, chamomile, cumin, star anise, and a "medicinal lichen." The list is long, deep, wide, and exhilarating.

Except for the industrial Pilsners, one thing that unites all this joyful chaos is the use of highly distinctive yeast. Most Belgian beers do not use truly wild microorganisms; those are limited mostly to the lambic family and the sour *oud bruins* of Flanders. But the yeast in Belgium is very diverse, and the strain employed in a beer definitely puts its unique stamp on the finished product. Brewers encourage this by fermenting some styles at relatively high temperatures, which encourages fruity and spicy aromas. You can, in fact, take any kind of wort and ferment it with Belgian yeast and the result will be a Belgian-tasting beer. There are some styles, like saison, that absolutely depend on particular yeast strains, and if they're not used, the beer really becomes something else.

On the whole, there is much more emphasis on malt than on hops. The Belgian hop varieties have traditionally been of good aroma but very low in bittering ability. Hop aroma is so assertive that it can mask other, more delicate aromas, and the Belgians would prefer a more layered, nuanced approach than hop bombs offer. And some of the malty flavors actually come from dark-cooked caramel syrups and other types of sugar. Sugar can be a bad thing if used in excess, but it is mainly used in stronger Belgian beers to thin out the body and make them more drinkable.

BELGIUM NEVER had a *Reinheitsgebot,* so the old traditions of herbs and spices other than hops still survive there. Not all Belgian beers employ spices, and even in the ones that do, it's not always obvious. Generally, if you can pick out an individual spice, the brewer is doing it wrong. Bitter orange peel (or the small unripe form, curaçao) and coriander are the dynamic duo, essential in witbier and slipped into many others. The bright peppery zip of grains of paradise (an African relative of cardamom) are often encountered in saisons and other strong pale beers. Richer, deeper dark beers take well to spices like licorice and star anise.

There is an abundance of strong beer, and many of these are cork-finished, a technique that makes a nice presentation and is being adopted for high-end beers in the United States and elsewhere. Carbonation varies widely, but many stronger beers have a huge mousse from carbonation levels, up to double what might be appropriate in "normal" beers. Bottle-conditioned beers are common as well. Yeast and a small dose of sugar are added at bottling, and the restarted fermentation creates carbonation, throwing a small deposit of yeast on the bottom of the bottle. For this reason, it is important to pour carefully or decant to avoid muddying things up when serving. It's not unhealthful, but the yeast mars the appearance and can sometimes add sludgy flavors to the beer.

Belgium is the only country to feature so many acid-tinged beers. The flavors of the ancient lambics really revolve around acidity, at times shockingly so. Sour Flanders red and brown ales live up to their names, and even in witbiers and saisons, the sharp crack of acidity adds life to these quenching styles.

The final thing to know about Belgian beer culture is that it's not just about the beer. There is a highly evolved gastronomic tradition that has beer as one of its important elements. Over there, you will find restaurants focused on *cuisine de la bière,* offering a fantastic way to appreciate Belgian beers in the proper context. With a little research, you can create your own version of that experience just about anywhere. The variety, subtlety, and never-overpowering intensity of the beers make them willing food partners.

Belgian Pale Ale

ORIGIN: The De Koninck brewery says its version was created by Johannes Vervliet in 1833; but Antwerp had long been known as a center of malt-based (as opposed to wheat) beers. Modern versions, Palm Spéciale in particular, were created in the early twentieth century to capture part of the market dominated by imported British pale ales. These really do have a lot of similarities to British ale, including a crisp palate, a definite hop presence, and a nutty, slightly crisp malt character.

LOCATION: Antwerp, Belgium; U.S. craft breweries

FLAVOR: light caramel malt, lightly hoppy

AROMA: clean malt plus spicy yeast notes; yeast character quite subtle compared to most other Belgian styles

BALANCE: evenly balanced; crisp, malty finish

SEASONALITY: year-round

PAIR WITH: wide range of foods, such as cheese, mussels, chicken, spicy dishes

SUGGESTED BEERS TO TRY: De Koninck, Palm Spéciale, Straffe Hendrik Blonde, New Belgium Fat Tire Amber Ale, Two Brothers Prairie Path Ale

GRAVITY: 1.040–1.055 (10–13.6°P)

ALCOHOL: 3.9–5.6% by volume

ATTENUATION/BODY: medium

COLOR: 4–14°SRM, gold to deep amber

BITTERNESS: 20–30 IBU, medium

Belgian Strong Golden Ale

ORIGIN: Moortgat's Duvel is the archetype for the style, but Duvel was a dark beer until 1971. The original strong Belgian golden-colored ale was Westmalle Tripel in 1934, which just points out the very slim differences between the Tripel and strong golden categories. The latter is supposed to be the simpler, cleaner version, but there is some degree of overlap, and as with many things Belgian, there is some degree of ambiguity. The complex fruitiness of certain yeast, the spiciness of the hops, and the crisp finish contributed by about 20 percent of the recipe being pure corn sugar are all important characteristics of the style.

LOCATION: Belgium, U.S. craft breweries

FLAVOR: super-crisp malt, clean hoppy finish

AROMA: spicy yeast plus malt plus hops

BALANCE: super-dry, but moderately bitter; highly carbonated

SEASONALITY: year-round

PAIR WITH: wide range of food; salmon, chicken, spicy cuisine like Thai

SUGGESTED BEERS TO TRY: Duvel, Delirium Tremens, Brooklyn Brewery Local 1, North Coast Pranqster Belgian Style Golden Ale, Victory Golden Monkey

GRAVITY: 1.065–1.080 (16–19.2°P)

ALCOHOL: 7–9% by volume

ATTENUATION/BODY: super-dry

COLOR: 3.5–5.5°SRM, straw to gold

BITTERNESS: 25–45 IBU, medium to high

Belgian Strong Dark Ale

ORIGIN: This really is a catchall category rather than a style with a specific history. As the work by Lacambre points out, there were a number of historic strong, darker beers, but there is no clear lineage from these older brews, with the possible exception of Gouden Carolus, a licorice-tinged deep amber beer that claims descent from the old Mechelen style (see Lacambre, page 192), although the taste and brewing process don't quite jibe with the old description. Modern versions include several Trappist beers (Rochefort and Westvleteren) and a number of more-eccentric brews. Sugar, as a body thinner, is quite common.

LOCATION: Belgium, U.S. craft breweries

FLAVOR: fat, caramelly malt, barely balanced by hops

AROMA: complex maltiness plus fruity/spicy yeast

BALANCE: malty to even; long, rich finish

SEASONALITY: year-round, but holiday versions abound

PAIR WITH: very hearty food; strong cheese; fabulous with chocolate

SUGGESTED BEERS TO TRY: Chimay Grande Reserve/Capsule Bleu, Het Anker Gouden Carolus, Van Steenbrugge Gulden Draak, Dogfish Head Raison d'Extra, Goose Island Pere Jacques

GRAVITY: 1.064–1.096 (16–23°P)

ALCOHOL: 7–11% by volume

ATTENUATION/BODY: very full

COLOR: 7–20°SRM, amber to brown

BITTERNESS: 20–50 IBU, medium

Brew Kettle, 1930s
This northern French or Belgian brew kettle reflects the rustic nature of many small breweries in the area at the time.

Abbey and Trappist Ales

THIS IS ANOTHER somewhat unruly group. The first thing to get a grip on is the differences. *Trappiste* is an appellation, which is a legal designation with the enforceability of a trademark, meaning that only brewers who meet certain requirements are allowed to use the name. In this case they must be brewed under the direct supervision of the monks at a brewery on the monastic property. Exclusive rights to the name *Bière Trappiste* or *Trappistenbier* were won for the group in 1962 as a result of a legal action spearheaded by Chimay. Abbey beers are of similar styles but are brewed by secular commercial breweries that may be under license to

CLASSIC TRAPPIST BREWERIES AND THEIR ALES

Achel (Brouwerij der Sint-Benedictusabdij de Achelse Kluis)

Founded in 1648, rebuilt in 1844. Some brewing was done in the late nineteenth century, but the brewery was dismantled by the Germans in World War I, and not rebuilt and certified as a Trappist brewery until 1998. Beers include an 8° (1.080/19 degrees Plato) Bruin, which is a fairly strong Dubbel, and an 8° (1.080/19 degrees Plato) blond, which is at the light edge of the Tripel style. Achel also makes 5° brown and blond beers available only at the brewery cafeteria, along with a 9° "Extra."

Chimay (Abbaye de Notre Dame de Scourmont)

Brewing since 1863, the brewery was rebuilt in 1948 by the prominent Belgian brewing scientist Jean DeClerck, who had a lot to do with the current recipes. Chimay produces several beers, including *Capsule Rouge,* a classic Dubbel at 1.063 original gravity (15.5 degrees Plato), 7 percent; *Capsule Blanche* (Cinq Cents), a briskly hopped Tripel at 1.071 original gravity (17.3 degrees Plato), 8 percent; and *Capsule Bleu* (Grande Reserve), a big, chewy, strong dark at 1.081 original gravity (19.1 degrees Plato), 9 percent. Chimay also produces a 4.8 percent *Dorée,* intended for local consumption only.

Orval

Founded in 1132, but rebuilt in 1926 after a period of abandonment after the French Revolution. Orval produces one beer for public sale, an orangish, golden ale broadly in the saison style, at 1.054–5 original gravity (13.3 to 13.5 degrees Plato), crisply hoppy and very dry, spiked upon bottling with *Brettanomyces* yeast, which after some months starts to develop rich, barnyard aromas. Alcohol is 5.2 to 5.7 percent.

an active abbey, named for a defunct one, or without any monastic name connection at all.

Trappist ales proper tend to reflect the beer traditions of the regions in which they're located. At present there are seven Trappist breweries (see sidebar, below) in Belgium and the Netherlands. The Trappist beers are highly individualistic, although two of them, Westmalle Tripel and Chimay Rouge (Dubbel), are archetypes of their specific styles. As a group, these are all superb beers. It's a rare beer fancier who doesn't have at least a couple of Trappist beers in his or her top ten. Singels are rare, often brewed just for the monks.

Abbey beers exist in greater numbers and tend to cleave to the convention of a brown Dubbel and a blond Tripel, with the occasional blond or strong dark tossed into the mix.

La Trappe/Koningshoeven (Onze Lieve Vrouw van Koningshoeven)

This brewery in the southern Netherlands has a somewhat complex history, having at times operated an on-site brewery and at others brewing under license. The current products are fairly recent (Dubbel, Tripel, 1987; blond, 1992) Classic dark Dubbel at 7 percent; pale Tripel at 8 percent; and a quadruple at 10 percent. The brewery also produces a 6.5 percent blond, a seasonal bockbier at 7 percent, and a witbier. The brewery was decertified as a Trappist brewery between 1999 and 2005, but has now resolved its dispute with the International Trappist Association.

Rochefort (Abbaye Saint-Remy in Rochefort)

Founded in 1230, closed in 1794, then reoccupied by monks in 1889. The brewery was established a few years later, in 1899. They produce a range of three beers designated 6, 8, and 10, but not following the degrees Belgian nomenclature. The 6 is actually 1.072/17.5 degrees Plato, the 8 is 1.078/19 degrees Plato, and the 10 is 1.96/23.4 degrees Plato. They share a rich, bittersweet chocolaty character. Alcohol is 7.5 percent, 9.2 percent, and 11.3 percent, respectively.

Westmalle (Abdij Onze-Lieve-Vrouw van het Heilig Hart van Jezus)

Founded in 1794, it began selling to the locals in 1856 and through commercial channels in 1921. The brewhouse was modernized in the 1930s, about when it launched their radical new pale Tripel. Three beers are produced: an "Extra" that is enjoyed by the monks, plus the famous Tripel at 1.080 original gravity (20 degrees Plato), 9.5 percent, and a rich Dubbel, the recipe for which comes from the earliest times but was reworked in 1926, at 1.063 original gravity (15.7 degrees Plato), 7 percent.

Westvleteren (The Abbey of Saint Sixtus of Westvleteren)

Established in 1831, the brewery started operations in 1871. It has never really expanded its operations, preferring to remain small. The brewery sells only to individuals, by appointment only, and with a strict limit. In fact, it recently has taken legal action to end gray market trading in its rare beers. The brewery produces a hoppy blond at 1.051 (12.6 degrees Plato), 41 IBU, and two dark, raisiny beers, the 8, or Blue Cap, at 1.072 (17.5 degrees Plato), around 8 percent, and the 12, or Yellow Cap, at 1.090 (21.5 degrees Plato), 11 percent. Author Stan Heironymous (*Brew Like a Monk*) reports considerable batch-to-batch variation.

Belgian Abbey Dubbel

ORIGIN: Abbeys brewed these in ancient times, but modern abbey styles were created in the past 100 years.

LOCATION: Belgium, U.S. craft breweries

FLAVOR: soft, creamy malt, considerable spiciness

AROMA: clean malt, soft hops, spicy/fruity yeast character; middle-color malts crucial to this style and may manifest as soft hints of cocoa or deep, dried fruit character, like raisins or prunes

BALANCE: malty, yet fairly dry on the palate due to the use of sugar (sometimes dark) as a body thinner

SEASONALITY: year-round

PAIR WITH: wide range of hearty food; perfect with barbecued ribs, abbey cheese, tiramisu, chocolate cake, medium-intensity desserts

SUGGESTED BEERS TO TRY: Affligem Dubbel, Chimay Première/Capsule Rouge, Ommegang Abbey Ale, Allagash Dubbel Reserve

GRAVITY: 1.062–1.080 (15–19.2°P)

ALCOHOL: 6–7.8% by volume

ATTENUATION/BODY: medium dry

COLOR: 10–20°SRM, amber to brown

BITTERNESS: 15–25 IBU, low-medium

Belgian Abbey Tripel

ORIGIN: Westmalle Abbey, in 1930s in reaction to Pilsner and pale-ale trends

LOCATION: Belgium, U.S. craft breweries

FLAVOR: complex clean maltiness with lots of spicy depth; highly carbonated

AROMA: spicy/fruity with clean malt, a bit of hops

BALANCE: honeyed, but dry, with clean, crisp finish

SEASONALITY: year-round

PAIR WITH: roast pork, rich seafood like lobster, creamy desserts like crème brûlée

SUGGESTED BEERS TO TRY: Bosteels Tripel Karmeliet, Westmalle Tripel, Stoudt's Tripel, Unibroue La Fin du Monde

GRAVITY: 1.075–1.090 (18–22°P)

ALCOHOL: 7.5–9.5% by volume

ATTENUATION/BODY: rich, but dry

COLOR: 3.5–6°SRM, pale to deep gold

BITTERNESS: 25–38 IBU, medium

Saison

ORIGIN: In the nineteenth century, the saisons were brown beers, so there are still some dots that need connecting. It is possible that modern versions owe more to the top-fermented originally blond beers popular in the Nord region of France, which is not far away from the francophone Wallonia and Hainault, where saisons are currently brewed. Lacambre also gives a perfectly sensible meaning for the name *saison,* which means "season." He says the small beers everywhere were brewed year-round because they were consumed so quickly that they didn't have time to go bad in the summer heat. Saison beers, he says, were brewed "in season," that is, between November and March, and would have been strong and clean enough to age through the summer, a theme we have seen many times before.

The current story is that saison came from Flanders, made in farmhouse breweries, where it was brewed for agricultural workers to sustain them in their summer "season" of labors. This is a nice story, and while there are undoubtedly elements of truth in this, it isn't entirely accurate. Historically, the name was applied to the very eccentric beers of Liège way over in the east, almost in Germany; but those beers were the same (according to Lacambre in 1851) as the beers of Mons, much farther west in an area now known as a saison region, so now this starts to make sense. The Liège beers were brewed with malt, wheat, oats, spelt, and, even at times, buckwheat or *fèves* (broad beans).

At some unknown point (I'm guessing midtwentieth century, like many other styles), the modern saison was born. Today, it may or may not contain wheat, although at least one version (Saison d'Epeautre) contains spelt. Many saison brewers offer a range of strengths; some of the stronger ones use sugar to improve drinkability.

One of the defining things about the style is the yeast. Believed to be related to red-wine yeast, the saison strains are tolerant of very high fermentation temperatures — above 90°F (32°C). The yeast produces a lot of peppery phenols, but not a lot of ester, which at these elevated temperatures would render the beer undrinkably solventy and reeking of nail polish remover. It's a slow and cranky yeast to deal with, so many brewers start their saisons with the proper yeast and then switch over to a more conventional yeast to finish the job. Spices are not required for the style, but grains of paradise, black pepper, and others are sometimes used to complement the character of the yeast.

LOCATION: Hainault and Wallonia (Francophone), Belgium

FLAVOR: creamy pale malt, clean hops; slight tang; may also use spices or *Brettanomyces* wild yeast; very crisp and dry on the palate, but soft and drinkable just the same

AROMA: complex, peppery spice, hints of malt, hops, sometimes a whiff of orange

BALANCE: super-dry, with clean, hoppy finish

SEASONALITY: traditional for summer and harvest, but good year-round

PAIR WITH: Substantial salads, chicken, richer seafood dishes; very nice with bloomy-rind cheese. Earthier versions great with ripened goat cheese.

SUGGESTED BEERS TO TRY: Brasserie Dupont Saison Dupont, Brasserie des Géants Saison Voisin, Jolly Pumpkin Bam Bière, Southampton Publick House Saison

GRAVITY: 1.055–1.080 (13.6–19°P)

ALCOHOL: 4.5–8.1% by volume

ATTENUATION/BODY: super-dry

COLOR: 6–12°SRM, gold to amber

BITTERNESS: 20–45 IBU, medium to high

Witbier/White Ale

ORIGIN: This once widespread style showed up in medieval northern Europe in the eleventh century or so. White beers were the first hopped beers, although ironically today they are thought of as one of the few styles for which seasonings other than hops are essential. There were many variations, from *kvass* in Russia to Devon white ale in England, that died out by about 1870. Berliner Weisse is a survivor of this family of beer.

Wit (or *weisse* in German) means "white," a name that describes the beer's pale color and cloudy appearance. White beers invariably contain wheat and often other grains as well.

By the late nineteenth century, the style was centered around Leuven (Louvain), Belgium, and to a lesser extent in the nearby town of Hoegaarde, where by 1955 the last traditional witbier brewery had closed its doors. Ten years later, Pierre Celis, who in his youth had worked at Tomsin, the last of the Hoegaarde breweries, decided to revive the style. He founded the Brouwerij Celis (renamed de Kluis in 1978) in a hayloft and launched a beer called Hoegaarden. Eventually, the beer found success, and witbier is now being brewed by many breweries in Belgium and elsewhere. Even the industrial giant Molson-Coors has had a reasonable degree of success with their quasi-craft version, Blue Moon.

A Very Young Pierre Celis (second from right), in the Tomsin Brewery, c. 1943
After the last witbier brewery closed in his hometown of Hoegaarde, Belgium, Celis saved the style by opening a brewery and producing Oud Hoegaards Bier, now sold by InBev as Hoegaarden Witbier. Note that he is holding a *stuikmand,* the brewer's wicker basket used to separate wort from spent grains.

TURBID MASHING AND *SLIJM*

Wheat beers go back many centuries in Belgium, and so matching the style nearly always demands special brewing procedures to extract much fermentable materials. In addition, the oddball excise regulation imposed on Belgian brewers between 1822 and 1885 and a tax on the capacity of the mash tun forever changed the way they brewed many types of beer. The Belgian brewers also produced "single" or "ordinary" beers at very low gravities, and for these styles it was useful to brew in such a way so as to end up with a lot of unfermentable materials, which gave small beers a richer, fuller taste. And in lambic brewing, these unfermentable dextrins are valuable as food for the *Pediococcus* bacteria, used for adding the bracing sourness so important to the style.

So, the game was to absolutely jam-pack the mash tun, which meant very little hot water was used. The normal false bottom wasted too much space, so to filter out the liquid, a *stuikmand,* or brewer's basket (a tall wicker basket), was forced down into the mash, letting liquid dribble in through the woven sides. This was then scooped out with big ladles. The most important feature of turbid mashing is that this cloudy, enzyme-rich wort, known as *slijm* (a Dutch term meaning "slime"), is immediately put into a kettle fitted with a set of rotating chains that drag the bottom and keep the starch from sticking and scorching. As the *slijm* boils, the enzymes are destroyed. The original mash is then reinfused with very hot water, and mashing proceeds. After a period of time, additional liquid is drawn off the mash and boiled. At this point the boiled *slijm* is reinfused into grain and mashed again, with more runoffs and boiling of wort. In actuality it's a lot more complicated than there is space here to discuss. The result of this Byzantine procedure is that the enzymes are seriously impaired in their ability to convert starch to fermentable sugar, so that the wort has a lot of remaining dextrin in it.

It's a difficult beer to brew well. The traditional recipe of 50 percent air-dried malt, 45 percent unmalted soft wheat, and 5 percent oats requires that the adjunct grains be boiled briefly to gelatinize the starches, a procedure not many small breweries are set up to do. Simple infusion or upward-step mashes can be used, but they don't always extract the proper milk-shake texture from the grains. Bitter orange peel and coriander are critical to the style, but the spices need to be chosen carefully to avoid vegetal or unpleasantly bitter flavors. Chamomile or the pungent spice grains of paradise are sometimes used as "secret spices."

Witbier is such a strong idea that it can support a fair amount of vamping, so occasionally one sees stronger or darker variants that have a high chance of being delicious.

LOCATION: Belgium, U.S. craft breweries, Japan

FLAVOR: dry creaminess; soft, acidic finish

AROMA: spicy yeast plus subtle notes of orange and coriander, and possibly hints of other spices

BALANCE: milk-shake texture, but dry, a touch tart

SEASONALITY: year-round, but best enjoyed in warm weather

PAIR WITH: lighter foods, such as mussels, salmon, chicken

SUGGESTED BEERS TO TRY: Hoegaarden Original White Ale, Brasserie du Bocq Blanche de Namur, Bell's Winter White Ale, Michigan Brewing Company Celis White, Unibroue Blanche de Chambly

GRAVITY: 1.042–1.055 (10.4–13.0°P)

ALCOHOL: 4.2–5.5% by volume

ATTENUATION/BODY: dry to medium

COLOR: 2–4°SRM, pale straw to gold, hazy

BITTERNESS: 15–22, low to medium

Lambic

ORIGIN: Lambic is an ancient beer brewed in the region surrounding Brussels. It's as weird as beer gets. Lambic has a high proportion (40 to 60 percent) of unmalted wheat and employs the turbid mash procedure discussed on page 202. The extremely diluted and protein-rich worts also require several hours of boiling (as opposed to an hour for most beers). Also, hops are aged for 2 or 3 years until there is very little bitterness or aroma left, as the lambic brewers are just looking for the antibacterial properties.

Lambic is considered to be "spontaneously fermented." The classic method is to expose the cooling wort to the night air, upon which drifts a whole zoo of microscopic critters that perform various roles in fermenting and souring the beer. In the old days, the region was rich in fruit orchards that served as the natural ecosystem in which the microbes lived. These days, the orchards are gone, and there is some feeling that the old ways are not as reliable as they once were. Part of the problem is that the whole process is so complicated; despite

Lambic Jug
This stoneware jug sums up the earthy sophistication of lambic.

LAMBICS TO TRY

Straight Lambic. Unblended sour beer, rarely available outside of Brussels. This can be mellow or scorchingly sour, depending on the blender. Usually served with little or no carbonation, the traditional method of serving was to provide the drinker with a bowl of sugar cubes and a "stomper" to crush the sugar in the bottom of the glass to add sweetness according to individual taste.
SUGGESTED BEERS TO TRY: Cantillon Iris, Oud Beersel Lambic

Gueuze. Bottled blend of young and old lambic that was created sometime between 1850 and 1875, when machine-made bottles were available and the taxes on them were eliminated. The word *gueuze* is probably related to our English word *geyser,* with the obvious meaning that conveys. Gueuze is bottle-conditioned.
SUGGESTED BEERS TO TRY: Cantillon Gueuze, Lindemans Cuvée René.

Faro. A diluted form of lambic, sweetened with caramel syrup and sometimes spiced up with seasonings, faro was by far the popular form of lambic in the nineteenth century, but is rare now.
SUGGESTED BEERS TO TRY: Lindemans Faro Lambic, Boon Faro Pertotale

Fruit Lambic. While it's reasonable to think that homemade versions of fruit lambic may have existed for centuries, fruit lambic as a commercial product was created only in the 1930s. Some examples include cherry (kriek), raspberry (framboise), peach, cassis, and many others.
SUGGESTED BEERS TO TRY: Cantillon Rosé de Gambrinus, Drien Fonteinen Schaerbeeckse Kriek, Lindemans Kriek or Framboise

A FEW BELGIAN ECCENTRICS

A great number of Belgian beers make no attempt to conform to any particular style. If you are used to the clear delineation of German categories, this can be confusing at first. Just lighten up, strap in, and enjoy the ride.

Kwak. From Bosteels in Bruggenhout, this beer is said to have been created by a brewer/innkeeper named Pauwels Kwak in 1791. It is a rich amber color and features a creamy, caramelly texture and a unique spice profile that is said to include licorice. Nicely balanced; 8 percent. Served in a bulb-bottomed "stirrup cup" that announces its coaching heritage.

De Dolle Brouwers. Literally, the Mad Brewers, this is a small brewery in Esen, outside Antwerp. Run by a mother-and-sons team, they produce a wide range, including a soft blond Easter beer, a hoppy 8 percent amber, a strong (9 percent) sour, and a stout.

Celis Grottenbier. A range of products from the man who saved witbier, Pierre Celis. The rich and creamy 6.5 percent Bruin was launched in 1999; the 7.7 percent blond came out in 2005. The "grotten" refers to the cave in which the beers are aged.

Wostyntje. From Brasserie de Regenboorg. Mustard-tinged (really!) blond ale with an English hop profile, this is a seriously crisp and refreshing beer.

Poperings Hommelbier. From van Eecke in Belgian hop country, this 7.5 percent blond beer is a bright, fresh nose full of hops, softened by the subtlety of the Belgian approach.

Bush/Scaldis. This extremely strong (12 percent) golden ale from Dubuisson has a slight toffeelike maltiness balanced by a bright Goldings kind of hoppiness, all smoothed out by a long, cool-temperature conditioning. Highly drinkable despite its strength.

Chouffe. This company in the Ardennes makes a range of character-filled brews, including a Scotch ale and an American-style IPA available only in the United States. All of the color in their beers comes from caramel brewers syrups rather than specialty malts.

Urthel. Another individualistic brewery turning out a range of character-filled products. Inspired by a gnomelike character, the beers are formulated to suit the life stages for these imaginary "Urthels." A husband-and-wife team, Hildegard and Bas van Ostaden, run the show: she brews the beer, he does the marketing.

a lot of scrupulous research, there are great swaths of the lambic science and practice that are still poorly understood. For instance, when the Lindemans brewery expanded some years ago, they sawed out a whole wall and bolted it in place in the new building, not wanting to take a chance that the needed organisms wouldn't be there when they needed them.

Fortunately, many of the bugs are quite happy living in the barrels in which lambic is fermented. The stories about lambic brewers never cleaning the spider webs off the casks is true. Everybody's walking on pins and needles trying not to upset the delicate balance required for great lambic. No other beer depends so highly on voodoo.

The spontaneous fermentation of lambic begins with an attack by enterobacteria such as *Kloeckera* and *E. coli,* which metabolize the small amount of glucose in the wort and then die off. Next is *Saccharomyces,* which converts maltose sugars to alcohol and carbon dioxide, doing the bulk of the fermentation. At this point things slow down a lot, and the *Brettanomyces*'s and *Pedioccocus*'s earthy, fruity aromas become apparent and a serious amount of acidity builds up. Long wood aging is required for these slow-acting bugs, which also allows harsh acidity to mellow. Naturally there is quite a lot of variation from barrel to barrel, so blending is essential to get any kind of consistency. Even so, some barrels are just too sour; in the old days, these were used to clean the brewery's copper kettles.

LOCATION: Brussels region; attempted with varying degrees of authenticity by U.S. craft brewers. The term *lambic* is a legal appellation, restricted to brewers in a specific region following approved recipes and procedures.

FLAVOR: sharp, acidic palate, amazing complexity

AROMA: yogurt, *Brettanomyces*, vinegar, fruitiness

BALANCE: very sharp and acidic, hints of sweetness

SEASONALITY: year-round

PAIR WITH: lighter food; cuts fat nicely; fruit versions perfect with dessert

SUGGESTED BEERS TO TRY: See page 203.

GUEUZE:

GRAVITY: 1.044–1.056 (11–14°P)

ALCOHOL: 5–6% by volume

ATTENUATION/BODY: medium

COLOR: 6–13°SRM, gold to amber

BITTERNESS: 11–23 IBU, low

Sour Brown/ Oud Bruin

ORIGIN: There are two regional focal points these days for sour brown ale in Belgium. One is in West Flanders, in Roeselare, home of Rodenbach, and the other is centered around Oudenaarde, in East Flanders. The two types have many similarities but are not identical. Brown beers, oak aging, and blending of young and old were fairly common prior to 1800, and a very few beers of this type have survived to this day. Interestingly, of the broad survey of Belgian beers by Lacambre in 1851, the only one that fits this description was brewed in Mechelen/Malines, a little farther east, halfway between Brussels and Antwerp. Way over east in Maastrict, there is another highly lactic sour brown style, so it's likely that these sour red/brown ales were much more widespread in former times.

West Flanders red is exemplified by Rodenbach. These reddish brown beers are brewed conventionally, then aged for close to 2 years in large wooden vats in which they pick up plenty of sourness from *Lactobacillus, Acetobacter* (vinegar bacteria), and the wild yeast *Brettanomyces*. This is not a spontaneous fermentation. It is the use of wood as a substrate that encourages the growth of these organisms. The wood lends an earthy touch as well as vanilla and other nuances that smooth out the sharp, acidic flavors.

The Oudenaarde Brown relies on yeast adulterated with *Lactobacillus* for its unique tart character. The Oudenaarde beers, typified by Liefmans Goudenband, have a complex earthiness about them and sometimes a touch of haze as well. Liefmans, at least, is not aged in oak, but their Goudenband is a blend of young and old beers.

The reds, in particular, show a variety of blending strategies. They may have a good deal of the sour "old" beer, usually for the more-premium products, or just a small amount for a sweet-sour flavor. Such "half-sour" beers like Jack-OP and Zotteghem were once popular, and a few remain on the market.

Sour ales are fine bases for fruit beers, as the acidity gives the fruit what it needs to taste right. Cherry and raspberry versions of both styles can be found and are well worth seeking out.

LOCATION: Flanders; sometimes attempted in the United States.

FLAVOR: mellow to sharp acidity with caramel malt or cooked sugar

AROMA: deeply fruity/estery, with acidic notes (vinegar/pickle notes in red ales), hint of malt

BALANCE: sweet-and-sour; almost no hops

SEASONALITY: year-round

PAIR WITH: tangy cheese, rich meat, fried dishes; try with a light fruit tart

SUGGESTED BEERS TO TRY: Liefmans Goudenband, Rodenbach Grand Cru, Verhaeghe Duchesse de Bourgogne, Jolly Pumpkin La Roja, New Belgium La Folie, New Glarus Wisconsin Belgian Red (with cherries)

GRAVITY: 1.044–1.057 (11–14°P)

ALCOHOL: 4.8–5.2% by volume

ATTENUATION/BODY: acid plus sweet

COLOR: 12–18°SRM, amber to brown

BITTERNESS: 15–25 IBU, low to medium

NOTE: While they're not for everyone, wild-fermented beers are being developed by a number of American craft breweries and are occasionally available in limited quantities. Look for such products from Cambridge Brewing Company, Jolly Pumpkin, Lost Coast/Pizza Port, New Belgium, Russian River, and others.

French Bières de Garde

ORIGINS: France has always been on the fence about beer. There are passionate beer lovers there, but the wine culture is so strong that beer has trouble getting much of the spotlight. Historically, two regions have been the fountains of beer culture in France. In Alsace-Lorraine, nestled against the lager powerhouse Germany, and with Germanic cultural affinities, a plenitude of blonds, bocks, and Märzens came right along with industrialization. In the Nord, up north just west of Belgium, brewers were turning out rustic, top-fermenting *brunes* and *blanches* like neighboring Flanders and Hainault. Parisians drank a lot of each type, by the way. The two regional proclivities come together in the present *bières de garde* style. The term, like *lager,* means "beer to store" and originally had no connection to any particular style. It was simply a French term for the "double" or stronger versions of their basic beers.

Then came trouble. In 1871, the Germans annexed Alsace-Lorraine as spoils of their victory in the Franco-Prussian war, which meant that the greater part of French brewing capacity was no longer under French control. This forced the government to try to improve the brewing capability of the Nord breweries, which were by no means highly industrialized. It also meant a ready market for anything remotely resembling the bocks, blondes, and *bières de mars* (Märzens) they had been drinking, even if the words *Fermentation Haute* were on the label.

Despite all this beer activity, the brewers in the Nord were still pretty unsophisticated; contemporary reporters (R. E. Evans, *Journal of the Institute of Brewing,* 1905) found them in some disarray. Like elsewhere, there were two terrible wars with a short, vigorous period between them. Breweries regained some strength in the gap, and started to brew export-quality luxury beers.

After the damage of the second war was repaired, luxury bottled beers became big business and the Northern French breweries, now in the hands of a more ambitious generation, started packaging up strong beers. Early on, these were mostly brown beers, but eventually, in our present state, became a mix of brown or *ambrée* and blond brews.

LOCATION: northern France, U.S. craft breweries

FLAVOR: caramel malt, hints of toast

AROMA: complex malt with earthy yeast character

BALANCE: definitely malty, barely balanced by hops

SEASONALITY: year-round, great in colder weather

PAIR WITH: hearty, rich food; steak, roast pork, beef stew; simple desserts

SUGGESTED BEERS TO TRY: La Choulette Amber, Brasserie La Choulette Bière Sans Culottes, Lost Abbey/ Port Brewing Avant Garde, Russian River Perdition, Two Brothers Domaine DuPage

GRAVITY: 1.060–1.080 (15–19°P)

ALCOHOL: 6–8% by volume

ATTENUATION/BODY: medium to full

COLOR: 6–12°SRM, pale to medium amber

BITTERNESS: 25–30 IBU, low to medium

CHAPTER 13

CRAFT BEER IN AMERICA AND BEYOND

CRAFT brews sprang from a passionate desire to save our palates from bland, industrialized products, to salvage the authentic flavors of the world's great beers, and restore the artist's hand in the making of this beloved beverage. Like so many of the social movements brought on by changes in attitudes during the 1960s, it had audacious and maybe even naive goals. Whether it has succeeded will have to be judged by history, but it sure is a lot of fun right now. The beer landscape is richer and deeper than ever, and just plain delicious.

Q: WHAT IS CRAFT BEER?

A. Tough question; this is one of those tricky terms that defies exact definition. Anyone who drinks decent beer in this country has a solid enough idea about what this term means, but the more you try to define it, the vaguer the dividing line becomes. Is it what is in the glass or who brewed it that makes the difference? Must it be all malt? If so, then what about wheat beer? Is it about ownership? Can large public corporations make proper craft beer? Does calling a beer a "craft beer" make it so?

As it stands today, IRI and Nielson, the two companies that collect supermarket scanner data, have two craft categories: Craft-Independent and Craft-Affiliated. The first follows the Brewers Association definition, and excludes those breweries with big-company or foreign connections. The second category covers all others, including craftlike beers such as Coors's Blue Moon.

The Brewers Association (BA) in 2007 released a definition of a craft brewer: producing less than the two million–barrel federal small-brewer's tax exemption; independence, defined by a less than 25 percent ownership by another company that is not a craft brewer; and "traditional" in the sense of having a flagship product that is all malt.

I was involved in these discussions as a member of the BA board of directors. The process was long and wrenching, and in the end there was not unanimity. To me, craft beer is art. This means that the ideas and recipes for the beers must come from the brewers, not from the marketing department. It takes a passionate and often highly personal point of view to create something unique, memorable, and meaningful.

Brewing with Purpose

THE UNITED STATES in 1975 was a pretty barren place for good beer. American breweries large and small had been battling it out over price in the decades since World War II, with the result that unbranded generic beer was being sold in supermarkets and the number of genuine specialty beers could be counted on one hand, with fingers to spare.

A number of factors came together to make craft beer a reality. First were the European experiences of military personnel and college students on backpacking adventures. In Britain they found beers with an intimate, personal sensibility; in Germany, a sense of order and righteousness; and in Belgium, an unlimited fountain of ideas and ancient taproots. These were profoundly great places to start.

The blind optimism of the baby boomer generation gave us the certain knowledge that we could make whatever kind of future we could envision. So what if nobody had started a brewery in fifty years. How hard could it be?

Humble Beginnings
Sierra Nevada brewery and brewer/owner Ken Grossman in the early days, c. 1981.

Born in the Boneyard

IN BOULDER, COLORADO, Charlie Papazian was leading a merry band of homebrewers that eventually coalesced into the American Homebrewers Association, which spread a fun, subversive message of self-reliance. Homebrewing was legalized in 1979, ushering in a real boom for the hobby brewers and homebrewers, who started to dream of bigger things. To this day, homebrewing provides the reservoir of energy, ideas, and manpower from which commercial craft beer springs.

Many of these early breweries were built from castoffs salvaged from the dairy industry. The failure (thanks in part to CAMRA) of the English brewers to gain traction on a plan to deliver bulk beers to their pubs led to a surplus of seven-barrel "Grundy" serving tanks, which were perfect for brewpubs. Starting small allowed these pioneer brewers to hone their craft and build a relationship with their markets. Most of today's best-known large craft breweries started this way.

The first brewpub, Yakima Brewing and Malting, was opened in 1982 by a retired hop consultant named Bert Grant. While the restaurant business is a difficult one, brewpubs have managed to thrive. Over the years they have been a highly visible manifestation of craft beer, introducing millions to its charms. As of November 2007, there were 967 brewpubs operating in the United States.

What is really significant about craft brewing is that a bunch of guys and gals who started in their basements with improvised breweries and family financing have managed to take over the conceptual helm of beer in this country. For well over a century, the biggest players determined the future of beer, be it pale, cold, fizzy, light, canned, cheap, dry, ice, or clear. The large public companies still wield an enormous amount of power and are by no means fading out of the picture, but the fact that they are now following the lead of the little guys and squirting out me-too, craft-ish brews shows where the creative energy lies. It's hard to point to another industry that has flip-flopped so dramatically.

An American Sense of Style

AT THE START, the beers were pretty simple: pure American pale malt with a big dollop of crystal malt, topped off with a heaping helping of citrusy hops and fermented with ale yeast — just an honest, handmade beer. For drinkers accustomed to the yellow fizzy stuff, these beers were a slap in the face. Once the shock subsided, relationships were built, and the rest is history. Old World tradition was the inspiration, but the result was uniquely ours. American hops in all their resiny, grapefruity glory just about define American craft beer.

Lagers have always been a part of the craft beer story, especially away from the coasts. But lagers pose a logistical problem: their extended lagering (storage) requires a lot of tank time, so a lager brewery needs perhaps twice the number of tanks as an ale brewery of the same capacity, an expensive requirement that has limited the number of craft lager breweries. In contrast to our freewheeling willingness to deconstruct ales, American craft lagers stay true to their original inspirations. Maybe it's an invisible *Reinheitsgebot* force field that resists efforts at deformation, but for whatever reason, you won't find distinctive craft reinventions of lager styles in this chapter. But who knows what the future holds?

Belgian-style beer started to come into focus in the early 1990s. New Belgium Brewing in Fort Collins, Colorado, and Celis Brewery in Austin, Texas, were the first breweries to focus exclusively on Belgian-inspired beers. A new generation, including brewers such as Lost Abbey Brewing's Tomme Arthur and Russian River's Vinnie Cilurzo, are leading the charge, but others are pursuing similar paths. A recent entry from Cambridge Brewing Company in the Festival of Wood and Barrel-Aged Beer was described as being "aged 12 months in Napa Valley French oak wine barrels with chardonnay and Semillon grapes, apricots, and a malolactic fermentation." Delaware's Dogfish Head just installed two 10,000-gallon tanks of exotic Palo Santo wood, the largest wooden brewery tanks built in this country since before Prohibition, just to age a special 12 percent alcohol brown ale. Interesting ideas are all over the place.

A Tempting Future

WHAT DOES THE FUTURE HOLD? Craft brewers in 2006 had about 3.5 percent of the overall beer market in barrels and about 5 percent in dollars. There is hope this could eventually rise to about 10 percent (barrels), as it is pushing toward in Oregon. The wine market might be a fair comparison: While there are some large players, no one company has anything close to a dominant share. As consumers move away from the mass-market brands, they seek a wide variety of constantly changing products, which has never been the big breweries' strong suit. They have yet to demonstrate whether they can make money with a large number of low-volume brands.

There will be consolidation as the founders of successful craft breweries reach retirement age and seek to cash out, and the transfer of equity to the big players will continue. There are many advantages a big brewer can offer: technical and marketing assistance, access to raw materials, and especially a ride on the truck — distribution has always been a very challenging aspect of craft brewing.

Craft beer is becoming a worldwide phenomenon. Small craft-style breweries are popping up in Europe and elsewhere. Italy has an

CRAFT BEER AROUND THE WORLD

Italy. Half a dozen brewpubs in the north have banded together to form a self-promotion group called Union Birra. Included is the Belgian-themed Le Baladin, whose products we see occasionally on American shelves.

Denmark. Here is very much an American-style scene, with plenty of creative and very hoppy beers. The Danish Beer Society has over 17,000 members!

Brazil. The scene is just getting going, but one brewer has named his brewery after the state of Colorado and is brewing an interesting range of beers, including a manioc Pilsner and an IPA made with the local rapadura sugar.

Argentina. Argentina has a strong and growing scene. Antares is producing a number of adventurous products, including a delicious barley wine.

Japan. Japan has a small but thriving scene. The products of Hitachino Nest are imported to the United States; these include a credible witbier and Pilsner brewed with a red rice that adds a sake flavor and a hint of pink color.

England. Lots of small, artisanal breweries are popping up. One has even made a beer with Cascade hops! Summer ales, wheat beers, eighteenth-century porter, and beers seasoned with ginger and ginseng have all been spotted recently.

enthusiastic smattering of breweries, largely driven by a love of Belgian beers. Cascade hop aromas are showing up occasionally in beers in England. Australia and Denmark have thriving scenes very much along the lines of craft brewing in the United States. Japan recently relaxed its rule on the minimum size of a brewery, making small breweries possible. Latin America is making strides, and there is interest in Africa as well.

Craft brewing adapts itself to the culture, market, and tastes of wherever it finds itself, but the basics are always the same: people passionate about the flavor of great beer, brewing up fresh, character-filled beers of all strengths, shades, and sensibilities. Quality beer is a part of a lifestyle that values the experience of living, of making every moment an adventure, every taste worth tasting. Craft beer is here to stay, but we need to reach out and turn people on to the world of choice, authenticity, and flavor it provides so well.

The Big, Bold Taste of Craft Beer

One thing you can say for sure about the craft-beer revolution: it has elevated hops from a bit part to a starring role. American brewers just love hops to pieces, whether spicy, floral, piney, resinous, citrusy, or herbaceous, and they are constantly finding new ways to showcase them in all their bitter and aromatic glory.

I used to think this was just a phase; an understandable overcompensation for the indignities of a century of declining bitterness in beer. For twenty years brewers have been jamming more and more hops into the beers. But I was wrong on this one: Massively bitter beers are here to stay.

This resiny madness has topped out at about 100 IBUs. Fortunately for our palates, something else is going on. It's no longer just about the raw power of this bitterness. Brewers are applying a more finessed approach, finding subtler ways of showcasing our favorite beer herb.

American Pale Ale

More than any other, this style defines American craft beer. They are built on a base of pure malt, usually with the caramelly, raisiny flavors of crystal, counterbalanced by the fresh, pungent flavors of Cascade and other American hops with their piney, citrusy notes. Almost every brewery has a pale ale in some form.

ORIGIN: around 1980, as American brewers tried to satisfy their thirst for hops

LOCATION: U.S. craft breweries and elsewhere

FLAVOR: fresh hops plus a nutty maltiness, hints of raisins and/or caramel, crisp finish

AROMA: malty, fruity, but with American (Cascade or related types) hops in the foreground

BALANCE: medium body; crisp, bitter finish

SEASONALITY: year-round

PAIR WITH: wide range of food; classic with a burger

SUGGESTED BEERS TO TRY: Anchor Liberty Ale, Boulder Brewing Hazed & Infused, Deschutes Mirror Pond Pale Ale, North Coast Ruedrich's Red Seal Ale, Sierra Nevada Pale Ale, Three Floyds Alpha King Pale Ale

GRAVITY: 1.044–1.060 (11–14.7°P)

ALCOHOL: 4.5–5.5% by volume

ATTENUATION/BODY: medium

COLOR: 6–14°SRM, dark gold to dark amber

BITTERNESS: 28–40 IBU, medium to high

American IPA

IPA is just a paler, stronger, hoppier style of pale ale. And like pale ale, American versions showcase American hop varieties.

ORIGIN: around 1985, as American brewers looked for other hop-delivery vehicles

LOCATION: U.S. craft breweries and elsewhere

FLAVOR: fresh hops plus a clean, bready maltiness, perhaps a hint of caramel, and a clean, crisp, bitter finish

AROMA: American (Cascade or related types) hops in the foreground and some malty, fruity aromas

BALANCE: medium body; crisp, bitter finish

SEASONALITY: year-round

PAIR WITH: wide range of food; classic with a burger

SUGGESTED BEERS TO TRY: Anderson Valley Hop Ottin' IPA, Bear Republic IPA, Bell's Two-Hearted Ale, Harpoon IPA, Victory Hop Devil

GRAVITY: 1.050–1.060 (11.4–14.7°P)

ALCOHOL: 5.5–6.3% by volume

ATTENUATION/BODY: crisp, dry

COLOR: 5–12°SRM, gold to light amber

BITTERNESS: 35–70 IBU, medium to high

Double/ Imperial IPA

Imperial is a term normally applied to beers that were brewed in Britain, then shipped to the imperial court of the Russian Empire during the nineteenth century. "Imperial" was also used in late nineteenth-century America as a designation for the top of a brewer's range, typically a pale "stock" ale of fairly high strength. The term was occasionally used in England around the turn of the twentieth century. Of late, craft brewers have embraced the term and applied it to anything that moves: stout, porter, brown pale, blond, Pilsner, and more.

Consumers have been enthusiastic about big bottles of strong, seasonal imperial or double beers, and so brewers have been happy to oblige them, making these beers very available.

ORIGIN: around 1995. More malt! More hops!

LOCATION: U.S. craft breweries and elsewhere

FLAVOR: hops in the foreground, but playing off a background of complex, creamy maltiness; big beers that should have plenty of complexity

AROMA: a massive blast of hops along with some serious maltiness

BALANCE: medium body; long, bitter finish

SEASONALITY: year-round, but better away from the heat of summer

PAIR WITH: very rich food, such as aged Gorgonzola or carrot cake

SUGGESTED BEERS TO TRY: Dogfish Head 90 Minute IPA, Great Divide Hercules Double IPA, Lagunitas Brown Sugga', Rogue I2PA, Stone Ruination IPA, Three Floyds Dreadnaught IPA

GRAVITY: 1.075–1.100 (18.2–24°P)

ALCOHOL: 7.9–10.5% by volume

ATTENUATION/BODY: crisp, dry

COLOR: 6–14°SRM, gold to amber

BITTERNESS: 65–100 plus IBU, very high

English and American Labels, 1890–1940
The term *Imperial* has been applied to many different styles, usually to indicate a luxurious, and possibly strong product.

OTHER IMPERIALIZED BEERS

Pilsner

- Dogfish Head
- O'Dell's
- Rogue Morimoto Imperial Pilsner
- Samuel Adams Hallertau Imperial Pilsner

Blonde Ale

- Ska Brewing True Blonde Dubbel

Red Ale

- AleSmith Imperial Red Ale
- Lagunitas Imperial Red Ale
- Rogue Imperial Red Ale
- Southern Tier Big Red

Brown Ale

- Dogfish Head Palo Santo
- Lagunitas Brown Sugga'
- Tommyknocker Imperial Nut Brown Ale

Porter

- Flying Dog Gonzo Imperial Porter
- Full Sail Top Sail (bourbon barrel aged) Imperial Porter
- Ska Brewing Nefarious Ten Pin Imperial Porter

Amber & Red Ale

A few years back everybody and his brother was brewing up a red ale and naming it after some furry woodland critter, hoping to make a fast buck in the craft-brewing business. Most of them went skulking back into the forest after the boom faded, and honestly, that's probably a good thing, because many of them were pretty insipid. But the style has more potential than has been demonstrated by this superficial craze.

Ambers are basically a beefy session beer, so good drinkability is important. The key to this is using hops in a way that is assertive without being tiring; building a malt base that is profound but not cloying. The emphasis should be on bitterness rather than aroma, although some aroma is a good thing. You just don't want it smelling like a fresh-cut grapefruit; malt aroma should have the upper hand.

ORIGIN: This was one of the first craft-beer styles and provided something different, but not too challenging. The term appeared in America in about 1990, as brewers searched for a way to find descriptors for beers that were neither intimidating nor linked to specific historical traditions.

LOCATION: U.S. craft breweries

FLAVOR: plenty of caramel malt, delicate hop finish

AROMA: clean caramel malt plus a hint of floral hops

BALANCE: malty to somewhat hoppy

SEASONALITY: year-round

PAIR WITH: wide range of food; chicken, seafood, burgers, spicy cuisine

SUGGESTED BEERS TO TRY: Bear Republic Red Rocket, Full Sail Amber, New Belgium Fat Tire, Tröegs Nugget Nectar

GRAVITY: 1.048–1.058 (12–14.5°P)

ALCOHOL: 4.5–6% by volume

ATTENUATION/BODY: medium

COLOR: 11–18°SRM, pale to dark amber

BITTERNESS: 30–40 IBU, medium

American Barley Wine

Like all the rest of the American craft versions of British beers, this style is differentiated by the enthusiastic use of hops, especially those that display all the piney, citrus qualities of American varieties. The term in England is applied to beers that by American standards are shockingly weak, but the American versions take no prisoners in the alcohol department.

LOCATION: U.S. craft breweries

FLAVOR: richly malty, sometimes a bit raisiny; may be fiercely bitter

AROMA: richly malty, with varying amounts of hops; often with leathery, sherrylike notes in aged examples

BALANCE: evenly to extremely hoppy

SEASONALITY: very nice in the dark days of winter

PAIR WITH: big food, especially aged cheese and intense desserts

SUGGESTED BEERS TO TRY: Bridgeport Brewing Old Knucklehead, Hair of the Dog Fred, Middle Ages Brewing Company Druid Fluid, Rogue Old Crustacean, Sierra Nevada Bigfoot Barleywine Style Ale

GRAVITY: 1.080–1.120 (19.3–28.6°P)

ALCOHOL: 7–12% by volume

ATTENUATION/BODY: medium to full

COLOR: 11–18°SRM, pale to dark amber

BITTERNESS: 50–100 IBU, high

American Brown Ale

Classic English styles have the barest whisper of bitterness, just to offset the maltiness. But American versions have a decidedly more even-handed balance and are sometimes downright hoppy. In addition, American browns are likely to be considerably bigger and browner than their English cousins, typically with a strongly toasty palate and some sweetness.

LOCATION: U.S. craft breweries

FLAVOR: plenty of caramel malt; delicate hop finish

AROMA: clean caramel malt plus a hint of floral hops

BALANCE: malty to somewhat hoppy

SEASONALITY: year-round

PAIR WITH: wide range of food; chicken, seafood, burgers, spicy cuisine

SUGGESTED BEERS TO TRY: Dogfish Head Indian Brown Ale, Brooklyn Brown Ale, Flossmoor Station Pullman Brown Ale, Surly Bender

GRAVITY: 1.045-1.060 (11.2-14.7°P)

ALCOHOL: 4-6% by volume

ATTENUATION/BODY: medium to full

COLOR: 18-35°SRM, deep amber to chestnut brown

BITTERNESS: 20-45 IBU, medium

Porter and Stout

Porter was the first beer in the world brewed and exported on an industrial scale. Yes, the Yankees did have a taste for porter. It is well known that George Washington was a fan, and after the Revolution, he regularly purchased bottled porter from Robert Hare's brewery in nearby Philadelphia. Eastern Pennsylvania was America's brewing capital, and it maintained that reputation until German immigrants brought their lager beers to America and shifted the center of gravity westward. In the early era, Philadelphia porter was famous for its quality. In fact, the area never completely lost its taste for porter. Yuengling still brews one in Pottsville, Pennsylvania.

For a recap of the particulars of porter and stout, see chapter 9. American versions tend to be pretty close to these, although they often use American hop varieties and may color outside the lines a bit when it comes to style rules.

American Wheat Ale

This craft-brewed style first achieved popularity in the Pacific Northwest. This new version forgoes the exotic fermentation character of the German styles; usually the brewery uses its standard ale yeast. Most contain between 30 and 50 percent wheat. American wheat beers are popular with young consumers looking for something truly different but who are not ready for some of the darker, more bitter beers.

ORIGIN: U.S. brewpubs and craft breweries; usually seen as a "starter" beer

LOCATION: U.S. craft breweries; British versions also popping up

FLAVOR: Super-clean and crisp; hoppier than German weizens

AROMA: soft fruitiness without the clove and/or banana of German weizens; sometimes a little hop aroma

BALANCE: crisp, with a little creamy texture from the wheat; sometimes a hint of tartness

SEASONALITY: year-round, but best in summer

PAIR WITH: salads, lighter food like chicken or sushi, simple cheeses

SUGGESTED BEERS TO TRY: Boulevard Unfiltered Wheat, Goose Island 312 Urban Wheat, Leinenkugel's Honey Weiss, Three Floyds Gumballhead Wheat Ale, Widmer Hefeweizen

GRAVITY: 9-14°P/1.035-1.055

ALCOHOL: 3.0-5.5% by volume

ATTENUATION/BODY: light to medium

COLOR: 3-6°SRM, straw to gold

BITTERNESS: 15-35 IBU, low to medium

Fruit Wheat Beer

"Chick beers" are what the beer geeks call these. You know the brews. Pink, fluffy little numbers, a bland wheat-beer base dolled up with a drop or two of raspberry essence. These have their charms on a hot summer day, and for that reason they are the most common type of fruit beer encountered in the United States.

There are a few breweries managing to get a good fruit buzz going with more-concentrated beers. Wisconsin's New Glarus brewery has put Door County cherries to good use in a big fruit bomb they call Wisconsin Belgian Red. They brew a raspberry offering as well. Not coincidentally, these two beers consistently medal at the Great American Beer Festival. Elsewhere, Kalamazoo Brewing has long made a cherry stout that delivers the goods, and Delaware's Dogfish Head offers beers made from currants, apricots, and blueberries.

ORIGIN: U.S. brewpubs, often thought of as appealing mainly to female customers

LOCATION: U.S. craft breweries

FLAVOR: Delicate fruitiness — raspberries, apricots, cherries, blueberries; clean, crisp finish

AROMA: soft fruitiness with not all that much else

BALANCE: crisp to somewhat sweet

SEASONALITY: year-round

PAIR WITH: salads and lighter food, lighter desserts

SUGGESTED BEERS TO TRY: Harpoon UFO Raspberry Wheat, Leinenkugel's Berry Weiss, Pyramid Apricot Weizen, Saranac Pomegranate Wheat. Also try a popular summer seasonal at brewpubs.

GRAVITY: 1.044–1.052 (11–13°P)

ALCOHOL: 3.8–5% by volume

ATTENUATION/BODY: medium

COLOR: gold to pink to deep purple

BITTERNESS: 15–25 IBU, low

Pumpkin Ale

ORIGIN: U.S. craft breweries; as a harvest-themed fall seasonal, pumpkin beers can be a lot of fun and help to point out the agricultural roots of beer. The Elysian Brewpub in Seattle holds a pumpkin-beer fest, featuring a couple of dozen pumpkin styles on tap, including a pumpkin barley wine and a beer conditioned in a giant pumpkin, was tapped right from the mighty vegetable.

LOCATION: U.S. craft breweries

FLAVOR: delicate pumpkin sometimes overpowered by traditional pumpkin pie spice mix; subtle is better; some caramel malt adds interest

AROMA: a nice spiciness, perhaps a little malt

BALANCE: usually a little sweet

SEASONALITY: autumn

GREAT WITH: Thanksgiving roast turkey and gingerbread

SUGGESTED BEERS TO TRY: Buffalo Bill's Pumpkin Ale, New Holland Ichabod Ale, Weyerbacher Brewing Imperial Pumpkin Ale. Also check out Seattle's Elysian Brewing Company's Great Pumpkin Beer Festival in October.

GRAVITY: 1.047–1.056 (12–14°P)

ALCOHOL: 4.9–5.5% by volume

ATTENUATION/BODY: medium

COLOR: 6–12°SRM, gold to amber

BITTERNESS: 10–15 IBU, low

That's a Big Pumpkin Beer
The folks at Seattle's Elysian Brewery thought a pumpkin would make the perfect keg for one of their pumpkin beers.

Up and Coming

VARIETY CONTINUES to be the mission for adventurous craft brewers wherever they are. Here are some of the trends and ideas that brewers are pursuing these days.

Historical Re-Creations and Fantasies

The past is always present in brewing. Whether dipping back just a few decades or to the very beginnings of beer, history is a ready resource of ideas for the creative brewer. So often the necessary details of ancient beers are gone forever; consequently most re-creations are just informed guesses. Sometimes there is some actual science, as when Anchor's Fritz Maytag collaborated with Sumerologist Solomon Katz to create a limited-edition beer called Ninkasi, named for the Sumerian goddess of beer.

Other examples include a range of ancient Scottish beers, including a Pictish heather beer called *Fraoch,* as well as pine and kelp brews; a coriander-tinged pre-industrial "Jacobite" ale from Traquair House, also in Scotland; spruce-tip beer from Alaskan Brewing Co., Kentucky common beer re-created by a brewpub in New Albany, Indiana; and an Italian version of an ancient Egyptian beer called Nora, made from kamut (an ancient wheat), from Le Baladin.

In addition to the beer discussed in chapter 1, inspired by King Midas, these resuscitated beers are always interesting, as they lend a kind of insight into the old traditions that you can't get from reading books. And as often as not, they are delicious as well.

Single-Hop Ales

The idea is to take a relatively straightforward recipe such as an American pale ale and dope it up with just one kind of hops, which lets the true

SOME NEWER AMERICAN HOP VARIETIES

Amarillo. This privately developed hop has been around for a few years. Loosely in the Cascade mold, it has a floral, citrusy character all its own. It is lovely for American pale ales and IPAs, and is 8 to 11 percent alpha acid.

Glacier. Introduced in 2000, it is broadly in the Fuggle family, but I'd call it more of a Super Styrian. At 5.5 percent alpha acid, it's great in Belgian-style ales — like saison — which display some hop character.

Santiam. Introduced in 1997, this variety has Tettnang and Hallertau parentage and character. Alpha acid is low, between 5 and 7 percent. It has a clean, noble hop character to lend to any Germanic beer.

Simcoe. A real hop blast, introduced in 2000; with 12 to 14 percent alpha acid, this has become a darling of the double IPA brewers. It has a unique, pinelike aroma.

Sterling. Introduced in 1998, this hop has a lot of spicy Saaz-like character. With 6 to 9 percent alpha acid, it is great for Belgian ales.

character shine through. This is a great way to learn about the unique character of individual hops. Aside from its educational aspect, it ties beer to the land and the seasons, and really creates a lot of excitement among consumers. A similar sense of excitement with single-hopped beers is percolating among British craft brewers.

Wet-Hopped Ale

Another technique gaining in popularity is "wet-hopping." This is the use of fresh, undried hops right off the vine. Many California breweries are harvesting the cones off plants grown on their own property for this purpose. Brewers farther from hop country are shipping the hops via overnight courier, often at great expense. Beers hopped this way have fresh, green aromas and a certain just-picked briskness. California brewers hold a Wet Hop Beer Festival in San Diego every November.

LOCATION: U.S. craft breweries

FLAVOR: varies by base beer, but should always have plenty of fresh bitterness

AROMA: very much a matter of specific recipe and especially hop variety: spicy, flowery, piney, resiny, herbal, grapefruit, and other hop aromas

BALANCE: definitely on the bitter side, but should be counterbalanced by some nice malt

SEASONALITY: harvesttime

PAIR WITH: bold foods like steak, lamb, blue cheese

SUGGESTED BEERS TO TRY: Drake's Brewing Harvest Ale, Harpoon Glacier Harvest Wet Hop Beer, Sierra Nevada Harvest Ale, Two Brothers Heavy Handed IPA

New Belgian-American Ales

A number of American brewers, inspired by Belgium, are using the ideas and techniques of that brewing culture to create uniquely American beers with some of the Belgian magic. Some have been reverential, interested in re-creating the classics like the Trappist beers, while others have taken a more freewheeling approach. Several processes are involved: adding wild microorganisms such as *Brettanomyces;* barrel aging; blending; incorporating sugar, fruit, spices; and more. There is even some partnering with breweries in Belgium, in which batches from both sides of the Atlantic are melded into a single cuvée. The flavors of these Belgian-American beers are as varied and distinctive as Belgium itself.

SUGGESTED BEERS TO TRY: Allagash Curieux and others; Goose Island Matilda; Russian River Salvation, Perdition, and others; Lost Abbey Cuvée de Tommy and others; seasonal specialties from New Belgium Brewing

Barrel-Aged Beers

The invention of the barrel is variously attributed to Bronze Age Celts, Vikings, or similar hairy, cloaked tribes. By Roman times barrels were in use across a wide area of northern Europe. Barrels served admirably in a pre-industrial world, but the difficulty of cleaning and maintaining them caused them to be phased out by brewers around 1950. Stainless steel suits the squeaky-clean nature of international lager perfectly, but if you love the funky depths of a truly handmade beer, wood can offer that extra dimension.

Wood contains chemicals that dissolve in the beer over time, which can add woody, oaky, and other flavors to the beer. Temperature swings cause the liquid to pump in and out of the wood, accelerating the process. Over a period of many months, one of these substances, lignin, transforms into vanillin, which is why vanilla notes are often found in whiskey and other barrel-aged spirits.

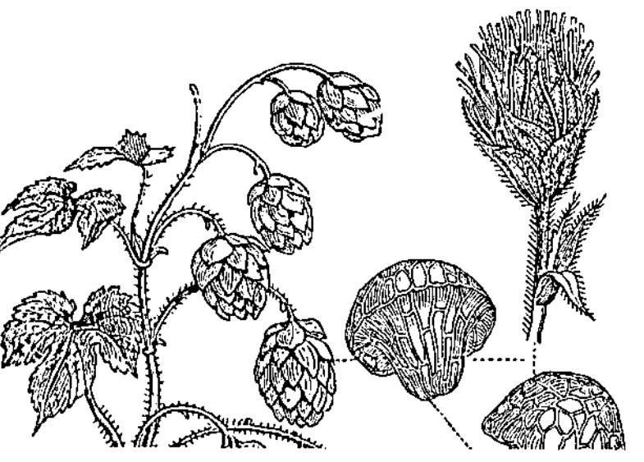

Barrel wood is porous, which exposes the contents to air, creating the potential for oxidized flavors, both good and bad. Porosity also means there are lots of little nooks and crannies for microorganisms to hide, and this is a fact that may be used to the brewer's advantage, or mitigated if necessary. Lambic and other sour-beer brewers depend on barrels as a safe harbor for their wild yeast and bacteria.

The bourbon industry uses the expensive charred-oak barrels only once for bourbon, so when emptied, they are relatively cheap to purchase. They can be great for aging beer. The first bourbon-aged beer I ever heard of was from a group of suburban Chicago-area brewers who brought five 10-gallon batches of a strong Imperial Stout together to fill a fresh bourbon barrel. Six months later they reconvened to bottle the beer. Shortly after that time, Goose Island Beer Company started experimenting with the style, one of the first commercial breweries to do so.

Barrel aging is not the best treatment for a Pilsner; strong and dark is the rule. Imperial Stout is the classic, and barley wine may also benefit. A super-strong weizenbock, blond barley wine, or triple bock might do with a dab of whiskey-barrel flavor as well.

LOCATION: U.S. craft breweries

FLAVOR: whatever the base beer is, plus rich, round, slightly caramelly flavors and perhaps a touch of woodiness

AROMA: malt and hops appropriate to the base beer, plus rich vanilla, toasted coconut, and perhaps hints of sherry or port-type oxidized aromas

BALANCE: generally a bit on the sweet side

SEASONALITY: best in cool weather

PAIR WITH: huge, rich desserts and Stilton cheese

SUGGESTED BEERS TO TRY: Allagash Interlude, Firestone Walker Rufus, Goose Island Bourbon County Stout, Great Divide Oak Aged Yeti Imperial Stout, New Holland Dragon's Milk Ale

Hyper-Beers

The trend for this type of beer began on the East Coast in about 1994, most famously championed by Boston Beer Company's Jim Koch; but Dogfish Head's Sam Calagione has also been there since the early days of this trend. We're talking about super-gravity beers containing as much as 25 percent alcohol, retailing for up to $200 a bottle for beers such as Samuel Adams Utopias, a price that company representatives say is just breaking even!

Beer yeast normally doesn't want to ferment much above 10 percent alcohol. It takes special strains adapted to the high levels of alcohol, which after an initial fermentation are then carefully dosed with sugar, a little at a time, while the alcohol content gradually adds up. Often wood aging is employed as well. The flavors of these beers have more in common with spirits and liqueurs, and indeed the Utopias has won numerous blind taste-offs against such competitors as port and Calvados.

LOCATION: U.S. craft breweries

FLAVOR: massive taste, sweetish, creamy, dried fruit, spice, alcohol; in darker examples, roast malt character; hops may or may not be big

AROMA: immense maltiness, along with barrel character of vanilla and coconut; plenty of fruity esters, alcohol

BALANCE: usually a little sweet

SEASONALITY: a contemplative tipple by the fire

PAIR WITH: Stilton, walnuts; a dessert in itself

SUGGESTED BEERS TO TRY: Dogfish Head 120 Minute IPA, Worldwide Stout, Hair of the Dog Dave, Samuel Adams Utopias

GRAVITY: 1.12 plus (29°P plus)

ALCOHOL: 14–26% by volume

ATTENUATION/BODY: medium to full

COLOR: 18–55°SRM, deep amber to fully opaque black

BITTERNESS: 50–100 plus IBU, medium to very high

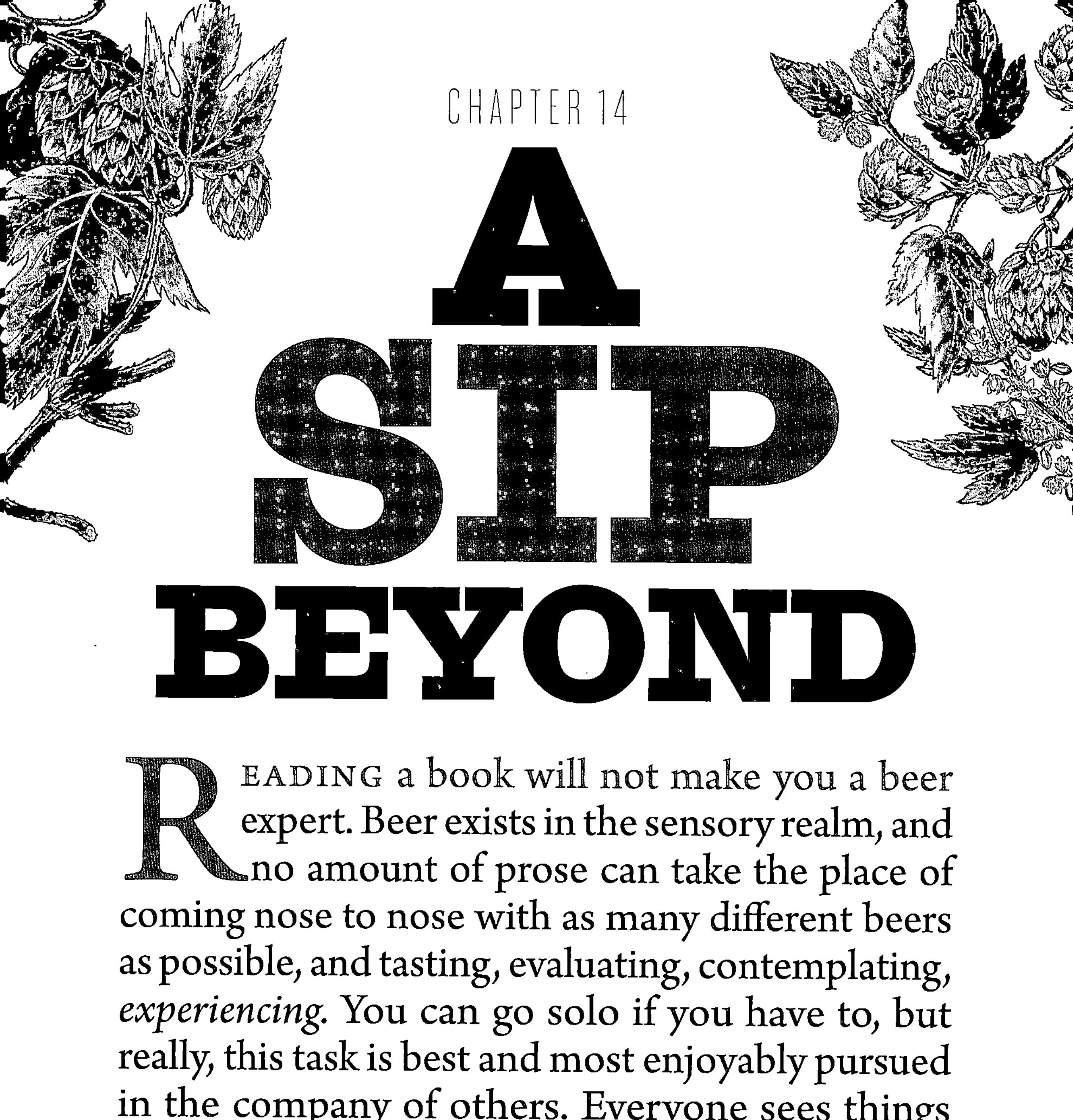

CHAPTER 14

A SIP BEYOND

READING a book will not make you a beer expert. Beer exists in the sensory realm, and no amount of prose can take the place of coming nose to nose with as many different beers as possible, and tasting, evaluating, contemplating, *experiencing*. You can go solo if you have to, but really, this task is best and most enjoyably pursued in the company of others. Everyone sees things differently. We bring our long histories to the table, and the interchange of insights leads to a richer, fuller understanding of beer as well as a stronger community. The two are inseparable, as far as I'm concerned.

The Joys of Beer Clubs

I USED TO CLEAVE to the old Groucho Marx adage of refusing to join any club that would have me as a member. But that was before I found out about beer and homebrewing clubs, which are some of the most welcoming organizations on earth.

Some of you may already enjoy their benefits: easy camaraderie amongst a willing pool of drinking pals; an exchange of information about beer, brewing, and life in general; organized activities; and an opportunity to achieve something bigger than one could manage alone. For those of you not yet hooked up, I urge you to connect with an existing club or, if need be, start your own.

Charlie Papazian started his club back in the late 1970s from the homebrewing classes he taught. With his fearless vision of a brighter, beerier tomorrow in mind, Charlie turned his club into the American Homebrewers Association, which eventually spawned the Association of Brewers, now the Brewers Association. This organization represents America's commercial craft brewers as well as its homebrewers.

Good beer in this country depends on the vital and dynamic culture that supports it. It was individuals working as a greater community that brought about the exciting beer culture we enjoy here, and those interpersonal connections will sustain and build it in the future.

Organizations exist at every level: local, national, and virtual. It may be worthwhile to participate on all of these levels. Right now, most of the local groups are homebrew-focused, but these folks are keen for all manner of authentic beer, and because of their familiarity with the brewing process, they are usually very knowledgeable and enthusiastic about commercial craft beer as well. And most craft brewers know that homebrewers are their most ardent and vocal supporters. There is a lot we can do together, and the benefits flow to everyone.

Many homebrewing groups run commercial events in addition to their homebrewing activities. The well-respected beer festivals in Madison, Wisconsin, and Portland, Oregon, are organized in large part by homebrewers. Depending on the size and experience of the club, there are a range of possible events, from beer and food–pairing workshops, style classes, and tasting dinners to festivals large and small to multiday extravaganzas such as the Spirit of Belgium, put on every few years by BURP, a renowned homebrewing club in the Washington, D.C., area. Homebrew clubs are your key to getting involved with the Beer Judge Certification Program, your single best way to build your tasting skills and vocabulary through experience as a beer judge. A list of existing clubs can be found at www.beertown.org.

My own Chicago Beer Society specializes in beer events featuring commercial beer. When properly run, we have found they attract new people into the club, promote great beer in general, offer a venue for commercial brewers to hang out with us and each other, and raise funds for less-profitable activities. We are a dues-paying member of the Illinois Craft Brewers Guild and do some events jointly with them. Over the past few years we have run a variety of beer and food events including our crowning glory, the Brewpub Shootout, during which local breweries compete in the categories of best food, best beer, and best pairing. If you're thinking of staging a competition with your local beer club, here's a hint: Awards generate participation.

Here are some of the larger beer enthusiast and brewing organizations.

The Brewers Association. This craft-brewing trade association, publishing company, and homebrewers organization was formed in 2005 with the merger of the Association of Brewers and the Brewers Association of America and now represents America's small, independent producers of craft beer. Much of its activities are aimed at promoting and protecting craft breweries, but the BA also produces the Great American Beer Festival, the huge annual beer expo held in Denver, usually around the end of September. In 2007 there were 2,793 beers from 473 breweries and over 46,000 attendees. Membership is open to breweries and others in the beer trade, as it is primarily a professional organization.

The American Homebrewers Association (www.homebrewersassociation.org). This organization is part of the Brewers Association and is America's national homebrew club. It is a membership organization that publishes a bimonthly magazine on beer and brewing (*Zymurgy*); runs the National Homebrewing Competition, the largest brewing competition the world has ever known; and organizes the National Homebrewers Conference, a yearly chance for homebrewers from all over to get together to share their knowledge, enthusiasm, and of course, beer. The AHA also runs a brewing e-mail forum, TechTalk, which is a collegial environment where brewers help each other with questions about beer, brewing, and beer-travel recommendations.

Support Your Local Brewery (http://supportyourlocalbrewery.org). This program of the Brewers Association is designed to create a ready force of volunteers willing to speak up to their government when their access to good beer is threatened. As legislatures react

to recent Supreme Court decisions regarding distribution, there are politics afoot in many states that could seriously impede your access to good beer. In many states, beer enthusiasts have helped repeal or change unreasonable state laws, such as North Carolina's limit on alcohol content in beer, and they have helped defeat legislation that would negatively impact small brewers in Wisconsin, California, and elsewhere. In these cases, beer enthusiasts do make a difference. Membership is free and open to all.

Beer Judge Certification Program (www.bjcp.org). Formed in 1985, the BJCP is responsible for procedures and judge certification for homebrewing competitions. It is a nonprofit association, run entirely by volunteers. Although it is dedicated primarily to homebrewing, there is a great deal of useful material on its site, including study guidelines for the certification exam, thoughtful and detailed style guidelines, and judging score sheets. To become a member, a prospective judge pays a one-time fee to take the exam, and then is a life member whose judging level and experience are tracked at no charge by the BJCP. An e-mail discussion group on the topic called JudgeNet can be accessed from the BJCP Web site.

Cicerone Certification Program (www.cicerone.org). This is a program recently set up by industry insider Ray Daniels as the beer equivalent of a wine sommelier, something that's been needed in the beer world for some time. The Cicerone program will serve as a testing and certification authority for beer servers, consultants, and others in the beer trade. Participants take a test and demonstrate industry experience to rise to three different levels of certification.

Beer Forums (www.beeradvocate.com and www.ratebeer.com). These threaded forums have developed into sizable communities, and BeerAdvocate has recently spun off a magazine. Both offer plenty of space to exchange views on the relative merits of favorite (and most despised) beers, although RateBeer is a little more narrowly focused in this direction.

Beeradvocate

Homebrewing Paraphernalia
Homebrewing is a relatively inexpensive hobby to get started in, and the rewards are great brews and a much better knowledge of beer.

PubCrawler (www.pubcrawler.com). This site is a forum for ratings of bars and restaurants based on their qualities as a pub. It's a great resource for locating good beer joints when you're traveling, or even for locating great places you might not know about in your own area.

Craft-Foods Movement. Beer is part of the broader craft-foods movement, so it makes sense to pursue it in those contexts. In organizations such as Slow Food (www.slowfoodusa.org) you'll find people who are already excited about high-quality, locally produced food and drink. Producers and retailers of artisanal foods are always looking for ways to get their products in front of willing customers, and they know that good beer is a powerful draw. As you probably already know, enjoying beer in the context of great, fresh, authentic food adds a delightful dimension to our favorite beverage.

Brew It Yourself

If you're of a creative bent, and especially if you like to cook, you might enjoy brewing some of your own beer. In its basic form, it is neither complicated nor expensive, and the results can be profoundly rewarding. Homebrewing is the only way to really get your hands on the process behind the beer, which I think gives you insights unavailable to the nonbrewer.

Everything one needs to brew great beer is at your fingertips these days. Malt in a rainbow of colors and flavors awaits your recipe. Hops may be had in dozens of spicy, herbal, citrusy, resiny varieties. Yeast, once by far the weakest link in the homebrew chain, is available in dozens of pedigreed strains, freshness dated for your brewing pleasure. Many of the thorny technical issues have been wrestled to the mat. Information flows in beery electronic rivers. Clubs abound.

Getting started doesn't have to be a big deal. A brewing kit at your local homebrew shop will run you between $50 and $100, depending on how luxe you want to get. Those truly dedicated to the hobby can eventually spend a lot more, but it is usually an incremental process, one stainless steel gizmo at a time. For now, the basics will do just fine.

But why go to the trouble of brewing your own? Great beer is all about the process and the choices made. Going through them actually tunes your senses to the amount of various flavor, aroma, and texture elements that make up a beer.

And once you start brewing, you become part of the community of homebrewers — a surprisingly passionate, collegial, and mystical society.

When you have a batch of beer under your belt (literally), you will have few answers and a lot more questions. Read, taste, listen, and grow. You will be rewarded with mightily good beer and an amazing feeling of accomplishment.

Breweriana

BEER HAS A WHOLE MATERIAL CULTURE associated with it in the form of packaging, marketing, branding, glassware, brewery buildings, and much more. This area of interest is every bit as fascinating for many people as the sensory aspects of beer.

Collecting breweriana has its own powerful allure, but it can also serve as a valuable tool to understand the attitudes, products, and role of beer in any given time and place. Breweriana can add another layer of understanding about beer itself, through the words, images, and methods used to advertise it. Although not

Labeled Beer Bottles, c. 1910
Old beer bottles are everywhere, but labeled examples are much harder to find.

a serious collector of the garage-filling type, I have gained several insights from keeping my eyes on breweriana as it flows through transaction paths such as eBay. The JPEGs are free for the taking and frequently reveal tidbits about beer styles not found in books.

People collect everything associated with beer, from bottle caps to delivery trucks. At its simplest, breweriana collecting can be a nice way of remembering your beer journey by saving coasters or bottles from beers you've enjoyed. These inexpensive trinkets, if framed or displayed properly, make evocative and eye-pleasing displays for your home pub. At the highest levels, collectors become experts on the history of a brewery or a region, shelling out thousands of dollars for items that may complete certain areas of their collections. Usually these serious collectors are generous about sharing their information, and they may make presentations, lead bus tours of defunct breweries or living bars, or write articles or books on their favorite subjects. Most beer-producing regions now have a book describing their brewing history, and these are well worth getting if you're interested in the beer history of your region.

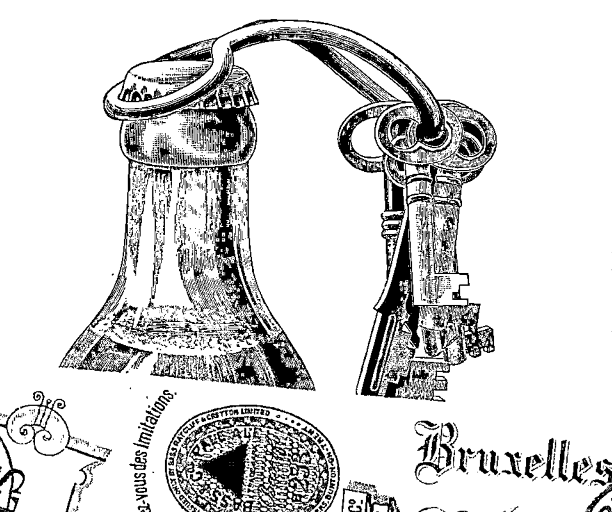

Glassware is especially fun to collect, because you can actually use it. Prices range from just pennies for modern or vintage glasses to thousands of dollars for rare, Georgian, twist-stem engraved examples. My own taste runs to handblown nineteenth-century glassware, which can be found without shelling out big bucks just often enough to keep me engaged in the hunt. It's fun to drink beers in period glassware. As you admire the glassware's charm, it's transporting to wonder what stories it could tell.

Beer on the Page

Old beer and brewing books are of obvious value to the student of beer. Period brewing texts can help decipher the pathways of historic beers. There are collections of lore, historical reviews, serious archaeology and history, and a wide array of brewery-published books, usually issued to celebrate some milestone. While they are generally scarce, copies of meaningful books turn up all the time in used bookstores, sometimes for very reasonable prices. The most reliable sources are the online bookseller networks like alibris.com and abebooks.com that have listings from all over the world.

Fortunately, many of the rarest and most valuable beer books exist in reprint versions, sometimes even available as free downloads. An excellent series of important reprints can be found at raudins.com. The eighteenth-century *A Vade Mecum for Ale Worms* was reprinted in the late nineteenth century; large numbers of the charmingly evocative 1889 *Curiosities of Ale and Beer* are easy to find, as it was printed in an inexpensive edition in 1965. Beerbooks.com and beerinnprint.com are two other good sources for hard-to-find beer books.

You may also find cookbooks published by breweries, most typically in the 1940s and '50s, which are designed to showcase their beers with the casseroles and other dishes of the era. I've had a great deal of fun collecting photos of anonymous people drinking beer in earlier times, and these, which are liberally sprinkled throughout this book, add one more dimension to our understanding of people's relationship to the world's best drink.

Beernog [and Other Concoctions]!

THESE DAYS WE'RE ACCUSTOMED to drinking our beer "neat" or without any kind of adulteration, but this was far from the case in earlier times. The sweet green or red syrup *Schuss* of Berliner Weisse, the old-school stout-and-champagne cocktail known as a Black Velvet, or simply the salt that Grandpa dashed into his beer are the last vestiges of this. Central heating wasn't what it is now, and people relied on warming drinks made from ale, spirits, and seasonings to take the chill off their bones. The line between liquid and bread wasn't so finely drawn either, and people tended to load up their brews with toast, oatmeal, eggs, cream, fruit, and more. The old line about beer and breakfast would fit right in here.

A few recipes have survived from Renaissance times. A thick drink called "ale-brue" or "ale-berry" was ale boiled with spices, sugar, and sops of bread, often with the addition of oatmeal. One ditty goes: "Ale brue thus make thou shall / With grotes [oats], safroun and good ale." Such porridgelike drinks later came to be known as "caudle" and were popular in the American Colonies.

No less a figure than Sir Walter Raleigh had a personal recipe for "sack posset," which actually sounds a lot like eggnog. "Boil a quart of cream with *quantum sufficit* of sugar, mace and nutmeg, take half a pint of sack [sweet sherry] and the same quantity of ale, and boil them together." He suggests letting it all mull together in a covered pewter bowl by the fire for a couple of hours. I would estimate between half and a whole cup of sugar and ⅛ teaspoon each of nutmeg and mace as "sufficit."

Seventeenth-century England saw a craze for "buttered ale," which was composed of unhopped ale (by then just about extinct) mixed with sugar and cinnamon, heated and topped off with a dollop of butter. Samuel Pepys mentions it in his famous diaries as a morning pick-me-up.

A century later, a wild profusion of "beer cups" were the rage. The particulars are lost now, but tantalizing names such as "Humpty Dumpty," "clamber-down," "hugmatee," "knock-me-down," and "cuddle-me buff" offer clues to the nature — or at least the effect — of these drinks. Not far from these are the slightly racy names of cocktails today. Here are a few to consider.

Flip. A beer drink also known as "yard of flannel," which is a reference to the long, smooth stream formed by the creamy liquid as it was poured back and forth between two vessels to froth it up. Flip had a good long run in England, the American Colonies, and elsewhere, and it was beloved for several unique qualities, not the least of which was having a red-hot poker thrust into it.

Place in a saucepan 1 quart of strong ale, a couple of ounces of good aged rum, 4 tablespoons of brown or muscovado sugar, a small piece of cinnamon, a couple of cloves, and a piece of lemon zest. Heat just to a simmer, but do not boil, then after the sugar is dissolved turn off the heat and remove the cinnamon and other solid ingredients. Beat 4 eggs, and gradually add some of the hot ale mixture to the eggs, stirring steadily. Then add the egg mixture to the ale in the pan and beat furiously until foamy.

Next comes the most dramatic — and some would say essential — step in the flip-making process. The warm beverage is further heated by the insertion of a glowing hot fireplace poker. This causes the mixture to boil violently and creates a smoky, caramelized flavor much prized by flipophiles. Needless to say, this is an operation that should take place outdoors and with all reasonable safety precautions. It is good for a holiday spectacle. Garnish with whipped cream, if you like, and a little freshly grated nutmeg.

Flip has a unique drinking glass associated with it. These are wide, tapered glasses, often decorated with molded or engraved designs, ranging in size from less than 1 pint to wastebasket-size behemoths holding 6 quarts or more. These were passed around the party, and must have been a test of coordination and strength, and possibly sobriety as well. One I own, circa 1800 and decorated with stylized palm trees, weighs more than 10 pounds when filled.

Crambambull (Beernog). It's just a short hop from flip to eggnog, which when made with ale is called Crambambull. At a holiday party last year, our host whipped up a batch of homemade eggnog sans alcohol, thinking that celebrants could enjoy it unadulterated or spike it with bourbon or rum as desired. As the host had also laid in a store of tasty beers, I seized on the opportunity to re-create history and use the ale to spike the nog. Gasps ensued, but after a few nervous sips, the nog got very beery. While the idea of adding beer to eggnog may seem strange to us, strong ale would have been pretty much essential in all such early drinks.

George Washington was kind enough to leave us a formula for eggnog, considerably more appetizing than his famous small beer recipe: "1 pint brandy, ½ pint rye whiskey, ½ pint Jamaica rum, ¼ pint sherry, [unspecified number of] eggs, 12 tablespoons sugar, 1½ quarts milk, 1 quart cream." The eggs are separated and the sugar is creamed into the yolks, then the milk and cream are added, and then beaten egg whites. He counsels, "Let set in a cool place for several days, taste frequently." Yeah, I bet he did.

A typical modern eggnog recipe has us separate 4 eggs. Beat the yolks with ½ cup of sugar until smooth, then mix in 1½ cups of milk and 1 cup of cream. Season with a little nutmeg or mace and sometimes a dash of vanilla, then beat the egg whites and fold them into the mixture. Many recipes call for the cream to be whipped before adding it, and I think this does improve the texture. I should mention that the prepared stuff sold in milk cartons is beneath consideration. Make it fresh or don't bother.

The recipe above makes an ideal base for experimenting with beernog. A reasonable approach is to fill a 12-ounce glass one-third full of hearty ale, add ½ ounce of bourbon, rye, or dark rum, and top it off with the prepared nog mixture, leaving room for a dollop of whipped froth on top. This is a concoction that really puts you in the holiday spirit.

But what kind of beer is best? In our little taste test, we had success with Anchor Christmas ale, and I expect any similar dark, wassail-type holiday ale would fit right in. Barley wine, Imperial Stout, doppelbock, and Scotch ale all work well, and we found that the sweet mixture made for a palatable drink even when mixed with a strong, hoppy pale ale, although the bitterness was not to everyone's taste.

On Christmas Eve, did you ever think that Santa might be sick of milk and cookies? What he would really like is beernog! That'll get the stockings filled to overflowing.

Note: These eggnog recipes call for raw eggs. While this is traditional and done every day with no harm, some health experts recommend against this. If you are dubious, specially processed eggs made for raw consumption may be available in a health food store in your area.

Bishop. Heat 4 cups of ale and 1 tablespoon of brown sugar in a saucepan. Stud 2 large oranges with 4 whole cloves each and bake at 250°F until very soft, about 25 minutes. Slice each orange into quarters, removing the seeds, and add the oranges to the beer mixture. Remove from the heat and let stand for 30 minutes. Reheat to a warm serving temperature, but do not boil. Serve hot in a stoneware mug with a piece of the orange.

Buttered Beer. Start with 1 quart of strong, brown or Scotch ale and add a couple of pats of unsalted butter, ¼ cup of brown sugar, and a pinch each of powdered ginger and powdered licorice (if you can find it — try an Indian grocery store). Heat to just below the boiling point while stirring gently to dissolve the sugar, then serve.

Crab Ale. The authentic recipe calls for roasting a wild apple (you can use a few crabapples) until it's hissing hot, then adding it to a soup bowl of ale that has been sweetened with 1 tablespoon of sugar. Top with a slice of toast and a garnish of ground cinnamon and nutmeg.

Crabapple Lambswool (Wassail). Heat 1 quart of ale with 1 pint of sherry and a healthy dash of freshly grated nutmeg nearly to boiling. Add 1 tablespoon of brown sugar and ½ teaspoon of ground ginger. Pour into a heated punch bowl and float 6 freshly roasted and cored crabapples, or any small, tart apples, on top.

Ale Punch. Add 2 ounces of brown sugar and the zest of 1 lemon to a punch bowl. Squeeze the lemon juice from the lemon into the sugar, straining out the seeds and pulp. Let stand for 30 minutes, then remove the lemon zest. Add 2 quarts of pale or amber ale, ½ pint of sherry, and a handful of ice cubes. Stir and garnish with lemon wedges or slices.

Black Velvet. Mix equal parts chilled champagne and stout in a large bar glass. Serve in flute glasses.

Brown Betty. Named after a famous bread maker in Oxford, England. Combine 1 cup of Cognac, 3 whole cloves, 1 quart of brown or amber beer, and ½ cup of brown sugar; stir gently to dissolve the sugar. Chill for 2 hours before serving.

Capillare. Combine 1 quart of pale beer, 6 ounces of sweet white wine, 2 ounces of brandy, the juice and zest of half a lemon, a dash of freshly grated nutmeg, and a few sprigs of borage or mint. Add the mixture to 1 pint of hot simple syrup (1 cup of sugar dissolved in 1 pint of boiling water) plus 1 ounce of orange-flower water (if you want to be really authentic, the orange-flower water should be poured over the fronds of a maidenhair fern). Add 6 ounces of orange curaçao and serve iced or cold in a large pitcher.

A Final Word

THREE INGREDIENTS — grain, water, and hops — are transformed by yeast. Beer is shockingly simple, yet dazzling in the range of rich sensations it can offer. Its amber depths contain more ideas, sensations, and stories than can fit into a single lifetime. It is my sincere hope that this book has given you some notion of this, and I can assure you that there is far more out there that will amply reward your attention. Your trip with me is at an end, but your journey continues.

We are fortunate to live in an age when all things are possible in the world of beer. This did not happen by accident. It took the efforts, imagination, and just plain contrariness of brewers, entrepreneurs, and informed beer lovers to make it happen. Beer, like any art, is an interactive experience. Great beer depends on a community to sustain it and give it meaning. Without this, it becomes just another industrial commodity. Beer is only as good as the people who seek it out, support it, keep it honest, and, most important of all, enjoy the genuine pleasures of it. Never take it for granted.

This book began with a beer, so perhaps it should conclude with one, too. Uncap something special and pour it into a treasured glass. Give it the time it needs to settle into perfection. Ahh, beer! Raise the glass, as have countless others before you, and toast someone special. Pause for a sniff, and then drink deep. Grain, water, hops — and yet so much more. Use your head, your heart, and your soul, and you can taste the whole world in it.

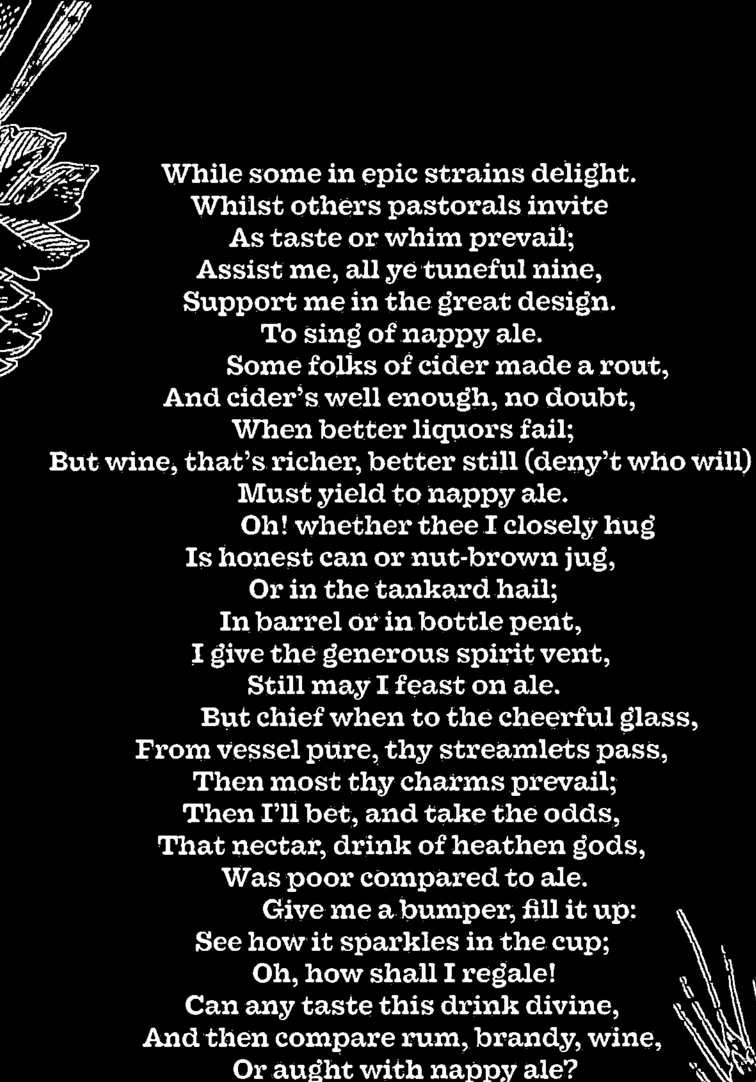

While some in epic strains delight.
Whilst others pastorals invite
As taste or whim prevail;
Assist me, all ye tuneful nine,
Support me in the great design.
To sing of nappy ale.
Some folks of cider made a rout,
And cider's well enough, no doubt,
When better liquors fail;
But wine, that's richer, better still (deny't who will)
Must yield to nappy ale.
Oh! whether thee I closely hug
Is honest can or nut-brown jug,
Or in the tankard hail;
In barrel or in bottle pent,
I give the generous spirit vent,
Still may I feast on ale.
But chief when to the cheerful glass,
From vessel pure, thy streamlets pass,
Then most thy charms prevail;
Then I'll bet, and take the odds,
That nectar, drink of heathen gods,
Was poor compared to ale.
Give me a bumper, fill it up:
See how it sparkles in the cup;
Oh, how shall I regale!
Can any taste this drink divine,
And then compare rum, brandy, wine,
Or aught with nappy ale?

O blest potation! still by thee,
And thy companion Liberty,
Do health and mirth prevail;
Then let us crown the can, the glass,
And sportive bid the minutes pass
In quaffing nappy ale.
Ev'n while these stanzas I indite,
The bar-bell's grateful sounds invite
Where joy can never fail.
Adieu, my muse! adieu, I haste
To gratify my longing taste
With copious draughts of ale.

— John Gay (1686–1732), "Ballad on Ale"

A GLOSSARY OF BEER AND BREWING TERMS

NOTE: For beer styles, refer to the index to find definitions and detailed information.

A

AAU. Alpha acid unit, the international measurement of bitterness in beer.

acetaldehyde. Chemical present in beer that has a green-apple aroma.

acetic. Aroma descriptor for vinegar aroma from *Acetobacteria.* Common in sour, wood-aged beers.

acrospire. The shoot of the barley grain, which develops during malting.

adjunct. Any fermentable added to barley malt for brewing, especially rice, corn, and roasted unmalted wheat, roast barley, sugar, etc.

adsorption. Physical process involving adherence of particles to one another at the microscopic level. Important in fining and other processes.

aftertaste. Lingering flavor after liquid has left the mouth.

albumen. Older term for class of proteins found in malt. Much of it coagulates or breaks down during brewing.

alcohol. A type of simple organic compound containing one or more hydroxyl groups (OH) per molecule. Ethanol is the type found in fermented beverages. Other types occur in beer and other fermented products, but in small quantities.

ale. Any beer produced with top-fermenting yeast. In the old days, a strong unhopped beer. In Texas, any beer above 5 percent alcohol by volume (4 percent by weight).

aldehyde. Group of important flavor chemicals found in beer and other foodstuffs. Most commonly associated with stale flavors in beer.

alkalinity. A measure of water hardness, expressed as ppm of calcium carbonate.

alpha acid. Complex of substances that are the bitter component of hop flavor.

alt or altbier. German type of beer made from top-fermenting yeast. Includes Kölsch and Düsseldorfer.

amino acids. A group of complex organic chemicals that form the building blocks of protein. Important in yeast nutrition.

amylase (alpha and beta). Primary starch-converting enzymes present in barley and malt. They both break the long chains of starch molecules into shorter, fermentable sugars.

ASBC. American Society of Brewing Chemists. Standards-setting organization for beer analysis in North America.

attenuation. The degree to which residual sugars have been fermented out of a finished beer.

autolysis. Self-digestion and disintegration of yeast cells. This can give rise to soapy off-flavors if beer is not racked of dead yeast after primary fermentation.

B

°Balling. European measurement of specific gravity based on the percentage of pure sugar in the wort. Expressed in degrees. The measurement system used in the Czech Republic.

barley. Cereal grains, members of the genus *Hordeum*. When malted, the primary ingredient in beer.

barrel. Standard unit in commercial brewing. U.S. barrel is 31.5 gallons; British barrel is 43.2 U.S. gallons.

Baumé. Hydrometer scale used to estimate alcohol content by subtracting post-fermentation reading from pre-fermentation reading.

beer. Broad term that describes any fermented beverage made from barley malt or other cereal grains. Originally denoted products containing hops instead of other herbs.

beta glucans. A group of gummy carbohydrates in malt. Some varieties have an excess, which can cause problems with runoff and fermentation, where they may precipitate as a sticky goo.

body. A quality of beer, largely determined by the presence of colloidal protein complexes and unfermentable sugars (dextrins) in the finished beer.

Brettanomyces. Genus of yeast sometimes used in brewing, capable of producing barnyard (horsey), pineapple, and other aromas.

bung. Wooden plug for beer barrel.

Burtonize. To treat water so that it approximates the water of Burton-on-Trent, England, long famous for pale ales.

buttery, butterscotch. Flavor descriptor for diacetyl in moderate to high concentrations.

C

calcium. Mineral ion important in brewing-water chemistry.

CAMRA. Campaign for Real Ale, Britain's traditional beer preservation movement.

caramel malt. See **crystal malt.**

Cara-Pils. Trade name for a specially processed malt used to add body to pale beers. Similar to crystal but not roasted. Also called dextrine malt.

carbohydrates. The class of chemicals including sugars and their polymers, including starch and dextrins.

carbonate. 1. To add carbon dioxide gas to the beer; 2. Alkaline water mineral ion associated with limestone.

carbonation. Fizz due to carbon dioxide (CO_2) dissolved in beer.

cask. British term for a barrel-shaped vessel used to serve beer.

cereal. Broad term for a group of grass plant species cultivated as food grains.

cheesy. Flavor descriptor for isovaleric acid, mostly found in old hops.

chill haze. Cloudy residue of protein that precipitates when beer is chilled.

chocolate (malt). Dark brown roasted malt.

cold break. Rapid precipitation of proteins occurring when wort is rapidly chilled.

colloid. A state of matter involving very minute particles suspended in a liquid. Beer is a colloid, as is gelatin. Especially related to body, haze, and stability.

conditioning. The process of maturation of beer, whether in bottles or in kegs. During this phase, complex sugars are slowly fermented, carbon dioxide is dissolved, and yeast settles to the bottom.

cone. The part of the hop plant used in brewing; properly called strobiles (catkins), not flowers.

conversion. Occurs in the mash, of starch to sugar.

copper. The brewing kettle, named for its traditional material of construction.

corn sugar. Dextrose, sometimes added as an adjunct.

crystal malt. A specially processed type of malt that is used to add body and caramel color and flavor to amber and dark beers. Comes in several shades of color.

D

decoction. Continental mashing technique that involves removing a portion of the mash, boiling it, then returning it to the mash to raise its temperature.

dextrin, dextrine. A family of long-chain sugars not normally fermentable by yeast. Contributes to body in beer.

diacetyl. A powerful flavor chemical with the aroma of butter or butterscotch.

diastase. An enzyme complex present in barley and malt that is responsible for the conversion of starch into sugars.

diastatic activity. An analytical measure expressed in degrees Lintner of the power of malt or other grains to convert starches to sugars in the mash.

diatomaceous earth (DE). Microfine fossil single-cell creatures of almost pure silica, used in the filtering of beer in preparation for bottling.

disaccharide. Sugars formed by the combination of two simple sugar units. Maltose is an example.

DMS. Dimethyl sulfide, a powerful flavor chemical found in beer, with the aroma of cooked corn.

dough-in. The process of mixing the crushed malt with water in the beginning of the mash operation.

draft, draught. Beer from a cask or a keg, as opposed to bottled beer. Generally unpasteurized.

dry hopping. A method of adding hops directly to the tank or cask at the end of fermentation, to increase hop aroma without adding bitterness.

dunkel. German word for "dark," as in dark beer. Usually refers to Munich dark style.

E

endosperm. The starchy middle of a cereal grain that serves as the food reserve for the young plant. It is the source of fermentable material for brewing.

entire. Old term meaning to combine the first, middle, and last runnings into one batch of beer. This began in the large mechanized porter breweries in London during the 1700s and is accepted common practice today.

enzyme. Proteins that act as catalysts for most reactions crucial to brewing, including starch conversion, proteolysis, and yeast metabolism. Highly dependent upon conditions such as temperature, time, and pH.

esters. Large class of compounds formed from the complete oxidation of various alcohols and responsible for most fruity aromas in beer, especially top-fermented ones.

ethanol. The (ethyl) alcohol found in beer; its intoxicating component.

ethyl acetate. A common ester in beer; fruity in small amounts, solvent at high concentrations.

ethyl alcohol. See **ethanol.**

European Brewing Convention (EBC). Continental standards organization for brewing. Most commonly encountered as a term applied to malt color: degrees EBC (about double degrees Lovibond/SRM).

export. Trade term usually for a higher-gravity or better grade of product.

extract. 1. Alternative word for gravity; 2. Term used to refer to concentrated wort in dry or syrup form.

F

FAN (free amino nitrogen). Type of protein breakdown products in the wort. Amino acids and smaller molecules are included. Indicates yeast nutrition potential.

fermentation. Biochemical process of yeast involving the metabolism of sugars and the release of carbon dioxide and alcohol, along with many important by-products.

fining(s). Clarifying agents that are added post-fermentation, which help pull yeast and other particulates out of the beer.

firkin. British cask containing 10.8 U.S. or 9 Imperial gallons (40.9 liters).

first runnings. The sugar-rich wort that drains off at the beginning of runoff. Used in former times to make a strong beer; nowadays blended in with the rest of the batch.

fusel alcohol. Higher (more complex) alcohols, found in all fermented beverages.

G

gelatin. Used in brewing as a fining agent.

gelatinization. The cooking of corn or other unmalted cereals to break down the cell walls of the starch granules. The resulting starch is in a colloidal state, making it accessible for enzymatic conversion into sugars.

germination. The sprouting of barley, the most important step of malting.

glucose. Corn sugar or dextrose. A simple sugar sometimes used in brewing.

gravity. Original gravity.

grist. Ground grain ready for brewing.

grits. Ground degermed corn or rice used in brewing.

gruit. Medieval herb mixture used in beer.

gyle. A single batch of beer.

gypsum. Calcium sulfate ($CaSO_4$), an acidic water mineral ion, especially welcome in the production of pale ales.

H

hardness. A term indicating the presence of water mineral levels, especially calcium.

heterocyclics. Important, ring-shaped aroma molecules responsible for the full range of malty aromas in beer. Produced by the Maillard reaction.

hop. A climbing vine of the Cannabacinae family, whose cones are used to give beer its bitterness and characteristic aroma.

hop back. A strainer tank used in commercial brewing to filter hops and trub from boiled wort before it is chilled.

horsey, horse-blanket. Terms used to describe the barnyard aromas contributed by *Brettanomyces* wild yeast.

hot break. The rapid coagulation of proteins and resins, assisted by the hops, during boiling.

humulene. One of the most plentiful of the many chemicals that give hops their characteristic aroma.

husk. The outer covering of barley or other grains. May impart a rough, bitter taste to beer if sparging is carried out incorrectly.

hydrolysis. The enzyme reaction of the breakdown of proteins and carbohydrates.

hydrometer. Glass instrument used in brewing to measure the specific gravity of beer and wort.

I

IBU (international bitterness unit). The accepted method of expressing hop bitterness in beer. Ppm of dissolved iso-alpha acids present in beer. See also International Bitterness Units in chapter 4.

infusion. Mash technique of the simplest type used to make all kinds of English ales and stouts. Features a single temperature rest, rather than a series of gradually increasing steps common in other mashing styles.

ion. Water minerals in the form of electrically charged half molecule.

Irish moss. A marine algae used during wort boiling to enhance the hot break. Also called carrageen.

isinglass. A type of gelatin obtained from the swim bladder of certain types of fish (usually sturgeon), used as a fining agent in ales.

iso-alpha acid. Bitter hop resins chemically changed by the boil and present in beer. Also, processed hop extract, sometimes used to add bitterness after fermentation.

isomerization. The chemical change during wort boiling that causes hop alpha acids to become more bitter and soluble in wort.

K

kettle. Boiling vessel, also known as a copper.

krausen. The thick foamy head on fermenting beer.

krausening. The practice of adding vigorously fermenting young beer to beer in the secondary to speed maturation.

L

lactic acid. An organic acid that is a by-product of *Lactobacillus,* responsible for the tart flavor of Berliner Weisse and some Belgian ales.

Lactobacillus. Large genus of bacteria. May be either a spoilage organism or purposefully added to such products as Kölsch or Berliner Weisse.

lactose. Milk sugar. Unfermentable by yeast, it is used as a sweetener in milk stout.

lager. Beers made with bottom-fermenting yeast and aged at near-freezing temperatures.

lauter tun. A great term for a sparging vessel.

lightstruck. An off-flavor in beer that develops from exposure to short-wavelength (blue) light. Even a short exposure to sunlight can cause this skunky odor to develop. Often occurs to beer in green bottles sold from lighted cooler cases. Brown bottles are excellent protection.

°Lovibond. Beer and grain color measurement, now superseded by the newer SRM method. Still commonly used in reference to grain color.

lupulin. The resiny substance in hops containing all the resins and aromatic oils.

M

Maillard browning. The caramelization reaction, also known as nonenzymic browning. Responsible for all the roasted color and flavor in beer.

malt. Barley or other grain that has been allowed to sprout, then dried or roasted.

malt extract. Concentrated commercial preparations of wort. Available as syrup or powder, in a wide range of colors, hopped or unhopped.

maltose. A simple sugar that is by far the predominant fermentable material in wort.

maltotetraose. Type of sugar molecule consisting of four molecules of glucose hooked together.

maltotriose. Type of sugar molecule consisting of three molecules of glucose hooked together.

mash. The cooking procedure central to brewing, in which starch is converted into sugars. Various enzyme reactions occur between 110 and 166°F (43 to 74°C).

mash tun. Vessel in which mashing is carried out. Has a perforated false bottom to allow liquid to drain through.

melanoidins. Group of complex color compounds formed by heating sugars and starches in the presence of proteins. Created in brewing during grain roasting and wort boiling.

milling. Term for grain grinding or crushing.

mouthfeel. Sensory qualities of a beverage other than flavor, such as body and carbonation.

N

nitrogen. Element used as a measure of protein level in malt, and important as a yeast nutrient. Also used to pressurize stout.

O

OG. Original gravity.

original gravity. Measure of wort strength expressed as specific gravity; the weight of the wort relative to the weight of water.

oxidation. Chemical reaction that occurs between oxygen and various components in beer, most often resulting in wet-paper or cardboard off-flavors.

oxygen. Element important in yeast metabolism, especially during startup, but may cause problems for long-term storage. See also **oxidation**.

P

parti-gyle. Antiquated brewhouse practice in which first runnings become strong ale, second runnings become ordinary beer, and the last and weakest runnings become small beer.

pasteurization. The process of sterilizing by heat. Used in almost all mass-market canned or bottled beer.

peptide. Short fragment of a protein. Also the bond holding amino acids into chains of protein.

pH (potential of hydrogen). Logarithmic scale used to express the level of acidity and alkalinity in a solution. 7 = neutral; 1 = most acid; 14 = most alkaline. Each step on the scale represents a tenfold change from the previous one.

phenol. Chemical family responsible for spicy, smoky, and other aromas in beer.

phenolic. Flavor term referring to phenol flavors and aromas.

°Plato. European and American scale of gravity based on a percentage of pure sugar in the wort. A newer, more accurate version of the Balling scale.

polishing. Final filtration prior to bottling in commercial brewing. Renders beer sparkling clear.

polyphenol. Tannins, important in beer in connection with protein coagulation and chill haze.

polysaccharide. Polymers of simple sugars. Includes a range from complex sugars through dextrins up to starches.

ppb. Parts per billion. 1 microgram per liter.

ppm. Parts per million. 1 milligram per liter.

precipitation. A chemical process involving a material coming out of solution.

primary fermentation. Initial rapid stage of yeast activity when maltose and other simple sugars are metabolized. Lasts about a week.

priming. The process of adding sugar to beer before bottling or racking to kegs. Restarts fermentation, pressurizing with carbon dioxide gas.

protein. Complex nitrogenous organic molecules important in all living matter. In beer, involved in enzyme activity, yeast nutrition, head retention, and colloidal stability. During mashing, boiling, and cooling, they may be broken apart and/or precipitated.

proteinase. Enzyme that breaks proteins apart into smaller, more soluble units. Most active at 122°F (50°C).

protein rest. During mashing, a 120 to 125°F (49 to 52°C) temperature rest for 20 minutes or more to eliminate proteins that cause chill haze.

proteolysis. The breaking up or digestion of proteins by enzymes that occurs in the mash around 122°F (50°C).

proteolytic enzymes. Enzymes naturally present in barley and malt that have the power to break up proteins in the mash.

Q

quarter. An English measure of malt equal to 336 pounds; of barley, 448 pounds.

R

racking. Transferring the fermenting beer from one vessel to another to avoid tainting by off-flavors that result from autolysis.

rauchbier. A dark lager beer made in Germany from smoked malts.

Régie. Belgian/French gravity scale still applied to some Belgian beers (e.g., 1.050 OG = 5.0 degrees Régie).

Reinheitsgebot. Bavarian beer purity law, enacted in 1516.

runnings. Wort that is drained from the mash during sparging.

runoff. The draining of wort from the mash during sparging.

S

saccharification. The conversion of starch to sugars in the mash through enzyme activity.

Saccharomyces. Scientific genus name of brewer's yeast. *Saccharomyces cerevesiae* is both top- and bottom-fermenting yeast.

salt. 1. Minerals present in water that have various effects on the brewing process; 2. sodium chloride.

secondary fermentation. Slow phase of yeast activity during which complex sugars are metabolized and "green beer" flavors are reabsorbed. May take weeks or months.

session beer. Lighter in gravity and alcohol, it is designed to be consumed without overtaxing the drinker in either flavor or intensity. It is typically less than 4.5 percent alcohol; examples include British bitter, witbier, and American adjunct pilsner.

set mash. Condition that sometimes develops during sparging that makes runoff difficult.

six-row. A type of barley most often grown in the United States and used in the production of American-style beers. High diastatic activity makes it ideal for the mashing of corn or rice adjuncts, which have no starch-converting power of their own.

skunky. Faint rubbery aroma caused by overexposure of beer to light. See also **lightstruck.**

sparge. Process of rinsing mashed grains with hot water to recover all available wort sugars.

specific gravity. A measurement of density, expressed relative to the density of water. Used in brewing to follow the course of fermentation.

spelt. A grain intermediate between barley and wheat that has been used in brewing since ancient times.

SRM (Standard Reference Method). Measurement of beer color, expressed as ten times the optical density (absorbance) of beer, as measured at 430 nm in a spectrophotometer. Nearly the same as the older Lovibond color series, measured with a set of specially colored glass samples.

starch. Complex carbohydrates, long polymers of sugars, that are converted into sugars during mashing.

starch haze. Cloudiness in beer due to suspended starch particles. Usually caused by: (1) Incorrect mash temperature resulting in incomplete saccharification; or (2) sparging temperatures over 180°F (82°C), which can dissolve residual starch from the mash.

steep. The process of soaking barley or wheat in water to begin malting.

step mash. Mashing technique using controlled temperature steps.

strike. The addition of hot water to the crushed malt to raise the temperature and begin mashing.

T

tannin. Polyphenols, complex organic materials with a characteristic astringent flavor, extracted from hops and the husks of barley.

terpenes. Group of flavor chemicals forming the main component of hop oils.

top fermentation. Ale fermentation. At warmer temperatures yeast stays on top of the beer as it ferments.

torrefication. Process of rapidly heating grain so it puffs up like popcorn. Commonly applied to barley and wheat. Often used in British pale ales.

trisaccharide. Sugar molecule consisting of three simple sugars linked together.

trub. Coagulated protein and hop resin sludge that precipitates out of wort during boiling and again at chilling.

two-row. The most common type of barley for brewing everywhere in the world except America. Has a lower protein content and a finer flavor than six-row.

U

ullage. Empty space at the top of a wooden barrel.

underlet. The addition of water to a mash in progress from below so the grains float a bit. Encourages quicker and more thorough mixing.

undermodified. Applies to malt that has not been allowed to malt to an advanced stage.

W

weiss. Term applied to German wheat ales of the Bavarian, or Süddeutsch, style.

weisse. German word meaning "white;" applied to the tart wheat beers of the Berliner style.

weizen. German word for "wheat." Synonymous with weiss.

whirlpool. Device used to separate hops and trub from wort after boiling. Wort is stirred in a circular motion and collects in the center of the whirlpool. Clear wort is drained from the edge.

wind malt. A type of very pale malt dried in the sun or by exposure to the air, without kilning. Once used in the production of witbier.

wort. Unfermented beer, the sugar-laden liquid obtained from the mash.

wort chiller. Heat exchanger used to rapidly cool wort from near boiling to pitching temperature.

X-Y-Z

yeast. Large class of microscopic fungi, several species of which are used in brewing.

zymurgy. The science of fermentation, also used as the name of the magazine of the American Homebrew Association.

Further Reading on Beer Styles, Flavors, History, and More

Aidells, Bruce, and Dennis Kelly. *Real Beer, Good Eats.* New York: Knopf, 1992.
Cornell, Martyn. *Beer: The Story of the Pint.* London: Headline Book Publishing, 2003.
Hornsey, Ian. *A History of Beer and Brewing.* London: The Royal Society of Chemistry, 2004.
Jackson, Michael. *Michael Jackson's Great Beer Guide.* New York : DK Publishing, 2000.
———. *Ultimate Beer.* New York : DK Publishing, 1998.
———. *The Beer Companion.* Philadelphia: Running Press, 1993.
Mosher, Randy. *Radical Brewing.* Boulder: Brewers Publications, 2004.
Ogle, Maureen. *Ambitious Brew.* Orlando: Harcourt, 2006.
Oliver, Garrett. *The Brewmaster's Table.* New York: HarperCollins, 2003.
Perrier-Robert, Annie, and Charles Fontaine. *Beer by Belgium, Belgium by Beer.* Esch/Alzette, Luxembourg:Schortgen, 1996.
Protz, Roger. *The Ale Trail: A Celebration of the Revival of the World's Oldest Style.* Orpington, Kent: Eric Dobby Publishing Ltd., 1995.
Sambrook, Pamela. *Country House Brewing in England 1500–1900.* London and Rio Grande, OH: The Hambledon Press, 1996.
Saunders, Lucy. *The Best of American Beer and Food: Pairing & Cooking with Craft Beer.* Boulder: Brewers Publications, 2007.
Wells, Ken. *Travels with Barley: A Journey through Beer Culture in America.* New York: Wall Street Journal Books, 2004.

Art Credits

Interior photography by © Randy Mosher, except
The Trustees of the British Museum: 7 (bottom)
Frances Duncan: 208
© 2009 Jupiterimages Corporation: 106 (middle right)
© Kevin Kennefick: i, iii, viii, 10, 17, 35, 37, 40, 61, 63, 73, 77, 99 108 (left three), 109 (top left, center right, bottom right) 115, 119, 122-127, 129, 130, 198, 224
Courtesy of the Massachusetts Historical Society: 19
© The Metropolitan Museum of Art: 3
© Randy Mosher, courtesy of The Oriental Institute, University of Chicago: 8, 9
© Museum of London: 106 (middle left, bottom right)
© National Museums Scotland. Licensor www.scran.ac.uk: 11
Courtesy North Carolina Museum of Art, Raleigh, Purchased with funds from the State of North Carolina: 106 (top right)
© Olgierd Nowicki/Alamy: 7 (top)
© Penn Museum object B17691, image # 152180: 106 (top left)
Rijksmuseum Amsterdam: 107 (top right)
© V&A Images, Victoria and Albert Museum: 106 (bottom left, 107 top left)
Mars Vilaubi: 65, 97

Historical photographs, illustrations and ephemera courtesy of the author, except
Antique hops illustration by © 2004 Visual Language®: i (repeated 5, 28, 36, 78, 96, 115, 133, 144, 165, 180, 188, 207, 220)

Infographics by Randy Mosher and Dan Williams: 32, 38, 43, 67–71, 75, 102, 134

Index

Page references in *italics* indicate photographs or illustrations; page references in **bold** indicate charts or graphs.

N

O

P

Q

R

S

***The American Craft Beer Cookbook* by John Holl**
The best beer-friendly recipes from breweries, brewpubs, and taverns across the United States.
352 pages. Paper. ISBN 978-1-61212-090-4.

***Brewing Made Easy*, 2nd edition**
by Joe Fisher and Dennis Fisher
A foolproof starters' guide to brewing great beer at home — includes step-by-step instructions and 25 recipes.
96 pages. Paper. ISBN 978-1-61212-138-3.

***Hot Sauce!* by Jennifer Trainer Thompson**
More than 30 recipes to make your own, plus 60 more recipes for cooking with homemade or commercial sauces.
192 pages. Paper. ISBN 978-1-60342-816-3.

Tasting Whiskey by Randy Mosher
A comprehensive guide to tasting and enjoying the world's whiskeys, including Scotch and bourbon as well as Tennessee, Irish, Japanese, and Canadian whiskey.
256 pages. Paper. ISBN 978-1-61212-301-1.

***Vintage Beer* by Patrick Dawson**
Learn how to identify a cellar-worthy beer, how to set up a beer cellar, what to look for when tasting vintage beers, and the fascinating science behind the aging process.
160 pages. Paper. ISBN 978-1-61212-156-7.

These and other books from Storey Publishing are available wherever quality books are sold or by calling 1-800-441-5700. Visit us at www.storey.com or sign up for our newsletter at www.storey.com/signup.